FAUST IN LITERATURE

UNIVERSITY OF DURHAM
PUBLICATIONS

Faust
in Literature

by

J. W. Smeed

LONDON

Oxford University Press

NEW YORK   TORONTO

1975

Oxford University Press, Ely House, London W.1

GLASGOW NEW YORK TORONTO MELBOURNE WELLINGTON
CAPE TOWN IBADAN NAIROBI DAR ES SALAM LUSAKA ADDIS ABABA
DELHI BOMBAY CALCUTTA MADRAS KARACHI LAHORE DACCA
KUALA LUMPUR SINGAPORE HONG KONG TOKYO

ISBN 0 19 713139 5

*Printed in Great Britain by
The Camelot Press Ltd., Southampton*

PREFACE

This book deals with various aspects of the Faust legend which have not, as far as I know, been treated in detail before. There are detailed studies of the major works, of course, and surveys which tell how the legend grew and developed, but not, for instance, studies of the Devil in Faust versions throughout the centuries or accounts of how Faust came to be confused with Fust, the printer. There does not even seem to be a detailed account of the several attempts to continue or rewrite Goethe's *Faust*. Faust and Don Juan have often been associated: in studies of the Faust legend one tends to find a brief chapter linking him to Don Juan, and in books on Don Juan a brief chapter linking him to Faust; it seemed to me that there was room for something fuller. For easy reference I felt that I ought to give a brief account of the history of Faust (Introduction); the more detailed studies of the 'Faust through the Centuries' type are mentioned in the Bibliography. Quotations are given in the original language, except in the cases of A. Tolstoi and Imry Madách. Here, since one of the main points made is the link with Goethe's *Faust*, I have quoted from German translations rather than in English.

A book such as this must necessarily from time to time mention very minor authors. Some I have brought in only to show how common a particular motif was or how persistent a particular fashion in interpretation had become. It would add nothing to the argument and merely swell the book unduly to give even brief accounts of these almost forgotten writers and so I have not attempted to do so. I have tried to keep plot summaries to a minimum, especially where the work is reasonably well known or where one of the histories of the Faust legend already gives a summary. Sometimes, however, particularly in the case of 'continuations' of Goethe (Chapter 7) and some of the 'faustian' Don Juans (Chapter 8), it has been necessary to give a résumé of the plot.

The problem with the Bibliography has been to keep it to tolerable proportions. So, since there are specialized Bibliographies concerned with Goethe's *Faust*, I have not listed all the editions, commentaries, and critical works used. Nor have I given all the versions of the Faust and Don Juan themes consulted. Many burlesques, parodies, trivial retellings of traditional incidents for popular consumption, and works which use the name of 'Faust' or 'Don Juan' for catchpenny reasons could add nothing to my argument and have therefore been omitted. My lists of Faust and Don Juan versions are therefore *not* intended to be exhaustive. In a few cases, especially where the title of a work could be misleading, I have included a brief description in the Bibliography, if only to spare others the trouble and disappointment of tracking down a hitherto unknown version which turns out to be quite spurious (e.g. Castillo's *Don Jouan*, *c.* 1870) or an apparently serious treatment of the Faust theme which is merely a silly burlesque of Goethe.

The Bibliography has been subdivided for easier reference. I have devoted two main sections to versions of the Faust and Don Juan themes respectively. These sections are arranged in chronological order; references to the various works in the text of the book therefore simply give author and date. To avoid unnecessary footnotes I have given no references for quotations from very short works (e.g. Platen's), line references only for quotations from Goethe's *Faust*, and scene references in the case of a familiar and easily accessible play (e.g. Grabbe's). Chapter 9 seemed to require a separate Bibliography; to sandwich Clerke's book on the Herschels in the General Bibliography between a study of Don Giovanni operas and a history of the popular Faust plays would have been merely confusing. Puppet plays which have, rightly, attracted a good deal of interest among historians of both legends, seemed to deserve separate sections in the Bibliography. Since they are impossible to date exactly, I have given them in order of publication.

I would like to express my gratitude to the Research Fund Committee of the University of Durham for grants made at various times between 1964 and 1972 and to the University's

Publications Board for taking up this book into its series. I am much indebted to Professor and Mrs. W. E. Yates for reading the greater part of the typescript and making all manner of helpful suggestions, to Dr. Hans Henning for many leads concerning treatments of Faust in this century, to various colleagues in Durham for their advice, and finally to Dr. W. E. Saxton for helping the book through the press.

Since writing the book, I have read Patrick Carnegy's study of Mann's Faust novel: *Faust as Musician*, London, 1973. This contains a great deal of interesting discussion of Leverkühn's compositions, both as stages in his development and in their relationship to actual composers of this century.

J. W. S.

Durham
May 1974

CONTENTS

ABBREVIATIONS

The following abbreviations have been used from time to time. The Roman numerals in parenthesis refer to the section of the Bibliography where full details may be found.

Bévotte	G. G. de Bévotte, *La Légende de Don Juan* (xiv).
Brukner and Hadamowsky	F. Brukner and F. Hadamowsky, *Die Wiener Faust-Dichtungen* (xiiia).
E. M. Butler	E. M. Butler, *The Fortunes of Faust* (xiv).
Dabezies	A. Dabezies, *Visages de Faust au 20e siècle* (xiv).
DLE	the series *Deutsche Literatur in Entwicklungsreihen*.
Geißler	H. W. Geißler, *Gestaltungen des Faust* (xiiia).
Scheible	J. Scheible, *Das Kloster* . . . (xiiic).
Tille	A. Tille, *Die Faustsplitter in der Literatur des 16. bis 18. Jahrhunderts* (xiiia). References are to items and not to pages, except where it is explicitly stated otherwise.
Weinstein	L. Weinstein, *The Metamorphoses of Don Juan* (xiv).
Wendriner	K. G. Wendriner, *Faust-Dichtung vor, neben und nach Goethe* (xiiia).

INTRODUCTION

The Development of the
Faust Legend from the sixteenth century
to the present day

'Jeder Mensch sollte einen Faust schreiben.'
(Heine)
'Le personnage de *Faust* et celui de son affreux
compère ont droit à toutes les réincarnations'
(Valéry)

DR. Faust is not of course a purely fictitious character. There
was a real Faust, whose Christian name, it is now thought,
was Georg and who was born in or around 1480, probably in
the small town of Knittlingen.[1] He must have had some formal
education and it is likely that he spent a number of years as a
wandering scholar, although it now seems certain that he styled
himself 'Doctor' without having any right to the title. He led a
restless life; he appears in Gelnhausen, Kreuznach, Erfurt,
Bamberg, Ingolstadt, Nuremberg, Würzburg, Wittemberg and
the Freiburg areas, to mention only those places for which we
have reasonably reliable evidence. He cast horoscopes (including
one for the Bishop of Bamberg in 1520) and practised medicine,
was probably a palmist, and may have possessed hypnotic powers.
He doubtless dabbled in alchemy and magic. What is certain is
that he was a flamboyant character who captured people's
imagination. There was a seedy and disreputable side to his
personality (he was turned out of various towns) but he must
have had a measure of genuine learning. If contemporary accounts

[1] A quantity of material concerning the historical Faust was published by A.
Tille in 1900 in his *Faustsplitter*. Further 'Splitter' have since been published from
time to time. The evidence regarding this historical Faust has been sifted and resifted;
I have tried to give an account containing only what would be fairly generally
agreed on. The earliest recorded statements about Faust (from 1507) obviously
contain a measure of truth. As time went on, this became overlaid more and more
with gossip and invention. Accounts dating from later than 1540 should be treated
with extreme caution.

are to be trusted, he boasted about this learning and also claimed
magical powers. Tradition has it that he died in Staufen (near
Freiburg) in 1540 or 1541; the house in which this is supposed to
have happened is now an inn.

We shall never know exactly what sort of a man this historical
Faust was. But Hans Henning is surely right in putting him
somewhere between the travelling conjurers, hypnotists, and
purveyors of 'wonder cures' on the one hand, and a genuine
student of the natural sciences on the other.[1] The theory—
advanced at intervals from the Age of Enlightenment onwards—
that he was a wholehearted and devoted seeker after truth who
was misunderstood and turned into a bogyman by the ignorant
and the prejudiced is certainly over-charitable to him. He was
doubtless something better than the boastful, prattling vagabond
devoid of true learning as depicted by Trithemius of Sponheim
in 1507, but he must have fallen far short of the subtle and
masterful scholar that Marlowe later made of him.

To pursue in detail the growth of the legend, to show the
gradual accretion of magical tales, would swell this account
unduly. Suffice it to say that, as time went on, the rumours
became wilder and wilder, and crude anecdotes about magic
came to preponderate more and more. The few scraps of fact
were quickly hidden under a mass of legend. The familiar in the
guise of a dog, the magical banquets and flights through the air,
the conjuration of Homeric characters for the benefit of students,
the wine made to flow from holes in a table—all these motifs
became attached to the figure of Faust and were bandied about
during the 1560s and 1570s. Even before his history came to be
printed for the first time in 1587, Faust had become something
resembling a character in fiction.

The *Historia von D. Johann Fausten*, published by Johann
Spies at Frankfort on the Main in 1587,[2] purports to be a 'true
history', but is in fact almost pure fiction. The anonymous
author's intention was clearly both to entertain and to construct
the 'improving' biography of a presumptuous man whose dissatisfaction with the God-given limits to human knowledge led

[1] Hans Henning, 'Faust als historische Gestalt', in *Jahrbücher der Goethe-Gesellschaft*,
xxi, Weimar, 1959, p. 138.
[2] For the best short account of the genesis of the Spies chapbook, see section iv of
the Introduction to Henning's edition, Halle, 1963.

to his downfall. The first part of the book shows this dissatisfaction, together with Faust's intellectual restlessness, and the resultant pact with the Devil. A long middle section depicts the fruits of the pact: questioning of the Devil, disputations, fame as astrologer and caster of horoscopes, journeyings, the favour of the mighty, magic powers—often put to very trivial purposes—the 'swinish and epicurean' life. The closing chapters describe Faust's last weeks on earth, his lament over his sinfulness and his gruesome death. The author moralizes sternly and ceaselessly, denouncing Faust's rebellious arrogance, appealing to the piety of the 'Christian reader', and constantly referring to the Scriptures. Even the Devil preaches Faust a sermon.

The style is naïve and unpolished (although, to be fair, it must be remarked that, apart from Luther and Fischart, hardly anyone wrote stylish German in the sixteenth century). But while a naïve and homespun manner seems perfectly appropriate for the recounting of Eulenspiegel's tricks or the innocent jests purveyed by Hans Sachs, it occasionally seems out of place in the story of Dr. Faust. Consider the homely way in which Faust is shown minimizing the dangers of an alliance with the Devil: 'Er meynet der Teuffel wer nit so schwartz, als man jhn mahlet, noch die Hell so heiß, wie mann davon sagte . . .' (p. 20). This is surely a little *too* homely for someone supposed to possess a subtle and powerful mind. One occasionally feels that one is listening not to exchanges between a learned doctor and one of the princes of Hell, but to the bickering of two apprentices or peasants in an inn: 'Laß mich zu frieden, sagt Doctor Faustus zum Geist. Antwort der Geist, So laß mich forthin auch zu frieden mit deinem Fragen' (p. 46).

However, when one thinks of the subsequent career of Dr. Faust, of the hundreds of works concerned with him and the profundities attributed to him, the most remarkable single thing about the book which, directly or indirectly, is the source of nearly all later treatments, is not so much the naïve style as the lack of sympathy that the author has for the main character. Whatever else may or may not be true of the historical Faust, he clearly thought knowledge a good thing. Yet his story is told as a fearful warning by a conservatively-minded Lutheran who thinks that the pursuit of knowledge (except in the most narrowly practical sense) is a bad thing. Nonetheless, despite the author's attitude, what we would regard as a certain intellectual nobility on Faust's part comes through. Mephostophiles [*sic*] urges Faust to make an end to his questions about Hell since the answers will merely distress him. But Faust replies: 'So wil ichs wissen, oder wil nicht leben, du must mirs sagen' (p. 38). If Faust has since come to be regarded as the personification of modern man's insatiable quest for knowledge, the germ is here. One must remember too that, censorious though the tone may be, some twenty chapters of the original Faust chapbook are devoted to Faust's attempts to satisfy his curiosity.[1]

In 1599 a new Faust book appeared independently of 'Spies', although the two works probably drew on a common (unpublished) source. The author was Georg Widmann, the work a monstrous compilation puffed out with all manner of learned and moralizing commentaries. Like the author of 'Spies' before him, Widmann is strongly anti-Catholic. This 1599 *Faust* was newly edited, with a few modifications, in 1674 by J. N. Pfitzer. Both Widmann and Pfitzer stress Faust's intellectual striving somewhat less than the Spies Faustbook had done, and play up the theme of loose living correspondingly. Pfitzer's chapbook was in turn reissued in the early eighteenth century in drastically shortened form—the story minus the commentaries—by an anonymous author styling himself 'a man of Christian persuasion' (*ein Christlich Meynender*). Since both this and Pfitzer's work were frequently reprinted in the eighteenth century[2] and since Goethe probably knew both of them, they have a certain historical importance in an account of the Faust legend, but no one would read them for pleasure today.

The legend also survived from the sixteenth to the eighteenth centuries in the drama. The 1587 chapbook had quickly been translated into English by an author signing himself P. F., a more stylish writer than the original German author and clearly also a man better fitted to understand the restlessness of the central character. The English version slightly plays down the idea of Faust's godlessness in favour of the theme of intellectual curiosity. The following examples speak for themselves:

[1] There were many reprints of the first Faustbook between 1587 and the end of the century. Some of the most familiar material goes back to the two 1587 reprints known as B and C[1].

[2] See K. Engel, *Bibliotheca Faustiana*, Hildesheim, 1963, pp. 224–9 and Henning's *Faust-Bibliographie*, i (1966), 326ff.

'Spies'	*P. F.*
... dann sein Fürwitz, Freyheit vnd Leichtfertigkeit stache vnnd reitzte jhn also ...	... for his Speculation was so wonderful ...
Denn so bald wir dein Hertz besahen, mit was Gedancken du vmbgiengest, vnd wie du niemands sonsten zu deinem solchen Fürnemmen vnnd Werck köndtest brauchen vnd haben, dann den Teuffel. ...	... for so soon as we saw thy heart, how thou didst despise thy degree taken in Divinity, and didst study to search and know the secrets of our Kingdom. ...
hette ich Gottselige Gedancken gehabt, vnd mich mit dem Gebett zu Gott gehalten, auch den Teuffel nicht so sehr bey mir einwurtzeln lassen, so were mir solchs Ubel an Leib vnnd Seel nicht begegnet ...	... had I not desired to know so much, I had not been in this case.[1]

It is on this English version of 'Spies' that Marlowe's *Dr. Faustus* was modelled. With Marlowe we have for the first time an author who has the subtlety of mind and the boldness to make Faust psychologically convincing. In 'Spies', Faust's excellence in learning is mentioned briefly in the opening chapter, but only to allow the author to stress Faust's arrogance and sinfulness in not putting this learning to 'lawful' uses. But in Marlowe's great opening monologue, we see learning criticizing itself for its own inadequacies. The dilemma of the Faust figure—man's ability to long for something more-than-human, coupled with the clarity of vision which enables him to realize that the longing is futile— this is not even hinted at by the author of 'Spies', but is well conveyed by Marlowe.

It is worth noticing that *Dr. Faustus* takes over the main sequence of events from the chapbook, using the Chorus for those parts that do not lend themselves to dramatization, so that the whole is given a clear dramatic shape. The general outline (characterization or self-characterization of Faust, pact, questioning of the Devil, adventures, displays of magic, love, growing despair as the end draws near, death) survives to dominate, or at least to influence, Faust works right up to this century.

From the 1590s onwards, itinerant troupes of actors took

[1] 'Spies', pp. 14 and 36; 'P. F.', pp. 111, 128, 129.

English plays to the Continent, and by this means Marlowe's
Faustus (or a popularized version of it) became well known in
Germany and Austria. Soon popular German plays were made in
imitation of Marlowe's work. Unfortunately we know these only
from playbills or a few brief descriptions or from very late and
debased examples, but it is easy to see how the Faust legend
became more and more sensational, how clowning and magic
gained the upper hand. There were also numerous puppet plays
of Dr. Faust, enormously popular in eighteenth-century Germany.
Here we do have a few surviving old versions, which show the
low ebb reached by Faust drama at this time. The puppet plays
start with a brief monologue which pays lip-service to the theme
of intellectual curiosity, but often gives more importance to lust
for fame or gold. Then follow the pact, magic tricks, Faust's
attempt at repentance (foiled by the appearance of Helen), and
his dreadful end. The comic element is provided by a clown, who
appears in the first part of the play as Faust's servant and in the
last act as night-watchman, so that Faust's last hour is punctuated
not, as in Marlowe's noble scene, by the striking of the clock,
but by feeble clowning.[1] Yet the passage of time and the demands
of a crude popular theatre have not been able to destroy the
broad outlines of Marlowe's play or to obscure the deeper
meaning of Faust as a character. It was not too difficult for Lessing,
the young Goethe and the *Stürmer und Dränger* to see that here
was a great theme waiting to be dealt with afresh.

It was Lessing who first 'reclaimed' Faust for serious literary
consideration in the seventeenth of his *Briefe, die neueste Literatur
betreffend* (1759). Writing at a time when naïve popular literature
was looked down on—especially if it contained magical elements[2]
—and when most cultivated Germans were looking to France
for their literary models, Lessing claimed that French neo-
classicism could never transplant successfully to Germany, that
the Germans were nearer to the English than to the French, and
that it would therefore be better to translate Shakespeare into
German than Racine and Corneille. He then pointed to the old

[1] There were also ballads about Dr. Faust, both in English and German (see
Bibliography). The English Faust-ballad is superior to the German both as poetry
and, since it was apparently always sung to the fine tune of 'Fortune my foe', in its
music; the tune to which the German ballad was sung is banal.

[2] Cf. A. Charitinus, *Von Betrüglichen Kennzeichen der Zauberey*, 1708: 'diese *miserable
piece* von *Faustens Leben* . . .' (quoted by Tille, *Faustsplitter*, p. 404).

play of Dr. Faust as containing a number of scenes worthy of a Shakespeare. Lessing still cautiously smuggles in the German piece via England, as it were, but he has prepared the ground for the *Stürmer und Dränger*: one reason for their fascination with the Faust theme was unquestionably that it was both popular and German.

As far as Lessing's own *Faust* is concerned, it is clear that he wanted to put the main stress on intellectual curiosity: Faust was to be tempted through his lust for knowledge and was to be saved because 'die Gottheit hat dem Menschen nicht den edelsten der Triebe gegeben, um ihn ewig unglücklich zu machen'.[1] No one was to follow Lessing in this precise view of what the Faust theme ought to express; the importance of Lessing's letter on Faust and of his Faust plan, the subject of much gossip and speculation in his day, is that he drew attention to the puppet play of Dr. Faust as something worthy of serious literary re-working.

Before the *Sturm und Drang* versions are discussed, something must be said of the 'allegorical drama' *Johann Faust* (1775) by the Austrian Catholic writer Paul Weidmann, who makes out of the theme an allegory of the struggle between good and evil powers for the soul of man, a struggle in which good ultimately prevails and Faust is saved. (In conception this seems to go back beyond the Faust story to those older Catholic legends, e.g. that of Theophilus, which tell of pacts with the Devil in which he is finally cheated of his prey.) The account of this cosmic struggle is combined with elements from the then popular middle-class drama. In fact, the links with Lessing's *Sara Sampson* are such that one nineteenth-century scholar, Karl Engel, actually put forward Weidmann's play—originally published anonymously— as Lessing's lost Faust work. It is difficult to understand how Engel came to believe this, however, for Weidmann's play is wooden in its characterization and stylistically flat and crude. Its main interest, viewed historically, is that it is the first Faust work in which Faust is saved. But Weidmann's Faust is an ineffectual figure; it remained for the *Stürmer und Dränger* to turn Faust into something resembling a hero.

In Goethe's *Urfaust*, Faust is an eminent scholar who turns to

[1] For a summary of the problems surrounding Lessing's *Faust*, see R. Petsch, *Lessings Faustdichtung*, Heidelberg, 1911.

magic believing that it will enable him to penetrate more deeply into nature's secrets than orthodox studies have done; in Maler Müller he is the would-be superman, *der große Kerl,* who feels himself to be more than a king, to possess limitless potentialities. Faust, it is worth noting, has become subjective. Goethe expressly tells us that he felt attracted to the figure of Faust because of a feeling of kinship, and Maler Müller says that Faust was a childhood hero of his;[1] Müller's Faust—even if not like his author—is clearly what his author would have wished to be.

The other major Faust work of the *Sturm und Drang,* the novel *Fausts Leben, Taten und Höllenfahrt* (1791) by F. M. Klinger, is set in the fifteenth century. Klinger's Faust is a moral idealist who wagers with the Devil, here called Leviathan, on whether men are good or evil. He hopes to force Leviathan to concede that they are good; Leviathan hopes to reduce Faust to his own misanthropy and cynicism. Faust loses the wager, being forced to witness the appalling wickedness and greed of mankind and to realize that his attempts to correct various injustices only increase the sum of evil and suffering. The work is not only a denunciation of man's inhumanity; it is an implied criticism—or so I believe— of that type of cosmic optimism so widespread in the eighteenth century, the optimism which saw the universe as manifesting the creator's benevolence and demonstrating the greatest possible preponderance of good over evil. Klinger's *Faust* is, in this respect, like *Candide.* Through his Leviathan Klinger questions the theodicy. When Faust demands that Leviathan help him avenge a savage injustice, the Devil replies: '. . . warum soll der Teufel Grausamkeiten ein Ende machen, da sie der geduldig ansieht, den die Menschen ihren Vater und Erhalter nennen?' (iv, 2). Later he will, it is true, paint Faust a picture of simple virtue in humble circumstances, a Rousseauesque vision of the good life in tune with nature. But this is hardly convincing within the context of the novel. For the whole course of action suggests that, if you gave such a humble virtuous man a bag of gold or helped him to a position of power, you would promptly destroy his virtue.

Heine called Goethe's *Faust* the 'secular Bible' of the Germans.[2] It certainly has its sacred texts and it has been made to yield almost as many interpretations as even the most puzzling parts of

---

[1] For Goethe, see *Dichtung und Wahrheit,* Bk. x; for Müller see Geißler, i, 314.
[2] *Romantische Schule,* First edition, Paris and Leipzig, 1833, p. 126.

the Bible. As with the Bible, so with *Faust*: everyone has managed to read out of it (or into it) a meaning acceptable to himself, his age or class, his political or religious temper. It is certainly a difficult work, difficult because of its contradictions; difficult because of its strange economy (Goethe spreading himself almost beyond measure in some parts and treating rather cursorily other, often quite important aspects of his theme); difficult, too, because of Goethe's unorthodox use of familiar motifs and symbols, and because of the way in which he uses the Faust legend to express a highly personal philosophy of life.

Goethe's *Faust* is not only the story of one man's destiny, but an elaborate attempt to demonstrate the unity behind the multifariousness of things and to show how a proper life must accord with this unity. As an elaborate synthesis and a response both to contemporary and perennial problems, it is approached in Faust literature only by Thomas Mann's *Dr. Faustus*, although not even Mann equals Goethe in his elaboration of detail within a unified structure. Faust moves towards salvation by gradually freeing himself from his overweening, ruthless and subjective impulses and seeking a more constructive and altruistic approach to life, an approach which draws its chief inspiration from nature and from the classical ideals of harmony and beauty.

A large number of Faust works were written during the Romantic era; more than a couple of dozen, if one includes poems, fragments, and parodies. The only important ones are by Chamisso (1804), Platen (1820), Lenau (1836) and—belonging to the *Spätromantik* in theme, style and mood, if not strictly according to date—Woldemar Nürnberger (1842). These four works have certain features in common. They are at best gloomy and, in three cases, tragic in their implications; Faust is doomed to a state of partial knowledge and insatiable longing. As already in the case of the *Sturm und Drang* Fausts, the Romantic Fausts tend to mirror their authors' personalities. It is worth recalling here that Novalis had, at the very beginning of the Romantic era in Germany, defined the human predicament in terms which positively invited writers to express it through the Faust theme: 'Wir suchen das Unbedingte und finden überall nur Dinge.'[1]

---

[1] First published in the *Athenäum* in 1798. Quoted here from Novalis, *Schriften*, Darmstadt, 1965, ii, 413.

Of the scores of *Fausts* written in the second half of the nineteenth century, the great majority are trivial. Certain things recur time and time again: sooner or later Faust turns away from Titanism and speculation and rejects hedonism together with Mephisto's magic arts in favour of altruistic activity and acceptance of the human condition. Many authors show the power of love as contributing towards Faust's salvation. Open imitations of Goethe's Gretchen episode are quite common, Gretchen nearly always being instrumental in Faust's salvation. Comparatively few *Fausts* written between Goethe's death and 1900 end with Faust's damnation. There seems to be some point in Rudolf Pannwitz's wry couplet:

> Wollt ihr dereinst in paradiesen leben
> Müsst ihr euch erst dem teufel übergeben.[1]

The chief reasons for this increasing tendency to save Faust are obvious: a belief that curiosity is good and the feeling, even among more or less orthodox Christians, that noble rebelliousness and a tendency to seek truth along unorthodox paths are to be tolerated. Conceptions of Faust as a character change and develop, of course, with each new work and each discussion of the 'Faust type', so that the works in which Faust is shown using his powers for unselfish ends, and those which show him loving one woman instead of lusting after many, all help to make attitudes towards him more indulgent. Furthermore, to 'damn' Faust becomes less and less meaningful as fewer and fewer educated people believe in Hell and damnation anyway. Most nineteenth- and twentieth-century works in which Faust is despatched to Hell do not imply damnation in a literal sense; they use the motif symbolically to imply that Faust is in some way doomed.

Late nineteenth-century *Fausts* are often somewhat chauvinistic in tone, and occasionally as virulently anti-Catholic as the sixteenth- and seventeenth-century chapbooks. It is often implied that Faust represents all that is best in the German spirit. Not infrequently there is an attempt to give weight and significance to these works by the introduction of renowned historical figures (Luther, Hutten, Gutenberg, Vittoria Colonna) or famous events (the Reformation, the Peasants' Uprisings of the sixteenth

[1] R. Pannwitz, 'Mechristophiles Himmelfahrt', in *Vierteljahrdrücke*, 1940, no. 3, p. 24.

century, the Sack of Rome). But such events are usually treated trivially and the great figures of the past often have little more than a walk-on part in an incident intended to illustrate some facet of Faust's character. The style is often highly derivative; few of these minor writers were able to escape from Goethe. Yet it is not surprising that so many men of decidedly modest talents should have attempted this great theme; it takes a van Gogh to astound us with a chair or a pair of boots and a Stifter to make the unsensational events related in *Kalkstein* interesting.

Heine's scenario for a Faust ballet (first published in 1851) stands out in this otherwise rather depressing period in the history of the Faust legend, for it is original, witty, genuinely dramatic. It is Heine's hymn of praise to his graceful and harmonious Hellenic dream-world, and a dramatic allegory of how pagan acceptance of life was destroyed by Christian asceticism. Heine felt that the Faust legend was an appropriate vehicle to express this, since he saw the historical Faust as a humanist deeply versed in the works of the ancients and it was, after all, the humanist scholars who unearthed the works of antiquity and began to make their implications clear.[1] The only other work of any stature in this period is Fr. Th. Vischer's parody-sequel to Goethe's *Faust*, first published pseudonymously in 1862 (see Chapter 7).

From the late eighteenth century onwards, there have, in fact, been innumerable satires, parodies and burlesques on the Faust theme. Many authors have relied on the over-optimistic assumption that a comic effect can be achieved by transferring Goethe's characters to new, incongruous spheres and altering the most famous situations and speeches (especially Faust's opening monologue) accordingly. And so Faust reappears in various trades and professions. As a chemist's assistant:

> Habe nun, ach! botanisirt . . .

—or as an army officer who dreams of finding the infallible recipe for victory:

> Habe die Taktik der Infanterie . . .

Those works which make fun of Faust as a *type* are of marginally greater interest. In them, Faust nearly always begins as a man tormented by his inability to achieve total and certain knowledge,

[1] See Heine's 'Erläuterungen' to his *Faust*.

but is soon cured of this *Wissensqual*: by a woman, by wine, even by a good meal. Most of these works will doubtless have proceeded from a feeling that the faustian self-torment was only possible because the learned doctor had nothing better to occupy his mind.[1]

The writing of Faust works has continued unabated in this century. The most important modern *Fausts* are the continuations of Goethe produced by Lunarcharski (1916) and Avenarius (1919), Valéry's fragment (1940), Thomas Mann's novel (1947), and Hanns Eisler's libretto (1952). Since these will be discussed in subsequent chapters, it is not necessary to give an account of them here. Of the others, many are sentimentally pious in tone, showing Faust returning to faith and humility and finding satisfaction in selfless activity (for example: P. Degen, 1924). Sometimes the Faust legend has been used to make polemic points about contemporary society and politics. The best example of this type of work known to me is J. Gaulke's *Der gefesselte Faust*, 1910. Where there is a close link with traditional events of the Faust legend, the indebtedness is usually either to Goethe or to the popular tradition. But in general, authors in this century have been attracted to Faust as a character or type, and the association with the legend has grown looser and looser. An example in which the *sole* link with tradition is to be found in the characterization of Faust as a tireless quester after truth, and in which the incidents of the Faust legend play no part whatsoever, is E. L. Engelhardt's *Faust, ein deutscher Mythos*, 1916. Sometimes the magical events are related or depicted but then, as a concession to modern scepticism, shown to have been nothing but a dream (examples: Gaulke's novel, mentioned above; Rudolf Payer von Thurn's novella *Doktor Faust. Ein Gelehrtenschicksal*, 1919).

There have been various Faust films and the legend has inspired many painters[2] and, of course, musicians. But although

---

[1] See *Faust, eine tragi-komische Fastnachts-Posse* . . . , Berlin, 1865, p. 5, and *Der militairische [sic] Faust* . . . , Berlin, 1891, p. 5, both anonymous. For Faust cured by woman, see J. F. Schink, 'Doktor Faust: ein komisches Duodrama' in *Theater-Journal für Deutschland,* Gotha, 1778, later republished as *Der neue Doktor Faust*, 1782; also J. E. Nürnberger's 'Faust Junior . . .' in *Ernste*(!) *Dichtungen*, Kempten, 1841. For Faust cured by Bacchus, see J. M. R. Lenz, 'Fragment aus einer Farce, die Höllenrichter genannt' of 1773. For Faust cured by food, see F. Held, 'Fausts Monolog' in *Trotz Alledem!*, Berlin, 1895.

[2] See R. Payer von Thurn, *Faust im Bilde*, Vienna, 1919, and W. Wegner, *Die Faustdarstellung vom 16. Jahrhundert bis zur Gegenwart*. Amsterdam, 1962.

composers—pre-eminently Schumann and Liszt—have provided excellent musical realizations of Faust works or comments on them, music has not been so important in the history of the Faust theme as it was in the case of Don Juan. For, as will be shown, Mozart's music to *Don Giovanni* came, through the influence of E. T. A. Hoffmann, to play a decisive part in the interpretation of Don Juan throughout the Romantic era and in the development of the legend for decades to come. This has no parallel in the history of the Faust legend. To my knowledge no Faust work has inspired music which provoked a new interpretation of the Faust legend or of Faust as a character.

The history of the Faust legend has its oddities: Goethe's *Faust* reworked in Bavarian dialect, the Faust theme used to provide a puff for an encyclopedia, even an early eighteenth-century Faust pantomime enacted by performing dogs.[1] There have been Faust postcards and china statuettes of Mephistopheles, there is a 'Liebfraumilch Dr. Faustus' and a floribunda rose 'Faust'.

---

[1] For the Bavarian *Faust*, see M. Ehbauer, *Der Faust in der Krachledern* . . . , Munich, 1960; for the commercial, see the anonymous *Faust. Der Tragödie Abschluß*, Leipzig, c. 1906; for the performing dogs, see G. Stumme, *Faust als Pantomime und Ballett*, Leipzig, 1942, pp. 88–91.

I

Faust as a Character and a Type.
Changes in interpretation and motivation

> Le magicien coupable et maudit—l'esthète ambitieux—
> le 'génie original' tumultueux et passioné—le surhumain
> ou l'homme intégral selon Goethe—le blasé romantique—
> l'utopiste d'un monde meilleur—Faust est cela tour à tour,
> selon le tempérament du poète et l'idéologie en faveur aux
> diverses époques.[1]

GENEVIÈVE Bianquis' list is not complete, but it is a useful corrective to the view that the sole or main motivation of most Fausts is the quest for knowledge. The changing attitudes towards Faust as a character in fiction and as a human type, and the different ways of interpreting what made such a figure dissatisfied with the conditions of ordinary human existence have been hinted at briefly in the preceding chapter; but they deserve consideration in detail. Faust is probably the figure most often treated in modern literature, and it is in an examination of how successive authors have stood to him and attempted to motivate his actions that the reasons for this popularity must be sought. Since so little is known for certain of the historical Faust, our starting point must be the Spies chapbook.

As already mentioned, this work devotes a good deal of space to the theme of intellectual speculation, dealing with, among other things, Faust's questions regarding Heaven, Hell, astronomy, astrology, meteorology, and so on, together with the voyages of discovery which he undertook with the Devil's aid. The treatment of these themes is naïve and limited, but it is nevertheless a curious fact that this author devotes a greater proportion of his work to Faust's curiosity than other, later authors who are much more in sympathy with this facet of Faust's character. In the Spies Faustbook, of course, the curiosity is sinful; the arrogance, pride

[1] G. Bianquis, *Faust à travers quatre siècles*, Paris, 1935, p. 7.

and envy which drive Faust into Lucifer's arms are in fact the same qualities which, according to the theologians, caused the fall of the angels. Lawless desire for knowledge, the life of pleasure, the practice of magic, showing off at court: these are all of a piece, all demonstrations of Faust's presumptuous nature.

The historical Faust, if some early testimonies[1] are to be believed, seems to have preened himself on his actual knowledge, rather than to have been obsessed with the need to find out yet more. If this is so, he was a fool in the Socratic sense: a fool because he thought himself wise. The chapbook at least shows Faust as wanting to know more at any cost (see above, p. 4), that is, it depicts a Faust who realizes the limitations of his present knowledge and wants to overcome them, even if this desire is portrayed as reprehensible.

In Marlowe, the desire to condemn is absent; he wishes to make Faust's arrogance and 'Titanism' psychologically comprehensible. The Chorus, it is true, opens and closes the play with an invitation to us to muse on the theme of wickedness finding its just reward, but the play itself is rather an attempt to make us understand. There is a danger of taking up an anachronistic stance here, but clearly there is—to put it no more strongly—a marked difference between the attitudes of Marlowe and of the anonymous chapbook author. It is interesting to see how Marlowe picks up a motif from the chapbook and gives it new meaning. Faust's 'Weheklag' begins with the lament that he is not a mere beast, for whom death is the end: 'O Ich armer Verdampter, warumb bin ich nit ein Viehe, so one Seel stirbet, damit ich nichts weiters befahren dorffte . . .' (p. 128). The burden of the lament is again Faust's sinfulness and the frightful torments that await him ('Schmertzen, Trübsall, Heulen, Weinen vnnd Zäenklappern'). Marlowe's Faustus, too, wishes that he were a beast. (Even at this moment, he pays due regard to learning and gives Pythagoras proper credit for his theory.)

> Oh *Pythagoras Metemsycosis*; were that true,
> This soule should flie from me, and I be chang'd
> Into some brutish beast.
> All beasts are happy, for when they die,
> Their soules are soone dissolu'd in elements,
> But mine must liue still to be plagu'd in hell.   (p. 291)

[1] Tille, Nos. 1 and 2.

Where the lament in the chapbook is at least as much a sermon to the reader as an expression of Faust's agony of spirit, Marlowe's passage is part of a skilfully constructed climax of terror. Marlowe has put himself inside his character, whereas the German author is observing him and moralizing about him from outside. Faust in 'Spies' is saying, in effect: 'I should either have been a beast without soul, or a virtuous man. Now I am damned.' But Marlowe, despite his reference to Hell, is not interested in such straightforward didactic effects. He is showing the tragedy of wasted human material. His passage, in which Faustus is shown longing to be less than man, harks back to the opening monologue in which he is twice shown desiring to be more than man (cf. lines 50 and 88).

After Marlowe came the long process of popularization. Evidence concerning the stage plays is, unfortunately, inconclusive. Theatre-bills understandably stress the sensational spectacle and the clowning. But two pieces of evidence suggest that the theme of intellectual curiosity stayed alive in these works and only became extinguished somewhat later, in the puppet plays. The account of a Faust play given in Danzig in 1669 contains the following: 'Hieauff begibt es sich, das D. Faustus mit gemeiner Wissenschaft nicht befreidiget [*sic*] sich umb magische Bücher bewirbet, und die Teüffel zu seinem Dienst beschwüret . . .', while the Faust play given in Vienna in 1767 by Felix von Kurz opened with: 'Fausti gelehrte Dissertation in seinem Musaeo, ob das Studium Theologicum oder Micromanticum zu erwählen'.

There is then some regard for the theme of learning in these old stage plays. But in the puppet plays little or no stress is placed on this side of Faust's character. The opening monologues tend to concentrate on ambition and dissatisfaction, while the pacts turn on pleasure, power, fame and material things. Where there is a brief mention of thirst for knowledge, it is shown as part of Faust's vulgar desire to impress his fellow men rather than as the will to become more than man.[1] The only puppet play which shows a Faust who turns to magic out of dissatisfaction with

---

[1] This idea, that Faust pursues learning merely for the fame it brings, occurs in one of Schink's treatments of the theme too: 'Theologie, Philosophei/Hatt' er bis auf den Grund durchbissen;/Er trieb das Jus, trieb Medicin,/Bloß um des Ruhmes Seifenblase.'—'Doktor Faust. Romanze . . .' (1800).

lawful scholarship is the Ulm version, probably the oldest extant, and therefore nearest to the stage plays.[1]

By the time that serious writers in the eighteenth century came to turn their attention to the Faust theme, the attitudes of educated men towards knowledge and faith had altered radically since the century in which Faust's story had first been written down. For Lessing, intellectual curiosity was the noblest of human characteristics. According to orthodox opinion in the sixteenth century, Faust had abused his understanding by seeking to pass beyond the permitted frontiers; in the eighteenth century men increasingly came to ask why we should have been granted the gift of reason if our use of this gift is bad, or only good within certain limits. Since the author of the Spies chapbook is so clearly a staunch Lutheran, it may be interesting to hear Luther on the subject of human reason. It is not surprising that Luther constantly stresses the powerlessness, indeed the irrelevance of reason in matters of faith and salvation. What can still surprise us is the way in which he sometimes restricts the application of reason to trivialities:

In äußerlichen und weltlichen Sachen, da laß man der Vernunft ihr Urtheil. Denn da kannst du wohl ausrechnen und gedenken, daß die Kuhe größer sei, denn das Kalb; item, drei Ellen länger sind, denn eine Ellen . . . und daß das Dach besser stehe oben über dem Hause, denn unter dem Hause . . . denn Gott hat auch dazu die Vernunft gegeben, daß man Kühe melken und Pferde zäumen solle, und wissen, daß hundert Gülden mehr sind, denn zehen Gülden . . . Aber allhie, wenn es dahin kömmet, wie man solle selig werden im himmelischen Wesen, und in Sachen des Glaubens, da thue die Vernunft zu, halt stille . . .[2]

Speculation regarding the hidden forces behind everyday phenomena was, for Luther, useless curiosity:

Darum, lieber Mensch, laß natürliche Kunst fahren. Weißt du nicht, was Kraft ein jeglicher Stern, Stein, Holz, Thier oder alle Creatur hat, darnach die natürliche Kunst trachtet . . . ; so laß dir begnügen an dem, das dich deine Erfahrung und gemein Wissen lehret. Es . . . ist genug, daß du weißt, daß Feuer heiß, Wasser kalt und feucht ist; daß im Sommer andere Arbeit denn im Winter zu thun ist: wisse, wie du deinen Acker, Viehe, Haus und Kind üben sollst; das ist dir gnug in

---

[1] 'Alles zu sehen und mit Händen zu greifen möchte ich wünschen . . .', i, 1.
[2] Luther, S. W., Erlangen, 1826ff, xlvii, 337f.

natürlicher Kunst: darnach denke, wie du nur allein Christum erlernest, der wird dir zeigen dich selbst, wer du bist, was dein Vermögen ist.[1]

This second passage hints clearly enough at the meaning of such phrases from the 1587 Faustbook as 'wolte alle Gründ am Himmel vnd Erden erforschen' and 'die Elementa zu speculieren' (pp. 14 and 22).

By contrast Lessing's treatment of the Faust theme is very much a part of that general praise of reason among men of the European Enlightenment. Dr. Johnson is very near Lessing when he says (30/7/1763): 'Sir, a desire of knowledge is the natural feeling of mankind; and every human being, whose mind is not debauched, will be willing to give all that he has to get knowledge.' The same point had been made wittily in the penultimate chapter of Voltaire's *Zadig* (1747), where an angel appears to the hero and speaks to him of the (for mortals) inscrutable interaction of good and evil in the universe. But supposing there were no evil? asks Zadig. Then this would be a different world with a different order, is the reply. Everything in this universe, as in all others, is subject to immutable decrees which it is not your business to question.

> Faible mortel! cesse de disputer contre ce qu'il faut adorer.—
> Mais, dit Zadig. . . .

Zadig's 'but' would have been condemned in the sixteenth century as being on a par with Faust's illicit curiosity; for the Rationalists of the eighteenth century it was man's duty to interject a 'but' whenever anyone told him to accept something unquestioningly.

The first thing that must be said about the *Sturm und Drang* Fausts is that the insistence on the quest for knowledge that dominates Lessing's plans and sketches vanishes—at least in so far as 'knowledge' has anything to do with conceptual understanding, reason, logic. These things are clearly regarded as arid in the *Urfaust*, whose hero is interested first in an intuitive grasp of nature, later in direct experience, but never in explanation. The desire for knowledge figures in Maler Müller, but only in a long list of Faust's desires: 'Geschicklichkeit, Geisteskraft, Ehre, Ruhm, Wissen, Vollbringen, Gewalt, Reichtum, alles, den Gott dieser Welt zu spielen . . .' (p. 353). Presently, in the temptation scene, Faust is enticed with material goods and pleasures but not with the prospect of knowledge (pp. 384f). Müller's Faust does, it is true, ask:

Warum hat meine Seele den unersättlichen Hunger, den nie zu erstillenden Durst nach Können und Vollbringen, Wissen und Würken, Hoheit und Ehre . . . ?   (p. 416)

—but his main preoccupation is not to get an answer to this question, but to overcome the limitations to which it refers. A practical Faust, so to speak. . . .

Klinger's Faust begins by asking, among other things, about the hidden principles governing the universe; he wishes to learn about the purpose of man's life and the causes of moral injustice (i, 8). It may be noted that, if one assumes the existence of God and of purpose in the universe, the single problem of moral injustice embraces a good deal of what is traditionally understood by Faust's 'rebellious' curiosity. But Faust is quickly made to realize that, as a mortal, he cannot hope for an answer; the theme of intellectual curiosity is dead by the end of Book 1 of Klinger's novel.

In fact, what distinguishes the *Sturm und Drang* Fausts from Lessing's Faust and, to some extent, from the Faust of the original chapbook is that they do not so much want to *know* more than other men as to *be* more than other men. They are nearer to Marlowe's Faustus in this than to any other previous Faust, although any similarities are fortuitous since Marlowe was not known to the *Stürmer und Dränger*. Where Marlowe's Faustus had dreamed of becoming 'a Demi-god' through magic, the hero of the *Urfaust* feels god-like as he gazes on the sign of the Macrocosm and arrogates to himself something like superhuman status when he claims equality with the Earth Spirit. He is rebuffed, it is true (lines 159f), but this is a rejection because he has demanded the impossible, not a condemnation because he is wicked. Other *Stürmer und Dränger* go further and, implicitly or explicitly, praise Faust's desire to be more than man. Maler Müller sees him as a giant, worth a whole universe of lesser souls, 'Pöbelseelen'.[1] For the first time in Faust literature Faust is likened to a

[1] Cf. Klinger, i, 7: '. . . ein Mann wie [Faust] ist mehr wert als tausend der elenden Schufte, die . . . auf eine alltägliche Art zur Hölle fahren.'

god *with approval*: '[Ich] fühl' den Gott in meinen Adern flammen
. . .' (p. 353). This conception of Faust shows not only the
admiration of the *Sturm und Drang* for the 'Titanic' figure, but
also the moral ambivalence of this ideal. Maler Müller's Faust
is a superman of whom it is hardly relevant to ask whether he is
good or bad. Greatness is all.

Klinger's Faust, too, is a colossus—'ein Genie' says Satan
himself, with reluctant admiration (i, 7). His boldness is such that
the devils grow pale (v, 8). His rebellion takes the form firstly of
railing against the moral injustices in the world, then of trying
himself to put them right.

The two most considerable Faust works of the *Sturm und
Drang* period, then, demonstrate in their different ways that even
the greatest and boldest of men will be frustrated if they try to
become more than man. Klinger's Faust tries to usurp God's
position as moral arbiter and creates yet more suffering and
despair; Goethe's Faust is first cut down to size by the Earth
Spirit, then mocked by Mephisto: 'Warum machst du Gemein-
schafft mit uns wenn du nicht mit uns auswirthschafften kannst.
Willst fliegen und der Kopf wird dir schwindlich.'[1] But man is
not *condemned* for wanting to be more than man. It is in his nature
or, at least, in the nature of any bold and free spirit. (These
Sturm und Drang Fausts are indeed not so far from the ideal of
'der freie Geist', which Nietzsche was to formulate a century
later.)

Goethe's completed *Faust* seems to confirm the move away
from intellectual curiosity as the main motive behind Faust's
alliance with the Devil. If one had to express Faust's ruling urge
in a phrase, it would clearly have to be something like 'desire for
experience' or 'restless activity' rather than curiosity: as in
Klinger, the pact has become a wager bound up with Faust's
view of human nature. In each case Faust bets on something
which he regards as essential in man (Klinger: moral goodness;
Goethe: that dissatisfaction which leads to ceaseless activity). This
shows up the triviality of most pacts in the popular Faust
tradition, where Faust sells his soul for perks, so that the Devil
becomes not much more than the bestower of gifts and the
impresario of magical displays.

For Goethe, then, the essence of Faust is an urge to experience

[1] This passage is from the antepenultimate scene of the *Urfaust*, ed. cit., p. 210

all that men can experience and perform all actions open to men, rather than anything as narrow as purely intellectual striving. In the second conversation with Mephisto, Faust actually describes himself as *healed* of this striving for knowledge (line 1768) and, in Part 2, Goethe goes still further. For previously, in all versions of *Faust* in which the theme of knowledge figured at all, Faust had at some point badgered Mephisto with questions. If there had been any reluctance, it had been reluctance on Mephisto's part to answer.[1] But in the scene 'Hochgebirg', Mephisto positively thrusts information on Faust, who however is bored, indisposed to probe into first causes (10095f) or, at best, ready to listen with faintly indulgent amusement (10122f). Now it is true that Mephisto's account of how these rocks and peaks came into existence (10075–88) has clear affinities with Vulcanism and so is unlikely to appeal to a Faust created by the Evolutionist Goethe— but the real reason for Faust's impatience goes deeper. Ideas and experiences that do not have any consequences for man's practical conduct are sterile. Mephisto's 'foolish legends' (10073) fail by this criterion, where Faust's experience of nature ('Anmutige Gegend') and of ancient cultures (Acts 2 and 3) stand the test. Even Mephisto realizes that Faust's latest desire to act boldly and constructively stems from his experiences of and insights into 'heroic' ages (10185f). It is not that, in *Faust*, Goethe preaches against the pursuit of ideas or of knowledge; only of such knowledge as has no bearing on man's practical conduct. (This point was often overlooked in nineteenth-century discussions of the work.)

As has been mentioned, the *Fausts* of the Romantic era are highly subjective works, the heroes projections of the authors' longings and dilemmas. Lenau, in the following famous passage from his *Faust*, is obviously characterizing himself through Faust: '. . . stets geneckt von Zweifeln und gezerrt,/Ein Fremdling ohne Ziel und Vaterland . . .' (p. 7). This Faust cannot find satisfactory answers to his questions about life, yet is unable to stop brooding in order to enjoy life without questioning. Faust rebels against the idea of submitting to God and is repelled by the thought of being merely a link in nature's chain of being:

---

[1] Traditionally, the Devil may not answer questions concerning the nature or the activities of God. Often, in the older versions, Faust asks Mephisto who created the world, but receives either no answer or a false one.

> Ist Christus Gott, und folg ich seinem Schritt,
> So bin ich, sei es auch auf Himmelspfaden,
> Der Schuh nur, den sein Fuß erfüllt und tritt. . . .
> Ists die Natur—bin ich ein Durchgang nur,
> Den sie genommen fürs Gesamtgeschlecht. . . .   (p. 86)

—and so he retreats into his own ego:

> Behaupten will ich fest mein starres Ich,
> Mir selbst genug und unerschütterlich,
> Niemandem hörig mehr und untertan,
> Verfolg ich in mich einwärts meine Bahn.   (p. 87)

This extreme of subjectivity is the Romantic variation on the old tune of Faust's arrogance and pride. In the same year as Lenau's *Faust*, J. I. Baggesen's parody *Der vollendete Faust* made the point that the book which Faust studies most intensively is the book of his own ego:

> Hab' auch fast keine Bücher gelesen;
> Denn das ist alles erbärmlich Wesen;
> Schlage mir auf ein einzigs nur,
> Nämlich die genial'sche Natur
> Meines eigenen großen Ichs—
> Such' ich etwas, da findet sich's.   (p. 140)

The manner of making the point is clumsy, but the point itself is a just one; the Fausts of Lenau, Platen and Chamisso all either feel themselves to be imprisoned within themselves, or retreat into the ego when the external world proves frustrating. The philosophical problem of perception, which is central to Chamisso's Faust fragment and figures also in Platen's poem, intensifies this feeling of subjective isolation; the world outside is felt to be either a projection of Faust's ego or, at best, filtered through his ego and hence coloured by it (see below, pp. 88f). The Faust theme has undergone a precise reversal since Lessing. Consider the following exchange from Chamisso:

FAUST: Erschuf zu ausgesuchten Qualen mich
              Ein Gott des Hasses, den der Schmerz erfreut?
GUTER GEIST: Das Glück umblühte deines Lebens Pfade.
FAUST: Es ist Erkennen mir das einz'ge Glück.
GUTER GEIST: Die Hoffnung blüht dem Dulder; lern' entbehren!
FAUST: Sie welkte in der schwer erkrankten Brust.
GUTER GEIST: Der Tugend Kranz umgrüne deine Locken!
FAUST: Auch diesen Kranz entriß der Zweifel mir.

Why should man be made unhappy because of his curiosity?
Lessing had asked. Chamisso: man is inescapably condemned
to unhappiness precisely because of his curiosity. From the
contrast—Lessing dating from before the Kantian *Critiques*,
Chamisso writing after Fichte's most radically subjective works
had made their impact—we can measure the blow dealt to intellectual confidence by Kantian and post-Kantian philosophy.

Chamisso, Platen, Lenau, W. Nürnberger, Vischer (in his early
cycle of poems 'Faustische Stimmen')—none of these authors
holds out any hope for Faust. Lenau is the most subtly pessimistic.
For his Faust, having failed to find certainty or pleasure or comfort
either outside himself or within himself, ends by persuading
himself that the whole thing was only a troubled dream in the
mind of the divinity, that the universe is an indivisible One, and
that his feeling of separation is a delusion. As he commits suicide
in this conviction, it is Mephisto who gloatingly reveals that the
conviction is itself a delusion. But even so, it is devastatingly
ironic that the only stilling of the faustian urge appears to lie in
ceasing to experience as a separate being at all, that the very
personification of modern subjectivity and individual self-
assertion is forced by the logic of his own nature to long for the
loss of selfhood.

In the Romantic era, then, Faust tended to be seen as a tragic
figure rather than as wicked. However, throughout the nineteenth
century, there were occasional throwbacks to the older view,
occasional works which depicted Faust with pious disapproval.
E. von Groote's *Faust's Versöhnung mit dem Leben* (1816) is a
didactic treatise attacking the faustian urge. The restless desire
for more and more knowledge, together with pride and arrogance,
are all condemned much as in the original Faustbook; intellectual
curiosity is responsible for man's continuing in his fallen state.
Men should cultivate patience and humility and accept that
certainty is not attainable in this life.

A somewhat similar view of Faust (haughty, ambitious, vain)
is presented in G. Soane's 'Romantic Drama' *Faustus* (1825), and
finds expression too in the various modernized versions of
the old chapbooks that continued to appear throughout the
nineteenth century.[1] Meanwhile, in reaction against what was

[1] Such as that by O. E. H. Schönhuth, 1844. The anonymous chapbook published in
Vienna in 1857 combines the old, wicked Faust with Klinger's would-be benefactor.

felt to be an idealization of Faust in Goethe's work and in the comments of some of his critics, there were a number of attacks against the 'immorality' of his Faust (see Chapter 7).

But such attempts to recast Faust as a villain are comparatively few. More commonly, as has been said already, Faust was reformed and saved (see above, p. 10). Faust, that is, is no longer regarded as a wicked man, or even as a character who, because he is what he is, is placed in a tragic situation, but as a good character who temporarily went astray. A surprising number of Fausts are shown as trying to do good with diabolical assistance, although their attempts are seldom successful. If we are to examine the development of this idea, it is necessary to retrace our footsteps for a moment.

The first hint of a 'philanthropic' Faust occurs, rather oddly, in the original Faustbook, which tells of a young man who fell ill out of unrequited love. Faust learns of this and turns the girl's heart towards her suitor by magic means. They marry and—for all that we are told—live happily ever after (Chapter 54 in the first edition). Widmann and Pfitzer tell the story too, but give it a new twist, mentioning that parents and friends were far from happy about this hasty wedding and adding darkly that the marriage will doubtless have been an unhappy one, being brought about with the aid of the Devil.[1] And so Faust has already been turned from a successful benefactor into an unsuccessful one, on the principle that any gift or benefit coming from the Devil is likely to turn sour (see too Chapter 4).

The theme re-enters Faust literature with Weidmann. Here Faust uses the Devil's services in an attempt to harm his enemy and benefit his friends, but brings about the opposite of what he desires. The enemy, ruined financially by Faust, finds happiness in a simple and humble way of life, while those whom Faust 'rewards' with riches, beauty, etc., are corrupted and brought to misery (see Act ii). The old superstition concerning the Devil's gifts has been freed from its magical associations: here it is the beneficiaries who turn the gifts into curses by their abuse of them (the man suddenly become rich turns into a miser, the beauty into a coquette, and so on). Already we are near to the situation in Klinger and, in fact, it is likely that Klinger was influenced by this part of Weidmann's play. Klinger, as might be expected, is

[1] Bk. ii, Ch. 6, Note ii; similarly ii, 18, Note iii.

both more savage in his treatment of the theme and more far-reaching in his implications. The effect of Faust's ill-advised attempt to play Providence will last for centuries, says Leviathan, and future generations will curse him for it (v, 5). Sudden benefits corrupt the recipients and Faust is totally unable to perceive the potentiality for evil in those whom he assists. A youth saved from drowning brings Faust's own family to ruin (v, 4); the apparently noble champion of freedom (Robertus) turns out to have been driven on by envy and brings about the most appalling disorder and violence (v, 6). These incidents are integral to the plan of the work as a whole. A Faust so obsessed by moral injustice as Klinger's Faust will inevitably try to correct it, if he has the power. But, given human corruption, such attempts are bound to go wrong.

This aspect of Klinger's *Faust* was much copied, although no one came near the misanthropic power of the original, and no one related the motif to the central theme of the work as successfully as Klinger. More or less open imitations of him can be found in Soden (1797), Schöne (1809) and Voß (1823). An account of some puppet plays which follow Klinger is given in Chapter 6. Schink (*Johann Faust*, 1804) takes up Klinger's point but shows Faust for once as successful in his attempts to do good. The imitators of Klinger are all minor talents; the importance of such examples is that they show one of the ways in which the new approving attitude towards Faust could manifest itself. The *Teufelsbündner* could at least be shown trying to use his powers for good.

From the middle of the nineteenth century onwards, attempts to show Faust working in the cause of political or ideological freedom have been common. Faust was often cast as a popular hero in the Peasants' Uprisings of the sixteenth century, or shown as taking part in the struggles of the Reformation (see Chapter 7). Fausts who use their powers to help humanity persist up to the present day (for examples, see Kratzmann, 1927; Mampell, 1962; Becsi, 1963).

It is curious that, where Faust has been represented as a benefactor, whether successful or unsuccessful, his efforts have almost invariably been directed either towards correcting the injustices of the moral order or supporting the people against tyranny (or both). Klinger's Faust invents printing[1] and Goethe's

---

[1] Although, oddly enough, *before* the pact. See Chapter 5 for further details. A number of authors copied Klinger.

sets the Devil to work reclaiming land from the sea, but I do not know of any subsequent Faust who directs his powers to scientific or technological ends until this century.

The stress on the active life is linked, as has been seen, with the movement away from abstract speculation. Often, however, Faust is shown as tiring of speculation in order to turn to the life of the senses. In the Spies chapbook, the sensual life is shown in all its aspects: good living, women, music, dancing and lavish spectacles. Goethe too is comprehensive. But the influence of the Gretchen episode was such that writers came to concentrate on the pursuit of woman almost exclusively. This tendency was particularly strong in nineteenth-century England. In H. P. Grattan's *Faust* (1842), the love interest predominates; in W. S. Gilbert's *Gretchen* (1879), it provides the *sole* motivation of Faust. W. G. Wills' adaptation of Goethe (1886) lays the entire emphasis on Faust and Gretchen—the quest for knowledge does not figure at all. (Perhaps there is an English distrust of German abstract philosophical speculation and 'mysticism' at play here, making these writers disinclined to show Faust as an intellectual brooder. Certainly Gilbert, who had managed to create a Faust quite untouched by intellectual curiosity, makes fun, in *Patience* and elsewhere, of 'transcendentalism' and 'mysticism', without showing much sign of understanding what the terms mean or to whom they may appropriately be applied.) Be that as it may, such versions are trivial compared with the original chapbook. For there, the urge to speculate and the urge to enjoy run parallel for much of Faust's life. But as his twenty-four years run out, the emphasis on the epicurean life grows stronger (Chapter 57); that is, Faust turns to sensual pleasures to take his mind off his approaching end. This is much more psychologically convincing than those works in which Faust simply throws off curiosity to wallow in sensuality:

> Und des Helden glüh'nder Drang nach Wahrheit
> Kühlte sich im Schlamm der Sinnlichkeit.[1]

Of course, sometimes the movement towards hedonism is an integral part of later *Fausts* too. Volumes have been written about this aspect of Goethe's *Faust*; it is not necessary to add to the

[1] 'W. Jemand' (= W. Langewiesche), 'Faust' in *Lies Michl*, Iserlohn, 1834. p. 319.

discussion here. In Lenau, Faust's sensual desires are awakened, only to show him their destructive nature and oppress him with guilt. In W. Nürnberger too, Faust is made to yield to the body only to despise it.

It will have become clear that, especially throughout the nineteenth century, Faust tended to become less and less of a highly specialized and exceptional human being and more and more generalized. With the benefit of hindsight, we can see that this was more or less inevitable after Goethe. For Goethe's Faust is made the subject of a wager between God and the Devil, a wager entered on as a result of a conversation about mankind in general. And what Faust demands is the greatest possible range of human experience. Moreover, it is not too difficult to see *Faust 2* as a sort of Odyssey of modern western man. That Goethe's Faust is in all sorts of ways a most *extra*ordinary man sometimes tended to be overlooked in discussions of what made him typical of humanity:

... jeder Mensch [ist] mehr oder weniger ein Faust; denn keiner ist so durchaus christlich, daß er nicht je zuweilen etwas anders wünschen sollte, als es wirklich ... ist; keiner ist so geduldig, daß er überall sogleich seinen Willen mit dem Allgemeinen ... zu identifiziren vermöchte.[1]

For Karl Rosenkranz, Goethe's Faust was 'the representative of human kind', typifying the 'modern Fall of Man'. Stolte talks of Faust in a similar way as 'der die Menschheit repräsentirende Faust' while, according to Tertullian Faber, Faust is man *tout court*: 'Faust ist der Mensch'.[2] Hango's *Faust und Prometheus* (1895) also sets up Faust in this typified role. In each case, the equation is only arrived at after a good deal of simplification and the exclusion of much that we would regard as typically faustian, whether by this we mean pertaining to Goethe's Faust or to the Faust type. Faber simply means that Faust represents the conflict between sensual urges and higher impulses, and Hango regards Faust as typical of the nineteenth-century spirit of doubt. The most interesting and witty modern variation on the theme that Faust can somehow stand, if not for man in general, at least for

[1] C. F. Göschel, *Über Göthe's Faust* ... , Leipzig, 1824, p. 297.
[2] For Rosenkranz, see Schwerte, *Faust und das Faustische*, Stuttgart, 1959, p. 136; for Stolte, the 'Vorwort' to his *Faust* (1860), p. xix; for Faber, *Der neue Faust* (1851), p. 13.

modern western man, is in Valéry's *Mon Faust*; here Faust is shown as *victim* of western European culture, conditioned to ask pointless and unanswerable questions involving the concept of purpose.

'Nicht *Faust* wär ich, wenn ich kein *Deutscher* wäre!' says Grabbe's Faust (*Don Juan und Faust*, i, 2). As has been seen, a major factor in the 'reclaiming' of Faust for literature in the late eighteenth century was the feeling that here was a typically German legend. Soon the character of Faust too (his speculative urge, his restlessness) comes to be regarded as typically German. The more naïve type of writer tended to underline this by bringing in all manner of figures and events from German history and culture, even if they were only marginally connected with the theme. Thus, in J. D. Hoffmann's Goethe-continuation (1833), there is a scene in praise of Dürer, a procession of trade guilds in Nuremberg, scenes in Strasbourg cathedral, and so on. These episodes are obviously intended first and foremost to awaken associations with 'old Germany', thereby showing how typically German the Faust theme is. Often a contrast is drawn between the Reformation (seen as essentially German) and southern European Catholicism. This antithesis is nearly always naïvely made and the presentation is highly biased. In Adolf Müller's *Faust* (1869) the link between Faust as a German figure and the Reformation as a German movement is perfectly explicit: 'Ich fühle mich glücklich und gehoben', says Müller in his introduction, 'dies Bruchstück [=Goethe's First Part] nach deutschem Wollen und Vollbringen zu einem Ganzen gestaltet zu haben.' Faust, he continues, has been brought into the sphere of the Reformation ('in die Bewegungen der größesten, eigensten Thaten des deutschen Geistes'). All the Faust plays in which Faust takes up the cudgel in the cause of the Reformation or allies himself to the rebellious peasants express the feeling that he somehow stands for the German people or for all that is best in the German spirit. (Heine's equation of Faust with the German people on the grounds that both rejected asceticism and wished at last to pay due heed to the rights of the flesh—*Romantische Schule*—is a personal and idiosyncratic reading which remained, as far as I know, without influence.)

In the second half of the nineteenth century, equations of

Faust with the German spirit (usually in an idealizing manner, nearly always Protestant and nationalistic in flavour) were quite common. August Spieß, writing in 1854, claimed that in Goethe's *Faust* was to be found 'jenes Streben nach dem Hohen und Wahren, welches *dem Deutschen vor den anderen Nationen eigen ist . . .*'[1] For an arbitrary interpretation of Goethe's *Faust*, which seeks to represent that work as an allegorical pageant of the German spirit and Faust himself as representing the German people, see F. G. H. Hoffmann's *Das Gerippe von Goethes Faust*, Frankfort on the Main, 1894. Nietzsche regards Faust as one of the extremes to which the German character tends. For him, the German is either Faust or a Philistine, either permanently dissatisfied or complacent; there is no happy mean. The implications are critical: Nietzsche is far from the chauvinism of Adolf Müller or August Spieß, but he is just as ready to set up Faust as a psychological type with specifically German characteristics: 'Wenn der Deutsche aufhört, Faust zu sein, ist keine Gefahr größer als die, daß er ein Philister werde. . . .'[2]

In Spengler's 'morphology' of human culture, *Der Untergang des Abendlandes* (1918–22), western European civilization itself is described as 'faustian'. Faustian, for Spengler, signifies everything dynamic and speculative, all impatience with restrictions, a dislike of anything cut-and-dried, a romantic longing for the unattainable and indefinable. The term has ceased to have very much to do with any character or characters in literature called 'Faust', and can be applied to such diverse manifestations of western culture as religious dogmatism, *Lear*, the cult of the Virgin, Kant's Categorical Imperative, modern science, *The Art of Fugue*, and Nietzsche's 'will to power'.

A few Faust works were directly influenced by Spengler, the most interesting being Ernst Kratzmann's *Faust. Ein Buch vom deutschen Geist*, first published in 1932. This novel—which does not draw on the traditional Faust legend for anything except the name of the hero—is virtually a chronicle of German life from the late thirteenth to the mid-fourteenth centuries,[3] with a very idealized Faust as its central character. As the title implies, the work

[1] Quoted by Schwerte, p. 105. For a somewhat similar passage by the young Raabe, see Schwerte, p. 102.

[2] Nietzsche, *Werke*, Kröner, Leipzig, i (1923), p. 426.

[3] Kratzmann himself cheerfully pleads guilty to various anachronisms in the work.

presents Faust as embodying everything which is best in the
German spirit. Where Kratzmann cannot actually ascribe something to Faust, he shows him as being in some way in tune with
it. Thus we find Faust inspiring the architects of Naumburg and
Cologne, and advising Master Eckhart on what to preach.
Broadly speaking, Faust stands for a spirit of free intellectual
enquiry, for all that is best in German artistic and intellectual
life, for German nationalism, a quasi-mystical reformative
position in religion, and a desire for political freedom (but not at
the cost of revolution or anarchy). Kratzmann is, of course, much
narrower than Spengler. *Der Untergang des Abendlandes* is free
from religious dogmatism and anything resembling chauvinism;
Spengler's 'faustisch' is truly European, embracing Kant and
Descartes, Bach and Dante. Kratzmann, on the other hand,
restricts himself to things German and also excludes all fruits of
Catholic philosophy and theology. But the debt to Spengler is
clear, for Spengler does indeed imply that a writer can appropriately take characteristics of a whole culture, relate them to
a single man and call him Faust. Hermann Ammon is another
writer who takes Spengler's 'faustisch' and makes something
nationalistic out of it: 'Goethes Faust ist die Darstellung der
Entwicklung der faustischen, d.h. deutschen Kultur'.[1] Goethe's
Faust had often enough been linked with the German spirit in
the nineteenth century of course, but the phrase 'faustische
Kultur' betrays the influence of Spengler. The recasting of
Spengler's ideas in overtly nationalistic and racialistic terms is
still clearer in Alfred Rosenberg's *Mythus des 20. Jahrhunderts*,
first published in 1930. Again Goethe's *Faust* is seen as an
expression of the German soul: 'Goethe stellte im Faust das
Wesen von uns dar, das Ewige, welches nach jedem Umguß
unserer Seele in der neuen Form wohnt.' It is noticeable that
Rosenberg's list of cultural achievements, achievements of
'faustian' man, includes nothing that is not German or at least
Nordic: '. . . eine nordische Heldensage, ein preußischer Marsch,
eine Komposition Bachs, eine Predigt Eckeharts, ein Faustmono-
log sind nur verschiedene Äußerungen ein und derselben Seele,
Schöpfungen des gleichen Willens. . . .'[2] From Rosenberg it is

[1] *Dämon Faust—wie Goethe ihn schuf,* 1932. Quoted by Dabezies, p. 278.
[2] Alfred Rosenberg, *Der Mythus des 20. Jhts.,* 143/146th edn., Munich, 1935,
pp. 515 and 680.

only a short step to those writers who gave the concept 'faustian' definite Fascist overtones (a development which will be discussed in Chapter 6).

Representations of Faust as a creative artist are not common, despite the fact that the equation of Faust with the German spirit would seem positively to invite the writing of Faust works in which the hero was shown as a typically German imaginative genius. A further obvious link with the Faust theme is that artists in various ways attempt the impossible. E. H. Gombrich talks of post-Renaissance art in terms of unremitting attempts to test and modify schemata until they cease to be ready-made formulae and come closer and closer to an expression of the artist's unique impression. Progress in art is achieved by 'sacred discontent'.[1] Some of da Vinci's sketches show him 'demanding the impossible' as surely as Faust did when he set off on his quest for Helen. I am thinking particularly of Leonardo's attempts to express the fluidity and the swirling effects of water in terms of fixed lines. In literature too: the enforced use of existing words and constructions (of a language, that is, ready-made in accordance with the experiences and perceptions of others) to express something unique and personal can pose almost impossible problems. (The dilemma has probably been best expressed in modern times by Hofmannsthal in the 'Chandos-Brief', 1902.)

There are all manner of legends and anecdotes suggesting both that the artist strives after the impossible and that in so doing he challenges the gods or usurps their function.[2] Thus the artist combines two of the main characteristics which occur in Faust after Faust. Ernst Kris and Otto Kurz point out how biographies of famous painters and sculptors frequently mention the creation of something so lifelike that it deceives the viewer—the artist has taken the copying of nature to such lengths that he seems almost to have achieved a magical act of creation. That birds could be induced to peck at the mere painted image of grapes implies a challenge to the god-creator by the artist-creator. In their different ways, the stories surrounding Prometheus' fashioning of men out of clay, Daedalus' moving statues, and the Tower of Babel

[1] E. H. Gombrich, *Art and Illusion*, 2nd edn., London, 1962, p. 148.
[2] Cf. Ernst Kris and Otto Kurz, *Die Legende vom Künstler*, Vienna, 1934.

all have to do with this challenge, this implicit or explicit claim
by the artist that he is godlike.

According to Kris and Kurz (pp. 63f) legends telling how
artists accomplished their great works with the Devil's aid—
either concluding a pact with him or else somehow tricking or
forcing him into service—are not uncommon. A late example
which has marked similarities with the Faust legend is that of the
eighteenth-century sculptor Franz Xaver Messerschmidt, an
eccentric recluse who worked fanatically at his character busts,
putting weird caricatured heads at the windows of his house to
discourage visitors. The local population came to believe that
Messerschmidt had made a pact with the Devil and contrived
these strange productions with supernatural aid.[1]

In view of all this—the persistence of legends concerning the
'godlike' activities of the artist, the glorification of the artist
type from the Renaissance on, the existence of stories telling of
artists who enjoyed diabolical assistance—it is surprising that
there are not more Faust works that represent Faust as an artist,
striving to achieve the ultimate in his chosen medium and
becoming convinced that, failing supernatural help, the limitations
of his faculties, techniques and materials will doom him to fall
short of his ideal.

Platen's Faust does, it is true, bewail his inability even to
express adequately his sense of frustration at being unable to
attain a state of perfect insight: 'So hauch' ich's (= das Weben
dieser tiefen Brust) feurig nun in ahnungsvollen Dichterklang,/
Doch ach, das Wort zerstückelt, kümmerlich, Unendliches!'—
but the poet's feeling of impotence *as a poet* is only the secondary
theme here, introduced almost as a side-issue at the end; the
body of the poem is concerned with man's feeling of insignificance
in the cosmos and his faltering attempts to understand God and
nature. The central figure of Ida Gräfin von Hahn-Hahn's novel
Faustina (1841) is painter, composer and poetess, and the hero of
Spielhagen's novella *Faustulus* (1898) is a writer, but it was left
to Thomas Mann to produce a major Faust work with a creative
genius as hero and a plot which took up and re-formed the Faust
legend so as to express the problems facing a creative artist.
Arnim, in his preface to a German edition of Marlowe's *Faustus*
in 1818, had imagined the possibility of an artist-Faust whose

[1] Cf. Albert Ilg, *F. X. Messerschmidt's Leben und Werke*, Leipzig and Prague, 1885.

pact with the Devil would involve neither knowledge, nor love nor pleasure but artistic genius:

Auch ließe sich ein Faust als Schriftsteller denken, der seine Seele und Seligkeit an ein Werk setzt . . .[1]

Not for a century and a quarter, however, was such a Faust to be created.

[1] p. 36 in the 1911 edn., ed. Badt.

2

The Devil

IT is obviously beyond the scope of this chapter to give a
'history of the Devil'. The reader can find this in Roskoff and
Graf (see Bibliography, xiv). Here it is sufficient to recall Roskoff's
demonstration of how a picture of the Devil gradually emerged
from study of the Old and New Testaments, how the Church
Fathers, and medieval theologians after them, elaborated and
systematized, how Neoplatonic, Talmudic, and Cabbalistic
concepts were taken up at different times, both enriching and
confusing the picture, how in the later Middle Ages and the
century of the Reformation there grew up a pathological obsession with the Devil, so that learned and ignorant alike saw him,
his legions and his works everywhere. Learned *and* ignorant: it is
worth stressing this fact, for it is a very unhistorical point of view
that distinguishes all too sharply between 'learned' and 'popular'
elements in the early chapbooks of Dr. Faust.

For Luther, the Devil is 'Lord of the world': cunning and
arrogant, envious of God and arch-enemy to mankind. He
afflicts men with all manner of diseases and misfortunes, tempts
them to sin, deceives and deludes them through false promises,
lies, visions, and dreams. He is hostile to marriage, encourages
men to break the Commandments and uses the Papacy to further
his ends. (All of this, except the last point, is traditional and can
be found in the Bible, the Church Fathers and/or the medieval
theologians.) Clearly the anonymous author of the 1587 Faustbook
was largely influenced by this Lutheran Devil in depicting his
Mephostophiles [*sic*]. He adds, of course, traits from the devils of
comic literature and legend, laughable and fairly harmless
workers of magical tricks, stewards of a magical *Schlaraffenland*-
pantry. But it would be idle to try to distil any sort of logical and
unified characterization of Mephisto from this chapbook, or
indeed from any of the popular treatments of the Faust-theme.

The characterization has taken second place to the author's didactic intentions. When Mephisto tells Faust of Lucifer's fall, of Hell, of what he would have done in Faust's place, and so on (Chapters 11–17), he is not really addressing Faust at all; he is talking to the readers, exhorting them to shun pride and rebelliousness. (Most critical accounts of the Mephisto of this earliest chapbook have tacitly admitted this by tending to trace Mephisto's ancestry rather than to characterize him.) In fact, it is Mephostophiles' fondness for sermonizing rather than any other character trait that influenced the Devils of succeeding popular Faustworks. In the Faustbook of the 'Christlich Meynender', Mephisto at one point steps right out of character and warns Faust against the course he is taking. The author's comment on this episode is that it demonstrates God's indescribable mercy, 'daß alle Kreaturen, ja der Teufel selbst wider seinen Willen die abtrünnigen Sünder zur Buße vermahnen müssen'.[1] This seems an anticipation (although in very limited and naïve form) of Goethe's view of a Devil who wills the bad, yet conduces to the good.

The popular Faust-pieces often follow the chapbooks in the naïveté of their presentation of Mephisto. In the Ulm puppet play Mephisto assures Faust that, in his place, he would have been virtuous in order to gain Heaven (ii, 6). Usually Mephisto affirms that he would be prepared to climb to Heaven on a ladder with sharp knives as rungs.[2] In one Austrian puppet play, he would be prepared to put up with still more: 'Glaube mir, wenn die ganze Welt mit glühenden Nägeln beschlagen wäre, so ginge ich bis zum jüngsten Tag barfüßig darauf herum, wenn ich die Himmelsseligkeit noch erlangen könnte.'[3]

None of this is surprising. One would expect to find a preaching Mephisto in didactic works, or in naïve works of entertainment. What *is* surprising is to encounter these out-of-character utterances in the Devil of more sophisticated, 'literary' *Fausts*. Thus, in Klinger's *Faust*, when countless demonstrations of the evil

---

[1] Scheible, ii, 84. A similar exchange is already present in Widmann (i, 22), although the point concerning the usefulness of the Devil is not made explicit.

[2] For example, in the version edited by Hamm, 1850, iv, 3.

[3] *Der Schutzgeist* . . . , 1885, p. 187. There is a moralizing Mephisto, too, in F. Brutschin's modern version of the puppet play (*Faust*, Lucerne, 1948). Here Mephisto has the traditional passages about the red-hot nails and the sharp knives, and a long moralizing speech in addition, in which he condemns Faust's desire to be an *Übermensch* (pp. 62f, 72f). Weidmann's Devil sermonizes too.

effects of civilization have driven Faust to despair of ever finding goodness in his fellow men, it is Leviathan who points the Rousseauesque moral: Faust has been looking in the wrong places—he should have sought out simple people in humble spheres. It is interesting that Leviathan abandons his 'devilish' tone as soon as he embarks on this idyll; his manner of evoking it is exactly like that of any sentimental eighteenth-century writer turning against the artificial civilization of his day: '. . . nicht den [hast du gesehen,] der unter dem schweren Joche seufzt, des Lebens Last geduldig trägt und sich mit Hoffnung der Zukunft tröstet. Stolz bist du die Hütte des Armen und Bescheidnen vorübergegangen, der . . . im Schweiß seines Angesichts sein Brot erwirbt, es mit Weib und Kindern treulich teilt und sich in der letzten Stunde des Lebens freut, sein mühsames Tagwerk geendet zu haben' (v, 6).

In J. F. Schink's pact-scene ('Doktor Fausts Bund mit der Hölle', 1796) Mephisto again mounts the pulpit:

MEPH.: Du vertraust dich bösen Geistern an, das endliche Geschöpf wagt das gefährliche Spiel mit dem unendlichen; ist das nicht Raserei?
FAUST: Ich glaube gar, du predigst?
MEPH.: Und Besserung. Aber dein Ohr ist taub für Warnung; sie mag von guten oder bösen Geistern kommen... (p. 82)

So, as already in the *Faust* of the 'Christlich Meynender', devils can warn men just as well as can good spirits. It should be added, however, that the rest of Schink's scene up to the point where Faust signs the pact is so confusing that it is difficult to form any clear idea of what sort of a Devil this is supposed to be. What is interesting in this connection is that Schink obviously sees no reason why the Devil should not help to drive the moral point home in the most explicit terms.

C. C. L. Schöne (*Faust*, 1809) copies Klinger and, like Klinger, allows Leviathan to point the moral at the end. But he goes much further than Klinger:

> Wo dir zu glauben auferlegt, war'st [*sic*] du
> Vermessen, stolzer Faust! Du wolltest gar
> Auf Kosten deiner Ruhe ein Geheimniß lösen,
> Was hier dem Sterblichen verborgen ist.

Die Hoffnung und der Glaube sind's, die hier
Das Herz des Guten im Gewirr der Welt
Erhalten, und zum schönen Ziele leiten.
Dein kühner Geist verwarf Geduld und Glauben,
Du wolltest Wahrheit und dir wurde Wahn!   (v, 13)

It is above all Schöne's choice of words that gives this speech its
false tone. That Leviathan should crow over Faust for taking the
wrong turn: this is well and good. That he should use 'vermessen'
und 'kühn' as terms of disapprobation much as the author of the
Spies Faustbook had done is just acceptable. But his reference to
'das Herz des Guten' and 'das schöne Ziel' are all wrong for this
evil and malicious character.[1] The falsity again comes from a
desire to make the message of the work explicit.

One last example of these moralizing Devils (tuppence-
coloured, where Schink and Schöne had been penny-plain) is
to be found in C. E. Mölling's tragedy *Fausts Tod* (1864), where
Mephisto soliloquizes on the enigma of man:

> Teufel in der Leidenschaft,
> Mensch in seiner schwachen Kraft,
> Engel oft in seiner Güte,
> Göttlich in des Schaffens Blüthe
> Ist's ein Räthsel unauflöslich!
> Er ist ewig und verweslich!
> Er ist Tag und er ist Nacht!   (ii, 1)

The notion that Satan commanded a legion of devils, who were
allotted quite specific tasks of temptation, has complex and
ancient origins. The Old Testament speaks of the spirit of
jealousy, a lying spirit, the spirit of whoredom, and so on.[2]
(These spirits are often represented as instruments of the Lord's
purpose, a point which is obviously important for any consideration of the role of Mephisto in the various Faust versions.)
Once the view that spirits embodied particular vices and tempted
men to practise these became joined to the New Testament idea
of a legion of devils,[3] the way was open to the notion of a whole
infernal army, with various devils concerned with particular

---

[1] The danger is already present in Klinger—cf. 'die himmlische Angelika', v, 6.
But Klinger sees the trap and tries to avoid it by making Leviathan periodically
stress the joy which he derives from seeing the innocent suffer.
[2] Num. 5:14; I Kings 22:21–3; Hos. 4:12.
[3] Mat. 25:41; Rev. 12:7–9.

D

vices or weaknesses. A satanic hierarchy was set off against the heavenly hierarchy, the devils having their precisely defined spheres of influence just as the good angels were thought to have specified duties or territories, or particular classes of people to protect. Systematized first by the Church Fathers, later by medieval theologians, the idea became common in morality plays and other works, where we often find 'specialized' devils tempting men by means of a particular sin (vanity, lechery, gluttony, etc.).[1] In the fifteenth chapter of the 1587 Faustbook ('. . . von Gewalt deß Teuffels'), there is some account of particular spirits sent out on particular tasks. Widmann gives us, as might be expected of him, a good deal more:

Denn gleich wie zu einem Reich viel Personen und ungleiche Empter gehören, also sindt ungleiche Empter unter den Teuffeln. Dann etliche sindt geringe Teuffel, die mit Hurerey, Ehrgeitz und dergleichen Sünden anfechten, andere aber sindt höhere Geistere, die da anfechten mit unglauben, mit verzweifflung und mit Ketzerey, wie die rottengeister und der Babst solche teuffel haben, etliche teuffel sind verordnet zu dieser sünd, andere zu andern Sünden, als etliche böse Geistere sindt, abgöttische Teuffel, Tyranneyteuffel, Zäuberteuffel, Fluchteuffel, Sauffteuffel, Eheteuffel, Hurenteuffel, . . . und dergleichen mehr, die die Menschen zu sölchen Sünden reitzen und blenden . . .[2]

Now, in some lists there appears a *Klugheitsteufel*—a devil who tempts men through their intellectual curiosity and arrogance. The account we have from the pen of Georg Schröder of a Faust play performed in Danzig in 1669 mentions this 'Klugheit-Teüffel', and seems to equate him with the devil sent to serve Faustus. This is the only such identification in any Faust version known to me, but it is clear that, by implication, the Mephisto of early Faustbooks and plays is the *Klugheitsteufel* of the popular imagination. If the lecher, the glutton, the quarreller—later even the smoker!—had devils to play on their weaknesses, why should not Dr. Faust have one too? The identification of Faust's tempter with the *Klugheitsteufel* of tradition is apparent in Lessing's Faust-plan and (arguably, at least) lives on in Thomas Mann's

[1] Cf. Roskoff, i, pp. 189, 219, 232, 381.
[2] Widmann's note to i, 21 ('Von der Ordnung der Teuffel'). In a shortened version in Pfitzer too. Some later writers take up the tradition, drawing on the puppet plays. Examples: Maler Müller, Holtei.

Devil, projection of Leverkühn's self-tormenting and self-destroying intellect. But in all too many *Fausts*, as the author turned aside from metaphysical debate to concentrate on the less demanding theme of Faust's love life, Mephisto is demoted from *Klugheitsteufel* to *Hurenteufel*. The wittiest example of this occurs in Heine's Faust-ballet, where Faust is tempted by a vision of beauty and the Devil is a ballet-dancer. In Heine's notes (*Erläuterungen*), he justifies this by mentioning the agreeable old anecdote that the Devil invented the galliard to tempt the faithful and annoy the puritanical. The first stage in the development which is to transform Faust from retiring scholar into man of the world takes the form of a dancing lesson from Mephistophela and her companions. In Lenau too we have the spectacle of a Devil who uses music to awaken slumbering lascivious desires in Faust ('Der Tanz'). For a much more sombre treatment of a Faust led astray by a 'Hurenteufel', see the account of W. Nürnberger's *Josephus Faust* (below).

It is with Marlowe that one first notices the tendency of the Devil to steal the show. Marlowe's Devil is there to tempt Faustus, yes, and to bargain with him and to serve him; to do all those things which he is represented as doing in the chapbook. (And it may be added that Marlowe's Devil still has the inconsistency of the chapbook Devil: he moralizes *and* tempts, warns *and* eggs Faustus on.) But what chiefly seems to concern Marlowe is to depict the Devil as a fallen angel, brooding on the Hell that he carries about with him. After his famous speech locating Hell wherever God is not (i, 3), it seems of little consequence whether he is entirely consistent in his attitude towards Faustus.[1] To find this Mephisto presently providing out-of-season fruit and magic means of transport seems tolerable only if he is represented as performing these feats in a spirit of bored indulgence, underlining the irony of the fact that this is the sort of thing for which Faustus signed away his soul.

But for nearly two centuries after Marlowe the Faust theme lived on only in popular and trivialized versions, and Mephisto became trivial with all the rest, part naïvely wicked and treacherous spirit, part provider of magical court entertainments

[1] Contrast 'O *Faustus* leaue these friuolous demandes' (i, 3) with 'What will not I do to obtaine his soule?' (ii, 1).

and exotic feasts, often permitting himself a little moralizing and occasionally acting as pander. Not until Goethe does he again come to dominate the scene.

Goethe did not read Marlowe's *Doctor Faustus* until long after the completion of his own Part 1, and manifestly the popular Faust versions known to him in his youth had little to offer by way of hints concerning the characterization of the Devil. He had to create his own Mephisto just as he had to 'look into his own heart' (*in meinen eigenen Busen greifen*) for Faust. I do not wish to add unduly to the enormous amount that has been written on this subject, only to say enough to present Goethe's characterization of Mephisto as an important stage in the history of the Devil in the Faust legend.

The Mephisto of the *Urfaust* is linked with that strange cosmogony which Goethe constructed for himself as a young man under the influence of Pietistic, mystical, alchemical, and Cabbalistic writings. From such sources, Goethe tells us, he had come to conceive of a godhead which reproduced itself from all eternity, giving rise to a trinity (rather a Neoplatonic than a Christian one) and, in due course, to a fourth member, Lucifer, from whom material creation emerged:

> . . . alles das, was wir unter der Gestalt der Materie gewahr werden, was wir uns als schwer, fest und finster vorstellen, welches aber, indem es, wenn auch nicht unmittelbar, doch durch Filiation vom göttlichen Wesen herstammt, eben so unbedingt mächtig und so ewig ist, als der Vater. . . .[1]

So this material world was imperfect but never, as it were, quite forgetful of its divine origin, so that individual souls had the opportunity of sinking further down (into the realm of the material) or of rising towards perfection. In this world too dwelt various spirits capable of communicating with and influencing mankind in sundry ways. It is easy to see how these views led Goethe to the conception of his *Erdgeist*, a spirit which dominates the natural life of our planet, is the living and visible garment of the divinity and represents both the dynamism and the constant death and rebirth which characterize the world of nature. That Mephisto was originally thought of as a spirit subordinate to, or as an emissary of the *Erdgeist* is tolerably clear from *Urfaust*

[1] *Dichtung und Wahrheit*, Book 8.

159f ('Du gleichst dem Geist den du begreiffst,/Nicht mir!'),
and from the passage in the prose-scene where Faust implies that
Mephisto first appeared to him in the form of a dog and at the
bidding of the *Erdgeist* ('Wandle ihn du unendlicher Geist . . .').
This linking of Mephisto with the *Erdgeist* was later to receive
confirmation in the words addressed by Faust to the *Erdgeist* in
the scene 'Wald und Höhle'.

But, say some critics, when we reach Part 1, with its Prologue
in Heaven, an ambiguity has arisen. For the passages from the
Urfaust and the *Fragment* which link Mephisto with the *Erdgeist*
remain, while the Prologue introduces a new framework of
references and one which is apparently, from its clear echoes of
the Book of Job, a more Christian one. In the most strictly
literal terms (who dispatched Mephisto to Faust in the first place?)
there may indeed be an ambiguity or at least an untidiness here,
but I think that the more general difficulties with regard to
Mephisto's role have been exaggerated. If we turn to the famous
speech of the *Erdgeist* (*Urfaust*, 148ff; Part 1, 501ff), we find
terrestrial existence described in all its imperfection—but also as
a reflection of the divine. It is easy to see how a servant of this
spirit could carry out the ambivalent role allotted to Mephisto
by the Lord and later defined by Mephisto himself (Part 1, 1335f).
Mephisto's nihilism corresponds to the constant dying and
destruction in the realm of nature (the *Grab* of the Earth Spirit's
speech). But since this dying constantly leads to rebirth,
Mephisto's nihilism must always be vain (Part 1, 1371f). And if
the law of terrestrial life is constant change and activity, and
if it is only through striving and activity that man develops
towards higher things, the spirit who goads men on *must* unwillingly help to carry out God's purpose. Here again, the words
of the Lord in the Prologue and those of the Earth Spirit carry
similar implications.

Goethe took over (from what sources is impossible to establish
exactly, and is anyway not important) a good deal of traditional
material concerning the Devil. There is the 'crazy hocuspocus'
(*das tolle Zauberwesen*) of the 'Hexenküche' and the 'Walpurgisnacht', treated ironically and grotesquely, as if to say: these are
all traditional trappings of Western witch and Devil belief, and I
suppose they must go in somewhere. But there are much more
serious links with tradition. Goethe's Mephisto, who knows

much but not everything (line 1582), is wholly in accord with the theologians' Devil, who was commonly represented as knowing more than man, but less than the good angels.[1] The discordant note introduced into the angels' hymn of praise by the 'spirit who denies' recalls the Devil's traditional role as accuser, as denier of man's moral worth. (The explicit link here is with the Book of Job, but there is also an echo, deliberate or accidental, of the old 'Trials of Satan', in which the Devil accused mankind of wickedness, with the Virgin as defender and, usually, Christ as judge—cf. Graf, pp. 225ff.) Goethe's view of the usefulness of the Devil as a goad has also theological sanction, although Goethe's position is clearly very unorthodox and rests on an altogether less cut-and-dried notion of what is a 'good' and what an 'evil' act. The orthodox view has been that God permitted a certain freedom of action to Satan, so that he might tempt and plague men. Thus men would remain alert, would not sink into slothfulness or moral complacency and would achieve greater moral deserts by resisting the Devil than would be possible if there were no tempter to resist.[2] Since the possible ultimate salvation of this highly useful Devil is faintly hinted at in Goethe ('Grablegung'), and since it was to become an issue in some later works,[3] it deserves a word here.

Origen had argued that not even devils were incapable of good, and that in the end Satan's hostile will would be destroyed in a return to harmony with God.[4] This view was taken over by St. Gregory of Nyssa, to be sternly denounced by St. Augustine as 'a pitiful error'.[5] But, as with most heresies, it pops up from time to time through the centuries. Luther finds it necessary to oppose the idea, by the way (xxii, 34), and it was still a subject of serious discussion in the eighteenth century. William Law, after some hesitation, became convinced that Satan, as the negation of the principle of love, would ultimately be saved when Divine love triumphed over evil and darkness.[6] Goethe himself will

[1] Cf. Roskoff, i, pp. 234 and 272; Luther, lx, 14.
[2] Roskoff, i, 277-9. See also St. Chrysostom, *Works*, vol. i (=*Library of the Nicene and Post-Nicene Fathers*, ed. Schaff, vol. ix), pp. 189 and 192; St. Augustine, *City of God*, xx, 8.
[3] See Chapter 7; also in Bailey's *Festus*. Schink too, in his *Johann Faust* of 1804, had hinted at Mephisto's ultimate salvation (ii, 329f).
[4] *De Principiis*, i, 8 and iii, 6.   [5] *City of God*, xxi, 17.
[6] *Address to the Clergy*, London, 1761, pp. 172ff.

assuredly have come across the idea in Georg von Welling's *Opus mago-cabbalisticum* (Homburg, 1735). Welling deals with Lucifer's rebellion in terms of the breaking-away of the earthly realm from the Divine whole, terms which curiously combine Neoplatonic, cabbalistic and Christian notions (i, 4–5). Given this theory of the Devil's origins, Welling can go on to argue that, after a period of purification, Lucifer too will participate in the general redemption:

... diese Reinigung wird ... fortfahren, biß alle Kreyse, ja selbst der Mittel-Punct und Ursprung oder Ursach aller Verdammnuß und Verderbens, der Lucifer, gantz entblösset, nach der ewigen Erlösung seuffzen, und also auch er, als der letzte Feind, aufgehoben, wiederum in seine erstere herrliche Lichts-Gestalt verwandelt worden, und also das gantze Geschöpff wiederum in seinem ersten *Principio* erscheinen wird. (p. 467)

Thus, from Welling, Goethe derived not only hints for the cosmogony of the *Urfaust* and the linking of Mephisto with the Earth Spirit, but also perhaps the idea of the Devil's possible salvation.

But to treat Goethe's Mephisto as if he were the personification of some principle or cosmic force and to note the links with the evil spirits of Christianity and other traditions is, although interesting, very partial. For, once introduced, Mephisto takes on a life of his own, begins to display individual characteristics, and adopts a mode of speech peculiar to himself. Hence he must be approached like any other character in a play, or else we are left, like Faust at the beginning of Goethe's drama, with 'Tiergeripp' und Totenbein', dry bones instead of living nature. For some of Goethe's readers, in fact, Mephisto became not only a vital, living character, but the hero:

Le diable est le héros de cette pièce; l'auteur ne l'a point conçu comme un fantôme hideux ... Goethe a voulu montrér dans ce personnage ... la plus amère plaisanterie que le dédain puisse inspirer, et néanmoins une audace de gâité qui amuse. Il y a dans les discours de Méphistophélès une ironie infernale qui porte sur la création toute entière, et juge l'univers comme un mauvais livre dont le diable se fait le censeur.[1]

[1] Mme. de Staël, *De l'Allemagne*, ii, 23

D. L. Sayers, in the preface to her own Faust play, *The Devil to Pay*, has the same point to make:

> ... as ... Goethe, and every other writer who has meddled with the devil has discovered, the chief difficulty is to prevent this sympathetic character from becoming the hero of the story.

'Hero' is obviously too much (Gretchen? Philemon and Baucis?), but it is clear that there is always some likelihood that Goethe's Mephisto will be the dominant figure. Here a subjective element enters, but most people would probably agree that it is Mephisto who dominates most scenes in Part 1 where he and Faust appear together, and that, even in Part 2, where he has less to do and certainly calls the tune far less, his presence is still felt far more than his effective role would lead one to expect. It is noteworthy how often he is given the last word—sometimes in scenes where he has played comparatively little part, as if to suggest that 'devilish' mockery and denial are the most appropriate reactions to human greed and folly, and that he is the ruler here, the stage-manager of these antics, even if they seem to be played out wholly or largely without his help.[1]

It is in Part 2 particularly that Mephisto's role becomes so complex that it is altogether pointless to try to define it by any sort of formula. He is in turn Faust's helper and adversary (continuing the ambivalent role suggested by lines 340–3 and 1335f). He appears as court jester, as personification of envy, as Phorkyas, as stage-manager both of a financial crisis and of a military campaign, and as overseer. Yet he remains recognizable under all his disguises:[2] less as an evil and sinister spirit (except in the Philemon and Baucis episode) than as the 'spirit that denies'. But from the moment when he declares himself unable to procure Helen for Faust (6209f), he either withdraws from the scene to leave Faust to act independently, or actively helps him! The Devil who unwillingly 'works the good' is now much more apparent than in Part 1. In fact, Mephisto's dilemma, hinted at in the Prologue, becomes acute in Part 2: to damn Faust, Mephisto must keep him alive (cf. 318–22). But life, in Faust's case, means action, and action conduces towards salvation. Moreover, as Faust grows older, his impulses become maturer, less hedonistic

---

[1] Cf. 5061–4, 6172, 6360, 6564f, 6815ff.   [2] Cf. 7134–7 and 8992f.

and subjective, so that Mephisto, in serving him, cannot but appear as unwilling altruist.

But this does not exhaust his role in Part 2. He also provides light relief and has an important part to play in the *Klassische Walpurgisnacht*. Here the exile from the Harz Mountains is made to stand for northern incomprehension of the classical ideal. Hence his bewilderment at all the creatures he encounters, hence his nostalgia for the familiar German mountain peaks (7678–82), and hence Homunculus' scorn (6923–7, 6945–7). The contrast between Faust and Mephisto is pushed to the point of farce when Mephisto is shown wooing the Phorcides at a moment when Faust is absent in search of Helen.

In the most general terms, Goethe's Mephisto is the adversary of all faith and optimism, the personification of mockery. Few escape his sardonic glance. Wherever characters take themselves too seriously (Faust), or fall into arrogance (Baccalaureus) or ignore the obvious (Wagner), Mephisto is there to underline the fact. Even at the last, when Faust is filled with noble aspirations, Mephisto is the realist who cuts him down to size. And Mephisto is a *witty* Devil, with a wit that can at times make Faust seem solemn and self-important. Perhaps it is this factor which, above all others, has made it possible for some readers to see the 'hero' in him and has blinded them to the objective (evil) consequences of his actions.

An account of some of the more successful attempts to copy Goethe's Mephisto will be found in Chapter 7. There has also been a witty musical comment on Goethe's 'spirit that denies'. Liszt's *Faust-Symphony* (1854–7) has, as its first three movements, orchestral portraits of Faust, Gretchen and Mephisto. But whereas Faust and Gretchen are given characteristic themes and motifs, Mephisto has no themes of his own; his movement is built up out of parodies of the Faust-themes from the first movement, as if to suggest that he is a spirit opposed to everything positive and creative, merely mocking what others have willed. Significantly the Mephisto-movement dies away into nothingness, for 'alles, was entsteht,/Ist wert, daß es zu Grunde geht.'

Klinger's Leviathan is an intriguing figure. He is clearly based on Milton's tragic Devil and has a few (accidental) similarities to

Marlowe's. Here he is on his first appearance before Faust, grandiose, bitter, obsessed with a sense of his deprivation:

in erhabner, kühner und kraftvoller Gestalt. . . . Feurige, gebietrische Augen leuchteten unter zwo schwarzen Braunen hervor, zwischen welchen Bitterkeit, Haß, Groll, Schmerz und Hohn dicke Falten zusammengerollt hatten . . . Er hatte die Miene der gefallnen Engel, deren Angesichter einst von der Gottheit beleuchtet wurden, und die nun ein düstrer Schleier deckt.   (i, 8)

He has adopted human form because this exterior best corresponds to the evil within him, and appeals to Faust because of his power to see through human pretensions. He has the nihilism and the devilish laughter of all the best Devils of Faust literature (ii, 11). It could be argued that, like others that have been mentioned in this chapter, he steals the show. Or does he? It seems to me that, if one looks more closely at him, one can already see traces of that decline of the Devil which was to become one of the characteristics of Faust literature in the nineteenth and twentieth centuries. In one way this is simply a natural result of treating this magical theme in a sceptical age. Leviathan himself makes merry over Faust for expecting him to appear with horns and cloven hoofs (i, 8); thus too Klinger's treatment of magic is ironic (cf. ii, 4: more of this later). But there is a deeper reason. The deal with Leviathan, after all, has very little to do with the traditional pacts according to which the Devil was to serve Faust, shower him with gifts and procure him power and fame; it is a bet in which Faust will try to convince Leviathan of the moral nobility of mankind and Leviathan will try to confound Faust's faith in his fellow-men. So, although there is occasional recourse to magic, Leviathan's main weapon is his cynical insight into human weaknesses. He hardly needs to corrupt men or tempt them; he merely uncovers, explains and interprets. Indeed, he comes near to declaring himself redundant!—

Brauchen Die des Teufels, die ihn durch ihr Thun beschämen?   (iii, 3)

The gradual decline of the Devil will form the theme of the last part of this chapter. But before this happened, he was to live through a sort of Indian summer in the works of the German Romantics.

Lenau's sombre and malevolent Devil is a combination of the exiled fallen angel of Milton and Marlowe and Goethe's nihilistic Devil. The work of damnation is explicitly stated to be an act of revenge on the creator:

> So will Verstoßner ich mein Leiden kühlen,
> Verderbend mich als Gegenschöpfer fühlen. (p. 28)

This is a treacherous Mephisto who saves Faust from accidental death at the beginning ('Der Morgengang'), only to destroy him at leisure. (Goethe's image of the cat playing with the mouse is, in fact, much more applicable to Lenau's Mephisto than to his own.) The pact itself is full of double-edged and misleading promises, and Mephisto's final treachery is, of course, his betrayal of Faust to Hubert. Mephisto's tactics are gradually to isolate Faust and to bring him to despair. He easily turns him against God, the 'despot' who fills a man with infinite desire and curiosity but gives him only a limited capacity to know and to experience. (One can see plainly the appeal that the Faust theme had for the Romantics.) Then he draws him away from his friends and his past life and involves him in a web of guilt culminating in a murder which estranges him from nature. (The argument is that the law of nature is to preserve and propagate life, so that Faust's murder has alienated him from nature.) And so Faust, alone, is driven back within himself—but finds only cause for disgust. Remorse is combined with a feeling of futility—for he has done all this and is just as much a mortal with mortal limitations as at the outset.[1]

There are clear traces of Lenau's Devil in the Mephisto of Adalbert Lenburg (*Faust*, 1860)—another treacherous character, who is not merely content with winning Faust's soul, but also wishes to cause him as much suffering and disgust as possible in the process. But the most striking successor to Lenau's Mephisto and one who makes him seem almost amiable by contrast is the Devil in Woldemar Nürnberger's dramatic poem *Josephus Faust* (1842). The author was admired by Storm, who vainly tried to persuade Heyse to include something of his in the *Novellenschatz*. The Faust poem remained neglected until E. M. Butler gave a glowing account of it in *The Fortunes of Faust* (pp. 294–300). This

---

[1] 'Der Ritter' in Grabbe's *Don Juan und Faust* is to some extent an anticipation of Lenau's Devil, although not so witty.

account conveys the atmosphere of the work well, but does not analyse it closely enough to do justice to its subtleties. As the work opens, Faust is seen turning away from a hopeless quest for truth, longing for experience of life instead of futile studies. (This beginning obviously derives from Goethe and Lenau, but the tone is more turbulent and desolate than in either.) He is visited in the night by Mephisto:

> Mephisto beugt sich traulich zu ihm vor,
> Und um den Hals er seinen Arm ihm legt,
> Dann flüstert er gar leis' ihm in das Ohr
> So rasch, so rasch, daß kaum den Mund er regt. (p. 15)

This seductive whispering in Faust's ear will recur twice in the work. Since it is unheard by the reader, he has to guess what is said. But this is not difficult; the course of the poem shows Faust embarking on a career of wild and destructive Donjuanism. Mephisto is cast as the *Hurenteufel* of tradition. As in Lenau, Faust is cut off from his old life, to find nothing but bitterness in the new. This is underlined by an extraordinary variation on a motif from Lenau. It will be recalled that Lenau's Faust at the dissecting-table rails against the futility of asking the dead for the secrets of life. But Nürnberger's Faust returns nostalgically to the anatomical theatre, and regards the corpse awaiting dissection almost lovingly—for this body can at least make no demands on him:

> An dieser Leiche ruh ich heute aus,
> Von dem bewegten, teuflisch wilden Leben,
> Von meines Neigens, meines Hassens Graus. (p. 95)

—But he is soon fetched away by Mephisto, to resume his course as Don Juan.

Mephisto is not only adept at temptation; he takes a sinister delight in it:

> Er hinkt und taumelt auf und ab im Sande,
> Von seinen Frevelplänen still ergötzet. (p. 102)

He is no fallen angel, still tormented by thoughts of what he has lost. He has never seen God; God goes his way, and the Devil his (p. 136). Nürnberger's Mephisto is shown to be 'God of this world' in a much more literal way than in any other Faust version known to me. Nature too is his 'whore' (p. 136: for more on this, see Chapter 3). But often he is bored with his role, obsessed with the pointlessness of it, longing to annihilate the whole universe (himself and God included). The devilish boredom, which we have already encountered in Goethe and Klinger, and the Devil's nihilism, which would give up even his own power over the material world in favour of nothingness (cf. Goethe, 11595ff) returns here in a more radical and even blasphemous form. You can say of me what you will, says Nürnberger's Mephisto, but at least I have never committed the most frightful of all crimes:

> —Nennt mich 'nen Hurensohn, nennt mich 'nen schlechten Affen,
> Ich sei nun, wer ich will, *ich habe nicht geschaffen!* (137f)

It is a measure of Nürnberger's nihilistic pessimism that Mephisto is not the real villain of this dark work; the true Devil is the creator. The hint for a nihilistic Devil may well have come from Goethe, but the mood is that of Büchner's *Dantons Tod*.

The malevolence of Nürnberger's Mephisto seems to be reinforced at all points by the settings and the tone of the work. There is, for instance, a wild scene in a ruined convent, where Mephisto, with a band of demons, apes the Crucifixion:

> Die mittelste von den drei Trümmersäulen
> Steigt er hinan; wie er sich äffisch schmiegt
> Um das Gestein, gleich einem Jesus, eilen
> Flugs zu den beiden seitlichen Basalten
> Noch zween andre nächtige Gestalten.[1]

Even Mephisto's magic tricks have an authentic Gothic horror about them, as when he frightens a company of diners by the apparition of a murdered youth's head in a dish of food.[2] Nature herself is wild and sinister in this poem, and the style is mysterious and fragmented, full of lacunae, hints and rumours, so that the work seems like some dire folk-ballad, whose very textual mysteries and corruptions seem to make the horrible more horrible. For this is not a question of a Faust damned in a context which suggests that goodness, order and salvation are possible; the whole world of this poem is made over to the Devil. Mephisto,

---

[1] P. 26. This scene was probably suggested by a motif in the Faust ballads and some of the puppet plays, where Faust demands of Mephisto to be shown Christ on the Cross.

[2] P. 85. A similar motif in Klinger, iii, 1.

witnessing a frenzied scene of drinking and gambling, says to
Faust:

> Du glaubst es nicht, wie sehr es mir geneigt,
> Das Völkchen, das da drinnen wogt und reigt.
> Was wetten wir, Doctoren nicht allein,
> Verschreiben sich den ew'gen Teufelein.
> Was wetten wir, in einer halben Stunde
> Sind insgesammt die drin mit mir im Bunde!   (146)

The surrealist imagery of this scene suggests, as so often in Jean
Paul's visions of Hell, a verbal equivalent to the fantastic Hell-
paintings of Bosch:

> Mit diesen Kuben die man Würfel nennt,
> Die ganze Schaar mir in den Rachen rennt.
> Sie saugen fest und tief sich in mein Bein,
> Als hielt ich's Egeln in den Teich hinein.   (ibid.)

—but Nürnberger's Hell is this world, and the existence of
Heaven is nowhere hinted at.

It will be recalled that Klinger's Devil makes a mocking
reference to the old popular belief in a Devil with a cloven foot,
horns and the rest. This mockery is, of course, in tune with the
attitudes of, at least, educated men of the Enlightenment.[1] But
even if the Devil had been banished, the wickedness that he had
seemed to personify and encourage remained:

> Er [Satan] ist schon lang ins Fabelbuch geschrieben:
> Allein die Menschen sind nichts besser dran,
> Den Bösen sind sie los, die Bösen sind geblieben.[2]

And so inevitably the Devil of the Faust plays, no longer the
stage representation of a spirit in whose objective existence
people really believed, became more and more a mere symbol for
the 'darker' side of man. Even in the naïve popular treatments
one can occasionally catch a hint, perhaps barely conscious, of
this. It will be remembered that Faust traditionally subjects the
various spirits of Hell to a speed test and that he finally chooses
Mephisto, who boasts that he is swift as men's thought. Swift
as thought? Must this not mean that he will be there at Faust's

---

[1] For further examples, see Pfeiffer, *Klinger's Faust*, Würzburg, 1890, pp. 65f.
[2] Goethe, lines 2507–9. See too Lenz, *Hofmeister*, v, 9.

side as soon as Faust thinks of him? And, if so, is he not something resembling the making-material of a certain mood of Faust's? The point is made more explicitly in the puppet play which Heine saw in Hamburg in the mid-1820s and of which he gives an account in the *Erläuterungen* to his Faust ballet. The devils had appeared veiled and shrouded ('tief vermummt in grauen Laken') and, when Faust had asked them what they really looked like, had replied: 'Wir haben keine Gestalt, die uns eigen wäre, wir entlehnen nach deinem Belieben jede Gestalt, worin du uns zu erblicken wünschest: wir werden immer aussehen wie deine Gedanken' (pp. 67f in the original edition). This could mean that the devils really exist and that only their appearance when they make themselves manifest to humans is determined by men's thoughts, but for the less naïve members of the audience the exchange must have sounded very like an admission that the devils exist only in the mind.

In the literary treatments of the theme, the tendency to turn the Devil into a symbol is more conscious and more marked. (Given the pessimism of men like Lenau and Nürnberger, it is plainly no contradiction to have a powerful, malevolent and dominating fiend who is, at the same time, little more than a symbol for certain aspects of human nature.) Some people would argue that this development away from an 'objective' Devil towards a 'subjective' one can already be seen in Goethe's *Faust* or, indeed, in Marlowe's. But it seems to me that Lenau is the real starting-point. By this I do not of course mean to suggest that the Mephisto in Lenau's *Faust* is 'in the mind' like Ivan Karamazov's or Leverkühn's Devils. Lenau's Mephisto is a superbly drawn dramatic character, and the progress of the work depends on the tragic conflict between him and Faust. Nevertheless, there are points where Mephisto seems, for brief moments at least, to be the projection of one side of Faust. He appears when Faust is ripe for him, and there are passages in their conversations which almost give the impression that Faust is arguing with his *alter ego*:

FAUST: Warum doch muß in meiner Seele brennen
      Die unlöschbare Sehnsucht nach Erkennen! ...
MEPH.: Dein Schöpfer ist dein Feind, gesteh dirs keck,
      Weil grausam er in diese Nacht dich schuf. (p. 8)

The deduction seems so logical in this context that it hardly needs anyone outside Faust to draw it. And when, later, Faust turns on Mephisto in disgust ('Der See'), he is in fact only feeling disgust at himself. Later still ('Das Waldgespräch'), Mephisto's temptation of Faust—that to assert himself truly and independently as an individual he must cut himself loose from God and nature—is again almost a case of Faust's tempting himself, for the arrogant subjectivity was there from the outset, and what follows in this scene is only the logical outcome of it. Mephisto's temptation can be summed up as 'dare to be yourself' and it hardly needs the Devil to whisper that to Faust.

The author of the other major late Romantic *Faust*, Nürnberger, takes the process further still. This may sound odd, after what has been said about Nürnberger's Mephisto. Unchallenged lord of this world, despoiler of mankind with no sly and seductive angels to rob him of his prey—surely this is the apogee of the Devil in Faust literature? And yet the question of this Mephisto's objective existence seems open to doubt. For, towards the end, in a strange anticipation of Dostoievsky and Thomas Mann, as Faust curses Mephisto, his adversary isn't there at all—Faust is ranting against the empty air. But the most significant instance comes in the final scene. Here a wretched, crippled, beggared Faust calls on Mephisto, as if longing for his traditional 'grewliches und erschreckliches Ende'. But no Devil comes to carry off this Faust; he is left to wander out the rest of his life in loneliness. This really seems to suggest that there *is* no Devil except the one within Faust that first drags him into guilt and then condemns him to a lifetime of remorse.

That the Devil, if he exists, is within man, is stated quite positively in Spielhagen's novella *Faustulus* (1898). This is a Faust story within a Faust story, since the hero, Arno, is both the author of a Faust tragedy and a man who feels some affinity with the Faust figure, a man whose fate, moreover, bears a slight resemblance to that of Goethe's Faust. Although this synthesis is not very well achieved, *Faustulus* is one of the few late nineteenth-century Faust versions which deserve respect and serious consideration. Our immediate concern here is with Spielhagen's conception of the Devil: 'Bei ihm [=Arno, in his Faust play] spielte sich der Kampf des Guten mit dem Bösen in der Seele seines Helden ab und nirgends sonst' (p. 73). When asked whether he believes in the Devil (a fair question to put to the author of a Faust tragedy), Arno replies: 'An den in uns: sehr' (p. 147).

As I have already said, some had seen this demotion of Mephisto to a principle within man as already implied by Goethe. Fr. Th. Vischer had argued something of the sort from the link of Mephisto with the Earth Spirit. If Mephisto is the servant and emissary of this spirit, then he is to be associated with the 'earthy' parts of human nature too, with the passions and impulses.[1] This view, which obviously gains support from what Goethe has to tell us of his youthful philosophy (see above, p. 40), can easily degenerate into a trivial and oversimplified equation according to which Faust embodies the good and positive, Mephisto the bad and negative parts of man. In fact, the banishment of Mephisto to a point within man had entered Goethe-criticism as early as 1845, when Julius Mosen had described Faust and Mephisto as 'ein in zwei Hälften zerrissener Mensch', and Mephisto as 'das gegen den Geist und seine Überschwänglichkeit gerichtete Menschentier in der Brust Faust's. . . .'[2] Such an interpretation would obviously commend itself to many who were both unable to believe in a 'real' Devil, and indisposed to pursue the complex question of exactly who or what Goethe's Mephisto was. And in fact several treatments of the Faust theme confront us with a Mephisto who is no more than spokesman for a pessimistic or cynically realistic view which opposes itself to Faust's idealism. This is the case with Geibel's scene of dialogue between Faust and Mephisto in 'Historische Studien' (1865), and there is a similar case in Turgenev's *Faust* of 1856. The process is taken a stage further in Julius Sturm's poem 'Faust und Mephistopheles', 1883. Here Faust himself has been demoted to an Everyman-figure, so that Mephisto is no more than the voice of doubt within each man's heart:

> Faust—Mephistopheles—es sind die Beiden
> Im Herzen jedes Menschen eingeschlossen.

Der gefesselte Faust by Johannes Gaulke (1910) is a sceptical and astringent twentieth-century variation on Klinger's *Faust*, in which Mephisto destroys Faust's faith in morality and progress

---

[1] *Goethes Faust*, 1875, p. 14.
[2] *Über Goethe's Faust*, Oldenburg, 1845, pp. 9f.

much as Leviathan had done in Klinger. But here God and the
Devil are one, and they *both* lodge in the human breast. 'Himmel
und Hölle sind eins; ein jeder trägt den Himmel, aber auch die
Hölle in seiner Brust' (p. 80). And presently Faust asks:

> Mephisto, . . . gib mir Antwort: Bist du der Gute und Böse in einer
> Person? . . .
>   Er lächelte ablehnend, aber aus dem Lächeln sprach etwas, das mich
> mit Grauen erfüllte: Gott und der Teufel eins! . . . Entsetzlicher
> Gedanke! (p. 81)

But Gaulke goes yet further; for his Faust, his faith in humanity
destroyed, awakens to find that he has dreamt the whole thing!
So Mephisto is but a figure in Faust's dream. 'Der Verneiner' in
Gstöttner's Faust play (*Der Wanderer*, 1933: see Chapter 7) is
similarly placed inside Faust, so that Faust's debates with the
Devil are arguments between the forces of affirmation and denial
within man:

> WANDERER: So lüstern hundsgemein
>   Kann wirklich nur der Satan sein.
> VERNEINER: (ironisch) Bin ja nur ein Teil von Eurem Ich! . . .
>   Bin nur Gestaltung Eurer eigenen Gedanken! (124f)

All this prepares us for the death-blows dealt, in their different
ways, by Valéry and Thomas Mann. If the Devil *is* in the mind,
he reflects men's views and feelings at any particular time, will
change as men change, can be reduced to insignificance or even
annihilated. By making his characters aware of the literary
tradition of which they are part, Valéry makes it possible for
Faust to comment to Mephisto on his waning influence: 'tu ne
tiens plus dans le monde la grande situation que tu occupais
jadis . . . tes méthodes sont surannées . . .' (294f). Man's intellectual
development and his scientific conquests have gradually made
Mephisto out of date, small-time, almost a joke.[1] But at least
Valéry's Devil is 'there' in the sense that he is permitted to appear
as a character. With Thomas Mann, we reach the end of the
road. His Devil, like Ivan Karamazov's, is a hallucination. To
characterize him would be merely to characterize part of Lever-

---

[1] For more on this, see Chapter 9. This patronizing attitude towards a pre-
technological Devil can be seen in more than one of the Science Fiction stories in the
collection *The Devil his Due*, ed. Douglas Hill, London, 1967. See especially 'Return
Visit' by E. C. Tubb.

kühn himself; his Devil's insights are things dimly realized by Leverkühn, his Devil's gifts are symbolical of the artistic genius already latent in Leverkühn. And even when we take into account the wider meaning of Mann's *Faustus*—that Germany is Faust and that the most fateful of all Faust's pacts with the Devil took place in 1933—the Devil is no more than a convenient symbol for the evil in men. As an earlier Devil had said: 'Den Bösen sind sie los, die Bösen sind geblieben.' Again, here is the Devil ('the Stranger') in Albert Lepage's *Faust et Don Juan* (1960) bowing out, as Faust finally comes to face the fact that the Devil has only ever been the invention of man and an alibi for the evil done by man:

FAUST: Je ne veux plus de cette lâcheté! Je suis la seule source du mal que je fais . . .
ÉTRANGER: Donc, je meurs!
DON JUAN: La mort d'un mythe! (p. 116)

In short then: the Devil lost much of his importance in this type of work, as men ceased to believe in him except as a symbol and as the magic which he was previously represented as working came to appear increasingly trivial compared with what science could achieve by perfectly natural means (see too Chapter 9). But it is arguable that there is another major factor which contributed towards his decline, that Mephisto was bound to become ineffective with the increasing tendency to save Faust. The two things are, of course, linked. Mephisto becomes the symbol for an evil which is bound to be vanquished. The defeat of the Devil need not *in itself* mean that he is represented as harmless (witness the accounts of the battles between the saints and their tempters). For example, Mampell (1962) manages to save Faust without reducing Mephisto to a nonentity. But as soon as the conviction that Faust can be made to symbolize the forces in man which deserve 'salvation' rather than 'damnation' coexists with disbelief as to the actual existence of Hell and the Devil, then the Devil (where he survives at all, as a convenient fiction or symbol) is doomed to ineffectiveness. The process begins for all practical purposes with Goethe. For all Mephisto's cynical wit and eloquence, he is beaten from the outset. The reference to Faust's 'confused' service to God (line 308) marks him for salvation and condemns Mephisto to unwilling collaboration. But what is acceptable in Goethe as a symbolic representation of a world-view involving a very complex interaction of 'good' and 'evil' becomes trivial in later writers, in whom we find a conflict in which Faust cannot lose and the forces of evil are unrealistically inept. In Müffling's *Faust* (see Chapter 7), for instance, Mephisto sends a chorus of spirits to sing seductively to Clementine—but she resists temptation effortlessly. Again, he sends his emissary, the *Zeitgeist*, to stir up unrest, but the people quickly return to order as soon as they see Faust and the Duke together. It would be depressing to give details of the witless devices adopted by successive Devils. They make cynical and disillusioned remarks intended to shake Faust's optimism, they break out into devilish laughter, they disguise themselves, hatch plots, stir up anarchy, preach hedonism and try to lure Faust away from virtue with the aid of Helen and other seductive creatures, but they cannot win; the heavenly choir is too patently waiting in the wings.[1]

Perhaps even worse is the situation in which Mephisto is relatively *successful* in his wiles, but is still robbed of his prize in the end. In Mölling's *Fausts Tod* (see Chapter 7), Mephisto does in fact quite easily win Faust over to all sorts of dastardly exercises, but still loses him—*has* to lose him. It is all rather like those old films in which the villain binds and gags the heroine and places her on the railway line. Who, even among the rawest novices in cinema-going, ever thought that the train would hit her?

A. Großmann's *Faust* of 1934 provides the most fitting conclusion to this chapter. As so often, Faust is manifestly predestined for salvation, so that Mephisto is a non-starter. But here he is also very halfhearted as a tempter and gradually loses all zest in his hellish enterprises until—in an exact reversal of the traditional situation—he is ripe for seduction into goodness by Faust! But who is this Mephisto anyway? Only one half of man's soul again:

> Faust und Mephisto
> Sind des Menschen Seele ... (p. 197)

So his 'salvation' is no more than the overcoming of the spirit of doubt within man. The final union of Faust and Mephisto, all doubt and discord now resolved at the foot of the Cross, heralds

---

[1] Examples of such feeble Devils in Schink, 1804; Braun von Braunthal, 1835; W. S. Gilbert, 1879; F. Keim, 1890; H. Schilf, 1891; P. Degen, 1924 and W. Webels, 1951.

the worst play on words in Faust literature: 'Mephaustus' (p. 247).

Poor Mephisto! Once the arch-enemy of mankind, now Faust's Siamese twin, co-redeemable with him. Perhaps 'decline' is too weak a word.[1]

[1] Mephisto is saved too in Rudolf Pannwitz's postscript to Goethe, 'Mechristo-pheles Himmelfahrt' (1940). Faust: 'Fehltest du wär ein riss/Durch Gottes wahrheit ...'.

3

Nature

IT is not my intention in this chapter to give an exhaustive account of the theme of nature as it figures in the various Faust plays and poems. To discuss every monologue in which successive Fausts have apostrophized nature and expressed their longing for an understanding of it or unity with it would be tedious. Instead I wish to concentrate on major Faust versions in which nature has an important part to play in the author's plan. In the course of this chapter 'nature' will be used in various senses. Even in English the word embraces a good many meanings—the associations of 'Natur' in German are yet richer and more complex. Regarding the original chapbook and Marlowe's *Faustus* the discussion will centre on the visible world and its laws. But in Goethe, who necessarily and obviously occupies the central place in this chapter, the conception of nature is very much wider. For the young *Stürmer und Dränger*, the author of the *Urfaust*, 'Natur' suggested the visible world of nature as well as the natural impulses within man and also the simple life as opposed to 'artificial' civilization. When discussing *Faust* Part 2 we must extend the term still further to suggest the ways in which the natural world influences human life both directly and indirectly, how man should model his attitudes and behaviour on what he learns from nature. To examine everything that Goethe understood by 'Natur' would fill another book; I have had to confine myself to what is important for an understanding of his *Faust*. From the Romantics onwards, the emphasis shifts to the problem of understanding the natural world; later still, to the question of whether or not such a quest for meaning in nature has any point. For the rest, I hope that the various senses in which 'nature' is used will make themselves clear as the argument progresses.

'Natur' figures for the first time as an important theme in the

Urfaust. But the natural world already has some importance in the original Faustbook. One of Faust's main motives for concluding the pact is 'die Elementa zu speculieren' (p. 22). This, of course, has to be seen in the context of an age in which the natural sciences and magic were inextricably confused.[1] 'Die Elementa speculieren' is only half concerned with what we would regard as a study of the natural world. Faust certainly disputes with his familiar on such subjects as astronomy and the seasons, he journeys through the heavens and visits various earthly kingdoms; but the main stress in 'Spies' is on the practice of magic. Faust constantly *interferes* with the course of nature for sensational effects, to impress the mighty, to achieve fame and riches, or to exact revenge. Nature, that is, is present in 'Spies' chiefly inasmuch as she has secrets to yield to the magician or wonders which the credulous will relish. This point—that the insights into nature as well as the command over nature are achieved by supernatural means—must be emphasized, for it is easy to overlook. The limitations of the anonymous author are such that the knowledge provided by the Devil would for the most part have come as no great surprise to any reasonably educated person of the late sixteenth century. (This is part of a more general difficulty bound up with the Faust theme: see Chapter 4.) When we read the chapters dealing with astronomy, say, or meteorology, it requires some effort of the imagination to realize that all this is knowledge which Faust is supposed to have come by *unlawfully*. The treatment of nature in 'Spies' (secrets raped, treasures plundered, natural laws demonically interfered with) is in accord with the didactic intention of the book: to condemn unlawful intellectual curiosity, the type which Luther described as 'eine schädliche Hure . . . eigensinnig . . . farbblind'.[2] The arrogant and rebellious nature of Faust's quest for knowledge is hinted at clearly enough in a famous passage near the beginning of the Spies Faustbook:

[Doctor Faustus] name an sich Adlers Flügel, wolte alle Gründ[3] am

---

[1] For an example of the confusion of alchemy and chemistry see Cornelius Agrippa, *De incertitudine et vanitate scientiarum et artium*, Antwerp, 1530, Chapter 90. Chapter 42 of the same work gives us a good idea of what was understood by 'natural magic' at that time. Agrippa's work was widely known and often translated. English: *The Vanity of Arts and Sciences*, London, 1684.

[2] *SW* xvi, 144; lviii, 326; li, 400. See, too, Chapter 1.

[3] 'Gründ[e]' here suggests the deepest, most hidden things: see Grimm, 'Grund', I F, i, 2.

Himmel vnd Erden erforschen, dann sein Fürwitz, Freyheit vnd
Leichtfertigkeit stache vnnd reitzte jhn also, daß er auff eine zeit etliche
zäuberische *vocabula, figuras, characteres* vnd *coniurationes,* damit er den
Teufel vor sich möchte fordern, ins Werck zusetzen, und zu probiern
jm fürname. (p. 14)

It is striking that this passage, stressing Faust's mutinous desire
to know all concerning the kingdom of nature, leads immediately into the description of his conjuration.

In Marlowe the treatment of the theme of nature is subtler,
more eloquent and more grandiose, but little of substance is
added to what the Faustbook had to offer. Faustus' comment
on his powers as a physician suggests that it is not enough to
combat nature by effecting sensational cures; he wants to *transcend*
nature:

> Are not thy bils hung vp as monuments,
> Wherby whole Cities haue escap't the plague,
> And thousand desperate maladies beene cur'd?
> Yet art thou still but *Faustus*, and a man.
> Couldst thou make men to liue eternally,
> Or being dead, raise them to life againe,
> Then this profession were to be esteem'd. (p. 165)

And so Faustus turns to magic to escape from mortal limitations,
to escape, among other things, from mortal man's subservience
to the elements; he dreams of being 'Lord and Commander' of
the realm of nature. He returns to this theme in his first conversation with Mephisto:

> I charge thee waite vpon me whilst I liue
> To do what euer *Faustus* shall command:
> Be it to make the Moone drop from her Sphere,
> Or the Ocean to ouerwhelme the world. (p. 179)

After the pact Faustus questions Mephisto about earth, Heaven
and Hell, and uses his magic powers to journey through the
cosmos, to trick and impress the naïve, to gain favour with
dukes and emperors and to avenge himself on his enemies.
The mixture as in 'Spies', in fact. The play, as has often been
remarked, becomes rather untidy and episodic, and one of the
themes which Marlowe disappointingly fails to pursue and

develop is that of Faustus' attitude to nature and to magic. But the main point is clear enough: Faustus desires to force nature to his will with the aid of magic—his attitude towards nature is part of his general arrogance.

So much has been written on the cosmogony of the young Goethe and of the ways in which the Sign of the Macrocosm and the Earth Spirit relate to this that it is not necessary to pursue these subjects here.[1] My concern is to show how nature as a theme runs through the *Urfaust* and holds it together, giving it its thematic unity.

The very beginning has something important to say on this theme:

> Hab nun ach die Philosophey
> Medizin und Juristerey,
> Und leider auch die Theologie
> Durchaus studirt mit heisser Müh
> Da steh ich nun ich armer Tohr
> Und bin so klug als wie zuvor.

The methods of university study have divided into categories something which should be perceived as indivisible. A further criticism of the way in which Faust has up till now sought knowledge of the natural world is implied by his description of his study, culminating in:

> Statt all der lebenden Natur
> Da Gott die Menschen schuf hinein
> Umgiebt in Rauch und Moder nur
> Dich Tiergeripp und Todtenbein.   (lines 61–4)

Symbolically, even the light of heaven is broken and obscured before it can enter this place of arid study (lines 45–9). So the *Urfaust* opens with the scholar's condemnation of his academic approach to nature: he has fragmented its unity, regarding the

---

[1] For Goethe's own account, see *Dichtung und Wahrheit*, Bk. 8. Cf. also H. M. Rotermund, 'Zur Kosmogonie des jungen Goethe' in *DVjs* xxviii (1954), 471–86; H. Jantz, 'Faust's Vision of the Macrocosm' in *Modern Language Notes*, lxviii (1953), 348–51; E. C. Mason, 'Goethe's "Erdgeist"' in *The Era of Goethe. Essays presented to James Boyd*, Oxford, 1959, 81–105; T. Whittaker, *The neo-Platonists*, 2nd edn., Cambridge, 1918; F. Koch, *Goethe und Plotin*, Leipzig, 1925; R. D. Gray, *Goethe the Alchemist*, C.U.P., 1952; Max Morris, 'Swedenborg im Faust' in *Euphorion*, vi (repr. in *Goethe-Studien*, Berlin, 1902, i, 13ff); also, of course, the various commentaries on *Faust*.

living reality as something dead and static, and has studied the whole at one remove from reality. His discontent leads him to long both for immediate and ecstatic contact with nature (39-44) and for more direct knowledge of her secrets (29f).

If I have gone over this very familiar ground in some detail, it is because in my view virtually the whole of the *Urfaust* answers this call of Faust's. We may regard the incident with the Sign of the Macrocosm as an invitation to mystical contemplation: superficially attractive but not in accord with Faust's personality and hence no fit solution for him. Then comes the confrontation with the Earth Spirit. This spirit represents nature in all those aspects which Faust's studies have combined to obscure for him:

> In Lebensfluthen im Thatensturm
> Wall ich auf und ab
> Webe hin und her
> Geburt und Grab,
> Ein ewges Meer
> Ein wechselnd Leben!
> So schaff ich am sausenden Webstul der Zeit
> Und würke der Gottheit lebendiges Kleid.   (149-56)

Nature is dynamic and alive; she is a constantly changing and indivisible manifestation of the divinity (Goethe using here the very ancient mystical image of the ocean as well as that of a garment; he will return to the latter image presently).

After this overwhelming vision, the appearance of Wagner must seem to Faust like a caricature of what he himself has been up to now, so that Faust's impatient rejection of Wagner's views has something of the character of a debate with himself, in continuation of the opening monologue. This is followed, in the *Urfaust*, by the scene in which Mephisto, impersonating Faust, advises the student. The scurrilous satire here, and perhaps too the fact that it is the Devil who is speaking, can blind us to the fact that this scene continues the argument of the opening. In the passage beginning 'Zwar ists mit der Gedanken Fabrick/Wie mit einem Weber Meisterstück' (353ff), Mephisto mocks analytical philosophy. The image of a piece of cloth recalls the 'living garment' evoked by the Earth Spirit. But Mephisto's academic philosopher examines the interdependence of the parts rather than perceiving the cloth as a whole; 'der Gottheit lebendiges Kleid' has become a demonstration piece in the lecture room. This caricature of the most pedantic type of teacher would apply to Wagner well enough—but it also comes uncomfortably close to Dr. Faust and again underlines the contrast between what he has been and what he wishes to become. Mephisto's 'Grau, theurer Freund, ist alle Theorie/Und grün des Lebens goldner Baum' (432f) sums this up yet again. The 'golden tree' is clearly linked with the 'living garment' of the Earth Spirit; the tree is another traditional symbol for the organic and everchanging unity of the natural world.

And so, after the frolic in 'Auerbachs Keller', Goethe shows us without more ado Faust confronting Gretchen. Goethe had already depicted the 'natural' being in the romanticized, Rousseauesque sense in a poem of 1772, 'Der Wanderer', a poem in which an unaffected and artless young woman is contrasted with the cultured and sophisticated figure of the Wanderer, the work suggesting that a simple life in tune with nature is superior to the pursuit of *Kultur*. Gretchen, too, is shown as simple, unaffected and unschooled. Her life has been circumscribed but 'natural'— at least if compared with Faust's. She has reared her baby sister: the young woman in 'Der Wanderer', too, is encountered with a child at her breast. Simple domesticity and the care of a child— these things are 'natural', while a life cooped up with one's books is 'unnatural'. It is worth noticing that Faust, in his ecstatic speech when shown Gretchen's room by Mephisto, falls into the same tone as in his hymn to nature in the opening scene of the fragment (cf. 33–44 and 561–75). Faust counters Gretchen's modesty by stressing not only the virtue of her simplicity and naturalness but also their superiority over worldly wisdom (929–32) and intelligence (950–3). Such exchanges recall Faust's weariness with conceptual reasoning and the whole trade of words, the weariness that runs through his opening monologue and his conversation with Wagner. He more than once affirms the impotence of words whenever feelings run deep (1037–9, 1144–50).

The naturalness of Gretchen's mode of expression is set off against Faust's more ornate and artificial way of speech as if, here too, Goethe were concerned with showing how 'civilized' man can be drawn away from directness and simplicity. Naturalness is contrasted with the *galant* manner:

FAUST: Mein schönes Fräulen darf ichs wagen
                  Mein Arm und Geleit ihr anzutragen.
MARGARETHE: Bin weder Fräulein weder schön
                  Kann ohngeleit nach Hause gehn.   (457–60)

or it is set off against the tones of a rather selfconscious, educated *Empfindsamkeit*:

MARGARETHE: Ich gäb was drum wenn ich nur wüsst
                  Wer heut der Herr gewesen ist.
                  Er sah gewiss recht wacker aus
                  Und ist aus einem edlen Haus
                  Das konnt ich ihm an der Stirne lesen.
                  Er wär auch sonst nicht so keck gewesen.
                  . . . .
FAUST: Willkommen süsser Dämmerschein
                  Der du dies Heiligthum durchwebst
                  Ergreif mein Herz du süse Liebespein
                  Die du vom Tau der Hoffnung schmachtend lebst . . .
                  In dieser Armuth welche Fülle!
                  In diesem Kerker welche Seeligkeit!   (530–46)

In this second passage Gretchen is thinking aloud in the most artless way, while Faust is almost composing his thoughts into a speech. She reacts naturally to a situation, he apostrophizes nature in his analysis of a situation.[1]

It has been noted often enough that Goethe underlines Gretchen's naturalness by giving her songs to sing which either are, or resemble, folksongs. But he goes further: he shapes the Gretchen episode so that the whole becomes like a dramatized folk-ballad. The opening exchange between Faust and Gretchen heralds this, for it recalls those folk poems in which the young gallant accosts and pursues a simple maiden. Consider the main events which follow: the introduction through a ruse, the wooing and surrender, the sleeping-draught and the series of catastrophes —the death of Gretchen's mother, Gretchen's dishonour and the killing of her child, her imprisonment. . . . For all the subtlety and eloquence of treatment, this action resembles that of some harsh folk-ballad, so that it is not inappropriate that Gretchen, half mad in prison, should see herself as a character in a folksong, saying that people are singing scornful songs about her. A

---

[1] For another exercise in contrasting styles, see 1145–53; similarly, with delicately humorous effect, throughout 'Der Wanderer'—especially lines 86–91 and 123–7.

remarkable feature of the Gretchen episode is the number of important events that Goethe omits to depict or even to relate directly (the death of Gretchen's mother, the birth and murder of the child). The 'prose-scene' gives only hints of Gretchen's disgrace and imprisonment and we have to piece together the details of her crimes from her ravings and snatches of song in prison. (And, of course, there is a gap between the scenes 'Marthens Garten ii' and 'Am Brunnen' as well.) Scene does not lead into scene as in a stage play of orthodox construction; rather do the individual scenes resemble the stanzas of a ballad, with the stages in the story being separated often by quite long gaps. Herder had commented on the lacunae of folk poetry, believing that these demonstrated the agility of the poetic imagination which could leap and bound where reason could only limp after. There is little doubt that Goethe was influenced by this simplified and romanticized view and that the disjointed and abrupt action of the Gretchen tragedy is a conscious attempt to make it resemble a folk-ballad.

Of the songs which Gretchen sings, 'Ein König in Tule' is particularly revealing. One of the things which the *Stürmer und Dränger* had admired about folk poetry was its concreteness; abstraction and reflection were cut to a minimum and the ideas and moods conveyed through things. In 'Ein König in Tule' the poet does not talk about faithful love; he traces the history of the goblet and allows the reader (or listener) to draw his own conclusions. Immediately after she finishes singing, Gretchen finds Faust's gift to her, the casket of jewels. As in folk poetry, so here: the concrete object stands for the abstract emotion. How much Goethe manages to convey through the implied contrast between the two objects!—

goblet	*jewels*
symbol of hospitality and good fellowship	mere show
gift proudly displayed in public	gift only to be enjoyed furtively, cf. 739–48
lover's present	Devil's snare

The choice of a ballad-like framework for the Gretchen tragedy was a fitting one. The folksong was felt to be natural and spontaneous (as is Gretchen too); it was associated with 'das Volk' who were assumed to be more genuine in their lives and attitudes than the rich and the learned; it recorded basic experiences, particularly the joys and miseries of love. Further, it was a native flower growing out of native soil, where most art poetry of the age was alien and remote from daily life.

If, in this account, I have seemed to set Faust off against Gretchen, always to his disadvantage, this has only been in an attempt to show to what an extent the *Urfaust* depends on a constant implied contrast between *Natur* and *Kultur*, in which the latter is always felt to be inferior.

The theme of Faust's quest for nature passes over into Part 1, although the picture is by now greatly complicated by the Prologue in Heaven and Faust's debates and wager with Mephisto, material which introduces questions concerning good and evil, the quality and scope of the experience possible to one man, the nature and implications of human restlessness and insatiability, and the meaning of magic. But the contrast between the 'natural' and the 'unnatural' was still clear enough to influence the Romantics profoundly and, in fact, their Faust versions make much of the contrast between nature perceived as something dead or as a living force, between nature fragmented or nature comprehended as a unity. Goethe's *Fragment* and Part 1 had also, of course, introduced the scene 'Wald und Höhle', which suggested that the quasi-mystical insights into nature's secrets which Faust had longed for in his opening monologue had been granted, but only at the price of enforced association with Mephisto. The precise significance of this scene has, from the beginning, puzzled many of Goethe's readers. But it has been much copied; many later authors were to make their Fausts mope among the rocks dreaming of perfect communion with nature.

That 'Anmutige Gegend' opens in an idyllic natural setting with the song of nature spirits accompanied by nature's instrument, the Aeolian harp, is an indication of the major role that nature will play in Part 2. Faust, shattered by Gretchen's fate, is soothed and healed by nature. More: it is nature which spurs him on to a new, higher activity (4681–5). All this suggests some sort of accord between man, nature and the (benevolent but unknowable) powers governing the universe. Nature, too, as a reflection of these powers, is benevolent but unfathomable. The symbolic turning away, dazzled, from the sun, to gaze upon the rainbow indicates that Faust can no longer hope to perceive the innermost secrets of the universe but must satisfy himself with such hints as can be gathered from natural phenomena. Contemplation of these and a willingness to be guided by them help man to find his destiny in fruitful, unresting activity.

This suggestion, that the right and proper life will be one in accord with nature, helps to explain why Faust will grow disenchanted with the Imperial Court and why it cannot provide the right setting for him to pursue his new ambitions. For the court and the state it governs—or misgoverns—are constantly represented as *un*natural in all sorts of ways.

The speeches of the Chancellor, the Army Commander and the Treasurer (4772ff) show how everything in the state is out of joint. (This almost Shakespearian account of anarchy hints at the possibility of an ordered state which would provide an analogy to the order of the natural world.) There follows the masque, in which nature is falsified and prettified to become nothing but a decorative backcloth. This masque, for all its references to Pan, to flowers, woods, valleys and the rest, is really a celebration of everything unnatural. The characters who really do live their lives in tune with nature (the woodman) seem clumsy and out of place (5199ff). Everywhere nature yields to art:

> Unsere Blumen, glänzend künstlich,
> Blühen fort das ganze Jahr. (5098; cf., too, 5132–7)

A state torn out of its 'natural' condition then, while the court amuses itself with the most artificial entertainments. Small wonder that Mephisto's highly 'unnatural' solution to the state's problems (paper money) is so eagerly embraced by such a court. I say 'unnatural' because, for Goethe, the rule of nature is one of gradual and organic development, whereas Mephisto's apparent panacea is an effortless and empty short cut. This *Unnatur* is stressed by Mephisto's references to superstition (4977ff) and by the weird metamorphoses brought about by him during the the masque (5783ff). The uncanny atmosphere thus evoked takes on greater meaning when we recall that magic was, in Goethe's eyes, an attempt to interfere with the patient processes of nature, to get or to do too much too quickly. (Faust himself is not yet free of this impatience; his attempt to snatch Helen from Paris is wrong in this same sense.)

The return to Faust's one-time study (Act 2) introduces us to another set of 'unnatural' attitudes. The Fichtean assertion of the Baccalaureus that the universe is a product of his act of cognition (6794–800) is a precise reversal of the truth: the 'Klassische Walpurgisnacht' will show that human consciousness is the result of a long process of natural evolution. After the Baccalaureus comes Wagner, with his attempt to construct life artificially. As Faust moves out of the laboratory, Wagner retreats yet further into it; as Faust resolves to live in accord with nature, Wagner attempts to bypass nature altogether. Presently we see these attitudes of the Baccalaureus and Wagner shown up by Homunkulus in his quest for a true, organic existence. But a new and very significant element enters into the 'Klassische Walpurgisnacht'. The elaborate mixture of motifs from art, mythology and nature hints at the ultimate unity of nature and culture. There are processes of change and evolution at work in both and both can influence human behaviour by helping man to know himself and his place in the universe. So Faust's quest for Helen and Homunkulus' quest for organic life are complementary.[1] So too Helen cannot be held in the alien milieu of a court by magic ('Rittersaal'); she must be sought out in her proper setting (cf. 7070ff). That cultural phenomena are subject to the same laws of organic development as are natural phenomena had been a commonplace in German thought since Herder—but an extraordinarily fruitful commonplace.

Faust's progress towards Helen is by way of all manner of mythical creatures, many grotesque and ugly, as if to suggest a parallel to the development of life itself through countless forms, including violent and bizarre ones. With many of these legendary figures it is as if nature had suddenly been given a voice, or as if some natural force had been personified (cf. 7249ff). By such means Goethe hints that the evolution of myths to express or bring to mind natural forces was one feature, conscious or unconscious, of Greek culture, indeed of all culture. Again nature and culture tend to come together. Although Homunkulus' quest takes place onstage and that of Faust offstage, the parallel

---

[1] Katharina Mommsen's book *Natur und Fabelreich in Faust ii* (Berlin, 1968) is, for all the invaluable facts and insights it contains, somewhat misleading in that Faust's quest is set off against that of Homunkulus in a way that suggests that the latter's activities are somehow superior to, or more 'real' than, Faust's.

is clear, and the evolutionary development prophesied for Homunkulus by Proteus (8260–4) is matched by Faust's gradual progress from 'lower' (bizarre, grotesque, violent) to 'higher' manifestations of the cultural spirit. The fundamental unity of the 'Klassische Walpurgisnacht' is shown again when Homunkulus dashes his phial to pieces on Galatea's throne: he finds his Helen and his path into life at one and the same time.

Much has been written about the dreamlike atmosphere of Act 3 and there has been much difference of opinion as to precisely how 'real' or 'unreal' Helen is. Less attention has been paid to the elements in this act which link it, through the theme of nature, to the 'Klassische Walpurgisnacht'. The opening of Act 3 shows Helen reliving her past; that is, it shows a legend gradually evolving as a natural form evolves. The end of the act and the beginning of Act 4 show Helen's influence living on and working through the generations in another implied parallel to natural processes of development and influence. And since Helen has already been represented to us as an ideal of beauty in the Platonic sense ('Finstere Galerie'), we have in her something akin to a force of nature which can run through countless rebirths and metamorphoses, ever different yet always recognizable. Here is one reason, at least, for the dreamlike quality of this part of *Faust 2*; Helen feels herself to be in all times and places at once (9411–15). The hymn to her fatherland (9506ff) again reminds us obliquely that the cultural ideal is subject to the same conditions of organic development which hold throughout the realm of nature, while the Chorus proclaims that the gaining and holding of Helen mean unremitting striving (9482–90). In fact, Faust talks of Helen in terms which strikingly anticipate the words he will use when musing on the need to rewin freedom constantly:

> Nur der verdient die Gunst der Frauen,
> Der kräftigst sie zu schützen weiß. (9444f)

Compare:

> Nur der verdient sich Freiheit wie das Leben,
> Der täglich sie erobern muß. (11575f)

It is made clear that both the pursuit of beauty and the achievement of freedom are subject to conditions analogous to natural laws.

F

In Act 4 Goethe shows us the effect on Faust of the fleeting possession of Helen. Hedonism is rejected (10176, 10259); the experience of classical antiquity and of ideal beauty urges Faust on to some noble and altruistic form of activity, just as the experience of nature had done earlier.[1] Faust's ambition is to modify nature in order to create an environment suitable for a free community. This is not, however, going against nature, as might at first glance appear. For Goethe, man is unique among living creatures in being able to alter and—to some extent at least —to control his environment (cf. the poem 'Das Göttliche'). In wishing to adapt his natural environment to suit himself, therefore, man is acting in accordance with his nature. That Faust chooses to do battle with the sea is significant. In the 'Klassische Walpurgisnacht' the sea is shown to be the realm in which life evolved and from which it emerged; now new life must be wrested from the sea. The unending pounding and battering of the sea reminds us too that a state of rest is foreign to nature and that anything worth the winning has to be won afresh each day. Human activity must obey and respond to nature's rule of incessant change and struggle. This harks back to the terms of the wager and shows that Faust's disposition is the natural one and that Mephisto, whenever he tries to make Faust satisfied with the present (11219–33) or to persuade him to accept an effortless hedonism (10160ff), is urging him towards attitudes which are *not* natural.

The last stage in Faust's struggle to achieve a life in tune with nature is heralded by his famous words in the scene 'Mitternacht':

> Noch hab ich mich ins Freie nicht gekämpft.
> Könnt' ich Magie von meinem Pfad entfernen,
> Die Zaubersprüche ganz und gar verlernen,
> Stünd' ich, Natur! vor dir ein Mann allein,
> Da wär's der Mühe wert, ein Mensch zu sein.   (11403–7)

Until recently he had still been sufficiently in bondage to Mephisto to rely on supernatural aid (in the battle and in the winning of land from the sea). But magic is a rape of nature; man must joyfully accept this world as his proper sphere of activity, must learn to depend on his human, his natural powers.

[1] Cf. 4681–5 with 10181–4, and see Mephisto's comment, 10186.

So, in a very broad sense, *Faust 2* is held together and given unity by the theme of nature. But, as we have seen, Goethe is throughout concerned with implying the wider unity of *Natur* and *Kultur*. Man's quest to understand nature as best he can and, through this understanding, to define his place and task in the universe and his attempt to plumb the cultures of past ages that they may help him to define his present ideal both of culture and activity—these two processes are, or should be, inseparable. To chop up *Faust 2*, of all works, and to label some sections as being concerned with 'nature', others with 'art', is to falsify the work and to misunderstand Goethe's lifelong desire to build a greater whole out of apparently separate and opposing parts.

> Natur und Kunst, sie scheinen sich zu fliehen
> Und haben sich, eh man es denkt, gefunden . . .

A feeling of helplessness in face of the visible world of nature, one of the major themes in the *Fausts* of the Romantic period, is expressed in Platen's 'Fausts Gebet' (1820). This poem of twenty-five lines is often underrated: in it Platen manages to say a good deal in a short space. The predicament which had come to be firmly associated in the German imagination with the Faust figure—the desire for full knowledge, coupled with the awareness that one is condemned to incomplete knowledge—is presented throughout this poem in terms of man's attempts to understand nature. Man is reduced almost to vanishing point as the known universe becomes vaster and vaster; he wishes to perceive the meaning of the world in one flash of insight, yet is forced to stumble along, interpreting his environment step by step; he feels that nature 'speaks' meaningfully, yet not in any language comprehensible to him with his limited perceptions. Already that very decided step towards pessimism which seems to distinguish the generation of the late Romantics from that of Goethe, Schiller and Herder is apparent. Faust is condemned to a hopelessly imperfect state of knowledge and has no prospect of ever reaching a position from which he will be able even to reconcile himself to this state of affairs. Here the contrast with Goethe's *Faust* is very clear. The assessment of man's ability to achieve insights into the natural world is not so different in the two works (cf. the end of 'Anmutige Gegend'); what is different is the reaction to this realization.

Lenau's *Faust* (1836) restates Goethe's view that it is folly to expect dead objects to reveal the secrets of living nature—but expresses it in much grimmer terms, which warn us that this is going to be a more savage and pessimistic work than Goethe's. One may contrast Goethe's Faust in the study:

> Statt der lebendigen Natur,
> Da Gott die Menschen schuf hinein,
> Umgibt in Rauch und Moder nur
> Dich Tiergeripp' und Totenbein. (414–17)

with Lenau's at the dissecting-table:

> Wenn diese Leiche lachen könnte, traun!
> Sie würde plötzlich ein Gelächter schlagen,
> Daß wir sie so zerschneiden und beschaun,
> Daß wir die Toten um das Leben fragen. (p. 4)

Nature reveals her phenomena to man but denies him knowledge of her inner secrets; again Lenau's Faust reacts bitterly to something to which Goethe's Faust had managed to reconcile himself:

> Und manch Insekt zerknickt des Forschers Hand,
> Weils ihm von seiner Schöpfung nichts gestand. (p. 2)

As in Platen, Nature has her language but it seems mere meaningless babbling to man:

> Steht ihr [Bäume] im Blätterschmuck, ist euer Rauschen
> Ein dummbehaglich Durcheinanderplappern;
> Zu Winterszeit vernimmt mein gierig Lauschen
> Von euren Ästen nur sinnloses Klappern.[1] (p. 10)

Already shut out from true understanding of nature, Faust estranges himself from her completely when he breaks her law and murders:

> Natur, die Freundin, ist ihm fremd geworden,
> Hat sich ihm abgewendet und verschlossen;
> Er ist von jeder Blüte kalt verstoßen,
> Denn jede Blüte spricht: du sollst nicht morden. (p. 74)

A quarter of a century later, when Darwinism was beginning to

---

[1] A somewhat similar point is made by Grabbe in *Don Juan und Faust*, ii, 1. In Lenburg's *Faust*, which is in various ways indebted to Lenau's, we encounter the image of the tree of nature, a tree of which we study only separate leaves and branches, and which we never know in its entirety (p. 38).

have its effect in Germany, Storm was to redefine the law of nature
as murder and brutality (in his novella *Im Schloß*, 1862). But
Lenau's 'Natur, die Freundin' is anyway somewhat misleading:
nature, in this dramatic poem, is represented as treacherous. She
does not only withhold her secrets from man, she helps to edge
Faust into the pantheistic delusion in which he takes his own
life, thinking to escape from Mephisto even as he runs into his
arms. The sympathy which Faust imagines as existing between his
own moods and those of nature helps him to persuade himself
that God, man and nature are one. The notion that man is in tune
with nature and can turn to her for sympathy, comfort and advice
runs strong in German Romanticism: but it is striking that all
Romantic Faust works reject both the pathetic fallacy and the
idea that nature can communicate with us. In this, as in other
respects, the Romantic writers, when treating the Faust theme,
seem to admit that Romanticism desires the unattainable and
claims the impossible. It is only in comparatively weak and derivative Faust works written much later in the nineteenth century that
we will encounter optimistic statements concerning man and
nature again (see below).

Nature figures as something wild and desolate in Lenau:

> In eines Urwalds nie durchdrungner Nacht
> Saß Faust auf einem Stamm, bemoost, vermodert . . . (p. 10)

Similar landscapes figure in W. Nürnberger's dramatic poem of
1842: rocks, wild forests, rushing streams. These landscapes are
peopled by bats, toads, owls, ravens, spiders—all creatures
traditionally associated with witches, the Devil and the Black
Arts. This is a turbulent and hellish nature, where the line between
empirical phenomena and hallucination is difficult to draw, where
malignant spirits seem to hover and dance in the wind:

> Es scheint kein Mond: im schwarzen Tannenhain
> Ging Faustus auf und ab, still und allein.
> Die Nacht sie schwieg so wie die Nächte schweigen,
> Ein dumpfig Flüstern: ein wahnsinnig Spiel,
> Von schwärzlichen Gestalten, dieses Neigen
> Der Gipfel und der Nadeln an dem Stiel. (p. 61)

The world of Nürnberger's Faust poem is not merely dark and
sinister, it is sick:

Dazu erstrahlt mit geisterhafter Bleiche
Das kranke, sieche Mondes Angesicht.   (p. 69)

Nürnberger's evocations of diseased landscapes seem to hark back to the hellish landscape of Jean Paul's 'Vernichtungstraum' and point forward to the famous description of the diseased forest in Mann's *Zauberberg*;[1] they are the only appropriate background to the fearsome events of this Faust version:

> in häßlichen Gewinden,
> Verfaulet hier ein ungeheuer Moor,
> Darin sich schon manch Menschenkind verlor.
> Hier war es grausenhaft und fürchterlich,
> Daß Sterblichen der Lebensmuth entwich, ...
> So starren hier in greller Irrlicht Scheine,
> Viel weiße, dürre, menschliche Gebeine,
> Zerrupft Gefieder treibt im nächt'gen Wind,
> Im Moor verwest der Balg von Schaaf und Rind.
> Wie bieget sich als unter Steingewicht
> Der Eichenast, der fast zu Boden bricht;
> So sitzt auf ihm in schwarzen, finstern Schaaren
> Der wüste Hauf von Geiern und von Aaren.   (p. 112)

But nature can be seductively beautiful and deceptively mild too; when Faust recalls with bitterness how Mephisto had tempted him, he curses the treachery of nature which had connived with the Devil:

> Wie war die Nacht so wild verführerisch
> Und reizend lag im Mondenschein die Welt ...
> Verflucht [sei] der träumerisch milde Mondenschein ...   (p. 17)

Nature is, in fact, a whore, used by Mephisto to tempt men:

> Die alte gute Mutter Natur,
> Ich brauche sie gar oft als meine Hur' ...   (p. 136)

We have moved very far from the optimism of Goethe's nature religion. From being a crafty but benevolent agent, working for man's benefit, although by methods largely unknown to

---

[1] For a discussion of the landscapes in Jean Paul's visions of Hell, see J. W. Smeed, *Jean Paul's Dreams*, O.U.P., 1966, Chapter 5, especially p. 37. For Mann's description of the forest, see *Zauberberg*, Chapter 7, 'Mynheer Peeperkorn (Schluß)'.

man,[1] she has become the sinister and perfidious instrument
of the Devil.

In the second half of the nineteenth century most treatments of
the Faust theme were, as already mentioned, a good deal tamer,
more optimistic and more sentimental. Faust was usually saved
and it was implied that the universe was in accord with man's
higher and more generous impulses and that God looks down
benevolently on the struggles of human existence. For most of
these authors it was as if Darwin had never written. Nature
becomes a heroine again. Three examples of such optimistic
works will suffice.

Geibel wrote two poems on the Faust theme: 'Fausts Jugendgesang' and 'Historische Studien', first published in 1865. The
former is an ecstatic hymn to nature, in which Faust is aware at all
times of his affinity with the natural world and confident that he
can understand nature's language:

> Die Wildniß lehrt mich ernste Worte
> Und Räthsel deutet mir die Nacht. (p. 10)

The contrast with the meaningless patter which is all that the
Fausts of Lenau or Platen had been able to make out could hardly
be greater. The poem ends with Faust's dream of union with
nature, and in this work it is suggested that Faust will achieve
what Lenau's Faust had been denied:

> O Blitzeslodern, Felsenkühle,
> O Sturm und Waldnacht nehmt mich hin,
> Und wie ich ganz mich euer fühle,
> Gebt Liebesantwort meinem Sinn!
> In euern Füllen untergehen
> Laßt dieses Herzens Einzelschlag,
> Bis ich von eures Odems Wehen
> Mein eigen Lied nicht scheiden mag. (p. 11)

The second of Geibel's poems concentrates on a different aspect
of nature: the constant renewal of life. Faust sees this as analogous
to historical processes (ceaseless development, the new emerging
from the old), so that both nature and history heighten man's
awareness of himself and of his environment, strengthening his

---

[1] See the 'Fragment über die Natur' of 1781.

determination to build the future on the foundation of the past. Mephisto does his best to pour cold water on Faust's enthusiasm, but it is affirmation which is dominant in this poem too.

In Mölling's tragedy *Fausts Tod* (1864) nature assists Faust in his attempts at regeneration. She calms him, and makes it possible for him to view his ambitions in true perspective:

> Wenn an ihren Busen die Natur mich drückt,
> In ihrer ew'gen Jugend üppig prangend,
> So scheint mir kindisch dieses Haschen, Streben
> Nach Rang und Ehre . . . (p. 79)

Later, when Faust is disgusted by the blindness and pettiness of his fellow-men, it is nature who provides a refuge:

> Die mächtige Natur, an deren Busen
> Das Zucken meiner kranken Brust sich legt,
> Wo ich vom Glanz des Himmels übergossen,
> Vom Flüstern trauter Bäume eingewiegt,
> Vergesse meine Sorgen, meine Qualen,
> Der Menschheit Jammer und der Menschheit Fluch. (p. 115)

Such starry-eyed attitudes, fairly typical of minor Faust works from the middle of the nineteenth century to the early twentieth, could not be expected to survive among the more thoughtful writers of this century. (The more thoughtful writers of the period 1850–1900 do not seem to have been interested in writing *Fausts*: for some suggested reasons for this, see Chapter 9.) Although, in this century too, minor Faust dramas and Faust poems continue to figure passages of 'fine writing' in which Faust, against a grandiose scenic backcloth, promises himself insights into nature, the view of man's ability to understand the natural world presented (or implied) by the two most penetrating minds to have treated the Faust theme is a good deal more guarded.

The main point of difference between Valéry's *Faust* and Goethe's, as far as the attitude towards the world of nature is concerned, is that Valéry's universe is one without purpose.[1] Since Valéry acknowledges his debt to Goethe and describes his fragment as 'un troisième Faust' (a variation or comment on Goethe, of course, not a continuation), we are surely justified in

[1] The implications of this for the Faust theme in general are discussed in Chapter 9.

relating the figures in Valéry's work to those in Goethe's. Thus Faust and Mephisto are aware of themselves as figures in a literary tradition and thus Lust and 'le disciple' may be regarded as Valéry's variations on 'das ewig Weibliche' and the student of Goethe's Part 1. Thus too 'le Solitaire', that strange intelligence musing gloomily on the impossibility of understanding—or at least of communicating any understanding of—perceived reality, may be regarded in some sort as a monstrous counterpart to Goethe's Earth Spirit. Not in the sense that 'le Solitaire' symbolizes or personifies the world of nature, but in the sense that he (it?) has something to tell Faust about man's urge to learn from nature.

What is 'le Solitaire'? There have been many answers. 'An intelligence which, from prolonged contemplation of purely abstract values, has become stark raving mad,' says K. W. Maurer. Or, according to F. Scarfe, 'An ironic conception of God, or else some potentiality in the mind of Faust.' Or an inhuman or superhuman intelligence which 'en est arrivé à mépriser toutes ces bassesses qui sont l'esprit, la pensée, le langage, la science et les merveilles de la nature' (Bémol). Bémol's view—much more tenable than the first two quoted—is restated in slightly different terms by Dabezies, who sees 'le Solitaire' as a sort of caricature of the type of intellect which wishes to explain the universe and as a demonstration of the self-destructiveness of logic.[1] Certainly 'le Solitaire' represents reality as incommunicable—life is to be lived, not analysed; nature accepted, not 'understood':

La réalité est absolument incommunicable. Elle est ce qui ne ressemble à rien, que rien ne représente, que rien n'explique, qui ne signifie rien ... (p. 389)

This is a far cry from the Earth Spirit's description of itself as the living garment of the Divinity ('der Gottheit lebendiges Kleid'). It is worth noting that Valéry goes further than even the Germans of the Romantic era. For Platen, Grabbe and Lenau nature did at least 'mean' something and 'say' something, even if man was

---

[1] K. W. Maurer, 'Valéry and Goethe' in *Publications of the English Goethe Society*, NS 17, 1948, pp. 74–100; F. Scarfe, *The Art of Paul Valéry*, London 1954, p. 307; M. Bémol, *Variations sur Valéry*, Saarbrücken, 1952, p. 129; A. Dabezies, *Visages de Faust au 20e siècle* ..., Paris, 1967, pp. 346–8.

incapable of understanding her language and thus of penetrating her meaning. But, for Valéry, the very quest for meaning is absurd.

The character with whom the study of the natural world is chiefly associated in Thomas Mann's Faust novel is not Adrian Leverkühn, but his father, Jonathan. What fascinates Jonathan is the mystery and deceptiveness of nature as well as her beauty. Nature is crafty; mimicry and trickery are means of survival, as in the case of the leaf-butterfly:

> . . . dessen Flügel, oben in volltönendem Farbendreiklang prangend, auf ihrer Unterseite mit toller Genauigkeit einem Blatte gleichen . . . Ließ dies geriebene Wesen sich mit hochgefalteten Flügeln im Laube nieder, so verschwand es durch Angleichung so völlig in seiner Umgebung, daß auch der gierigste Feind es nicht darin ausmachen konnte. (p. 19)

Sea-shells, too, fascinate Jonathan by their mysterious loveliness and, sometimes, the uncanny contrast between the beauty of the shell and the poisonous creature inhabiting it. One shell, in particular, obsesses Adrian's father because of the enigmatic and intricate markings it carries. Is this not, argues Jonathan, a language, albeit an indecipherable one, 'eine unzugängliche Mitteilung'? (p. 22).

If we are to find the further meaning implied by Jonathan Leverkühn's 'half-mystical' interest in nature, we have to take up the hint which Mann gives us when he describes Jonathan's studies in terms from the original Faustbook: 'die elementa spekulieren' (p. 17). The link is strengthened by Mann's frequent references in this same chapter (Chapter 3) to magic, alchemy, and witchcraft. This is, I believe, Mann's way of pointing to an association between his hero's heritage and the origins of the Faust legend. Adrian is both the son of his father and a descendant of the original Faust. Adrian's interests are different from those of his father; he 'speculates' about the 'elements' of the Western musical tradition. But Jonathan's pursuit of nature's secrets has been described in terms which will carry over into the account of Adrian's pursuit of the secrets of *his* art. Mann thought of music as a mysterious and daemonic art and of the composer (or indeed any artist) as an ambiguous and suspect being. The parallel to Jonathan's interest in the most ambivalent phenomena of natural history is unmistakable. Nature is ambiguous, says Jonathan; music is the ambiguous made into a system ('die Zweideutigkeit als System') says his son (p. 53). And where Jonathan had brooded on the secrets of nature, Kretzschmar recognizes in the last works of Beethoven the fruits of the deepest thought about the possibilities and boundaries of music, and the potentialities of each motif. His terminology makes the Beethoven who composed Opus 111 into something resembling a Faust figure: 'ein Exzeß an Grübelei und Spekulation . . .' (p. 58). Later the Devil will describe Adrian's turning to music in phrases which recall Faust's attempts to force nature to yield her secrets:

Von früh an hatten wir ein Auge auf dich, auf deinen geschwinden, hoffärtigen Kopf, dein trefflich ingenium und memoriam. Da haben sie dich die Gotteswissenschaft studieren lassen, wie's dein Dünkel sich ausgeheckt, aber du wolltest dich bald keinen Theologum mehr nennen, legtest die Heilige Geschrift unter die Bank und hieltest es ganz hinfort mit den figuris, characteribus und incantationibus der Musik, das gefiel uns nicht wenig. (p. 266)

(Certainly the whole passage is full of echoes from the first Faustbook.) It is no coincidence that the Devil, lord of this world, describes his own changing appearance in words which inevitably remind us of the natural phenomena which had fascinated Jonathan Leverkühn:

Das ist reiner Zufall, wie ich aussehe, oder vielmehr, es macht sich so, es stellt sich so je nach den Umständen her, ohne daß ich auch nur acht darauf gebe. Anpassung, Mimikry, du kennst das ja, Mummschanz und Vexierspiel der Mutter Natur, die immer die Zunge im Mundwinkel hat. (p. 245)

It is the Devil, too, who implies that the amoral criteria governing biological success in the world of nature also apply to the creation of works of art. 'Good' and 'evil', 'healthy', and 'diseased': these are artificial, man-made distinctions. What matters is whether a particular means is effective. The Devil is talking to Adrian about the conditions necessary to artistic creativity, but he constantly uses terms which could just as easily apply to the evolutionary process in nature:

Was krank ist, und was gesund, mein Junge, darüber soll man dem Pfahlbürger lieber das letzte Wort nicht lassen . . . Was auf dem Todes-, dem Krankheitswege entstanden, danach hat das Leben schon manches Mal mit Freuden gegriffen und sich davon weiter und höher führen lassen. . . . Was krankhaft und gesund! Ohne das Krankhafte ist das Leben sein Lebtag nicht ausgekommen. Was echt und unecht! (pp. 253–4)

According to this doctrine, 'right' and 'wrong' in the realm of nature mean tending to or threatening biological success; in the realm of art, propitious for or inimical to the production of great works.

Both Mann and Valéry oppose any view that the phenomena of nature have a 'meaning' (in any normal, human sense of the word) which they will yield even to the most determined investigator. Valéry, as we have seen, makes the point quite explicitly. Mann is more oblique: he presents Jonathan's attempts to discover meaning in shells and the like in a slightly ridiculous light and has Zeitblom describe such investigations as dreaming rather than research (p. 22). Nature is 'illiterate' (ibid). Markings on a shell: why should they mean anything? One may recall Günther Anders on Kafka. Kafka's demonstration that life is meaningless, says Anders, is achieved through an attempted interpretation of its meaning, an interpretation which is so absurd that it proves its own futility:

[Kafka ist] wie ein Mann, der Risse im Schiefergestein übersetzt, als seien sie Hieroglyphen, um denen, die daherzureden pflegen, das Gestein der Welt habe Sinn, durch die Absurdität des Übersetzungstextes zu beweisen, daß die Risse wirklich nur Risse sind.[1]

---

[1] G. Anders, *Kafka, pro und contra*, Munich, 1951, p. 99.

4

Problems bound up with
the Theme

(i) *The unanswerable questions*

Stets weichst du aus den ernstgemeinten Fragen!
Ich merke wohl, der Hölle Wissenschaft
Besteht darin: den Staub des Weges aufzujagen,
Und reizen die Begier ist ihre ganze Kraft.
(G. Pfizer, 'Faustische Szenen', 1831)

THIS complaint of Faust to Mephisto hints at a difficulty encountered by author after author who has treated the Faust legend. Where Faust is motivated by a craving for more than human knowledge, there will come a time when, after the pact, he will demand answers to his questions. Now the Devil has traditionally been thought of as knowing more than man, although less than the good angels. He *should* be able to answer some at least of Faust's questions. In electing to treat this legend, writers have therefore saddled themselves with the problem that their hero will, at some stage and with a reasonable expectation of being satisfied, ask a number of strictly unanswerable questions (unanswerable for the author, that is). How has this difficulty been surmounted?

For those who were concerned with showing Faust moving away from intellectual curiosity and finding his destiny, for good or ill, elsewhere, the problem did not exist. Such authors include the many nineteenth-century writers who represented the faustian curiosity as either arrogant or sterile and who showed Faust coming to prefer the active life to the speculative. Other Fausts are shown being dragged down by the Devil, deflected from their desire for knowledge into a wild and destructive hedonism. Again, some Faust works are not concerned with intellectual curiosity but with some other form of striving (for example, the desire to produce music of surpassing excellence, as in the case of Thomas Mann's Faust figure). And in the most famous *Faust* of all, the pursuit of ultimate certainty is shown to be futile; Faust quickly comes to accept that partial knowledge—the surface or reflection, not the heart of things—is all that he can and should hope for (cf. line 4727).

If we go back to the oldest printed version of the Faust story we find that the author was quite unaware of the hidden pitfall. Mephisto does, it is true, give one false answer to a question of Faust's (concerning the creation of the world—pp. 50-2), but the object of this is to show the Devil as a lying spirit who is reluctant to give God credit for the act of creation. The question is not wrongly answered because the author felt himself unable to give a correct answer; the episode has a didactic function. For the rest, the author seems quite happy to allow Mephisto to give conventional and orthodox answers to Faust's questions and obviously sees nothing incongruous in the fact that Faust has sold his soul to obtain information which would have been readily available to him by legitimate means. The Faustbook of Widmann/ Pfitzer is similar in this respect. The long section devoted to Faust's questioning of Mephisto (Part i, Chapters 16-23) demonstrates only that Faust has signed away his soul to get his head stuffed with nonsense which (as the authorities quoted by Widmann in his notes to these chapters show) he could have got from any learned theologian. Again there is a question which Mephisto fails to answer, and again the point is clearly didactic (cf. Chapter 19). There are unanswerable—or unanswered— questions in the puppet plays too, but always of a very naïve nature.[1]

Among all the *Fausts* written before the *Aufklärung*, it is only in Marlowe that we find any hint of awareness that the theme has a built-in difficulty. There is much in Marlowe that was present in his source: the description of Hell (subtler than in the chapbook but still not worth the price Faust pays), the references to secret books and magic travels, even the question that Mephisto refuses to answer (here less to make a didactic point than to show the continuing conflict between good and evil impulses in Faust).[2]

---

[1] See the Ulm and Strasbourg puppet plays, both in Scheible, vol. v, ii, 6 and v, 2.

[2] II, 1-2. Dédéyan (*Le Thème de Faust* . . . , Paris, 1954ff, vol. i, p. 64) points out that Mephisto's replies to Faustus show no more than the wisdom of a sixteenth-century Humanist.

But at the point where Faustus and Mephisto 'argue of divine astrology', Marlowe seems to show some realization of the dilemma into which his theme has led him. This Mephisto gives the same sort of answers as the Devil in the chapbook had given. But where the German Faust had seemed quite content with the information offered, Marlowe's Faustus turns on Mephisto:

> These slender questions *Wagner* can decide:
> Hath *Mephostophilis* no greater skill? (p. 201)

There is the problem, put as succinctly as one could wish. Within the framework of the legend—within the play, that is—Mephisto certainly should be able to do better than that. (And according to the theologians, he could do better.) But no author can show him doing better.

There is a hint that this dilemma had occurred to Lessing. In the so-called 'Berliner Scenario', the Devil, taking on the likeness of Aristotle, appears to Faust:

> Er . . . antwortet dem Faust auf seine spitzigsten Fragen. Doch, sagt' er endlich, ich bin es müde, meinen Verstand in die vorigen Schranken zurückzuzwingen. Von allem, was du mich fragst, mag ich nicht länger reden als ein Mensch und kann nicht mit dir reden als ein Geist. . . .

The suggestion is clearly that spiritual truths cannot be communicated in human language. It is a pity that we shall never know what one of the acutest minds ever to brood on the Faust theme could have made of this point. A pity, above all, that we cannot tell what the 'spitzige Fragen' would have been, and at what moment the Devil would have declared himself too weary to go on answering.

Klinger's Devil, Leviathan, makes two excuses for his inability to satisfy Faust's curiosity. Firstly, he has forgotten many 'sublime secrets' since the Fall; secondly, what he does know is communicable only in a language which would be meaningless, indeed terrifying, to man (i, 8). Here Klinger combines a traditional theological argument concerning the extent and limits of diabolic knowledge with a philosophical point regarding the interdependence of ideas and language (implicit, too, in Lessing's sketch). So Faust, convinced that, as a mortal, he cannot achieve ultimate truth, settles for knowledge of mankind's behaviour on earth instead. Klinger's argument concerning the limits of man's possible knowledge is not an easy way out of a difficulty; it is a necessary stage in the development of his theme. For when Faust, having hoped that man can achieve God-like insights, is persuaded that this cannot be, he is left only with his faith in man *as man*. This faith Leviathan systematically destroys, thus bringing Faust to despair.[1]

In lesser authors than Marlowe, Lessing and Klinger we often get the impression of mere side-stepping on the part of the Devil. In A. W. Schreiber's *Szenen aus Fausts Leben* (1792), Faust binds himself to the spirit (here: Helim) in the first place for one specific reason, to solve the mysteries of existence:

FAUST: Habt ihr Wahrheit, die der Mensch nicht hat?
DIE STIMME: Die haben wir.
FAUST: Ich bin Euer. (pp. 72f)

But when he presently questions Helim on specific points, he gets no satisfaction:

FAUST: Kannst du mich das unbegreifliche Wesen kennen lehren, das über uns waltet?
HELIM: Gott kennt sich allein. (p. 88)

In J. F. Schink's 'dramatic fantasy' *Johann Faust* (1804), the method used to wriggle out of the difficulty is somewhat different. As in Schreiber, so here: the pact-scene stresses Faust's demands for insights never before achieved by a mortal.

FAUST: Laß mich erblicken, was kein Auge sah,
Vernehmen, was kein Ohr von Fleisch und Bein
Noch je vernahm, was für den Sohn des Staubes
Nicht Laut und Namen hat.
MEPH.: Ei, weiser Faust,
Du traust dem Teufel große Dinge zu!
Er soll dir tönen heißen, was nicht tönt;
Dein Ohr will hören, was nicht hörbar ist? . . .
FAUST: . . . Hinweg von mir, wenn du *dies* nicht vermagst!
MEPH.: Nun denn! Was noch? (i, 120f)

It will be seen that Mephisto's agreement is curiously informal

---

[1] F. J. H. von Soden (*Dr. Faust*, 1797) has a passage probably indebted to Klinger. When Faust asks Mephisto about the power behind and within the visible phenomena of nature, Mephisto replies menacingly: 'Schweig! oder bei den Mächten der Hölle, ich hebe den Schleier, und ein Blick verzehrt dich zu Staub!' (iii, 1).

and ambiguous. For anyone versed in the ways of the Devil and familiar with the elaborate conditions and precautions prescribed in the manuals of conjuration, this should in itself be a warning. And in fact, when Faust finally comes to demand answers to his questions, Mephisto is in a quandary. He has no knowledge which will satisfy Faust.

> Da zwingt er mich, despotisch mir gebietend,
> Zu halten ihm, was ich nicht halten *kann*.
> Ich soll ihn lehren, was ich *selbst* nicht weiß:
> Der tiefverborg'nen Kräfte der Natur
> Geheimnißvolle, nie begriff'ne Kunde.
> Was kann ich thun, als ihn durch *Blendwerk* äffen?   (ii, 185f)

And so he stages an elaborate magical entertainment, in which allegorical figures representing Truth, Riches, the Elements, etc., appear to Faust. The whole is as rich in secret lore as a run-of-the-mill seventeenth-century court masque. Schink, faced with this major problem inherent in his theme, simply beats a retreat.

Other authors exploit the old notion that any bargain made with the Devil is likely to contain a hidden snare, and show Faust tricked out of his answers by a Devil who, quite simply, uses the literal wording of the pact as a means of outwitting Faust. Before these works are discussed, something must be said in general concerning the sharp practices of the Devil when dealing with mortals.

(ii) *The catch in the pact*

Wendelin, in Nestroy's comedy *Höllenangst* (1849), has the following to say about the Devil:

Der Teufel is überhaupt nicht das Schlechteste, ich lass' mich lieber mit ihm als mit manchem Menschen ein . . . er erfüllt seine Verträge weit prompter als manch irdischer Schmutzian. Freilich nacher am Verfallstag, da kommt er auch auf d'Minuten, Schlag zwölfe, holt sich sein' Seel' und geht wieder schön orndtlich nach Haus in seine Höll'; 's is halt ein G'schäftsmann, wie sich's g'hört. (i, 9)

But not all would agree with this picture of fair dealing. There are numerous folk proverbs which suggest the need for extreme caution in compacts with the Devil. If he *does* resemble a business-man he is more like the type who dazzles his customers with lavish offers and hides away the less advantageous clauses in small print. There are many popular legends in which the Devil's gifts turn out to be worthless. One of the most persistent tells of gold or jewels which vanish away overnight or turn into trash. This notion is referred to in the early nineteenth-century puppet play published by Oskar Schade in 1856. Here, when Faust demands riches from the Devil, he adds:

Aber kein solches Geld, das wieder unter Menschenhänden ver-schwindet, nein ein solches Geld das von Menschen ist geschlagen und geprägt worden. (iii, 2—p. 288)

In popular legend, agreements with the Devil often entail catches turning on place-names (usually Rome or Jerusalem) or on a stipulated number of deadly sins. In this last type of bargain, the magician agrees that his soul shall be rendered to the Devil only if he commits a certain number of mortal sins, usually three or four. But he forgets that the agreement already counts as one.[1]

The most common type of catch in bargains with the Devil in the popular Faust pieces concerns the period of service. Faust pledges his soul on condition that his familiar shall serve him for twenty-four years. But at the end of only twelve the Devil claims his due on the grounds that he has worked night and day for Faust, and should be paid double time, so to speak.[2] This incident is elaborated wittily in the puppet play given by Bonneschky in Leipzig in the mid-nineteenth century (edited by Hamm, 1850). In this version, Mephisto agrees to Faust's demand for twenty-four years' service but adds in an aside: 'Ich will ihn schon betrügen, er rechnet die Nächte nicht' (i, 5). Meanwhile Faust is planning to cheat Mephisto:

[1] For proverbs and legends concerning the hazards of dealing with the Devil, see Graf, pp. 80 and 87; for examples of the 'topographical' catch, see Kiesewetter, *Faust in der Geschichte und Tradition*, Hildesheim, 1963, p. 119 and Graf, pp. 139 and 141. It is, for instance, related of Pope Sylvester II that the Devil agreed to serve him until he celebrated mass 'in Jerusalem'. This seemed an easy condition to evade. But one day the Pope celebrated mass in an unfamiliar chapel in Rome, which, he afterwards learned, was called the Jerusalem Chapel. . . .

[2] It is not possible to tell whether this motif had figured in the popular stage plays of Dr. Faust but it is common in the puppet plays. Like all those catches previously mentioned, this Devil's trick is much older than the Faust legend. For something similar in the stories of Pope Alexander VI and the Devil, see Kiesewetter, pp. 125f.

Und habe ich, wenn die Hälfte der Zeit des Contraktes verflossen, nicht durch meine Kenntnisse Macht genug, mich seinen Klauen zu entreißen? (ibid.)

But in due course Mephisto reveals the catch: '. . . . rechne nur die Nächte dazu, und Du wirst sehen, daß unser Contrakt zu Ende geht' (iv, 5). When Goethe's Mephisto promises Faust that he will not be cheated of any part of his bargain (1416f), it is probably this shrinking of twenty-four years into twelve that is being referred to.

This notion of the catch in bargains with the Devil, like many other motifs from the popular Faust tradition, was taken up into literary treatments of the theme. Klingemann, in his *Faust* of 1815, takes over the 'trick' bargain concerning four mortal sins, while, more than a century later, Hanns Eisler exploits the old theme of the halving of Mephisto's period as Faust's servant. But where Klingemann takes over an idea from folk legend naïvely, without in any way adding to its significance, Eisler gives the traditional motif a new twist. His Devil makes the point about double time in terms that cast Faust as a ruthless capitalist exploiter:

> Wenn der Bauer sich einen Knecht dingt:
> Ob Regen, ob Schnee, ob Hitzplag,
> Zwölf Stunden ist der Werkeltag.
> Zwölf Stunden kriegt er als Nacht,
> Dann kommt ihm wieder seine Kraft.
> Tag und Nacht hast mich gehetzt,
> Daß aus vierundzwanzig Jahr
> Jetzt geworden sind
> Zwölf Jahr. (iii, 6)

This is wholly in tune with Eisler's treatment of the legend for his Faust is, after all, presented as the friend of the great, the betrayer of the common people.

This brings us to a second, more interesting snare in the pact with the Devil in this version. One of Faust's conditions is:

Die Herrn der Welt müssen vor mir sich neigen, die Sorg im Blick, ob ich auch guter Laun. (i, 6)

Faust does indeed gain the somewhat apprehensive recognition and favour of the ruling classes—but only at the cost of being hated by the common people, so that he comes to despise himself.

The catch is that he is given exactly what he asked for, but in circumstances which disgust and horrify him.[1]

This point, that the catch is hidden away in the precise literal meaning of the words in the contract, is central to Chamisso's Faust-fragment of 1803. And here we return to the point about Faust's unanswerable questions. The agreement between the 'böser Geist' and Faust includes the promise: 'Und was der Mensch vermag, sollst du erkennen'. Now Faust, in his opening monologue, had expressed the Kantian view that his knowledge of external reality *must* be imperfect because of the limitations both of his sense-perceptions and of his reasoning powers. Presently, when he has signed his soul away, the Evil Spirit makes clear the meaning of the small print in the agreement:

> Es kann der Staubumhüllte nichts erkennen,
> Dem Blindgebornen kann kein Licht erscheinen. . . .
> Du kannst nur denken durch den Mittler Sprache,
> Nur mit dem Sinne schauen die Natur,
> Nur nach Gesetzen der Vernunft sie denken.

(The last three lines quoted are closely similar to Faust's own formulation before the pact, when he had talked of 'Der Sinne Lügen, der Vernunft Gesetze'.)

So Faust, although enough of a philosopher to define his problem in Kantian terms, is cozened by the Evil Spirit through a form of words which unobtrusively makes capital out of that same problem of perception. The Evil Spirit keeps his bargain to the letter—and manages to damn Faust without having to render any service or give any information whatever. Why is Faust, of all people, fooled by a form of words in which any student of philosophy would see a hidden meaning? The answer probably lies in Faust's overbearing pride. The exchange between the 'guter Geist' and Faust, immediately before Faust allies himself to the powers of evil, gives us the hint. Faust insists on his freedom to will and to act, stresses the importance of the temporal world as opposed to a hypothetical eternity, and ends by cursing God. To someone so fanatically committed to the value of the individual

---

[1] Perhaps the popular notion that the Devil's gifts are likely to turn sour was in Goethe's mind when he composed the Gretchen tragedy. For it is in good faith that Faust gives Gretchen the sleeping draught that causes her mother's death (cf. 3510–16). It is nowhere made explicit that this potion is supplied by Mephisto but we must surely assume it.

and so hostile to external authority, the phrase 'was der Mensch vermag' must suggest limitless promise. What would man not be capable of, if he were truly free? In the last resort, Faust is played false not by the Evil Spirit but by his own vanity.

Grabbe's Faust falls into a somewhat similar trap, finding that he too can only know external appearances, without ever being able to penetrate to their inner meaning. Here the emphasis is on human language, which determines and limits man's power to understand the world (*Don Juan und Faust*, ii, 1). Julius von Voß (*Faust*, 1823) has a 'small print' clause in the pact, which is very like that in Chamisso, again turning on the Kantian philosophy:

FAUST: Wenn ich den Himmel dir verpfänden mag,
                Wird mir der Schleier von den Dingen weichen?
LEVIATHAN: (nach kurzem Bedenken)
                So weit der ird'schen Sinne Maaße reichen,
                Des Denkens Formen Sein und Nichtsein gleichen,
                Umhelle dich der Wahrheit Tag! (i, 7)

And so the old popular notion that the Devil's gifts will turn out to be trash and his promises double-edged is given a new, philosophical twist by these writers. That man's powers of perception and understanding are limited by his modes of experiencing and categorizing sense-data provides the Devil with a means of trapping Faust—and the author with a way out of a dilemma.

(iii) *Magical elements in the Faust legend*

The 1587 chapbook is the product of an age in which science and superstition, empirical and non-empirical attitudes, were inextricably mixed. The alchemists practised some chemistry, as we would understand the term, but chemistry combined with astrology and magical lore and rendered hopelessly unscientific (in anything resembling the modern sense of the word) by an ingenuous belief in the significance of analogies and correspondences. Just as, in alchemy, it is hardly possible to distinguish between science and magic, so too the dividing line between astrology and astronomy hardly existed.

Still more important: Faust lived and his legend grew up in times when nearly everybody believed in magic. The notorious 'Witch Bull' of Pope Innocent VIII (1484), together with the *Malleus Maleficarum* of 1486, had codified popular and learned superstitions concerning witches and the Devil and had given these superstitions the official sanction of the Church. In the resultant epidemic of witch trials, confessions exacted under torture seemed to provide objective corroborative evidence for these beliefs. The scholars of the Renaissance discovered classical sources which told of sorcerers, Striges, magical transformations and the like, adding, as it seemed, the authority of classical antiquity to the authority of the Church. The Reformation, far from weakening the belief in witches and demons, probably strengthened it and helped it to survive rather longer. For in the polemical writings of the sixteenth century, it became natural and common for each side to represent the other as allied to the Devil or as doing the Devil's work. Moreover, Luther's enormous personal influence bolstered up the belief in witches and in a Devil who roamed about the earth, tempting and tormenting mortals. Most men of the sixteenth century, Catholic and Protestant, educated and uneducated, believed that an alliance or pact with the Devil was possible, that the Devil and those in league with him had the power to transform themselves into all manner of shapes and to plague men through magic. Those who bound themselves to the Devil were formally required to renounce the Trinity and the Sacraments and to oppose the Christian religion. They could fly through the air, and they copulated with incubi and succubi. All these (to us) fantastic notions were the subject of learned deliberation.[1] There were, of course, individuals in the sixteenth century who rejected certain of these superstitions (for instance, a man might believe in the Devil, but not in the possibility of sexual intercourse between a human being and a demon, or in magical flights). But doubters were in a minority. The events related in the first Faustbook will not have seemed impossible to most sixteenth-century readers. Marlowe's *Dr. Faustus* reflects a much more sophisticated and sceptical attitude than 'Spies', of course, and it seems probable that Marlowe wished the magic inherent in the legend to be taken only in a symbolical sense, as signifying Faustus' desire to be more than man (cf. 'A sound Magitian is a Demi-god'). But the popular Faust pieces on stage and in puppet theatre treat the magic naïvely and credulously again. The magic tricks and spectacles

---

[1] Cf. J. Hansen, *Zauberwahn, Inquisition und Hexenprozeß im Mittelalter*, Munich and Leipzig, 1900, especially p. 179. I am much indebted to this work.

are made much of and are given prominence in the theatre bills. It is safe to assume that, for a century at least, audiences accepted these magical elements as 'true'. But when the Faust theme came to be taken seriously by educated men in the eighteenth century, the situation had, of course, changed.

In 1701 Christian Thomasius produced his *De crimine magiae*, a work which was translated into German three years later by Thomasius' pupil, Johann Reiche, under the title *Kurtze Lehr-Sätze von dem Laster der Zauberey*.[1] In this work, Thomasius attacks the superstitions concerning witches and the Devil, points out the frightful consequences of such credulity (notably the whole machinery of the witch trials), and denies point blank the possibility of pacts with the Devil. He was not the first writer to have done this[2] but his work was certainly the main factor which led to increasing scepticism regarding the Devil and his works in eighteenth-century Germany. Brüggemann is unquestionably right when he says that Thomasius helped to create the belief—at least among educated men—that the story of Dr. Faust was legend and fantasy rather than fact.[3] From the early eighteenth century onwards more and more people came to realize that the story of Dr. Faust was a fantastic invention woven around a person who had actually existed. The magical elements were regarded as products of superstitious imaginations.[4] Thus we have the situation that the Faust theme re-entered serious literature at a time when the majority of cultivated men had ceased to take magic and demonology seriously. The magic came to constitute an embarrassment.

This feeling of embarrassment can already be detected in the 'Vorbericht' to Weidmann's *Johann Faust* (1775). The whole

---

[1] Edition used: *Herrn D. Christian Thomasii . . . Kurtze Lehr-Sätze von dem Laster der Zauberey . . . und anderer gelehrter Männer Schrifften*, herausgegeben von Johann Reichen, Halle, 1704, pp. 580–621. Extracts from Reiche's translation are given in *Deutsche Literatur in Entwicklungsreihen: Aufklärung*, vol. i, edited by Brüggemann, 1928.

[2] Balthasar Bekker in Holland had covered the same ground in his *De Betoverde Weereld* ('The Bewitched World') of 1691. There were a number of German translations, of which the first appears to be *Die Bezauberte Welt . . . Aus dem Holländischen nach der letzten vom Authore vermehrten Edition*, Amsterdam, 1693 (translator not named).

[3] DLE, *Aufklärung*, i, 'Einführung', p. 9.

[4] For examples, dating from the early eighteenth century, of this view, see Tille, *Faustsplitter*, nos. 164, 174, 184, 192.

preface is a masterpiece of doubletalk, but the most likely interpretation is that Weidmann disbelieved in the magical elements,
regarding them as symbolical. He did not quite bring himself to
say so outright, however. Lessing too seems to have found the
magic in the Faust legend inhibiting for, if we are to believe
Staatsrat Gebler, he had treated the theme twice, once according to
the popular legend and once without any supernatural aspects.[1]
We find him, too, praising Maler Müller for approaching the
theme 'ironically'; a modern writer who presented such a subject
credulously would, he says, be doomed to failure.[2]

In the anonymous farce *Faust im Achtzehnten Jahrhundert*, which
takes up Schink's idea of the woman (here called Sidonia) who is
in love with Faust and impersonates the Devil in order to 'cure'
Faust, Sidonia herself mocks the credulity of those who believe
in pacts and magic:

> Alles Beschwören, Pakt machen, Teufel holen, ist elende Erfindung
> von Leuten, die sich in dummen Jahrhunderten die Gewalt anmasten
> unsre Seelen zu verwalten. Glaube mir, wann man die Teufel nöthigen
> könnte Geld zu bringen, so hätte schon mancher König aus der Hölle
> geborgt um eine Universal Monarchie zu errichten. (Brukner and
> Hadamowsky, p. 79)

From the time of the *Aufklärung* onwards, then, authors of
Fausts began to find that the magic bound up with their theme
presented them with a problem. In serious Faust works, the
magic has usually been given some symbolical meaning. Thus it
could still be represented as an important element in the story,
even if no longer regarded as 'true' in any literal sense.

In Klinger, the magic tricks carried out by Faust and the Devil
are linked with the central theme of the novel, human corruption.
Faust uses magic to mete out a grotesque, even surrealistic, form
of justice. When the Burgomaster and the council of Frankfort are
to be punished for their greed and servility, they are magically
transformed into the pitiable creatures which, despite their self-
importance and pretensions, they truly resemble:

> Der Bürgermeister trug einen Hirschkopf zwischen den Schultern,
> alle die übrigen, Weiber und Männer, waren mit Larven aus dem

---

[1] Gebler to Nicolai, 9/12/1775. Quoted in Petsch, p. 44.
[2] This is from a conversation between Lessing and Müller in 1777, as reported by
Müller. Quoted by Petsch, p. 45.

launigen Reiche der grotesken und bizarren Phantasie geziert, und jeder sprach, schnatterte, krähte, blökte, wieherte oder brummte in dem Tone der Maske, die ihm zu teil geworden. (ii, 4)

A more savage example of how Faust uses magic to make the punishment fit the crime occurs when a peasant, unable to pay his dues to the Bishop, commits suicide in despair. Faust remonstrates with the Bishop, a *bon viveur*, who will hear nothing of peasants and tithes while eating. So Faust causes Leviathan to turn the calf's head, which the Bishop is about to cut, into the head of the dead peasant (iii, 1). There is nothing facetious or tongue-in-cheek about these episodes. The first is genuinely grotesque, the second genuinely horrific. Klinger is evidently content that magic should figure in his Faust novel, since it was traditionally an important part of the legend, but he is not prepared to take over the trivial and often pointless traditional tricks and exploits. The magic, like everything else in this sombre work, must be made relevant to the central theme.

In his 'Helena' essay of 1828, Carlyle, after remarking that the days of magic are past and that witchcraft 'has been put a stop to by Act of Parliament', says that Goethe, in his treatment of the Faust legend, 'retains the supernatural vesture of the story, but retains it with the consciousness, on his and our part, that it is a chimera'.[1] In the most narrow and literal sense—that Goethe did not believe in rejuvenating potions, compacts with the Devil, and so on—this is obviously true but it is nevertheless slightly misleading. Even at the earliest stage of planning *Faust*, Goethe committed himself to some of the magic traditional to the legend. (There is the scene 'Auerbachs Keller' and the reference in the antepenultimate scene of the *Urfaust* to Mephisto's having appeared in the form of a dog.) This suggests that Goethe was attracted to the 'old German' and 'popular' aspects of the theme, while the inclusion (in 'Auerbachs Keller') of the Song of the Flea, with its political and social comment, implies that he was at the same time concerned to make the traditional episodes less trivial. Also we know that in the years in which the *Urfaust* was conceived, Goethe was fascinated by magical, cabbalistic and Neoplatonic lore, and it seems likely that even at this early stage he began to brood on the symbolic meaning of magic, the way

[1] *Critical and Miscellaneous Essays*, London, Chapman and Hall, i (1869), pp. 181f.

in which it could be made to express the relationship between man, the visible world and the invisible powers that govern both; the way, too, in which man's turning to magic could be seen as manifestation of a desire to become more than man.[1] For not only does Goethe take over magical elements from the Faust tradition, he introduces new material, both into the *Urfaust* and Part 1: the Sign of the Macrocosm, the conjuration of the Earth Spirit, Faust's magical rejuvenation in the 'Hexenküche' scene, and so on. Some of this material is not much more than magical trappings, one might even say: innocent showing-off on Goethe's part (cf. 1257ff, 1393ff). But the sign of the Macrocosm and the apparition of the Earth Spirit seem to symbolize the unity of the cosmos and the material world respectively, while the rejuvenation sequence shows man trying to overcome the laws of organic existence through magic. That is, magic is *introduced* by Goethe in order to make points of the utmost seriousness and importance. The sign of the Macrocosm suggests a constant interaction between divine and terrestrial, an eternal process by which finite existence refreshes and renews itself at the fount of all being. This process is expressed in near-mystical terms which rely for their force on Neoplatonic concepts, but it clearly anticipates and links up with the Christian imagery of the closing scene in Part 2. In fact it is in this last scene of the work that Faust is finally shown that the vision suggested by the sign of the Macrocosm is *not* a mere show ('ein Schauspiel nur'). The Earth Spirit, too, symbolizes something central to *Faust*, the dynamism, the imperfection, and the constant dying and rebirth which characterize and determine finite existence. In the 'Geburt und Grab' of the Earth Spirit's speech (504) is implicit the debate concerning human endeavour which is one of the main themes of this work. The phrase hints at why Faust will be wrong when he promises himself lasting and concrete results from his endeavours[2] although, if understood correctly, it implies that Mephisto's nihilism is wrong too. The rejuvenation in 'Hexenküche' is the first and most dramatic way in which Faust profits from magic. Much later, as an old man, he wishes that he might renounce magic, and is blinded. Much has been written about the

---

[1] This we have seen hinted at in Marlowe; it is worth repeating that Goethe did not, at this stage, know Marlowe's *Faustus*.

[2] Contrast 11583f with 11546ff.

meaning of the scene 'Mitternacht'; it seems likely that one meaning, at least, of the blinding of Faust is to show that he is at last fully subject to the infirmities of old age. His renunciation of magic must also involve renunciation of the fruits of his association with the Devil, one of which was renewed youth. Thus, (magical motifs from Part 1 are only revealed in their full meaning towards the end of the work: Goethe is both able to infuse profound meaning into Faust's cultivation of magic and also to use the theme of magic in its various aspects as one of the means by which his vast structure is held together and given unity.) The *tone* of some of the supernatural incidents is ironic, of course, but this does not mean that the episodes themselves lack significance. [1]

Lenau seems a little uncertain as to how to treat the magical elements in his theme. There is a brief, half joking reference to Faust's familiar, 'Fausts Hund, Prästigiar genannt' in the scene 'Das arme Pfäfflein'. The treatment of the spell cast on the peasants to prevent them from attacking Faust (ibid.) and of the magic flight on the cloak ('Das Lied') suggests that Lenau did not expect his readers to take such things very seriously, and certainly did not himself attach much importance to them. The situation is very different from that in Klinger and Goethe. More interesting is the scene in the village inn, 'Der Tanz'. Here Mephisto borrows a fiddle from the village musicians and plays in such a fashion that Faust becomes inflamed with sexual desire. There is no magic at all in this scene, but it is recognizably a variation on the old motif of the magical, 'devilish' music with which Faust is regaled in chapbooks and early plays. Lenau restates the theme in perfectly natural terms, exploiting it to show how Faust's sensual urges were waiting on the catalytic effect of sensual music.

Many authors have simply dismantled the magic and produced *Fausts* which are almost or entirely free from supernatural elements. Those authors who have taken over Faust as a type but have constructed their own plots independently of legendary material belong in this category. [2] Even in Faust plays which retain Faust's association with the Devil, the magic is often pared

[1] See especially the 'Mummenschanz' and the battle in Act 4. Some passages come dangerously near facetiousness (cf. 10664–78). Magic had already been treated with more than a touch of levity in Part 1, of course: cf. 1714–40 and the 'Hexenküche'.

[2] See account of Kratzmann, above, pp. 29f.

away almost to nothing. Adalbert Lenburg's is such a *Faust* (1860).
Here Mephisto appears, unbidden, to Faust after the monologue:
when Faust is ripe for him, that is. There is thus no need for
conjuration formulae, one of the chief elements that seemed to
link the Faust theme with a credulous past age. Neither is there
a pact in this version, merely a verbal agreement.[1] And once
Faust *is* associated with the Devil, Mephisto encompasses his
ruin without much need for magic: Lenburg's Devil operates
through sinister duplicity and a cynical insight into human
nature. He is more like Iago or Edmund than the Devil of tradition. At one point one of the characters, hearing that his wife has
been seduced by Faust, exclaims that this is the Devil's work.
Mephisto's rejoinder is:

> Das wäre möglich—, vor zweihundert Jahren;
> Doch jetzt—der Teufel kam zu Falle;
> Frei ist des Menschen Wille und Gebahren.   (p. 64)

Like Goethe's Devil (cf. *Faust 1*, 2507–9) Mephisto ironically
bows out. If men claim free will, they cannot blame evil on the
Devil. The action of Lenburg's play does, in fact, confirm the
implications of this speech; evil comes about because of qualities
in men, not because of the Devil and the aid he can give Faust
through his magic arts. This idea is taken to its logical conclusion
in Louisa M. Alcott's *Modern Mephistopheles* (1877), a variation on
the Faust theme which dispenses entirely with the supernatural.
The 'modern Mephistopheles' is an embittered and cynical
invalid whose driving force and only remaining pleasure is to
exert power over his fellow men, to corrupt them and cause
suffering. The action is a variation on Goethe's Gretchen tragedy
but is presented in purely human and natural terms. In W. S.
Gilbert's *Gretchen* of 1879, too, once Mephisto has approached
Faust and shown him a vision of Gretchen, the tragic events that
follow spring entirely from human motives and passions. Albert
Geiger's long episodic poem 'Ein moderner Faust' (1893) has no
magic and no pact with the Devil but simply deals with Faust's
restlessness and dissatisfaction. The 'modern' of the title probably
refers to this total banishment of traditional elements from the

---

[1] In F. Reinhard's *Faust* of 1848, the Devil is present as spokesman of a cynical
philosophy of negation, but there is no conjuration or pact to explain how he got
there, nor are there any displays of magic on his part.

poem, for there is nothing else that is particularly modern about it. Faust's dilemma is stated in terms that recall Lenau and the verse style and nature settings are strongly reminiscent of the late Romantic poets of half a century earlier.

There are Faust works in which the magic proves to have been merely a dream, or which represent the magical legends which grew up around Faust as rumours passed about by the credulous, egged on by theologians jealous of Faust's learning.[1] But by far the most subtle and ingenious sceptical retelling of the Faust legend occurs in Thomas Mann's *Dr. Faustus*, where traditional features of the legend are either replaced by events which have a natural explanation or are shown to be hallucinations, both symptoms and causes of Leverkühn's approaching madness. The supernatural structure, which has traditionally given the Faust story its characteristic shape and has provided a framework for the inner meaning which the theme is capable of yielding, is not denied or swept aside by Mann, but is presented as susceptible of a natural explanation (see below, p. 126).

These, then, are some of the ways in which successive authors have dealt with the problems presented by the magic in the Faust legend. To retain the magic without treating it either symbolically or ironically or showing it in the end to have been no more than a dream is hazardous. In an age which believed in magic there were certain conventions: rules to be obeyed or broken, fixed forms and legalistic conditions governing magical practices, especially conjuration. But a writer who takes up magical elements without believing in them and in the knowledge that most of his audience or readers will not believe in them either, will almost inevitably appear arbitrary. The suspension of natural laws will lead not to situations in which a different but equally 'valid' set of laws operates, but to situations in which anything goes. This is common in modern stories and, especially, films in which magic figures. Works which present a self-contained and convincing world combining natural and supernatural elements are in a tiny minority. Since 1800 or so, simply to take over traditional magical features, incorporate them in a *Faust* and hope for the best has nearly always led to unhappy or ambiguous situations. K. F. Benkowitz (*Die Jubelfeier der Hölle*, 1801) treats the magic with

---

[1] For examples of the first, see above, p. 12; for the second, see G. Pfarrius, 'Sein und Schein', 1862–3.

great zest; there is no more reserve or embarrassment here than in the puppet plays of Dr. Faust. But the supernatural events co-exist unhappily with the realistic-bourgeois elements in the work. The magical episodes stand out incongruously from the main part of the play, in which events are carefully motivated according to human emotions and impulses.[1] It is possible, of course, for a sceptical author to make magic convincing, or at least acceptable to a sceptical public. W. Nürnberger achieves this by exploiting the sinister *atmosphere* which the supernatural can create; Eisler takes over the magic as an integral part of a popular legend in order himself to create a popular work. But lesser writers are all too often both unable to bring themselves to exclude the magic and incapable of treating it with conviction or of giving it a meaning which would integrate it into their conception of what Faust as a human type 'means'. The result is lame (examples: Braun von Braunthal, 1835; Linde, 1887; Hutschenreiter, 1895–6). In the worst cases we have facetiousness total and disastrous, situations in which Hell and the Devil, conjuration and magic are made the subject of feeble jokes born in the minds of those for whom Faust's bargain is itself a joke. This is what occurs in E. J. Byng's novella of 1958, *Die Wiederkehr des Dr. Faust*:

'Hier Hades. Wen wünschen Sie, bitte? Den Verein für den Schutz junger Mädchen? Bedauere, falsch verbunden!'
  Da plötzlich: 'Hier Hades. Wie, bitte? Dringendes Staatsgespräch? Wer spricht denn dort? Wie, bitte? Wie war der Name? Mephistopheles? Mit "M", wie "Medusa"? Jawohl, ich habe verstanden. Fürst Luzifer persönlich? In welcher Angelegenheit, bitte? Bitte sehr, ich kann Ihnen nur das Privatbüro des Fürsten geben . . .'   (p. 3)

This is hardly better than the arch treatment of the supernatural in some of the comic operas of Offenbach or Gilbert and Sullivan.

---

[1] For the plot of Benkowitz's play, see R. Warkentin, *Nachklänge der Sturm- und Drangperiode in Faustdichtungen des 18. und 19. Jahrhunderts*, Munich, 1896, pp. 56–8.

5

Faust and Fust

Viel verbreitet im Volke ist der Irrthum, unser Zauberer
sei auch derselbe Faust, welcher die Buchdruckerkunst
erfunden.

(Heine)

MANY of the *Faustdichtungen*, especially in the late eighteenth
and early nineteenth centuries, attribute the invention of
printing to Dr. Faust. The process by which Fust the printer came
to be confused with Faust the magician is a long and interesting
one. First, the salient facts regarding Fust.

Johann Fust was born in Mainz and died in Paris in or about
1466. Around 1450 he advanced money to Gutenberg, who set
up a printing-shop in an attempt to exploit his invention. But
Gutenberg was no businessman, and he failed to meet Fust's
financial conditions. Fust sued him for repayment and, after a
lawsuit, gained possession of the equipment and stock. Fust then
continued to run the press on his own account, aided by
Gutenberg's one-time foreman, Peter Schöffer, who later married
Fust's daughter.

The first step in the series of events which led to the identification of Fust with Faust was the attribution of Gutenberg's
invention to Fust—for even the most credulous age would
hardly believe that a speculator needed the Devil's help in order to
foreclose on an unbusinesslike partner. The claim that Fust was
the inventor first seems to have been made by his grandson,
Johann Schöffer, elder son of Peter, in books printed from 1515
onwards. [1] Since Fust's name appeared in these attributions more
often than not in the form 'Faust', it is easy to see how the confusion arose. For in the seventeenth and early eighteenth centuries

[1] For details see C. A. Schaab, *Die Geschichte der Erfindung der Buchdruckerkunst*,
Mainz, 1830–1, i, 72–7, 99f, 557, and ii, 465ff.

few knew of the 'true' Dr. Faust, whose exploits and boasts had led to the writing of the chapbooks. The search for the historical model behind the Dr. Faust of popular literature seemed to lead back to the inventor of printing.[1]

This identification was served by another factor. It so happens that many early accounts of the history of printing tell that Fust was suspected of magical practices. The origin of this very persistent anecdote seems to be J. Walchius' *Decas fabularum humani generis . . .* , Strasbourg, 1609.[2] Before the art of printing was widely understood, says Walchius, Faust [*sic*] went to Paris to sell his newly printed Bibles. He sold them as manuscripts, for greater profit. But when his customers came to compare their copies, they found them so alike in all particulars that they concluded that they had been swindled and demanded compensation. Faust fled from Paris. . . . Now it is true that the early printed books were often very ornate, and made to look as much as possible like handwritten books. It also appears to be true that the earliest printers jealously guarded the secrets of their trade. All else in Walchius' account seems to be legend. It may be noted that he does not mention accusations of magic. Many writers were to repeat his story: Chr. Besoldus in 1624, G. Naudé in 1630, A. Rivinus in 1640, Z. von Beichlingen in 1669. Here is how it appeared in Naudé's influential and widely read *Addition à l'Histoire de Louys xi*:

. . . que ledit Jean Fust en ayant apporté grand nombre [of his printed Bibles] à Paris pour les distribuer, la pluspart desquelles aussi estoient sur du velin, et ornées de grandes lettres et vignettes d'or, il les vendit au commencement pour manuscriptes, et ne les bailloit à moins de soixante escus piece: mais venant par apres à les lascher à vingt ou trente, et ceux qui en avoient acheté des premieres s'estant apperceus qu'elles estoient en trop grand nombre et trop semblables pour estre escrites à la main, ils intenterent action de survente contre luy, et le poursuivirent si chaudement que s'estant sauvé de Paris

---

[1] For outright denials of the 'historical' Dr. Faust, see W. Schickard, *Bechinath Happeruschim*, Tübingen, 1624, p. 126, and G. Naudé, *Mascurat*, Paris, *c.* 1650, p. 519. More noncommittal judgements in G. C. Wagner, *Eruditi spirituum*, Leipzig 1715, p. 24, and P. F. Arpe, *De Prodigiosis Naturae*, Hamburg, 1717, p. 125f.

[2] Pp. 181f.

à Maience, et ne s'y trouvant pas en assez grande seureté, il passa à Strasbourg. . . .[1]

Walchius and those who followed his account had said no more than that Faust's customers could not understand how so many books could be produced so quickly and so similar in appearance. But soon a new twist was given to the story: since no one could find a natural explanation, Faust came to be suspected of magic. And so it became possible to believe that the (wicked) Dr. Faust of popular legend had been based on the (good but misunderstood) Faust who invented printing. The first such identification appears to be in a letter from J. C. Dürr to S. Führer of 18 July 1676.[2] Dürr's theory is that monkish scribes, embittered and alarmed because printing seemed to represent a threat to their interests, put about the story that Faust was in league with the Devil and owed his skill at producing books to magic arts. In the early eighteenth century writer after writer repeated this story, using it to explain the rise of the legend of Dr. Faust, the magician. Whether Dürr was the first to form this theory must remain uncertain; there was much curiosity in Germany at this time regarding the origins of the Faust legend, and the story of Fust and his detractors was, as I have tried to show, widely known.[3] There were a number of writers in the early eighteenth century who held the view that Dr. Faust was a fictitious character based on a much-maligned printer of the same name.[4] F. W. Bierling (1724) mentions this theory but remains noncommittal.[5]

It is worth noting that this identification of Fust with Faust involved four distinct misapprehensions. Fust was transformed from a speculator and exploiter into an inventor, his name was

[1] Paris, 1630, pp. 290f. For Besoldus, see 'De inventione typographiae' in *Pentas dissertationum philologicum*, iii (Tübingen, 1620), pp. 22–4; for Rivinus, *Hecatomba . . .*, Leipzig, 1640, ii, 14f; for Beichlingen, *Wahrer Unterricht von Uhrsprung . . . der Buchdruckereyen . . .*, Eisleben, 1669 (no pagination).

[2] Printed by J. G. Schelhorn in *Amoenitates literariae*, Frankfort and Leipzig, 1726. Given by Tille, nos. 126 and 215.

[3] The first history of printing to contain the story that Faust was accused of magic is, as far as I know, that by Jean de la Caille: *Histoire de l'Imprimerie*, Paris, 1689, p. 12.

[4] See H. Prideaux, *The Old and the New Testament connected . . .*, 5th edn., London, 1718, i, 174; G. G. Zeltner, *Vitae theologorum . . .*, Nuremberg, 1732, p. 508; D. E. Baring, *Clavis Diplomatica*, Hannover, 1737, Preface, pp. 8–9; F. C. Lesser, *Typographia Iubilans . . .*, Leipzig, 1740, p. 38.

[5] See Tille, no. 210.

H

changed, real and imagined events of the fifteenth century became mixed up with real and imagined events of the sixteenth, and the Dr. Faust with whom this study is primarily concerned was denied any actual (historical) existence at all.

However, as the eighteenth century wore on, more and more writers came to deny that Faust and Fust were one and the same. Fassmann, writing in 1738,[1] tells the story of Faust [*sic*] and Gutenberg rather more accurately than was usual in those days, although still with the story concerning accusations of sorcery when the printed Bibles were offered for sale. Was this the Dr. Faust of legend? Or were there two Fausts who had become confused? Fassmann favours the second theory. H. C. Schütze's *Abhandlung von Aberglauben* (1757) contains such an ingenious attempt to explain how the confusion between the two Fausts arose that it deserves quoting. The magic flights on the cloak, the fabulous wealth, the appearances in different places at unnaturally short intervals of time, even the title of Doctor are accounted for by this engaging theory:

Als Johann Faust mit seinen beyden Gehülfen, Johann Guttenberg(!), und seinem Schwiegersohn Peter Scheffern, die Buchdruckerkunst erfunden und die erste lateinische Bibel gedruckt hatte, begab er sich mit vielen abgedruckten Exemplaren auf die Reise, und verkaufte dieselben auf öffentlichem Marckte, in Paris und andern Orten. Er mogte [*sic*] die Exemplare . . . wol unter einem Mantel haben. Die Käuffer der Bücher konten, weil die Buchdruckerkunst noch neu war, nicht begreiffen, wie es möglich wäre, daß in allen Exemplaren, auf allen Blättern und Seiten, nicht mehr und nicht weniger Reihen stünden, und daß nicht ein eintziges Strichlein anders wäre, so hielte man ihn für einen Zauberer. Weil er auch unbeschreiblich viel Geld aus den Büchern lösete, und sich mit seinem Mantel bald wieder fortpackete, wenn er brav Geld gesamlet hatte, auch bald in dieser, bald in jener Stadt, auf dem Marckte sich sehen ließ, so kan das zu dem Mährlein Gelegenheit gegeben haben. Hierzu kommt noch, daß Johann Fausts Gehülfe . . . , Peter Scheffer, auch ausgereiset war, und eben die Bücher verkaufte. Weil nun Scheffer eben einen solchen Mantel umgehabt, so haben die Leute leicht auf die [*sic*] Gedancken kommen können, das wäre eben der Johann Faust, und also daraus den Schluß machen können, Faust wäre in einem Augenblick wo anders. Wenn nun Johann Faust, wie vermuthlich, auf die folgenden Bücher, die er gedruckt, gesetzt hat, Dr. Johann Faust, das ist, druckts

[1] *Gespräche in dem Reiche derer Todten.* Repr. Tille, no. 240.

Johann Faust, so hat, zu den damaligen duncklen Zeiten, leicht der Irrthum entstehen können, daß man gemeinet, dieser vermeinte Zauberer sey ein Doctor.[1]

From this time on most accounts either of Dr. Faust the magician or of the development of printing recognize that Fust and Dr. Faust were two different persons. There was still confusion enough: the name 'Fust' still nearly always appears as 'Faust' and Fust is still, more often than not, credited with Gutenberg's invention. But the main point—the distinction between Fust and Dr. Faust—is made clear in work after work between the 1750s and the 1790s.[2] Gradually the evidence for the existence of the historical Dr. Faust began to see the light of day, and a simple reference to dates was enough to make the distinction clear. There are brief accounts of the real Dr. Faust by Zedler (1735), Heumann (1759), and others. The first detailed attempt to separate fact from legend and to reconstruct the life of Dr. Faust seems to be J. F. Koehler's *Historisch-kritische Untersuchung über das Leben und die Thaten des . . . Dr. Johann Fausts . . .*, Leipzig, 1791. It is interesting that, in his preface, Koehler tells us that he was moved to write his book because some people doubted the real existence of Dr. Faust, while others had confused him with Fust (p. 3).

So by the third quarter of the eighteenth century it was hardly possible for an *informed* person still to hold that Gutenberg's associate and Dr. Faust were the same man. Yet the myth lives on in many of the novels and plays on the Faust theme. Perhaps the authors did not bother about one more improbability in what was anyway a fantastic tale. At all events, if to make Dr. Faust the inventor of printing added a dimension to the work, or even simply afforded the opportunity for a satirical quip or two, he was duly made the inventor of printing.[3]

Komareck (*Faust von Mainz*, 1794) approaches the affair with printing, rather than Dr. Faust, as his main concern. The setting

[1] *Vernunft- und schriftmäßige Abhandlung von Aberglauben*, Wernigerode, 1757, pp. 135f. Repr. Tille, no. 272.

[2] See Tille, nos. 280, 300, 308, 335, 340, 342, 346. Also J. D. Schoepflin, *Vindiciae Typographicae* (c. 1760), trans. and ed. C. A. Nelson, New York, 1938, p. 156.

[3] The motif does not seem to have figured in the popular tradition until *after* Klinger. That is: the puppet plays in which Dr. Faust appears as the inventor of printing are examples of popular *Fausts* influenced by Klinger or, less probably, by his imitators.

is fifteenth-century Mainz, and Faust is an honest and pious citizen ('Edel und heiter, fromm ohne Scheinheiligkeit, freund-schaftlich und munter . . .', p. 10), concerned only with perfecting his invention, so that God's word may become freely accessible. For this he draws upon himself the envy and suspicion of scribes and monks and gains the reputation of being a magician. This is not, then, a work dealing with Dr. Faust, rather an almost wholly fictitious account of the invention of printing and the way in which this came to be the object of superstition. Of all the works to be mentioned in this chapter Komareck's is nearest, both in spirit and in detail, to the fanciful accounts of F(a)ust in the early histories of printing. This Faust reappears in Hermann Schiff's novella 'Johann Faust in Paris, 1463', dating from 1835. But to find the theme of printing entering Faust literature proper, we must turn to Klinger, on whom most later writers who introduce this theme draw, directly or indirectly.

The situation in Klinger is odd; but the oddity is so tersely contained in the first three sentences of the novel that it is likely that most of those who copied Klinger read over the implications of these sentences. Here is the opening:

Lange hatte sich Faust mit den Seifenblasen der Metaphysik, den Irrwischen der Moral und den Schatten der Theologie herum-geschlagen, ohne eine feste, haltbare Gestalt für seinen Sinn heraus-zukämpfen. Ergrimmt warf er sich in die dunklen Gefilde der Magie und hoffte nun der Natur gewaltsam abzuzwingen, was sie uns so eigen-sinnig verbirgt. Sein erster Gewinn war die merkwürdige Erfindung der Buchdruckerei.

Klinger adds in a footnote: 'So die Tradition, welcher man hier allein folgt.' Klinger, therefore, represents printing as developed with the aid of magic, but *before* the pact with the Devil. When Faust does finally conjure the Devil, the immediate cause of this is his despair of ever profiting from his invention (i, 3). Those who follow Klinger in placing the invention before the pact will, as we shall see, always represent it as a perfectly natural process which, however, drew down upon Faust unjust accusations of necromantic practices. The situation in Klinger, it must be admitted, is less telling. But this was anyway not the main point for Klinger. He exploits the printing motif as one more element in his misanthropic attack on human society and culture. Thus

Satan gleefully paints the evils which will result from Faust's invention. Books, the 'dangerous toys' of mankind, will spread doubt, dissatisfaction, and religious bigotry; they will create more darkness than light. So demons acclaim Faust as the 'poisoner' of mankind (i, 5), and later, when Faust is safely in Hell, Satan will return to his praise of the invention of printing, so useful to Hell (v, 8). It has often been pointed out that, when denouncing human civilization in his *Faust*, Klinger took Rousseau's *Discours sur les Sciences et les Arts* of 1750 as his textbook. And sure enough, an attack on printing had already been made by Rousseau in that work. Rousseau's point, rather more limited than Klinger's, is that printing ensures the survival of noxious works which would otherwise have perished without doing lasting harm:

Le Paganisme, livré à tous les égaremens de la raison humaine, a-t-il laissé à la postérité rien qu'on puisse comparer aux monumens honteux que lui a préparé l'Imprimerie, sous le règne de l'Evangile? Les écrits impies des Leucippes & des Diagoras sont péris avec eux. On n'avoit point encore inventé l'art d'éterniser les extravagances de l'esprit humain. Mais, grace aux caractères Typographiques & à l'usage que nous en faisons, les dangereuses rêveries des Hobbes & des Spinosa resteront à jamais.[1]

The printing motif was then no mere piece of trimmings with Klinger; it added significantly to his attack on human nature and institutions. (This ironically foreshadows Faust's disastrous attempts to be a benefactor, for Faust thinks that he ought to be *rewarded* for his invention—it is the Devil who foresees the evil consequences of printing.) But as with other aspects of Klinger's *Faust*, the motif was often copied mechanically, without much understanding of how, in Klinger, it had both derived its meaning from, and reinforced the central idea of the work.

C. C. L. Schöne's *Faust* (1809) is an unskilful combination of ideas lifted from Klinger and original (but very confused) material.[2] Schöne simply represents his Faust as having invented printing but having failed to profit from it. So he turns to magic. But Schöne takes the point no further. Here, as in his treatment of Faust's attempted good works, he has plundered Klinger without

---

[1] Geneva, n.d. (=1755), Cl. and A. Philibert, pp. 49f.
[2] For a brief analysis, see Warkentin, pp. 28–32.

really grasping the meaning of what he took. The same point (printing without profit) is made in E. A. F. Klingemann's Faust tragedy of 1815.[1] Again the 'unnatural' art of printing is shown as leading to the charge that Faust is a magician. As nearly always in such works, the point is made in crudely anti-Catholic terms:

> Und mich nun gar, mit meiner Druck-Erfindung,
> Mich zählt man zu den Ketzern, und die Mönche,
> Sie schreien laut aus ihren Klosterlöchern,
> Daß ich dadurch sie um den Wein bestehle
> Für ihren Schreiberlohn;—und noch um mehr,
> Sobald die Menschen wirklich lesen lernen. (p. 21)

Julius von Voß (*Faust*, 1823) also shows Faust as inventor of printing, bitter because his skill has brought him neither money nor fame, but has provoked slanderous tales. Since the puppet-masters took so much from Klinger's *Faust* (see Chapter 6) it is not surprising to come across the confusion of Faust and Fust, treated in terms very similar to Klinger's, in the Strasbourg puppet play:

Johannes Faust, ein kühner Sterblicher, der die Kunst erfunden, die Bücher, das gefährliche Spielzeug der Menschen, die Verbreiter vieler Irrthümer, auf eine leichte Art tausend- und tausendmal zu vervielfältigen . . .[2]

Needless to say, this fits into the scheme of the puppet play no better than the theme of Faust's 'good' deeds and their consequences, taken up by more than one impresario of the puppet theatre. Before we leave the question of Klinger's influence, an English play of about 1849 remains to be mentioned: 'The Devil and Dr. Faustus' by Leman Rede. The author identifies Faust with Fust (again as inventor, not exploiter), gives him Schöffer as a servant and disinters the old chestnut about the magic arts:

. . . because the rare novelty of the printing-press suggested itself to his . . . mind, it was bruited abroad that the Prince of Darkness gave him the hint . . . (from Rede's Introduction).

We encounter Faust in Mainz in 1466, old and embittered because, despite his learning and his invention, neither honour nor

---

[1] Accounts in Warkentin (pp. 35–42) and Butler (228–32). A similar point is made in Gérard de Nerval's immature Faust fragment.

[2] I, 3 (=Scheible, v, 855). Cf. Klinger, i, 5.

riches have come his way, only an evil reputation. So in resentment he turns to magic and signs a pact with the Devil for the
sake of renewed youth, pleasure and a glimpse into the future.
He duly turns up, rejuvenated, in mid-nineteenth-century London.
But he gets no joy from the pleasures offered him because he is
haunted by remorse over Bertha (yet another reincarnation of
Goethe's Gretchen) whom he had loved and deserted. In the end,
the pact turns out to have been a dream and the spirit of Bertha
appears to him to reveal that 'fiends have no power over the soul
of man' (p. 36), and that Faust's remorse and her love for him
ensure his salvation. Another piece, then, in which the printing
motif is taken over without much thought of its possible meaning
for the work as a whole. There is not even the suggestion, which
we shall find in two later German treatments, that printing is
honest and altruistic work which qualifies a man for salvation.
This Faust is not saved through activity; he is saved through
love.

The two works which see printing as one of the activities
through which Faust comes to merit salvation are both attempts
to continue or rewrite Goethe: *Fausts Tod* by C. E. Mölling 1864,
and *Faust* by F. Stolte, 1869.[1]

Where other writers had represented Faust as concluding a
pact with the Devil because, among other reasons, the invention
of printing had brought nothing but suspicion and persecution,
Mölling introduces the motif long after the pact. His Faust,
aghast at the violence and suffering which his association with
Mephisto has caused, seeks salvation through honest work and
throws in his lot with Gutenberg. Their relationship is quite
unlike that between the historical Gutenberg and Fust, for here
Faust acts as selfless encourager and benefactor. As nearly
always in such treatments of the theme, he is accused of magic
and vainly tries to persuade his enemies that his mysterious
process is perfectly natural and above-board. However, this
episode is rendered nonsensical by its placing. For, since this
work is intended as a sequel to Goethe's Part 1, Goethe's pact
is pre-supposed. So where other printer-Fausts had been un-
justly accused of magic, Mölling's Faust has long since allied
himself to the Devil. At worst, the accusations levelled at him are
a little out of date (since by now he is trying to break his ties with

[1] For accounts of these works, see Chapter 7.

Mephisto) and are applied to the wrong episode in his career. Even Mölling's main point—that Faust has renounced magic and has turned to honest and *natural* activities—is untidily worked out. For he renounces his riches, too, as part of his rejection of the Devil (v, 1), but later is shown to have retained a ring precious enough to buy off apprentices who threaten to wreck his works and denounce him as a magician (v, 3–5). Can one really cast aside magic and seek rehabilitation as a human being pure and simple if one prudently keeps some Devil's wealth for use as hush-money?

In Stolte, too, we find Faust turning to printing and helping Gutenberg, here too out of a feeling of revulsion against what Mephisto has to offer him and with a desire to serve humanity. As Faust himself puts it, in the wooden rhymed verse that bids fair to make this 1,000-page work the most unreadable of all *Fausts*:

> Ich meine, daß die Bücherdruckerei
> Ein practisch, sichres Mittel sei,
> Um *Einsicht, Kenntniß* zu verbreiten,
> Und gegen Obscuranz zu streiten. (i, 73)

Presently Gutenberg disappears from the scene and the middle part of the work is taken up with complicated political intrigues. In Part 4 we encounter him again, living in rural retirement with wife and son. Faust tries to tempt him back to the printing-presses:

> Und würde es, mein Freund, Dich nicht erfreuen,
> In zweckvoll ausgedehnter Thätigkeit
> Die Kunst, die uns verband, jetzt zu erneuen?

But Gutenberg refuses:

> Nein, mit der Welt hab' ich mich abgefunden . . . (iv, 172)

This is surely the oddest twist ever given to the Fust–Gutenberg affair. Far from edging Gutenberg out of the business for selfish reasons, Stolte's Faust tries—from the most highminded motives —to draw him back into it.[1]

---

[1] The theme of printing is mentioned perfunctorily in the anonymous *Faustus. A Fragment of a Parody*, 1793; in Soden's *Dr. Faust*, 1797; further in Vogt's *Färberhof*, 1809. Two of the Faust burlesques introduce the motif for trivial satirical purposes. F. X. C. Gewey has his Faust prophesy that publishers will grow fat while authors starve (Brukner and Hadamowsky, p. 128). Engel (*Der traverstirte Dr. Faust*, 1806) brings it in solely in order to make a quip about the proliferation of books (p. 15).

This is, then, a chapter of misunderstandings and falsifications. Not only did the original confusion between Fust and Faust arise out of a complex of misapprehensions, but the literary treatments of the theme take these over and add a fresh one. For Faust is still represented as inventor rather than exploiter and is, at the same time, shown to be motivated by the highest and most philanthropic considerations. For Mölling and Stolte, he is a disinterested benefactor. They share none of Klinger's doubts as to the value of printing to mankind. Where Klinger follows Rousseau, they are closer to those eulogists of printing who felt that it would help to ensure man's moral, intellectual and artistic progress:

Say what was man ere by the PRESS refin'd,
What bonds his glorious energies confin'd?
Did genius, thro' the dull chaotic waste,
Court the fair forms of beauty and of taste,
Tho' strong his ardour, and tho' pure his love,
Small was the sphere wherein those powers could move.
The meteor beam that science lent mankind,
Darting effulgence on th'inquiring mind,
Oft gleam'd—a weak and transitory light,
A moment glar'd—then sunk in endless night:
Man knew no means to hold the flitting race
Of art's coy forms, that courted his embrace,
His only hope in memory's stinted power,
The oral record—changing every hour.[1]

---

[1] John McCreery, *The Press, a Poem*, Part i, Liverpool, 1803, p. 2. For other examples, see M. Maierus, *Von den hochnützlichen herzlichen Erfindungen und Künsten* . . . , Frankfort on the Main, 1619, Chapter 5; J. Rompler von Löwenhalt, 'Von löblicher erfindung der Buch-trukkerej . . .' (1640), in *Des J. R. von L. erstes gebüsch seiner Reim-getichte*, Strasbourg, 1647, pp. 48–61; John Harris, *A . . . History of the first Inventers and Instituters of the most famous Arts, Misteries . . .* etc., London, 1686, pp. 101f; W. E. Tentzel, *Discours von Erfindung der löblichen Buch-drucker-Kunst* . . . , Gotha, 1700; F. Burges, 'Some Observations on the Use and Original [*sic*] of the noble Art and Mystery of Printing', 1701 (repr. in the *Harleian Miscellany,* vol. iii). C. L. Thiboust, *L'Excellence de l'Imprimerie*, Paris, 1754; Scott's *Quentin Durward*, Chapter 13.

6

The Popular and Literary Traditions

THE history of literature is full of examples of literary themes passing into popular forms and vice versa. The Faust legend is particularly interesting from this point of view of interaction and cross-fertilization. To study it is to see what serious authors regarded as usable in the popular versions as well as what the impresarios of the popular *Fausts* felt could be taken up from the serious, literary versions and assimilated into these popular pieces. (For want of better terms, I use 'popular' here to designate the chapbooks, dialect comedy, folk drama and puppet plays, ballet, *Singspiel* and pantomimes; 'literary' for treatments of the Faust theme by poets, dramatists and men of letters. The terms are obviously not wholly satisfactory, but are useful as labels when one thinks of the clear contrast between, say, Marlowe and his chapbook source or Goethe and the German puppet play tradition on which he drew.)

The original Faust chapbook was clearly intended to combine moralizing with entertainment; the chapters dealing with Faust's magic tricks link it with other popular compilations of the age (for instance, the chapbooks telling of Eulenspiegel, or of Fortunatus). Although the *Faustbuch* falls fairly neatly into sections (pact, disputes, magic tricks, despair, and death), it is all of a piece as regards the tone: the same naïveté informs the accounts of Faust's motives and his questioning of Mephisto as is apparent in the chapters devoted to his magic and showmanship. With Marlowe we have an incomparably sharper and more subtle examination of Faustus' character and motives and of his relationship with Mephisto, but also scenes which are simple dramatizations of various 'magical' chapters from 'P.F.' (I am leaving out of consideration the unsettled question of exactly how much Marlowe himself wrote, since it is the effect of the play as a whole which concerns us here.) Faustus' opening monologue is serious, subtle, learned and eloquent; the episodes with the knight and the horse-courser are much as in Marlowe's source, once the difference in medium is allowed for. It can be argued that there is some implicit link between these disparate elements, that the magic tricks and adventures are Faustus' attempts to ward off awareness of what he has done and to make him forget the passing of time. But even when this is said, one is left feeling that it is inappropriate for Marlowe's Faustus to dissipate his time and his power on these petty conjuring tricks; the opening has been treated too seriously and too eloquently to allow us to accept the middle part of the play.

Profoundly serious motivation of Faustus but trivial demonstration of his use of magical powers: it is clear enough which aspect of Marlowe's work would be stressed and which played down in the long process of popularization that led via the versions of itinerant players (*englische Komödianten*) to the German folk theatre and finally to the puppet plays.

As already mentioned, not one of the *early* popular German stage plays on the Faust theme is extant but we can deduce a good deal from the many detailed theatre bills which have survived. These plays usually open with a conference of demons, after which Faust is shown, discontented with his lot, making the decision to conjure the Devil. From the general tone of the play-bills and the indirect evidence of the puppet plays, we may safely assume that Faust's monologue was brief and shallow. After the pact, court scenes, magic tricks and (sometimes) episodes with Helen and with a pious hermit who tried to move Faust to repentance, Faust was shown being dragged off to Hell, there to be tormented (often to the accompaniment, we are assured, of a splendid display of fireworks).[1] Most versions had an important part for the traditional clown figure (Hanswurst, Pickelhäring, Crispin, etc., according to locality), who played the part of Faust's servant, aped his magical practices, but survived at the end, thus affording yet another example of the fool in popular

---

[1] A somewhat similar popularization went on in England, in such pieces as W. Mountford's *Life and Death of Dr. Faust* ... (1697), although here at least the last scene is free from comic interruptions and a good deal of Marlowe's original text has been taken up. Later Faust pantomimes were more farcical: cf. Stumme, p. 29.

drama and literature who comes off better than the great and the learned.[1]

With the puppet plays we are on somewhat firmer ground, although even here most extant versions were recorded too late to give much absolutely reliable information about Faust on the puppet stage of eighteenth-century Germany. These plays clearly carry on the tradition of the popular stage plays. Faust's motivation is usually superficial, his opening monologue no more than a few lines. There is more naïve moralizing than would appear to have been the case in the stage plays (although it may simply have been that the more morally edifying aspects of these were not stressed in the playbills, as being far inferior as a selling point to the clowning and magic). The clown figure seems to assume yet more prominence: dismissed from Faust's service for treachery or ineptitude, he usually reappears in the last act as night watchman, so that Faust's last hour on earth is punctuated by inane fooling. Yet it would be wrong to assume that the puppet plays treated the Faust figure as a joke. Faust may be trivialized, but he is not made funny. In a way, even, the puppet plays helped to ensure that Faust could be regarded as a figure deserving serious attention, for *his* appearances are always treated with gravity and he speaks—always allowing for the limitations of the unknown authors or patchers-together of these pieces—with a sort of wooden earnestness. The older puppet plays still even observed the convention of verse for Faust's serious scenes and prose for the clowning.[2]

The travelling players had liked to stress the popularity of the Faust theme; their playbills often refer to it as something universally familiar and beloved. There is plenty of evidence that this popularity persisted throughout the eighteenth century. J. H. Zedler, writing in his famous *Universal Lexikon* in 1735, had this to say:

[1] In A. Borrow's *John Faust* of 1958 Caspar shows unheroic, hedonistic acceptance of life while Faust torments himself with insoluble problems. Caspar refers to himself and Faust as 'the silly fool and the clever fool' (p. 48). Since the play ends with Faust's learning to accept life as it is, it is easy to see which of the two types of fool is, by implication, the wiser.

[2] The lowest ebb in the fortunes of Faust was reached not in the puppet plays but in the feeblest of the Faust parodies and the type of Faust farce popular in Vienna in the early nineteenth century (Gewey, c. 1805; Bäuerle, 1815; Nißl, 1818. See Brukner and Hadamowsky).

Und ist die Fabel, oder Historie von seinem [=Faust's] Leben und Thaten in Teutschland so bekannt, daß auch die Comödianten selbige, als eines von ihren vornehmsten Stücken, auf allen Schau-Bühnen vorstellen.

Gottsched frowned on this and hoped that Dr. Faust was on his way out:

Das Mährchen von D. Faust hat lange genug den Pöbel belustiget, und man hat ziemlicher maßen aufgehört, solche Alfanzereyen gern anzusehen. (*Versuch einer critischen Dichtkunst*, 1730, Chapter 5)

The theatre of an enlightened age would be able to do without cheap sensation and the supernatural, for these offended against decorum and reason.

But Faust was not to be expelled so easily; twenty-four years later Lessing wrote of *Dr. Faust* as the best known of Germany's traditional popular plays (17th *Literaturbrief*), and there is evidence that it was not only the 'mob' who continued to find him fascinating. Nicolai, visiting the puppet play in Augsburg in 1781, found cause for surprise on just this score:

Ich fand eine viel vornehmere Gesellschaft, als ich mir vorgestellt hatte, die auch mit ihrem hohen und gnädigen Beyfall nicht sparsam war. (Tille, No. 333)

The reasons why the Faust theme came to be taken seriously by men of letters in the third quarter of the eighteenth century and especially by the young men of the *Sturm und Drang*, are clear. They wanted to escape from subservience to foreign models and Faust offered them a native theme. They felt that contemporary literature was artificial and esoteric whereas Faust was genuinely popular and, because naïve, 'natural'. (The confusion of naïveté and naturalness in Germany at this time owes much to Herder and, less directly, to Rousseau. The uncritical cult of folk poetry was another of its manifestations.) Yet this 'naïve' fable seemed capable of expressing profundities. For Lessing, the nobility of intellectual curiosity; for the *Stürmer und Dränger*, man's ambition to be more than man. It is worth repeating that the puppet plays, whatever their shortcomings, treated Faust seriously and therefore encouraged these authors to do likewise. In a famous passage in *Dichtung und Wahrheit*, Goethe recalls the impact made on him in his early years by the 'significant' puppet play of Dr.

Faust. It is easy to exaggerate the intrinsic value of the puppet plays (and a number of critics from Simrock to E. M. Butler have done so), but it would be difficult to exaggerate their influence.

In the case of Lessing the evidence is fragmentary and uncertain, but it is clear that the folk plays were the model for his *Faust*. It is worth remembering that, for him, the puppet plays contained hints of exalted origins (see above, p. 7). The fact that Lessing's version of the 'speed-test' scene is in some respects arguably inferior to some puppet play versions is of less consequence than Lessing's view that here was the place to seek dramatic themes and stimuli, not among the works of the neoclassicists. The various accounts of Lessing's lost *Faust* put it beyond doubt that this was (or was to have been) a recognizable variation on the puppet plays: the opening was a conference of devils, and this was to have been followed by the established study-scene and the conjuration. All else is surmise but, even if we accept Gebler's testimony that Lessing had treated the Faust theme twice (once according to the popular legend and once without any 'devilry'),[1] the fact remains that he had regarded the puppet play as worthy of serious reworking and had encouraged other dramatists to follow him in this.

Similarly Maler Müller's attempts to treat the Faust theme are indebted to the puppet plays, probably also to the chapbooks. Again the popular theatre provided the main model although the conception of Faust (as, one might almost say, a Nietzschean superman a century before Nietzsche) is far from the Faust of the puppet plays. Weidmann's Faust play, that indigestible combination of sentimental family drama and elements from the popular Faust tradition, has already been described briefly (see above, p. 7).

Now we must look at the greatest *Faust* of all and try to see in what relation it stands to the popular tradition. We know that the puppet play was Goethe's main inspiration and that he pondered long on Faust because he felt some affinity with him:

Die bedeutende Puppenspielfabel des andern [=Faust] klang und summte gar vieltönig in mir wider. Auch ich hatte mich in allem Wissen umhergetrieben und war früh genug auf die Eitelkeit desselben hingewiesen worden ... (*Dichtung und Wahrheit*, Bk. 10)

[1] To Nicolai, 9/12/1775. Quoted Petsch, p. 44.

The puppet play (and, we may add, the chapbooks) set Goethe off, then. But the fact that Goethe brooded over his kinship with Faust before writing anything down, and the circumstances under which the *Urfaust* was eventually written, mean that the actual thematic links with popular forms of the legend are very loose and of secondary importance. Faust, Wagner, and Mephisto are taken over but they become virtually new characters. 'Auerbachs Keller' is traditional, of course, but the only other important element in the *Urfaust* which derives from traditional material is Mephisto's impersonation and parodying of Faust. It will be recalled that Mephisto first impersonates Faust before the student and later apes his courtship of Gretchen in a travesty wooing of Frau Marthe. Now in some of the puppet plays Mephisto had offered to impersonate Faust (or to have another spirit do this) in church and in the lecture room, two places forbidden to Faust by the pact. Furthermore, the clown had travestied Faust's actions in a variety of ways. It seems likely that such incidents influenced Goethe. What is interesting is what he made of them. The notion that a spirit could play Faust's part for him led to the elaborate satire on academic life and the devilish student-guidance of the 'Schülerszene'; the hint that Faust's activities could be parodied by other characters within the play probably helped Goethe towards the conception of the contrapuntal scene in which Mephisto and Marthe play out a sardonic variation on the lovers' courtship. But for the rest, Goethe went his own way in the *Urfaust*, drawing on quite different sources (arcane books, subjective elements, events witnessed by and people known to Goethe, folk poetry, and so on). And when Goethe came to complete Part 1 and to pay his outstanding debt to the 'barbarous' Northern elements inherent in his theme, he did not draw specifically on Faust material, apart from a few details concerning Mephisto's appearance to Faust and the signing of the pact. But, in Part 2, important traditional elements from the puppet plays are taken up and worked into Goethe's plan. Here Goethe plays Beethoven to the puppet-masters' Diabelli, turning brief, naïve episodes into highly elaborate symbolic events. Thus Faust's demonstration of magical powers before the Emperor reappears as a complex satire on the frivolity and irresponsibility of court life. The court is shown as being too mindless and hedonistic to provide a suitable sphere of activity for Faust with his newly awakened desire to strive for a higher existence. Thus, too, Helena from being the mere symbol of sexual temptation as the Devil's snare becomes the central figure in an intricate allegory of modern man's quest for classical Greece. In the puppet plays an instrument in the damnation of Faust, she comes in Goethe to contribute towards his salvation.

The popular tradition is only one of a complex of influences and experiences that went into Goethe's *Faust*. But it was the popular treatments of the theme that first suggested to Goethe that he should deal with Faust at all and important parts of the finished work derived from the popular tradition. In the case of the court scenes and the Helen episode there is no doubt that Goethe meant these to be *recognized* as his variations on traditional material.

Holtei's *Dr. Johannes Faust* (1829)[1] is based more closely on puppet play material than any work yet discussed, although there are also debts to Goethe. From Goethe, Holtei took the idea for Margarethe (his Gretchen) and a few other details but in general his work is an attempt to construct a 'legitimate' Faust drama on the basis of the puppet plays. Holtei's court scenes and his treatment of the Helen episode make this perfectly plain. But difficulties and inconsistencies can arise if popular and literary elements are combined in any but the most painstaking and fastidious way. This becomes clear if we look at Holtei's Wagner. For Wagner begins by playing the part of Faust's faithful servant, trying to hold him back from conjuring.[2] But suddenly, at the beginning of Act 2, he turns into the clown figure of the puppet play and goes through the traditional comic business, clenching his fist because he has been forbidden to let his master's name pass his lips (Faust=fist), extricating himself from a tight corner in which he was required to perform magic feats himself, and so on. But presently (ii, 4) he becomes Wagner again, urging Faust in perfectly serious terms to repent. Yet later (iii, 10) he appears in the traditional clown's role of night-watchman but, appropriately for his double role, without the *lazzi* which accompany this

---

[1] For an account of this, see E. M. Butler, pp. 237–46.

[2] For other examples, see Klingemann and Schink. One occasionally finds a moralizing Wagner in the puppet plays (e.g. in Geißelbrecht's version, Scheible, vol. v)—but the fully worked-out 'faithful-servant' Wagner is, on the whole, a feature of the literary *Fausts*. In fact, in most puppet plays, Wagner is more or less pushed aside by the clown.

episode in the puppet plays. This curious veering to and fro between virtuous servant and clown seems to reflect the rather unhappy middle position of Holtei's play. An ill-advised attempt to introduce puppet play material into a pretentiously serious treatment of the Faust theme is to be found in F. Marlow's *Faust* (1839)[1] at the point where Faust turns up in Rome with Caspar as his servant (2. Abt). The scene, which must be intended to bring to mind similar comic scenes between master and servant in the puppet plays, is full of long punning speeches which are far more wearisome than the feeblest of traditional *lazzi*. Heine, too, draws on the court scenes of the puppet plays in his ballet of 1851, taking up the old motif of the Duke's jealousy when Faust flirts with the Duchess. But, seen as a whole, Heine's ballet has little in common with the puppet plays—far less than critics have held. They have perhaps been tempted to exaggerate Heine's debt to the popular tradition because Heine himself overstated the case, saying that he had held 'ganz gewissenhaft an den vorhandenen Traditionen, wie ich sie zunächst vorfand in den Volksbüchern . . . und in den Puppenspielen . . .' (*Erläuterungen*, p. 57 in the original edition). But in fact only Act 2 of the ballet shows any debt to the puppet plays and what Heine makes of the episode is entirely his own.

The above examples show how 'literary' Fausts drew on popular Fausts, not always felicitously. At the same time the puppet-masters, alive to the fact that Faust was constantly being reinterpreted by serious writers, attempted to integrate elements from these versions into the traditional puppet play with results often nothing less than ludicrous.

Towards the end of the Plagwitz puppet play of J. Dreßler, Faust challenges Mephisto: have I not performed many good actions? But Mephisto shows him the consequences of these:

Erblicke deiner Aussaat verfluchte Ernte. Jenem Mädchen gabst du den Geliebten; er ist ein Landstreicher. Sie floh mit deinem Gelde ihm nach, weil der edle Vater, nicht eingenommen gegen die Armut des Verführers sondern gegen seine Laster es war und die Einwilligung versagte. Auf die Nachricht von der Flucht seines einzigen Kindes erhing er sich. Die Unglückliche, von ihrem Manne Verlassene endigt mit einem Dolchstoß ihr Leben . . . Jenem Bettler gabst du Geld im Überfluß. Er verschwendete deinen Reichtum in schwärmerischen

---

[1] An account of this version will be found in E. M. Butler, pp. 276–80.

Taumel, und als er nichts hatte und an Müssiggang gewöhnt war,
wurde er Straßenräuber und fiel durch Henkers Hand . . . Jenem
Greise gabst du seinen Sohn wieder. Er lebte diesem ungeratenen
Kinde zu lange. Um schneller sein Vermögen zu erhalten, räumte er
den Alten durch Gift aus dem Wege. Er selbst aber starb auf dem
Hochgericht.   (Part 2: ii, 4)

This is the 'accursed harvest' as in Klinger (v, 4), except for minor
details. The *point* is certainly the same: man, with his imperfect
insights, should not try to play Providence. But this is the first we
have heard of this; the puppet play Faust has *not* tried to play
Providence as far as the audience can tell. Such unthinking adoption of material from a totally different treatment of the legend is
doubly incongruous: it has nothing to do with the action proper
and it introduces a false note into the characterization of an
otherwise hedonistic Faust. (There is an exactly similar situation
in the Augsburg puppet play; and the motif from Klinger is
taken up yet again in the Strasbourg version.)[1]

It was hardly to be expected that Goethe could avoid Klinger's
fate and, in fact, Gretchen figures in more than one puppet play.
In the Lower Austrian example recorded by Kralik and Winter in
1883 or 1884, Kasperl delivers the moral after Faust's descent to
Hell:

> O Faust, o Faust, o Faust!
> Schrecklich hast du gehaust . . .
> Du verließest deine Gretel
> Und hängtest dich zu einem andern Mädel.
> Diese hieß Helene
> Und that dir gar so bene.   (p. 192)

This is another totally unintegrated reference to an episode
from a well-known 'literary' Faust. For, firstly, Gretchen has not
figured in the piece at all until now and, secondly, Helen's
appearance had been motivated in the usual way: as Mefistofilus'
[*sic*] answer to Faust's attempts at repentance. Hence it is confusing, to say the least, to have her suddenly presented as a
successful rival to Gretchen.[2]

Lest it be thought that this process was confined to Faust

---

[1] Both in Scheible, vol. v.

[2] Traces of a feedback from Goethe's *Faust* may also be found in the Oldenburg
puppet play—in Engel, vol. viii—and in a more recent version by Paul Braun,
Munich, 1924.

plays, let me mention a late example of a Faust chapbook which combines—not always successfully—the material of the old chapbooks with motifs from literary treatments of the Faust theme, notably Klinger's novel. This is *Dr. Faust's* . . . *Kreuz- und Querfahrten*, 1857. As in Klinger, Faust wishes to find out the causes of moral evil (Chapter 5). The description of the Devil is lifted straight out of Klinger: 'Er hatte die Miene der gefallenen Engel, deren Angesichter einst von der Gottheit beleuchtet wurden...' (Chapter 10; cf. Klinger, i, 8). The spirit-language, in which alone the Devil's secret knowledge can be expressed, figures here too (Chapter 11), together with many other details. Eventually the Devil horrifies Faust by the recital of how his 'good' deeds led to evil consequences (Chapter 31), although here, as in the puppet plays, this is the first we have heard of most of these attempts at benefaction. And yet much also is based directly on the Spies chapbook and on that of the 'Christlich Meynender'. The attempt to combine two quite different types of Faust novel resulted in an unhappy fusion of two different Fausts: the wicked character of the old chapbook and Klinger's tormented questioner and rebel.

After these confused examples[1] it is pleasant to find that two of the most significant twentieth-century *Fausts* have redressed the balance by going back to old, popular sources and finding genuine inspiration there: I am talking of the Faust works of Thomas Mann and Hanns Eisler.[2]

Mann's *Dr. Faustus* certainly carries within itself a number of implicit references to Goethe's *Faust*. It has often been noted that the relationship of Leverkühn to Zeitblom is something like that of Goethe's Faust to his Wagner and some critics would go on to say that this and other parallels are intended to force the comparison on us, to invite us to see *Dr. Faustus* as a 'refutation' of Goethe's *Faust*, rather as Leverkühn's last composition is a 'refutation' of Beethoven's Ninth Symphony. But Mann's chief

[1] I have given only a selection. For a popular, somewhat bowdlerized retelling of Klinger's novel, see *Faust, der große Mann* . . . , 1798; for a Tirolean stage play influenced by Weidmann's *Faust*, see *Das Zingerlesche Faustspiel*; for pantomimes and ballets based on Weidmann, Müller and Goethe, see Stumme, pp. 66, 71ff, 95ff.

[2] There is a combination of motifs from Marlowe and Goethe with chapbook elements in R. H. Ward's rather slight play *Faust in Hell*, Ilkley, 1944. For a modern reworking of the puppet play, into which elements from Marlowe have been introduced (especially in the opening monologue), see F. Brutschin, *Faust. Volks- Schauspiel in 4 Akten*, Lucerne, 1948.

source was manifestly the Spies Faustbook. The appearance
of a phrase straight out of 'Spies' near the beginning of Mann's
novel gives the first clear sign: 'die elementa spekulieren' (Mann,
Chapter 3; 'Spies', Chapter 6). Leverkühn's similarity to Faust is
soon made apparent: he has an impatient and easily bored intelligence, and regards intellectual curiosity as more potent than
any of the emotions.[1] The Manichean lectures of Schleppfuß
signal the entry of the Devil into this modern *Faust* and the pact
is transformed into the escapade with Esmeralda, the signature
in blood becoming an infection of the blood. Leverkühn's
conversation with the Devil, in which the terms of the 'pact' are
agreed, is Mann's equivalent to the numerous confrontations in
'Spies', restated in terms which owe a great deal to a somewhat
similar episode in *The Brothers Karamazov* (xi, 9). The fruits of the
pact for Mann's Faust are, of course, his gifts as a composer but
even here Mann slyly reminds us of the chapbook from time to
time. Leverkühn's symphony *Wunder des Alls* is an ironic counterpart to Faust's initiation into the secrets of the universe (Mann,
Chapter 27; 'Spies', Chapters 25–7), and his *Apokalypse* occupies
the place of the journey to Hell in the old version (Mann, Chapter
34; 'Spies', Chapter 24). Faust's confession to the students and
his 'Weheklag' have their equivalent in Mann's scene in which
Leverkühn invites his friends to hear his Faust cantata but breaks
out into a mad confession of his diabolism.[2]

Mann's central purpose in this novel was to restate his views on
the 'questionable' nature of the artist (and, more particularly, the
technical predicament of the modern artist) in allegorical terms.
A composer was chosen partly because music seemed to Mann to
display in the most radical way that ambiguity which he found to
a certain extent in all art forms (see above, p. 79). The young
Adrian Leverkühn at first means this in a narrow, even slightly
naïve sense: 'Nimm den Ton oder den. Du kannst ihn so
verstehen,—oder beziehungsweise auch so, kannst ihn als
erhöht auffassen von unten oder als vermindert von oben . . .'
(p. 53). That is, the same note can be read as A♯ (with one set

[1] Chapters 5 and 8. This is Mann's more sophisticated equivalent to the 'trefflich
ingenium vnnd *memoriam*' mentioned in 'Spies'.

[2] Further parallels have been noted by Butler, Bergsten and others, but those
given here are sufficient to show how closely Mann based at least the general
shape of his *Faustus* on 'Spies'. There are of course many verbal echoes and near-
quotations from 'Spies', too.

of references implied) or as B♭ (with a quite different set of references). But this is only Adrian's first groping towards this truth: the 'ambiguity' goes much further. For instance, individual notes and chords depend for their 'meaning' on their context, and can change meaning suddenly and uncannily according to context. One need only think of the device (popular with Schubert) of keeping one note in a chord while changing all the other notes, or of Bartok's use of innocuous common chords in 'advanced' harmonic contexts, chords which suddenly come to sound most *un*common. Ambiguity concerning the function of an individual chord is wittily exploited by Haydn in the slow movement of his Symphony No. 64 in A major where, on a number of occasions, what is technically the final chord of a half-close is, by means of a pause, made to form the opening chord of a new phrase. Our enjoyment of this rather sensuously melodic movement is enhanced by an intriguing element of doubt as to 'where we are'. But perhaps the ambiguity implicit in the diatonic harmony of Western music is best illustrated by the chord of the diminished 7th, a chord which can be resolved in so many different ways that it can virtually destroy our sense of harmonic orientation (see illustration). (Of course, one does not need to understand the

technical reason for the ambiguity in order to experience it as one listens; I am not suggesting that these or similar considerations necessarily passed through Mann's mind.) The ambiguity applies to motifs and tunes as well, for these can appear to change quite radically according to instrumentation, tempo, context, or even pitch. Furthermore, music can appear to be progressive and regressive at one and the same time. To Zeitblom's remark that the 'new' music (the 12-note music, that is) seems sometimes to look backwards even as it looks forwards, Leverkühn replies: 'Interessantere Lebenserscheinungen . . . haben wohl immer dies Doppelgesicht von Vergangenheit und Zukunft. . . . Sie zeigen die Zweideutigkeit des Lebens selbst' (p. 208). Yet again, music is both the most intellectually pure and abstract and the most intensely and directly emotional of the arts; the disparity between the technical discipline and mastery involved in a great work and the apparently spontaneous emotion expressed in it and released by it—this disparity is probably greater, or seems greater, than in other art forms. And so the composer must have appeared to Mann to demonstrate in the most striking way the charlatanry which he found in all artists. Perhaps, too, Mann had in mind the 'ambiguity' of a genre like opera: highly artificial in form yet, at its best, profoundly 'true' in emotional content.

But the main reason for the choice of a composer rather than any other type of artist must have been that, for Mann as for many before him, music seemed the deepest and purest of the arts and also the quintessential expression of *German* artistic genius. This is what he had in mind when, in 'Deutschland und die Deutschen', he wrote that it had been a mistake on the part of authors of past *Fausts* not to present Faust as a composer. It is interesting that one at least of those critics who rather vaguely extolled 'faustian' man and equated him with their ideal of German manhood saw music as the prime means of expression for this faustian soul: 'Die Sprache des faustischen Menschen ist die Musik.'[1] Music is also an art that can still remind us of its ancient magical origins—there are many references to its daemonic and magical characteristics in Mann's *Faustus* (especially in Chapters 2 and 15). Both the magic and the uncanny mathematical ingenuity are implied by the 'magic square', for which Leverkühn has such a liking.

16	3	2	13
5	10	11	8
9	6	7	12
4	15	14	1

[1] Fritz Strich, *Dichtung und Zivilisation*, Munich, 1928, p. 80.

(The 'magic' resides in the fact that all lines of figures add up to the same total.) The choice of this magic square to characterize the new, 12-note music is felicitous. The square is symmetrical, logical, and orderly and yet, through its 'magic' it seems to transcend the logic of its structure, to be more than the sum of its parts. A good serial composition should do this, as do the more traditional devices of canon and stretto.

Further, music is seen as an art which constantly re-examines its own basic elements, refreshing and renewing itself out of these. This is Kretschmar's theory, 'daß unter allen Künsten gerade die Musik . . . niemals sich einer frommen Neigung entschlagen habe, . . . ihre Elemente zu zelebrieren' (p. 69). Kretschmar's examples concern the spinning-out of music from the elemental material contained in, or implied by, common chords. (He instances the opening of Wagner's *Ring*; the first movements of Beethoven's Moonlight and Appassionata sonatas would be equally apposite.) Kretschmar uses architectural imagery ('Bausteine der Welt . . . Quader von Urgestein'—p. 69), and indeed music—or Western music, at least—can be seen to build itself up out of chords, arpeggios, basic rhythmic patterns, even intervals. We have seen how extended passages may be based on a common chord or, to be exact, more usually on the arpeggio figures which can be derived from it. Or a movement may parade its basic rhythm before us in its opening notes (Beethoven's Violin Concerto). Or, as with the first four notes of the slow movement of Brahms' Double Concerto, we may be given the melodic elements of which the movement will be an elaboration. Organic development, the derivation of enormously complex material from comparatively simple beginnings, has been taken to extreme lengths in ingenuity by some composers (for example by Dohnányi in his Cello Sonata). Schumann and Haydn have bewitching tunes which consist, if analysed coldly, in nothing more than the ascent and descent of a major scale. Fugues, variations and those older forms of music based on plain-chant or on a *cantus firmus*—these all depend on the elaboration of basic elements. The art of development in sonata form, from Haydn to Brahms, shows the composers brooding and 'speculating' over the potentialities of the musical material on which the movement is based.

Where *Der Zauberberg* invites us to muse on the question 'what is life?', *Dr. Faustus* sets us wondering 'what is music?' As regards

the link between Leverkühn and Faust, the matter with which this
discussion is immediately concerned, Mann's point is surely that
Kretschmar's phrase echoes 'die elementa spekulieren', so that
this is another way of suggesting that Leverkühn's 'speculation'
will be in and through music. And when he develops the 12-note
system, he is indeed breaking up Western music into its elements,
speculating about them, trying to renew music out of them.

But Leverkühn is, so to speak, only one of two Fausts in
Mann's novel. The other is Germany itself. It has been shown
how many writers in the nineteenth and early twentieth centuries
had seen in Faust an archetypal figure, standing for qualities felt to
be essentially German: 'faustisch' came to be equated with
'deutsch'.[1] Goethe's *Faust* was usually the starting-point for
such speculation and it was Faust's restless drive to action, his
Tatendrang, that came to be stressed more and more. Goethe's
extremely subtle presentation of a basic dilemma (passivity is less
than human; action involves man in guilt with seeming inevitability) was passed over in favour of a vague but ecstatic
glorification of *die Tat*. As time passed, eulogies of 'faustian' man
became more and more nationalistic in tone; Faust seemed to
more and more writers a symbol of the 'national soul' and the
'faustian' urge to action came to be linked with such policies or
activities as led to national aggrandizement. With the rise of
German Fascism, interpretations of 'das Faustische' and of
Goethe's *Faust* took off into realms of fantasy. Karl Gabler,
writing in 1938, sees Goethe's *Faust* as a hymn to everything that
is best in the German spirit and a prophetic allegory of the course
which German history, shaped by this spirit, was to take.[2]
Georg Schott, writing two years later, ransacks and misinterprets
Goethe's *Faust* to find contemporary significance in it, talking of:

. . . der zweite Teil des Dramas . . . , in welchem die Gestalt des
faustischen Führers von Goethe in einer Weise herausgearbeitet ist,
daß man zuweilen geradezu betroffen steht, wenn man Dichtung von
einst und Wirklichkeit von heute vergleicht . . .[3]

---

[1] See above, pp. 28ff.

[2] K. Gabler, *Faust-Mephisto, der deutsche Mensch*, Berlin, 1938, 'Vorwort'.

[3] G. Schott, *Goethes Faust in heutiger Schau*, Stuttgart, 1940, p. 8. One could
multiply examples. For instances of *Faust* made into propaganda at the time of
World War I, see Dabezies, pp. 90ff. For a dramatic poem which seems to suggest
that unity and progress can only be ensured for mankind by the German spirit
(represented by Faust), see *Jung Faust an die Menschheit*, 1932, by M. Blümelhuber.

In this twisted interpretation, Mephisto becomes equated with
the type of modern intellectual journalist who seeks to spread
confusion and 'negative' values, and presently is identified with
the Jewish spirit. Schott is fond of phases like 'jüdisch-mephisto-
phelische Teufelei' and 'der mephistophelische (jüdische) Geist'
(p. 29). Hitler, who did not much like Goethe, was ready to
forgive much for the line 'Im Anfang war die Tat'.[1]

In view of such truly frightening distortions of what Goethe's
Faust stood and stands for, it is easy to see how Mann came to the
idea of showing Germany as Faust and 1933 as the year of this
modern Faust's pact with the Devil. The parallelism Faust/
Germany is kept before our eyes through Zeitblom's narration
as he refers to contemporary events while narrating past events.
The close of the novel makes the point perfectly explicit:

Deutschland . . . taumelte dazumal auf der Höhe wüster Triumphe,
im Begriffe, die Welt zu gewinnen kraft des einen Vertrages, den es zu
halten gesonnen war, und den es mit seinem Blute gezeichnet hatte.

Once this dual identification of Faust with the artist and with
Germany is borne in mind, the scarcely veiled references to
Nietzsche in the work fall into place too.[2] (The trick played on
Leverkühn when he is taken to a brothel instead of to a hotel is
taken from Nietzsche's life, as are various minor details. And of
course Leverkühn ends, as Nietzsche ended, in madness.)
Firstly, Nietzsche seemed to many of Thomas Mann's generation
the very personification of the lonely, tormented, uncompromising man of genius, the man who had intoxicated many with
his idea that truly free spirits must cherish their apartness fasti-
diously. Secondly, his cult of the 'superman', his insistence that
it is the strong and bold man's first duty to realize his own
potential and that humility and remorse hinder the achievement
of this—all these things help to suggest an association between
Nietzsche's ideal being and the Faust type.

But the implicit introduction of Nietzsche into the plan of
Dr. Faustus must also have been intended to refer to Nietzsche's

---

[1] 'Ich liebe Goethe nicht. Aber um des einen Wortes willen bin ich bereit, ihm
vieles nachzusehen: "Im Anfang war die Tat" . . . Der Mensch ist zum Handeln
da . . . Jede Tat ist sinnvoll, selbst das Verbrechen.'—H. Rauschning, *Gespräche mit
Hitler*, Europa Verlag, New York, 1940, p. 211.

[2] For parallels between Nietzsche and Leverkühn, see M. Colleville, 'Nietzsche
et le *Doktor Faustus* de Thomas Mann' in *Études Germaniques*, iii (1948), 343–54.

contribution to Nazi ideology. I do not wish to add to the library that has already been written on this controversial subject, but merely to suggest that Nietzsche's two moralities (one for the ruling classes and one for the slaves) are as easily applicable to nations as to classes, and that speeches by the Nazi leaders often showed a combination of Nietzschean ideas and pseudo-scientific racialism. That Nietzsche was distorted by the Nazis is true but it is also true that he despised egalitarianism and democracy, that he believed that an élite should have its own moral criteria—and that he was convinced that any philosophy worth its salt should be translatable into action. . . . It is not as unreasonable as some of Nietzsche's apologists have made out to seek links between this philosophy and Nazism, and hence it is not as tasteless as some of Mann's critics have maintained to introduce Nietzsche into this Faust novel.

Mann's chief technical problem in this novel, then, had been so to manipulate and transmute the old fable of Dr. Faust that it could be made to express a complex of ideas. A great part of this problem clearly concerned the magical elements; these had to be transformed into 'natural' events in such a way that the parallels and correspondences were still plain.[1] So, in Mann, the Devil becomes a university don who lectures on evil and, later, a figment of Leverkühn's imagination. The pact, too, is shorn of its magic, to become an allegorical statement of what the artist's gifts are and what must be paid for them. Mann's elaboration of various articles in the bargain between Faust and the Devil is very interesting. Traditionally, Mephisto 'sells' Faust twenty-four years in return for his soul (the moralizing point of the older versions being greatly strengthened by the infinite contrast between this brief span and eternity). There is a reference to this transaction when Leverkühn asks: 'So wollt Ihr mir Zeit verkaufen?' (p. 247). But this Devil is much subtler and more precise in his definition of the quality of his wares. It is not perhaps too fanciful to see here a veiled comment on the use to which the traditional Fausts had put *their* twenty-four years:

Zeit? Bloß so Zeit? Nein, mein Guter, das ist keine Teufelsware. . . .
Was für 'ne Sorte Zeit, darauf kommts an! Große Zeit, tolle Zeit . . .

---

[1] It is clearly possible to appreciate Mann without close knowledge of 'Spies' but it is equally clear that such a reading misses much.

Denn wir liefern das Äußerste in dieser Richtung: Aufschwünge liefern wir und Erleuchtungen, Erfahrungen von Enthobenheit und Entfesselung . . . (p. 247)

The twenty-four years which the chapbook Faust had very largely filled with trivial activities—these are to be replaced in Mann by 'ein ganzes Stundglas voll genialer Teufelszeit'. And Mann's Devil keeps his word, for Leverkühn's time of genius does indeed come and he composes with uncanny fluency and brilliance.

Another example of how Mann deepened and elaborated on a motif from the Faustbook concerns Faust's attempted marriage. In 'Spies', Faust desires to marry but is frightened off the idea by the Devil, who procures him mistresses instead (Chapter 10). In some puppet plays a clause forbidding Faust to marry actually figures in the pact. Mann's version of this motif is: 'Liebe ist dir verboten, insofern sie wärmt. Dein Leben soll kalt sein—darum darfst du keinen Menschen lieben' (p. 268). That is to say, the traditional prohibition of marriage (because it is a sacrament) has been turned into an allegorical statement of the loneliness to which the artist's singleminded pursuit of excellence condemns him. Decades before, Mann had put into Tonio Kröger's mouth the weariness and bitterness which the artist felt at having to portray human feelings without being permitted to share them ('das Menschliche darzustellen, ohne am Menschlichen teilzuhaben').

For all his subtlety and obliqueness, Mann holds closer to his naïve model than anyone who, since Marlowe, had treated the Faust theme. Why this adherence to 'Spies'? Partly, I believe, to escape from that dependence on Goethe's Faust that had trammelled so many during the past century; also, perhaps, to make sure that his Faust had none of the chauvinistic overtones that Goethe's had acquired, especially in the 1930s. Partly, too, to dissociate himself from the optimistic message of Goethe's Faust, by going back to a more pessimistic interpretation of the pact with the Devil and of its consequences.[1] Furthermore, if

---

[1] But it seems as if Mann was unwilling to end his account of Leverkühn on a note of utter hopelessness. The *Weheklag* is seen as a work expressing despair, as the denial of the optimism associated with Beethoven's Ninth. Yet it ends with a high G on the cello, pianissimo, suggesting, says Zeitblom, the possibility of renewed hope out of despair (p. 526).

Mann's Faust was, in some respects, to symbolize the German people, it must have seemed only logical to use as a basis for his work that version which was rooted most deeply in the German past, the first printed version of the Faust-theme. Lastly, there must have been an aesthetic element at work: Mann's delight in making elaborate and ironic play with a fundamentally naïve and crude mass of material.

The introduction of a narrator was something of a novelty in Faust literature. (There had been a narrator in Tertullian Faber's *Der neue Faust* of 1851, but this is an isolated case.) Zeitblom serves to produce a criterion of normality against which we may evaluate the—in all respects—abnormal character, gifts and motives of Leverkühn. (The parallel between Zeitblom and Goethe's Wagner has already been mentioned; both in Mann and in Goethe, a comparatively simple and unproblematic person is set off against the complex and tormented man of genius.)

An interesting illustration of Zeitblom's role occurs at the point where he introduces the account of Leverkühn's conversation with the Devil (Chapter 25), presenting the manuscript in a reverential, puzzled, gingerly fashion like the editor of some strange, ancient scroll of uncanny import. Before imparting the contents to us, he describes the manuscript together with the handwriting and Leverkühn's method of accommodating music manuscript to the needs of ordinary writing. The manuscript is undated but, like a good editor, Zeitblom dates it as best he can. The pedantry of all this is set off against the strange and daemonic content of the writings themselves. Nowhere is the contrast between hero and narrator more acute than in Zeitblom's agonized attempts to understand the precise psychological conditions under which this 'dialogue' was written. Or was it a dialogue? One would have to be a madman to believe that. A hallucinatory conversation with Leverkühn's other self then? But this forces one to the terrifying conclusion that the Devil's cynical mockery is Adrian's. . . .

Some readers of *Dr. Faustus* find that Zeitblom's rather pompous style interferes with their enjoyment of the book. Tastes differ, but it seems to me that the juxtaposition of narrator and Faust figure enriches the work, as we see this affectionate but puzzled 'ordinary man' trying to plumb Leverkühn's soul.

Unquestionably the most original, even startling twist given to traditional material by Mann concerns the fruits of the pact. Where, in 'Spies', Faust had lost his soul to the Devil in return for benefits throughout the remainder of his earthly life, Mann's Faust allies himself to the Devil in order to *gain* his soul as an artist, but at the cost of ordinary enjoyment of life. It is the Devil who points out how difficult it is to be a modern composer (a real one, an honest one): 'Das Komponieren selbst ist zu schwer geworden, verzweifelt schwer' (p. 257). The pact becomes a symbol for the desperate effort needed to compose 'with soul' in a genuinely new, genuinely logical idiom; the madness and disease, the cold and lonely life—all these things make up the Devil's price.

Before Leverkühn ever actually composes anything he devises and solves technical problems in music (p. 80). This is truly music without soul. Zeitblom's accounts of his friend's early works stress the element of irony (pp. 232, 282) and the fastidiousness with which the composer has avoided any cheap or hackneyed effects (p. 284). That is to say, Leverkühn is put into the position of a composer who is too austere to continue writing in the lush, emotively chromatic post-Wagnerian style. He could never develop into a super-Reger. Yet pastiche and persiflage will not satisfy such a serious and self-critical artist for long. Again it is the Devil who points this out: '[Die Parodie] könnte lustig sein, wenn sie nicht gar so trübselig wäre in ihrem aristokratischen Nihilismus. Würdest du dir viel Glück und Größe von solchen Schlichen versprechen?' (p. 260). The quest for a musical idiom which would be intellectually rigorous enough to satisfy a Leverkühn, yet truly expressive, is not worked out at all schematically but the progress can be perceived if one reads the descriptions of Leverkühn's later works attentively. The first important stage is the *Apokalypse*. (As already mentioned, the title and the theme remind us that this is to be regarded as one of the fruits of the pact, so that it should not surprise us to see some progress towards the acquisition of an artistic soul in it.) The central paradox of the work is that Hell is associated with concord, Heaven with dissonance (p. 402). Heavenly dissonance suggests opposition, striving, unwillingness to sink into passivity, while Hell is represented as banal and commonplace. To underline this, the music contains parodies of various idioms which the pitiless Leverkühn regards as insipid: drawing-room

music, French Impressionism, Tschaikovsky, jazz . . . (p. 403).
So parody is used to help to make an oblique metaphysical statement about the composer's view of Heaven and Hell—parody
begins to acquire, or yearn after, soul. And, in fact, what Zeitblom
sees in this work is precisely this yearning for soul: 'Verlangen
nach Seele' (p. 405). The process continues in the *Tempest*
settings and reaches its climax in the *Weheklag*.

It will be recalled that this work is a setting of a lament uttered
by Faust in the chapbook of 1587. Leverkühn's 'gaining of soul'
in this, his last composition, consists in a combination of intellectual discipline and expressiveness, in the rebirth of freedom
out of the ultimate of formal strictness: 'die Geburt der Freiheit
aus der Gebundenheit' (p. 520). The work, in the 12-note system,
is so tightly constructed that each note is integral to the plan and
determined by logic. Yet the music is liberated as a means of
expression: 'vermöge der Restlosigkeit der Form eben wird die
Musik als Sprache befreit' (p. 522).[1]

Where most of Adrian's earlier works had displayed the logic
without the soul and had tended to explode in mockery, his
musical logic now paves the way for true expressiveness. His
happiness and sanity may have been destroyed but he has found
his soul as a composer.

Hanns Eisler's Faust libretto of 1952 places Faust against the
background of the Peasant Rebellions of early sixteenth-century
Germany. For Eisler, the Marxist, Luther is to be condemned
because he supported the princes against the insurgent peasants,
while the true hero of the revolt is Thomas Müntzer. The origin
of this view is to be found in Fr. Engels *Der deutsche Bauernkrieg*,
1850, which sees Luther as a 'bourgeois reformer' and Müntzer
as a 'plebeian revolutionary'. Engels' account of Müntzer's
career shows him as gradually becoming less concerned with
theological matters and more with social aims, and stresses the
near-Communistic implications of his teaching. This interpretation of Müntzer's career became the received version among
Marxists and Eisler must have been influenced by it.

The account of Faust's history in Eisler owes much to the

---

[1] Mann, as is well known, acknowledged that he had borrowed the 12-note
system from Schönberg and credited Leverkühn with the discovery and development of it. This does not of course mean that Leverkühn can be identified with
Schönberg or his music with Schönberg's.

puppet plays. He enters on a pact with the Devil for wealth, power, and fame and is found demonstrating his powers at court and impressing the mighty with his riches. So, in due course, the recognition and favour of the great come to him—but too late, for he has seen the suffering and injustice around him and has bought the favour of the rich at the cost of self-respect and the respect of the common people. He sees himself as a man of peasant stock who has betrayed his class.

This is one of the few genuinely original conceptions of Faust since the Romantics and also one of the comparatively few works to possess real intrinsic merit. It has wit and rough humour, something of the simple eloquence of old folk-ballads and also something of Brecht's 'concreteness' of diction. Eisler's intention was to produce a workmanlike and popular libretto:

In der Oper wird es von Volksliedern, Versen von Hans Sachs und ähnlichem Volksgut nur so wimmeln. . . . Ich bin nicht ein Gymnasial-professor in Pension, der ein Drama—spät aber doch—der staunenden Mitwelt offerieren will, sondern ein Komponist, der sich einen Text baut und dazu Vorlagen nimmt . . .[1]

What of Eisler's models, then? There are a few echoes of Lessing, the *Stürmer und Dränger* and Goethe. Further, Eisler takes up a hint from those who had followed Fr. Th. Vischer's lead and had placed Faust in the context of the Peasant Wars. But the main source, as already hinted, is the puppet plays. Faust's conjuring, his choice of a familiar after testing various demons for their speed, the terms of the pact, the court scenes, all these are taken over directly. Hanswurst figures, too, taking the parts of servant and night-watchman as in the puppet plays and enacting many of his traditional *lazzi*.

Yet the traditional elements have been given new meaning by Eisler. The apolitical court scenes of the puppet plays have been replaced by court scenes which stress the injustice and terror of the regime. The magical spectacles staged by Faust also have class-significance; the incidents and characters ordered for the entertainment of the ruling classes appeal instead to the watching slaves and subvert them. Faust and Hanswurst fly back to Wittenberg to escape the ruler's wrath. But even Hanswurst's

---

[1] Eisler to Brecht, 27/8/51. In *Sinn und Form, Sonderheft Hanns Eisler*, Berlin, 1964, p. 14.

escape is not lighthearted as in the popular tradition but is made
to illustrate a characteristic of terror regimes old and new:
guilt-by-association. For the hapless servant girl who has been
seen together with him must suffer. The scene depicting Faust's
death again has many traditional elements but these, too, have
been changed to underline Eisler's theme of class-betrayal.
Hanswurst, as night-watchman, accuses Faust:

HANSWURST: . . . Erst gestern hab ich wieder einen im Vorbeigehn
              'Hackfleisch' sagen hören. Und warum? Weil Ihr ein
              Mörder seid.
FAUST: Ich bin krank.
HANSWURST: Leut wie Ihr sind immer krank. Was macht Euer Freund,
              der Kaiser? (p. 81)

'Your friend, the Emperor': that is where Eisler's originality
lies. He was shrewd enough to realize that the historical Faust
(from what little we know of him) or the Faust of the chapbooks
and the puppet plays would be on the side of the rich and powerful.
All other Faust versions known to me which put Faust into the
context of the Peasant Uprisings place him on the side of the
people and make a *Freiheitsheld*, a champion of freedom, out of
him. Eisler is much more plausible. 'Eine neue, *sehr* neue
Version des Faust-Stoffes . . .' writes Mann to Eisler (5/11/1952).[1]
It is fitting that this account of the resuscitation of the old
'popular' Fausts should end with a tribute from the man who
gave new meaning to the chapbook to the man who did the
same for the puppet play.[2]

[1] Ibid., p. 247.
[2] Eisler never composed the music for his libretto. There is one other example of
a Faust opera based on the puppet plays, an opera in which the composer is again
his own librettist. This is Busoni's *Doktor Faust* (1914–24). Busoni differs from the
puppet plays in that he ends his work on a note of hope.

7

Imitations and Continuations
of Goethe's *Faust*

'Goethes Faust ist ins Unendliche fortsetzbar.'
(Fr. Th. Vischer)

'Es ist immer ein Wagnis, einen bereits bearbeiteten Stoff
zu verwenden oder im Anschluß an frühere Arbeiten dem
Leser neue Gesichtspunkte über ein Thema eröffnen zu
wollen, das von Meisterhand behandelt wurde.'
(Torbrech)

IT is probably true to say that Goethe's *Faust* has had more
influence than any other single work of German literature.
In one way this influence is quite incalculable. The work has
come to form part of the consciousness of the educated German;
Faust is as full of quotations as *Hamlet*. Again, Goethe's *Faust*
was obviously the greatest single factor leading to the epidemic
of Faust versions in the nineteenth and twentieth centuries, and
it was Goethe's *Faust*, too, which was instrumental in causing
many Germans to regard Faust as a sort of symbol for the German
soul. So, indirectly, even the most eccentric 'Faust-fantasy' and the
most woolly and chauvinistic musings over 'faustian' attributes
derive from Goethe's poem. At the same time the work was
directly imitated by author after author.

Faust's character and motivation are perhaps too closely bound
up with Goethe's era and with Goethe's own spiritual and
intellectual development to have exercised much influence on
men of other generations and views—indeed, more or less wilful
misunderstandings seem to have been common through much
of the nineteenth century. But Goethe's work certainly helped
to popularize the view that a Faust should turn away from
abstract, speculative pursuit of knowledge to some sort of active
life:

K

Nun, Faust, an's Werk! Dir ziemt die Muße nicht![1]

But few authors allowed themselves to be guided at all closely by Goethe when it came to determining what type of activity should lead to Faust's salvation. The influence of the court scenes, the journey to the Mothers, the Helen-act and the regaining of land from the sea was largely negative; these episodes were rejected as irrelevancies or as unworthy of Faust.

Of the various characters in Goethe's *Faust* it is Gretchen who has been most copied; her successors lisp and sing their way through countless Faust dramas. In his poem 'Marguerite' of 1846 Henri Blaze de Bury was to describe Gretchen as the ideal and the obsession of the Germans. The poetry, the essentially *German* charm, the pathos, and the simplicity of the Gretchen episode had made her a sort of national folk-heroine. Moreover, for any aspiring author of a work on Faust, it was easier to follow this aspect of Goethe's work and produce a love tragedy than to deal poetically and dramatically with the crisis of knowledge, the application of science, the acquisition of power, the problematic nature of ambition, and similar questions. Czilski's *Faust* of 1843 is in large part an open imitation of the Gretchen tragedy, while Jordan's 'mystery' *Demiurgos* (1852) even contains *two* figures reminiscent of Gretchen (one confusingly called Helene). In Julius Große's poem 'Ein Bild' (1859) the poet dreams of the domestic bliss which Faust would have enjoyed had he remained faithful to Gretchen:

> Hättst du dem Gretchen Wort gehalten,
> Wie glücklich wart ihr, nun ein holdes Paar!

Gretchen spins contentedly, Faust is only occasionally disturbed by a passing restlessness, the poodle (no devil in disguise, but 'ein frommes Tier') gnaws a bone at Faust's feet. In fact, Goethe's *Faust* was a lot of fuss about nothing:

> Im engen Kreis auch winkt das höchste Ziel.[2]

We shall see that such implied criticism of Goethe's *Faust* was one of the main forces at work, whenever attempts were made to rewrite *Faust* or to provide a sequel to it.

Goethe's Mephisto, too, has been much copied. In particular

[1] A. Lutze, 'Doctor Faust . . .', c. 1840.
[2] R. Baumbach's poem 'Der Adept', 1880, makes a similar point.

there have been many attempts to catch his cynically witty tone. Close to Goethe's 'Geist, der stets verneint' is Lucifer in Imry Madách's *Tragödie des Menschen* (1861), often referred to as 'the Hungarian *Faust*':

> Dies Hemmungselement heißt Luzifer,
> Und sein Beruf ist: ewig zu verneinen.
> (p. 9: cf. Goethe, lines 338–43 and 1338)

Lenau, Woldemar Nürnberger, and, in more modern times, Gstöttner, all influenced in different ways by Goethe's characterization of Mephisto, have nevertheless all developed their own conception of the Devil. Minor authors who have produced feeble imitations of Goethe's Mephisto need not concern us. Perhaps the most interesting works inspired by Goethe are those in which copying in the narrow sense plays comparatively little part, works which represent the authors' personal variations on Goethe's theme.[1] One of the most important has already been mentioned: Madách's *Tragödie des Menschen*.

This begins with a Heavenly Prologue clearly based on Goethe, in which Lucifer introduces the one discordant note into an angelic hymn of praise to the Creator. This leads to a deal between God and Devil, again not unlike that in Goethe:

> Luzifer . . . . ich will mein Teil.
> Der Herr (spöttisch) Es soll dir werden. Blick hinab zur Erde.
> Im Garten Eden sieh die beiden Bäume.
> Ich fluche ihnen—und ich geb' sie dir.   (p. 10)

And so the scene changes to the Garden of Eden, with Adam and Eve before the trees of knowledge and immortality. Lucifer has a fairly easy job of temptation, holding out prospects of maturity and scoffing at a God who places part of his creation out of bounds to his creatures. Adam and Eve eat of the fruit of knowledge and are banished. Adam now expresses a 'faustian' desire for full knowledge:

> Aus meinem Wahne [the innocence of unknowing] hast du mich
> gerissen:
> So gaukle nicht und laß mich alles wissen!   (p. 28)

[1] Valéry's *Faust* which is, in its way, a commentary on Goethe's, is dealt with elsewhere. Of the attempts to imitate Goethe's Mephisto, that by Fr. Reinhard in his unfinished Faust play of 1848 is one of the most successful.

What follows is a series of prophetic visions in which various eras of human history are depicted,[1] with Adam and Lucifer playing a number of roles. Lucifer attempts so to appal Adam with the thought of the potential cruelty and folly of men that he will lose any wish to sire such a race, will, so to speak, 'return his entrance ticket' like Ivan Karamazov. (This is all closer in spirit to Klinger's *Faust* than to Goethe's.) But the work ends on a note of hope, as Adam resolves to take the responsibility of man's future on himself. The issue, for all the superficial dissimilarity, is not so different from that in Goethe's *Faust*. Madách is concerned with showing that, despite latent wickedness, despite the futility of various human endeavours, despite obstacles to light and progress, despite the dangers which accompany man's urges and instincts, it is on balance better to be than not to be. This is, after all, the point made rather less directly by Goethe when he sets off Faust's (and God's) doctrine of ceaseless activity against Mephisto's nihilism. The famous 'irony' of the scene 'Großer Vorhof des Palastes' becomes rather less ironic than some commentators maintain, when one considers that Mephisto—although no doubt right in his prediction that Faust's deeds will have no lasting effect (11544–7)—is wrong in his conclusions (11595–603). Both Madách's Lucifer and Goethe's Mephisto come to appear mistaken in their nihilism. The chief difference between the works is that Madách is drawing up a balance sheet for mankind in general rather than showing one man finding his destiny. There is no question of copying Goethe. But Madách's dramatic poem was clearly inspired by Goethe's. There are sufficient reminders of scenes, characters, and motifs from Goethe to make it quite clear that Madách intended it to be his *Faust*.

A somewhat similar case (although the work is intrinsically much inferior) is P. J. Bailey's *Festus*, first published in 1839 and added to throughout succeeding decades so that the eleventh edition of 1889 reached upwards of 40,000 lines! This was an open attempt to answer or to 'correct' Goethe's *Faust*, putting forward a less 'worldly' view. In fact, several nineteenth-century reviewers compared the two works, from the point of view of their moral message, to Goethe's disadvantage. (Tennyson was among the admirers of *Festus*.)

[1] Plan in Appendix II.

This work has its 'Prologue in Heaven', in which Lucifer obtains permission to tempt Festus, and a long Heavenly Epilogue. The general framework thus bears some resemblance to Goethe's. Further, there are all manner of references to Goethe's *Faust*, or variations on scenes and motifs from it. *Festus* has its 'Wald und Höhle' and its 'Vor dem Tor'. The echoes of Goethe's verse are sufficiently close to show that Bailey had steeped himself in *Faust*, even if he emerged only with a desire to refute what he thought to be its teaching. But when one tries to define what Bailey's attitude is, why Festus is saved, one becomes lost in a maze. At most one can say in general terms that Festus gradually abandons 'superhuman' ambitions, conquers hedonism and turns to God:

> With all his doubts, he never doubted God:
> But from doubt gathered truth, like snow from clouds. . . .
>
> (p. 556)

From Madách, who was prompted by Goethe's *Faust* to pour his philosophy into something resembling Goethe's mould, and Bailey, who clearly thought of Goethe's *Faust* as something that needed to be redone with sufficient reminiscences of the original to make clear to any attentive reader what was going on, it is only a short step to those authors who actually took up Goethe's pen for him. Between 1808 and the appearance of Part 2, impatient poets attempted to provide their own Part 2; after 1832 a surprising number of writers were sufficiently discontented with Goethe's solution to unravel the wool and remake the garment according to their own pattern. In some cases, even, a third part was added.

Firstly, the attempts to provide a suitable sequel to Goethe's Part 1 during his own lifetime. Goethe could be severe towards such presumptuous undertakings. When introducing his 'Helena' in *Kunst und Altertum*[1] he looks back on overhasty continuations of the First Part and wonders that the authors had not hit on the 'so obvious thought' that any Second Part should lead from the 'wretched' (*kümmerlich*) sphere of Part 1 into higher regions. Yet he had no right to be greatly shocked if people took up his *Faust*; had he not, decades before, produced a fragmentary second part to the *Zauberflöte*,[2] in which Papagena lays a number of

---

[1] Bd. 6, Stuttgart, 1827, Heft i, p. 201.   [2] Written 1795, published 1802.

eggs, she and her husband experience the joys of parenthood, and Sarastro, before setting off on a kind of Masonic Sabbatical leave, lectures the happy couple on how to bring up their offspring!

As early as 1812 Grillparzer had the idea of continuing Goethe's *Faust*, although only a fragment of forty-nine lines has survived. But a diary entry of 1822 tells what the outcome should have been. Faust was to take up a modest, restful life, seeking only peace. He would come into contact with a humble family and learn to know simple domestic pleasures. The daughter would grow to love him. But Faust would be ever troubled in his happiness by feelings of past guilt. Tormented by the innocent girl's love, he would try to turn her from him by revealing his past and, when this failed, would summon Mephisto and ask for the pact to be fulfilled before the time was up; that is, he would sacrifice his last years in order to save the girl. Between 1822 and 1830 K. E. Schubarth made three sketches for a possible continuation of Part 1. These are not plans which Schubarth intended to work up in dramatic form—he was not a creative writer—but merely his speculations as to how *Faust* might be continued. But for all Schubarth's intensive study of Goethe, his ideas for a Part 2 are totally un-Goethean. All his sketches embody in different ways a tepidly hedonistic view of life and they all tend to reduce Faust's role to little more than that of a spectator.[1]

The first full-scale attempt to provide a second part to *Faust* was C. C. L. Schöne's *Fortsetzung des Faust von Göthe* (1823). In his Dedication, Schöne explains why it was necessary to jump into the breach:

> O, möchten Deine Jahre sich erneuen,
> Und würde Dir des Grabes Ziel entrückt!
> Ja, dann!—Du schwiegst, Du willst den Faust nicht enden.
> So wagt' ich's zitternd denn ihn zu vollenden.   (p. vii)

Goethe was unmoved by this and described the work, which he saw in manuscript in 1821, as a repetition rather than a continuation.[2] Schöne picks up the action where Goethe had left

---

[1] The 1822 version was published by Max Hecker in the *Jahrbuch der Goethe-Gesellschaft*, xxi (1935), 185ff. The two later versions can be found in Schubarth, *Über Goethes Faust*, Berlin, 1830, 12. Vorlesung, and his *Gesammelte Schriften*, Hirschberg, 1835, 137ff.

[2] Letter to Zelter, 14/12/1821.

off, with Faust's bitterness and despair, his remorse over Gretchen's fate—but then produces a copy of the Gretchen episode all over again with the daughter of the Doge of Venice in the role of a second, higher-born Gretchen. Faust approaches despair again but achieves a moral regeneration touched off by the ennobling and purifying influence of art in Rome. The play ends with Mephisto thwarted and Faust saved. All reviewers and critics of the work known to me have been severe. 'Machwerk', 'klägliches Produkt'—these are the phrases one encounters. Yet Schöne had an insight or two. He perceived that the arts of antiquity must play some part in redeeming a Faust created by Goethe, and he showed Faust accepting that voluntary self-limitation which is the theme of all Goethe's mature work:

> Von Wissensdrang und Wissens Stolz gebläht
> Wollt' ich ein Gott, wollt' ich ein Ganzes sein.   (p. 15)

It is the senseless introduction of the second Gretchen and the feebleness of the verse which make Schöne's Part 2 so poor:

> Du frommes Kind, o, weile! weile!
> Sie hört mich nicht, denn sie hat Eile . . . .   (p. 87)

1831 saw three attempts to complete Goethe's *Faust*. Karl Rosenkranz modestly described his *Geistlich Nachspiel zur Tragödie Faust* as a little chapel added to Goethe's mighty cathedral. There is a Prologue in Heaven in which God talks of man's struggle to achieve truth and foresees that Faust will be saved, since the shattering effect of Gretchen's execution will lead him back to virtue. We meet Faust (disgusted with Mephisto and all he has to offer) looking back nostalgically on his earlier attempts to discover the truth, attempts which he is perfectly content to take up again with renewed hope. And so he returns to his study:

> Wo ich wiederum mich ergeben habe
> Dem alten Triebe zur Wissenschaft,
> Wo ich wieder, wie einst, studire
> In der Schrift göttlicher Offenbarung . . .   (p. 20)

Now Mephisto, seeing that his influence over Faust is waning, decides to set various cliques of poets, scholars and theologians on this upstart who claims to know the path to truth. But they are routed and Faust is left in peace again to devise his formula for true knowledge: not feelings alone, for these are not to be trusted, but a combination of feeling, reasoning and reliance on scripture:

> Wenn Schrift, Vernunft und Fühlen sich verbünden,
> Dann wird das ächte Wissen sich entzünden!   (p. 84)

So Faust is saved by being taken back to a point before Goethe's starting-point and by being transformed into a totally different person. This is not Part 1 continued; it is Part 1 blown away in a puff of smoke.

In the British Museum there is the manuscript of a play in rhymed verse by the soldier, administrator, and diplomat, F. C. F. von Müffling: *Zum Faust, der Tragödie von Göthe*.[1] Set in an unnamed *Residenzstadt* in Italy, it owes much to the traditional court scenes of the puppet plays and to *Tasso*, rather less to the already published court scenes of *Faust 2*. Faust and Mephisto are discovered in a picture-gallery where they are joined by the Duke and his daughter Clementine. She and Faust discourse about pictures, beauty, and truth, while Mephisto keeps her companions diverted. As the play progresses, Faust, with Mephisto's help and encouragement, tries to win Clementine. However, she is dismayed to find this soulful and intellectual companion taking an altogether too sensual interest in her (here the influence of *Tasso* is obvious). Meanwhile, Mephisto has been engaged in rabble-rousing in the general cause of disorder. Helped by a hellish spirit called *der Geist der Zeit*, he has been trying to provoke the people to revolt, although the Duke's regime is expressly described as just and good. If Faust leads this revolt, he can depose the Duke and simply take Clementine, kingdom and all. But Faust changes sides, boxes the ears of the *Zeitgeist* and forces Mephisto to return the pact. Mephisto's rueful comment recalls Goethe's Prologue:

> Meine Wette geht verloren,
> Denn der Alte hatte Recht ...   (p. 92)

In a passage clearly intended to offer a contrast to the famous curse of Goethe's pact scene (lines 1583–1606), Faust curses the

[1] Dated 1831. I give a fairly detailed account of this, since it has not, as far as I know, been published.

Devil and all his works. The play ends with Faust's voluntary renunciation of Clementine and his departure to work in the cause of freedom, a sort of Prussian Posa.

This play is an exception to the general run of continuations in that it concentrates on one aspect of the traditional Faust material (the court scenes) and ignores the question of Faust's guilt towards Gretchen (unless his giving up of Clementine is meant to imply remorse and regeneration which, in the absence of any hint from the author, seems unlikely). It is very Prussian in spirit in that the revolutionary *Zeitgeist* is explicitly represented as a servant of the Devil and Faust's nobility manifests itself chiefly in his opposition to this spirit. It is clear that his championship of freedom as prophesied in his last speech is not going to be in any revolutionary or even mildly subversive sense. Poetically the work is without merit, full of woolly abstractions and often not far from bathos.

The last, and best, of the 1831 continuations is Gustav Pfizer's 'Faustische Scenen'. These scenes follow on naturally and logically from the end of Part 1, making more sense both in themselves and as an informed guess of what Goethe might be expected to do than any other of these early continuations. And Pfizer shows at least an honest competence in his verse.

He opens with a monologue in which Faust expresses his remorse and bitter disappointment; the pleasures offered by the pact have proved to be empty ones and he sees the folly of his earlier Titanism. In the next scene he demands to know of Gretchen's fate. Her spirit appears to him and summons sylphs and elves to lull him to sleep:

> er ist nun umfangen
> Vom Schlummer kräftig und tief;
> Es klagen die blassen Wangen,
> Daß er lange so süß nicht mehr schlief!

> Gretchens Geist.
> O güt'ge Macht, die diesen ew'gen Kindern
> Das harmlos–schöne Spiel erlaubt:
> Hold zu umschweben ein verfluchtes Haupt,
> Und unverstandnes Weh zu lindern!   (Nr. 161, p. 641)

This resembles Goethe's already published scene 'Anmutige Gegend', and is doubtless an attempt to relate Faust's anguish and restlessness more explicitly to Gretchen. (It is perhaps even a criticism in a sense of 'Anmutige Gegend' in which, many thought, Faust had been let off much too lightly.) In due course Faust awakens out of his dreams to the odious reality of finding Mephisto by his side. But Gretchen's spirit appears again, urging Faust to repudiate the pact and go to Rome, and presently we find Faust, Mephisto, and Wagner in the Holy City. In this episode there are clear enough echoes of the 'Römische Elegien':

> Schwer wird's den Steinen, solcher Vorwelt Zeugen,
> Was sie gesehen, zu verschweigen. (Nr. 166, p. 663)

Faust dismisses Mephisto (after a certain amount of legalistic quibbling) and turns to Rome, there to seek inspiration for new forms of activity by contemplating the artistic achievements of the past. Shortly after this the fragment breaks off but it is clear that Faust is heading for salvation.

J. D. Hoffmann had the misfortune to be pipped at the post by Goethe, for *Faust, Eine Tragödie von Goethe. Fortgesetzt von J. D. Hoffmann* only appeared in 1833. It is not worth pursuing the plot of this work in detail; it is sufficient to say that it is a bizarre mixture of traditional Faust material, satire, knockabout, sentimentality and earnest moralizing. If Rosenkranz, with his Part 2, had placed a little chapel beside Goethe's cathedral, Hoffmann's is no more than a ramshackle fairground booth, filled with garish and ill-assorted trinkets.

So, of these four attempts to give Goethe a helping hand, only Pfizer's fragment can lay claim to intrinsic value. The others combine in varying degrees some reasonably good guesswork with much plain silliness. They all pick up the hint that Faust is to be saved and all but one make much of his remorse over his treatment of Gretchen. Two versions assign importance to an aesthetic experience. Pfizer comes nearest to Goethe's spirit, for the guiding and encouraging role he gives to Gretchen can be regarded as his narrower idea of 'das ewig Weibliche', while the Roman experience and the explicit renunciation of Titanism are wholly Goethean. This degree of understanding means that Pfizer's is the only continuation in which the frequent echoes of Goethe's verse are other than embarrassing.

Before the conscious attempts to re-do Goethe's Second Part are considered, there must be a brief mention of two writers remarkable in that, long after the 1830s, they appeared to be totally ignorant of the fact that there had ever been a *Faust 2*! *Der neue Faust* (1851) by Tertullian Faber (Xaver Schmid) is described by E. M. Butler (pp. 272f), so that there is no need to treat it in detail here. Suffice it to say that Faber tries to show how Faust lifts himself up from the moral depths to which he had sunk at the end of Goethe's Part 1 and achieves regeneration through a pious and philanthropic life. *Faust's Tod. Eine Tragödie in funf Aufzügen* by C. E. Mölling (1864), also intended as a sequel to Goethe's Part 1, is more interesting. The action opens in Florence, where Mephisto promises Faust new pleasures. A new character, Julia, is introduced, with whom Faust at once becomes infatuated. This episode reaches a tragic climax somewhat similar to the Faust/Gretchen/Valentin episode in Goethe. We next find Faust weary of love and longing for action. Mephisto contrives to pass him off at court as a prince and, later, engineers a conspiracy to depose the king and install Faust in his place. Eventually, Faust, horrified at all the violence, turns from Mephisto and seeks satisfaction in honest, humble work—assisting Gutenberg in his printing shop. But he is accused of practising black magic and, in a fit of disgust at human blindness and pettiness, comforts himself with the thought of death:

> Komm' an mein Herz, du Bote stillen Friedens! (p. 120)

Now Mephisto arrives to claim his soul, for:

> Wenn jemals du im öden Erdenlaufe
> Bekenntest, daß dein wilder Drang gesättigt,
> Dann wärst du mein. . . . (p. 122)

There follows an argument concerning the rights and wrongs of the agreement but Faust continues to defy Mephisto and finally hears a 'Stimme von oben' proclaim:

> Du hast gestrebt! Du bist gerettet! (p. 124)

Mölling's preface to the English edition of 1865 has this to say:

This drama is based on the old legendary tale of man seduced to sin by the evil spirit, here Mephistopheles. The author has taken the two leading characters from the '*Faust*' of the illustrious GOETHE, and in a manner commences where the latter has broken off. . . .

—which certainly seems to imply ignorance of Part 2. In any

event, Mölling intends Part 1 to be understood as forming the prelude to his tragedy. Goethe's wager is taken over, and, in fact, the dubious and disputed outcome (should Mephisto really have lost, according to the letter of the agreement?) is the only thing which might lead us to wonder whether Mölling might not, after all, have had some knowledge of Goethe's Part 2. It must be said that Mölling's taking up of Goethe's wager is not convincing; his Faust is not bidding time stand still because of the richness and beauty of the passing moment, but is longing for death in a mood of resignation. In fact, very few 'continuations' of Goethe have taken over and developed the wager of Part 1 at all successfully and Mölling unwittingly gives us a hint as to why. So much of Goethe's philosophy of life is implicit in 'verweile doch . . .', that an author cannot build on it convincingly without entering quite intensively into Goethe's thought. But this is precisely what the authors of these new Second Parts were unwilling or unable to do.

> Nun ja, zum Himmel führ' ich ihn ein
> Und das zweite Mal soll es gültig sein.

—thus the Lord in Fr. Th. Vischer's Faust parody. Vischer was not alone in thinking Goethe's salvation of Faust 'invalid'. The harvest of new 'Second Parts' and even 'Third Parts' thus represents a sort of oblique criticism of Goethe, and these pieces cannot be fully understood without some knowledge of the attacks made on *Faust 2* throughout the nineteenth century.

First and foremost among these are the moral objections to *Faust 2*, strongest in Goethe's Catholic critics. Paul Haffner, writing in 1880, criticizes the facile manner in which Faust's guilt is washed away (he is referring to the scene 'Anmutige Gegend'):

... wo ist die sittliche Idee? Ist Schlafen und Vergessen genügend, die Menschenseele aus der Todesnacht der Sünde zu erheben?

After very offhand treatment of 'die Mütter' and the Helen episode, in which Haffner makes no effort to penetrate a spiritual world foreign to him, he comes to the final Act. Any notion that Faust's ideals are particularly worthy or that they represent moral improvement or expiation is mocked; Faust has become merely 'Direktor einer Land-Urbarmachungs-Action-Gesellschaft', and the final scene in Heaven is 'mehr eine launig-fromme Comödie, als eine ernste Darstellung des Geheimnisses der göttlichen Barmherzigkeit'.[1]

Egon Ipse is yet more severe. Faust himself is a pitiful character and the work as a whole is symptomatic of the modern disease of doubt. Faust's ills are put down to hypochondria; exercise and a few doses of Carlsbad salts would work wonders. The macrocosm-episode is dismissed as mere conjuring tricks ('Seifenblase und Gaukelei'), and Ipse has this to say of the *Erdgeist*:

Der Geist müßte nach der Beharrlichkeit, mit welcher er vom Weben spricht, der Webergeist heißen. . . .

Ipse's account of Part 2 is equally wilful and distorted. Of Act 5:

Nach tausend Abenteuern und Irrfahrten findet Faust irgend eine Uferparzelle am Meer und einen Sumpf am Fuße eines Berges, und diese gefallen ihm. Das Ufer gegen das einstürmende Meer eindämmen, den Sumpf kanalisiren zu lassen, ist sein höchster Wunsch . . . Wäre es noch wenigstens ein Gotthardttunnel oder ein Suezkanal gewesen—aber ein Sumpf in einem Lande, das nicht an Übervölkerung litt: das ist bescheiden![2]

A good deal of criticism concerning the moral implications of *Faust 2* came from non-Catholic quarters, too. Gutzkow, in *Wally die Zweiflerin*,[3] pours scorn on the elaborate machinery which Goethe finds necessary to effect the 'canonization' of Faust. A more detailed attack appeared in the *Telegraph für Deutschland* (1838, pp. 1259–62), in what was ostensibly a review of C. Schönborn's study of Goethe's *Faust*. The Titan of Part 1, says Gutzkow, has been destroyed in Part 2. (This criticism will reappear in Spielhagen's lecture on 'Faust und Nathan' of 1867.) There follows—to return to Gutzkow—a mocking account of Faust's activities in Part 2, intended to show that his salvation is undeserved. The review concludes with the words:

Der wahre zweite Theil des Faust, im Lichte des Jahrhunderts, *Faust, kein Egoist*, sondern sich *aufopfernd* und dadurch versöhnend, Faust

---

[1] 'Goethe's Faust als Wahrzeichen moderner Cultur', in *Frankfurter zeitgemäße Broschüren*, neue Folge, i, Frankfort on the Main, 1880, pp. 29, 34, 36.

[2] *Faust und kein Ende*, Crefeld, 1883, pp. 41, 42, 14f. For a yet more savage comment on Goethe's *Faust*, see Adam Müller, *Ethischer Charakter von Göthes Faust . . .*, Regensburg, 1885.

[3] Book iii. See *Deutsche Neudrucke*, v, 2, Göttingen, 1965, p. 221.

schaffend und ringend für die Menschheit und dadurch den Geist des Neides und der Lüge, den Teufel, von sich bannend, dieser zweite Theil des Faust soll erst noch geschrieben werden.

Others echoed Gutzkow's views on the Catholic 'machinery' of *Faust 2* and the inappropriateness of Faust's activities, regarded as expiation. It may be added that nearly all the writers who put forward ethical objections criticized the work also from an aesthetic point of view, dwelling on its obscurity, its unduly allegorical nature and, sometimes, on its want of earnestness. Heine, of all people, criticized the frivolity: '. . . das schauerliche Teufelsbündniß . . . endigt wie eine frivole Farce.' He added that the only good thing in this 'allegorical wilderness' was the Helena Act.[1] One of the many attacks made on *Faust 2* during the second half of the nineteenth century must be singled out because it is by a scientist and treats Faust as a man of science. This is Emil du Bois-Reymond's lecture 'Goethe und kein Ende' (Berlin, 1882). After maintaining that Part 1 is full of psychological implausibilities and complaining that Faust is there shown as making trivial use of his magical powers, du Bois-Reymond moves into the attack on Part 2 with a passage which was to become notorious:

Wie prosaisch es klinge, es ist nicht minder wahr, daß Faust, statt an Hof zu gehen, ungedecktes Papiergeld auszugeben, und zu den Müttern in die vierte Dimension zu steigen, besser gethan hätte, Gretchen zu heirathen, sein Kind ehrlich zu machen und Elektrisier-maschine und Luftpumpe zu erfinden . . .   (p. 16)

The foregoing pages have obviously not set out to give a balanced picture of the reception of *Faust 2* in the nineteenth century. I have concentrated on hostile attitudes because views such as these underlie most of the attempts to rewrite Part 2. In Germany Adolf Müller seems to have been the first in the field with his *Faust. Tragödie in fünf Acten. Als zweiter Theil zu Goethe's Faust* (1869). The work is clearly indebted to Fr. Th. Vischer's

---

[1] Some of the attacks on Goethe can be found in Schwerte. Gervinus, in his influential history of German literature, is severe on *Faust 2*. For Heine, see pp. 56 and 82 in the original edition of his *Faust*. Meanwhile, some well-meaning Protestant admirers of Goethe distorted *Faust 2* in order to show that it was, essentially, Christian in spirit. Examples: C. J. Th. Gantzer, 'Das Christliche in Goethe . . .' (1839), reprinted in *Geistige Feldzüge*, Berlin, 1857, 313ff; or P. Tube, *Die Faustsage und der religiös-sittliche Standpunkt in Göthe's Faust*, Dresden, 1869.

sketch for a possible 'new' Part 2,[1] intended, says Vischer, as a 'positive criticism' of the existing Part 2. Faust's salvation, Vischer argues, must be achieved through political activity, Faust taking the side of progress in a struggle for freedom. What, then, would be more natural than to cast Mephisto as a reactionary, opposing Faust in order to preserve a rotten status quo? Everything combines to lead one to the choice of the Reformation as the most appropriate historical setting. There follows a long sketch in which Faust is first seen in an agony of grief over Gretchen's death. He resolves to expiate his guilt through noble actions and is fired to assist in the Reformers' cause by a visitor who is like a 'poetic version' of Hutten. After an abortive and, as he later realizes, misguided attempt to further the popular cause by exercising influence on the powerful, Faust becomes a leader of the peasants. Mephisto, in various guises, seeks to trap him and drag him down anew, but he is saved in the end because each offence had been followed by a sincere attempt at betterment and because his life had culminated in a noble death for a worthy cause.

And so to Adolf Müller. The preamble to his tragedy expresses the sort of criticism that, as we have seen, was current at the time. Goethe's work, despite its greatness, remains a fragment because Faust's regeneration has not been satisfactorily depicted.

In warmer, lebensfrischer That muß Faust sich aufraffen . . . nicht etwa, wie es der alternde *Goethe* gewollt, mit einer Nützlichkeits-beschäftigung vor uns treten—nein! er soll aus seiner Theilnahm-losigkeit wieder heraus *sich zur reinen, thatkräftigen Menschenliebe bekehren*.

Faust hears of the Reformation and is enthusiastic. He joins Luther and offers his services(!). Exactly what he *does* in the Reformers' cause remains obscure, for after Luther's death he is disillusioned (temporarily at least) with the new church and desires to return to 'des Lebens Freudenstrom'—perhaps Müller hesitated to rewrite history to the extent of allowing Faust a major part in the struggles of the Reformation. Nevertheless, the usual and obvious objection to literary works which recklessly mingle history and fiction applies here; it is ludicrous to have Faust and Luther

---

[1] *Kritische Gänge*, neue Folge, Stuttgart, 1861, Heft 3, 135–78. Müller had been anticipated in France by Eugène Robin (*Livia*, 1836), a sentimental piece in which Faust sheds tears over Gretchen's fate and is finally saved by the power of love.

confront each other as friends, when we know what Luther thought of Dr. Faust. This play is in fact an unhappy combination of the most soft-centred 'salvation of Faust' type of work and a quasi-historical play celebrating the Reformation in crudely partisan terms.

In the latter part of the play Faust meets Margaretha who is, although he does not know it, his daughter by Gretchen(!), and they fall in love. Finally, Mephisto reveals Faust's incest and betrays him to the Inquisition, charging him with black magic. Faust renounces Mephisto and is freed from prison by his students. But he is by now near death and presently dies with a hymn to the Reformation and with prophesies of future enlightenment and progress on his lips. Mephisto claims his soul but is repulsed by Gabriel. So Faust is saved; why is not clear. (Müller did, in fact, have second thoughts and reworked his material in *Doctor Faust's Ende*, 1888. This new version is not a continuation of Goethe's Part 1, but begins at the beginning. There is thus no Gretchen and no daughter with whom to commit incest, so that Faust's nobility as a hero of the Reformation can shine forth much more brightly. Müller also inserted a new episode, showing Faust pleading the Reformers' cause at the court of Charles V, thus bringing his version nearer to what had been envisaged by Vischer.)

In his long dramatic poem, *Faust*, of 1869, Ferdinand Stolte too begins with a criticism of Goethe: due remorse as a prelude to betterment is lacking, Faust wallows in pagan beauty, the 'Catholic' ending is all wrong. . . . And so Stolte has ventured to rewrite the Second Part, retaining Goethe's Part 1 as the prelude, the given past. Stolte opens with the by now usual scene showing Faust's reactions to Gretchen's fate. (We later learn that he even spends his nights at her grave.) He now longs for faith, turning away from the 'curse of thought' and from the hedonism urged on him by Mephisto. He resolves to serve humanity and decides to do this by advancing money to the penurious Gutenberg, thus sharing the glory of having furthered the development of printing. (As always in such episodes, there is little link with the hard-headed Fust of history—see Chapter 5.) The ensuing parts of Stolte's poem transfer us to the political sphere, and show Faust working to restore a rightful ruler to a throne occupied by a fratricidal usurper. Since the work is strongly Protestant in spirit and since Part 3 shows Mephisto aiding tyrannical and reactionary forces also backed by Rome, it is possible that Vischer's influence is at work here too. Mephisto tries to tempt Faust in various ways (there is, for example, a variation on the Helen motif of the popular tradition), but Faust's newly won purity and strength of purpose are inviolable. So at the end Mephisto is defeated and Faust dies, full of optimistic visions of mankind's future, to be greeted by the *Erdseele* and by choruses of blessed spirits. Thus the formula for Faust's salvation is the already familiar one: remorse, renunciation of hedonism, political action on the side of progressive and humane forces. The work is remarkable not for the way in which Faust is saved but for the time it takes. There are council scenes of nearly a hundred pages; one of Faust's monologues fills fifteen. Even Mephisto, who ought to be terse, holds forth for six pages. The work is so long that Stolte himself advises the reader as to which 'didactic debates' can be cut at a first reading.

Stolte devotes much of the Preface to Part 2 to quoting favourable critical reactions to date. He tells us that he had read parts of the poem to Gutzkow, who had commented: 'Das ist ein vollkommen gelungner Wurf. . . . Sie machen es der Welt begreiflich, was sich Göthe hat entgehen lassen, indem er sich in seinem zweiten Theile in poetische Düfteleien verlor' (p. xi). Clearly, Gutzkow's hostility towards Goethe's Part 2 had completely clouded his professional judgement for, even by the standards of run-of-the-mill nineteenth-century poetic drama, Stolte's *Faust* is lamentable. But any stick was good enough to beat Goethe with.

Ferdinand von Feldegg's tragedy *Der neue Faust* (1902) is another work intended as a sequel to Goethe's Part 1. Appended to it is a 'reflection' on the Faust theme, in which Feldegg argues that Goethe's Part 2 does not satisfactorily work out the problems posed in Part 1. An appropriate sequel would have to show that Faust, in passing from pure knowledge to the practical application of knowledge, would necessarily involve himself in guilt: 'daß Fausts Charakter, indem er sich von der bloßen Erkenntnis zur Tat durchringt, eine Schuld auf sich ladet' (p. 145). (This is a noticeably less cheerful view than those of most other completers of *Faust*.) In Feldegg's play, Faust is reincarnated in contemporary Germany as a scientist, Dr. Heinrich. He wishes to demonstrate the primacy of soul in an age where various trends threaten to reduce it to a function or product of the physical. He tries to prove his ideas by means of highly dangerous hypnotic experiments on a young girl Klara, who, however, dies as a result of his final, most daring experiment. But in the epilogue, a debate between God and Mephisto, it is stated that this age, like all others, is filled with God's spirit and that the ruthless quest for knowledge that characterizes it is a phase in God's plan. The children of this age, as of all ages, participate in the general redemption of mankind through Christ. A vision of Calvary ends the work and we must suppose that Faust, too, is to be saved, although the treatment of his salvation seems curiously impersonal.

For all that the setting is contemporary and only Mephisto, the Lord and Faust/Heinrich are common to Goethe's Part 1 and Feldegg's play, there are sufficient references to Goethe to make it clear that this *is* a sequel. Klara is obviously intended as the Gretchen of this new Second Part. Like Gretchen, she abandons herself completely, yet not without an uneasy feeling that there is something sinful about her love; like Gretchen, she looks up to Faust in adoring half-comprehension; like Gretchen, she is destroyed by Faust, who raves at her fate and is mocked by Mephisto. But Goethe's situations have been taken over and his characters reincarnated in order to make such a wholly un-Goethean point that one cannot help feeling that the author would have been better advised to start from scratch with his own characters. We have already seen something similar in Rosenkranz, who virtually turned Goethe's Faust into a different person in order to save him according to his own recipe.

Ferdinand Avenarius's *Faust. Ein Spiel* (1919) is the best of the attempts to provide a new Part 2. It has its faults (lack of economy, too much rhetorical pathos, a more than usually humourless and self-obsessed Faust), but it stands far above anything yet discussed in this chapter.

The prologue shows the effect of Gretchen's death on Faust more forcefully and poetically than in any previous version.[1] Faust, in his misery, is persuaded by a monk to go to Rome in search of absolution, but comes to realize that he must himself expiate his sins; he cannot have them taken off his shoulders by another. After a Helen episode, which marks Faust's final turning

[1] For a short description, see E. M. Butler, p. 280.

away from the lusts of the flesh, we find him in conversation with Michelangelo, who seems to him the perfect example of a man who unquestioningly uses his gifts in the service of mankind (Act 1). The second Act depicts Faust in an unnamed German university town as the assistant of a Humanist professor of anatomy, who incurs the wrath of the Church for proclaiming that the earth goes round the sun. The professor is arrested and Faust sees that the new spirit of learning is threatened by a lack of freedom. So this Act is presumably intended to show Faust fired by the example of a man fearlessly dedicated to an ideal. But Faust's path will not be the pursuit of knowledge through research;[1] rather the furtherance of the cause of freedom, without which the new learning will wither.

And so, as often before, to the Peasants' Revolt (Acts 3 and 4). As in Vischer's sketch, we find Faust trying to lead the peasants towards moderation, while Mephisto, as a rival leader, encourages them to ever greater brutality and more savage reprisals. There follows a court scene in which (again as in Vischer's sketch) Faust tries to plead the peasants' cause before the Emperor. Act 4 closes with a scene in the Expressionist manner, in which Faust battles with an invisible Mephisto (the voice of denial) and defies him. In the final Act, Faust demands of Mephisto to know the future of the human race. Mephisto shows him in a vision all that is most bestial in human nature. This vision culminates in the apparition of a terrible face, distorted with fury and madness, which fills the horizon. This, says Mephisto, is the face of your 'sacred' humanity (p. 130). But the distortion gradually vanishes and is replaced by a peaceful expression; that is, the struggle between good and evil in man and the ultimate victory of good are played out on these features. The final words of the apparition are:

> Die *Gottheit* bin ich, die im Menschen *wird*.

—to which Faust rejoins:

> In *mir* auch wird!
> Wie sucht ich, Gott, nach dir,
> Und was mich suchen hieß,
> Warst du in mir! (p. 132)

---

[1] 'Du bist kein Forscher, Faust', says the Professor (p. 52)—rather oddly, one feels.

The sense in which Faust had previously described himself as a quester (*Sucher*—p. 38) is now made clear.

Other 'Second Parts' involving Faust's remorse, the redemptive effect of Gretchen's love, work in the service of humanity, and the repudiation of Titanism and hedonism include J. Ernstlieb's *Faust. Zweiter Teil* (*c.* 1884), F. Keim's *Mephistopheles in Rom* (1890) and R. A. Édon's *Mephisto* (1923). Keim and Édon again link Faust to events of the Reformation. The most recent reworking of Part 2 is A. Schmid's *Faust der Denker* (1952). The author's criticism of *Faust 2* is that Goethe represents Faust as turning away from thought to action. It may be noted that this criticism is only possible if one has a mental picture of Faust as a brooding intellectual—which hardly accords with the Faust of Goethe's Part 1—and if one postulates a dichotomy of thought and action quite foreign to Goethe's way of thinking.

We must now turn to a curious attempt to popularize Part 2. In his *Faust-Phantasie* (1920) C. P. Torbrech has, he informs us, retold Goethe's Part 2 because, as it stands, it is incomprehensible to the great mass of the people. Furthermore, the popular imagination cannot perceive any moral justice in the manner of Faust's salvation (*Einleitung*, pp. i–iii). So he, Torbrech, has tried to show 'wie heute . . . eine volkstümliche und mehr zeitgemäße Fassung des zweiten Teils möglich sei und auf das Volk wirken würde' (p. xiii). To enter into Torbrech's reasoning, one has to recall the many attempts, from the middle of the nineteenth century onwards, to establish Faust as a kind of symbol for the German spirit. Now if Faust is really the expression of the 'German soul', then the greatest of all German works devoted to him ought to be comprehensible to all Germans. Clearly, the tritons and cabiri, Proteus and Nereus, the great ants and sphinxes and griffons have to go. . . .

Two examples of Torbrech's methods will perhaps suffice. Where Goethe hints at the healing of Faust through nature in a scene of great poetic beauty ('Anmutige Gegend'), Torbrech fobs us off with a magic potion which induces forgetfulness. And where Goethe's Faust wins land from the sea, Torbrech's regains lost stores of gold from the sea-bed like any modern adventurer with his diving-kit and his dreams of sunken galleons. Torbrech is both trivial and vulgar compared with Goethe; the German people would be better off with the original Part 2 and a good commentary.

There have been several attempts to provide Goethe's completed *Faust* with yet a Third Part.[1] Most of the writers who did this were prompted by the feeling that Faust's salvation as presented by Goethe was undeserved: by the same motive that led many to rewrite Part 2, in fact. In his parody *Faust. Der Tragödie dritter Theil*, first published in 1862,[2] Fr. Th. Vischer makes all the main criticisms of *Faust 2* which we have already encountered in commentaries, pamphlets and, by implication, in serious Faust plays. He jibes at the obscurity by setting Faust himself to explain the work and showing him quite incapable of the task. He makes the familiar points about the abstraction, the symbolism, the excess of learning and the 'Catholic' ending. But the main point of attack, and the point at which Vischer's parody touches the serious continuations most nearly, concerns Faust's salvation. Mephisto is made to say:

> Der Mensch hat ja im Grunde nichts gethan,
> Und dafür langt er nun im Himmel an? (50f)

So Faust must pass various tests to make himself worthy of Heaven: he is set as schoolmaster over unruly boys and forced to interpret *Faust* to them; he is put on a miserable diet while Mephisto and his cook tempt him with all sorts of delectable foods, and so on. Implicit at all times is the view that Goethe had made it all too easy for Faust. For all its lightheartedness, Vischer's 'Third Part' makes this point better than do most of the serious attempts. Some of these may indeed be passed over very quickly. Both C. A. Linde's *Faust . . . iii. Theil zu Goethe's Faust* (1887) and Hannah Stahn's *Faustus redivivus* (1921) seem to have been prompted by the feeling that Goethe had been too ready to save Faust in his wickedness. In both pieces Faust is brought back to earth and the struggle for his soul is fought out

---

[1] The first attempt (anon., 'Der Dritte Theil des Faust', 1838) is the merest fragment. F. W. Gubitz's 'Faust und Mephisto in Mitte des neunzehnten Jahrhunderts' of *c.* 1840 lays the chief stress on Mephisto, taking up Goethe's point that the greatest danger to mankind is inertia and that the Devil's task is to spur men to activity. In the political field, progress will come only through unrest. Hence Mephisto's task is to ensure this.

[2] For a zestful account of this work, see E. M. Butler, pp. 311-20.

anew. In Karl Zapfe's *Faust. Der Tragödie dritter Teil* (1929) a reincarnated Faust debates with Mephisto; the work is one long discussion piece. Zapfe's conclusion seems to be that Faust is doomed to wander, seeking knowledge in ever new incarnations. If this reading is correct (and Zapfe's style is very obscure), this is virtually the only Goethe continuation in which Faust is not saved or at least brought to some optimistic insight.

The best serious attempt to devise a sequel to Part 2 is by a Russian, A. V. Lunacharski, whose *Faust and the City* was written in 1908 and published, after pruning and recasting, in 1918. Lunacharski, a revolutionary, takes as his starting-point the situation in Goethe's Act 5, where Faust dreams of a community of free men living on the land which he has reclaimed from the sea. Lunacharski permits himself the fancy that Faust lives on to found his city, Trotzburg. In the play, we find him as Duke of Trotzburg, a benevolent despot, still working paternally for the people's good but without much understanding for the growing desire for self-determination. The profligacy and arrogance of his son Faustulus trigger off a popular uprising led by a worker, Gabriel. Faustulus is defeated and the city comes under a form of popular tribunal. Meanwhile Faust, faced with the prospect of limited power under this new constitution, has chosen to stand aside altogether. His daughter, Faustina, has allied herself to the popular cause by marrying Gabriel.

Mephisto, having failed to conquer the rebellion with Faustulus as his tool, now tries to undermine it from within by appealing both to the selfishness of the merchant classes and to lumpen-proletariat extremists, but is foiled by Gabriel's good sense. At the end, Faust is reconciled to his daughter and son-in-law; he lives to see a grandson by whom the struggle will be maintained and dies after having bequeathed his invention of a steam-engine to the city, to assist in the conquest of nature and the easing of man's lot.

To pretend that Faust never died is no doubt as great a liberty as bringing him back from Heaven to start all over again. But once one has decided to swallow this, it can be seen that the play is much closer to Goethe's spirit than any other Second or Third Part yet discussed. Faust's dream of founding a community on freshly-won land is treated seriously and with respect. But Luna-charski also shows that merely to have founded the city is not enough; freedom (here in a strictly political sense) must constantly be won again (cf. *Faust*, 11575f) and man must constantly be ready to accept and respond to a ceaseless process of change (again, here, in a political sense—but the thought is Goethean).

It was a happy touch and one that showed considerable understanding of Goethe's work, to present Faust at the beginning as somewhat patrician and paternalistic in attitude, only slowly coming to accept the new revolutionary ideas. (One need only think of Faust's possessive attitude towards 'his' future kingdom in Goethe's Act 5 and the paternalism displayed in 'Vor dem Tor'.) Two rather intriguing coincidences remain to be mentioned: Lunacharski's 'Faust 3' achieves something like a twentieth-century working out of the central idea in Vischer's Faust plan (Faust allied to the people's cause), while the bequest of the steam-engine recalls du Bois-Reymond's comment that Faust should have employed his talents and powers in the service of technology (see above).[1]

It now remains to discuss a handful of works which in some way continue, or adapt, or vary Goethe's *Faust* but which do not belong in any of the categories already described.

Artur Gstöttner's *Der Wanderer* (1933) is, according to the author, an attempt to restate Goethe's *Faust* in contemporary terms, a sort of anniversary tribute:

> Was würden heut nach hundert Jahren
> Ein Faust und ein Mephisto sagen. (p. 7)

Gstöttner starts with a monologue in which Faust, disillusioned with learning, summons Death, who comes only to mock him. Here the Faust tradition and the Everyman tradition are joined:

DER TOD: Mich ruft man nicht!
Zu kommen ungerufen ist meine Pflicht! (p. 16)

Faust must live on. There follow Gstöttner's variations on the 'Schülerszene' and on the Gretchen episode (Gretchen is again

[1] H. von Beguingnolles' *Hilario* (1849) is not a continuation of Goethe's *Faust* in any normal sense of the word, but it is certainly a sequel to it. The Devil, furious at having lost Faust, resolves to damn Hilario, a contented man, by destroying his happiness and causing him to lose his faith. But the attempt fails. The last '*Faust 3*' seems to be A. Großmann's *Faust* of 1934, in which Faust, returning to earth, is saved largely because of his pure love for Roselieb, a reincarnation of Gretchen. The play is chiefly remarkable for the bathetic treatment of Roselieb who, at one point, recommends herbal tea to cure Faust of his *Weltschmerz* (p. 72).

ruined by Faust). The place of the 'Walpurgisnacht' is taken by a visit to Rome. This then, the first part of *Der Wanderer*, roughly corresponds to Goethe's Part 1. In Part 2, Faust, the Wanderer, is forced to witness instances of man's greed, brutality, and corruption, as the Devil (here called 'der Verneiner' but unmistakably related to Goethe's Mephisto) tries to shake his faith in the goodness of man and the justice of the world-order. But when Faust is at last fetched by death, it is to be saved, for his faith and optimism have always resisted these assaults.

The first thing to say about Gstöttner's Faust version is that, despite his claim, there is nothing particularly up to date about it, apart from a few details (aeroplane instead of magic cloak, etc.). Gstöttner, like most authors of a serious work on Faust, is concerned with perennial questions regarding the mysteries and limitations of human existence, man's relationship with nature and with God, the conflict of hope and despair and so on. It is a measure of this that the scenes in which 'der Verneiner' tries to wreck Faust's optimism are strongly reminiscent of Klinger. Changes in the manner of interpreting man's inhumanity to man, of which one might reasonably expect to find traces in a work written nearly a century and a half after Klinger, are lacking.

But if one is prepared to accept the fact that Gstöttner hacks away at these perennial problems as if Darwin and Freud, to name no others, had never existed, the work can be read with pleasure. Stylistically it is uneven, but in general Gstöttner is abler than most of the rash spirits considered in this chapter. He is, for instance, one of the few who have managed to hit off something of the tone of Goethe's Mephisto. Here is 'der Verneiner' mocking Faust's enthusiasm for nature in the scene 'Die Schlucht':

> Im Wasserfall, im Lärm, Gespritze und Getöse
> Ich finde keine Spur von einer Größe! . . .
> —Doch Ihr seid inkurabel, weil Ihr prompt erbaut
> Darob, daß Euer Gott Euch Wasser in das Antlitz haut!
> (224f)

The chief fault of the piece is that—although a heavenly choir sings of Faust as

> Die Seele, die nach vielem Ringen
> Heimkehrend wir zum Lichte bringen   (p. 242)—

Faust's salvation is a good deal more difficult to understand than it is in Goethe; the struggles referred to are no more than battles of words with the spirit of denial. Faust actually does less than in almost any version known to me.[1]

Michl Ehbauer's *Der Faust in der Krachledern. Als Tragikomödie volkstümlich nachgeschrieben* (1960) is a curiosity:

> I setz den Fall—es kunnt ja sei—
> Der Goethe war a Bayer gwen
> Und fallert eahm des gleiche ei
> Und war mit uns erst heut am Lebn—
> Wia hätt er da den Faust wohl geschriebn? (p. 28)

So this play is not a Faust parody but a semi-serious version of *Faust* in popular, local vein. It is made up of scenes which are metamorphoses of the main scenes of Goethe's Part 1, so that the general shape is unmistakably that of Goethe's work—but Goethe retold from the point of view of a Bavarian local patriot and a good Catholic. The cosmogony of *Faust*, with all its implications concerning Mephisto's role and the interrelationship of good and evil, is abandoned in favour of more orthodox attitudes, the anti-Catholic quips are cut out and a happy ending is provided. Wendelin (Valentin) is only wounded in the fight; he recovers and is reconciled with Gretchen, who has meanwhile borne Faust's child and is bringing it up. Faust repents of his misdeeds in a churchyard scene in which he talks with the spirits of the departed who urge him to virtue:

FAUST: I glaub, iatz lern ich wieder betn,
Ma muaß bloß mit de Toten reden. (p. 215)

He returns, makes his peace with Wendelin, and the play ends with the driving-off of Luze (Mephisto) and with a Bavarian wedding.

Der Faust in der Krachledern has a certain innocent charm and it may seem churlish to criticize it. But Ehbauer does fall into the trap awaiting anyone who tries to rewrite a national work in a local dialect. The Bavarian versions of serious passages are likely to strike the reader as funny. Not only does God speak in the Bavarian dialect but the *Erdgeist*, when making itself manifest on Bavarian soil, does the same:

[1] W. Webel's *Ein Spiel vom Doktor Faust* (1951) is another redoing of Goethe's *Faust*, but feeble and sentimental in comparison with *Der Wanderer*.

Du möchst di wohl mit mir vergleicha?
Woaßt was, i wer mi wieder schleicha.
Du spinnst komplett, mehr sag i net.   (p. 34)

A last item, although not the last chronologically, is even more
of a curiosity: the poem 'Faustulus' by the Bohemian poet, Emil
Frida (writing under the pseudonym of Jaroslav Vrchlický).[1]
In this poem Faustulus (Gretchen's son by Faust) survives and
is brought up by the jailer, a former admirer of Gretchen. The
boy finds joy and liberation from the daily round in music. One
day in old age, as if seized by his father's spirit, he breaks out, in
the middle of a church service, into a wild organ improvisation
which seems like a musical summing up of Faust's demand for
totality of experience. At the end he is found dead at the instrument. . . . This poem was set as a *Melodrama*—that is, to be de-
claimed to a piano accompaniment—by J. B. Foerster.[2] The
music is characterized by a naïve determination to be 'pictorial',
to match each motif in the poem with descriptive or evocative
keyboard writing.

If one sets aside poems, fragments, parodies, burlesques and so
on, and takes only serious, full-length works into consideration,
it actually seems to be the case that, between 1830 and 1900, more
authors elected to rewrite or continue Goethe than attempted
independent works on the theme. Goethe's *Faust* was a vast
monument. One could not escape it or lose it from sight for very
long. Even many of those who disapproved heartily of some of the
views and values it expressed found that they could not free
themselves from it sufficiently to rely on their own invention.

What is one to make of a chapter of German literary history
in which a whole platoon of minor talents have refused to let
Germany's most famous poet do what he liked with his own most
famous character? Faust has laboured with Gutenberg at the
printing presses, has led the Peasants' Revolt, been present at the
Sack of Rome (Keim) and has written a pamphlet in support of the
Reformation. He has been incarcerated in the prisons of the Inquisition and has even been blown up in his own castle (Linde).
He has been put on a diet in Heaven and prescribed herbal tea on

[1] Dating from about 1888, the poem was translated into German by E. Albert.
[2] Published by Otto Janne, Leipzig, n.d. The style of the music and the layout
of the cover suggest the late 1890s.

earth, has spent his nights weeping at Gretchen's grave and his days as a schoolmaster, trying to interpret his own destiny to a mob of urchins. He has had to make and (worse) listen to some of the most abstract and turgid speeches imaginable.

Certain motifs recur frequently. In practically every case we sense the strong conviction that Goethe's Faust had not been made to suffer due remorse after Gretchen's ruin and death. (We know now that Goethe simply took this remorse for granted, but the resentment felt by many in the nineteenth century, when they found the prison scene followed by 'Anmutige Gegend', is at least understandable.) Nearly all reworkings and continuations of Goethe follow up Faust's remorse with his renunciation of hedonism in general and the flesh in particular, and with some attempt on his part to serve humanity. Often his sphere of activity is political and, where the setting is the Reformation, the tone tends to be crudely anti-Catholic. Titanism is repudiated and there is often a return to some more or less orthodox religious faith.

This last point concerning religious belief brings us to the central absurdity of most of these versions. Nearly all the authors discussed in this chapter seem either ignorant of, or impatient with, Goethe's views on man and the gods, good and evil, immortality, moral responsibility, and so on. The main point at issue was always the feeling that Faust's salvation, as shown by Goethe, is undeserved. But this is a semantic confusion, for what Goethe understood by salvation was something quite unlike the more conventional sense in which most of his critics would have used the word. The argument is thus reduced to the level of: 'I disagree with the salvation of Faust in Goethe because it is not what I understand by "salvation" and I resent his use of Christian symbols because that is not how I would use them.'

Now, clearly, anyone is free to disagree with Goethe and, having disagreed with him, to write a new *Faust*, putting forward a different view. This is what many did. But to disagree with the basic ideas of Goethe's *Faust* and to express that disagreement in a form which involved taking over Goethe's characters and their past—that is, taking over an elaborate machinery which only makes sense in terms of Goethe's world-view in order to put forward a different world-view—that was ill-advised.

One recalls Fr. Th. Vischer's description of his Faust sketch as 'positive criticism' of Goethe. But it is arguable that a 'Dramatic

Poem' or a 'Tragedy in Five Acts' is a very impractical form of criticism. The reader's response is made complicated and difficult. For he is invited to follow the action, to link it to the given past of Goethe's Part 1, and to compare critically the new treatment of Faust's redemption with what Goethe had done. New (or resurrected) characters and new twists in the action must be constantly related to characters and episodes in Goethe's work. Certainly the reader must have the parallel actions of the old and the new Second Parts constantly in his mind if the new continuation is to be fully meaningful to him. And there is the further complication that most of the continuers or rewriters misunderstood, or only partially understood, various key issues in Goethe. (The question of salvation, discussed above, is one such; another is the exact meaning of Faust's wager with Mephisto.) I cannot feel that any work discussed in this chapter, with the possible exceptions of those by Avenarius and Lunacharski, is a success either in its own right as a work of literature or as 'positive criticism' of Goethe. If it is possible to generalize, these reworkings prove that the best thing for the budding author of a *Faust* to do is not to subordinate his invention to that of another man, but to start afresh. Most Faust versions of any value since 1832 have, in fact, done just that.

8

Faust and Don Juan

(i) *Faust and Don Juan come together*

> '. . . jeder Don Juan endet als Faust und jeder Faust als
> Don Juan.'
>
> (Hebbel)

HEBBEL'S remark may seem odd, at first, in view of the apparently total contrast between a Faust brooding in his study and a Don Juan lurking under a balcony with a mandoline. (It cannot, surely, simply be intended to mean that Faust turns from speculation to the pursuit of woman and that Don Juan ends defying God.) Yet a link has been perceived time and time again. For Carl Helbig, Faust plus Don Juan could even be equated with Everyman: 'Gewissermaßen setzt sich jeder Mensch aus Faust und Don Juan zusammen'.[1] Most critics see the convergence of the two figures as dating from the Romantic era, following E. T. A. Hoffmann's famous interpretation of Mozart's *Don Giovanni*. But, in fact, Franz Horn had already associated Faust and Don Juan in an article of 1805, appearing in the periodical *Luna* (see below), and there are works of literature in which the two characters are brought together before Hoffmann wrote on *Don Giovanni*. To see how this came about, it is necessary to know something of the growth of the Don Juan legend.

El Burlador de Sevilla, generally attributed to Tirso de Molina, was first published in or before 1630. Unlike the *Historia von D. Johann Fausten*, it does not appear to have been based, even very loosely, on an actual individual or on actual events, although it may well include a generalized portrait of a certain type of rich young profligate to be encountered in Spain in the early seventeenth century. *El Burlador* seems to be the source, direct or

---

[1] Carl Helbig, 'Die Don-Juan-Sage . . .', in *Westermann's Jahrbücher*, xli, Brunswick, 1876–7, p. 650.

indirect, of all subsequent Don Juan works, thus holding the place in the history of that legend that 'Spies' occupies with regard to Faust. All works which show Don Juan impersonating a girl's betrothed or lover in order to seduce her and killing her father when he arrives on the scene, all works which feature the wooing of a fisher girl and/or a rustic beauty, all works which depict Don Juan confronting the statue of his victim, the invitation to supper, the call to repentance and the taking of the statue's hand—all are indebted, although often very indirectly, to *El Burlador*. The characterization of Don Juan in Tirso is largely dictated by the author's didactic purpose: the play sets out to show how wickedness and the failure to heed repeated warnings are finally punished. Tirso's Don Juan is a womanizer both out of lust and from delight in deception as such. He is proud and self-assertive, at odds with morality and religion, a reprobate who thinks that he can always put off repentance for a little longer. But, like the author of the first Faustbook, Tirso created a character destined to fascinate as well as shock.

From Spain the Don Juan theme quickly passed to Italy. Here Don Giovanni becomes yet more depraved and arrogant than the original Spanish character, while the part of the servant is expanded and comes to involve a good deal of clowning.[1] By the 1650s the theme had been taken into the repertoire of the *Commedia dell' arte*, and a Don Giovanni play became popular in Italy and France. From these Italian pieces, one line of development goes via seventeenth-century French theatre into popular stage plays and puppet plays; another line leads directly to Italian *opera buffa*.

In seventeenth-century France the Don Juan theme proved so popular that four versions were produced within twenty years. As far as their plots are concerned, these versions are all heavily indebted to Italian sources. The plays of Dorimon and Villiers, both entitled *Le Festin de Pierre* and first published in 1659 and 1660 respectively, depict Don Juan as yet more wicked, callous, violent, and blasphemous than in previous versions.

---

[1] Cf. *Il Convitato de Pietra* by J. A. Cicognini (1640s). There was at least one other mid-seventeenth-century play dealing with Don Juan which has not survived.

Molière's *Dom Juan*, first performed in 1665 but not published until 1682, is much less of a morality play and much more of a psychological examination of the main character than anything to date. This Dom Juan is a complex character. He is brave and has a certain sense of honour (although very limited in its application, one must confess). He is a fearless rationalist, doubting the existence of God and Devil alike, believing only 'that two and two are four'. He gives alms, but for the love of humanity not for love of God. With Molière, as in the case of early treatments of the Faust legend, we must be careful not to allow anachronistic judgements to colour our interpretation: Molière is undoubtedly concerned with showing the arrogance and the excesses to which intellectual boldness and scepticism could lead. For, coupled with these good, or partially good qualities, are evil ones. Dom Juan is a hypocrite, an unscrupulous libertine and a moral sadist. Yet to the end, as supernatural powers gradually break down his rationalistic and anthropocentric convictions, he retains a certain obstinate nobility. He remains true to himself.[1]

When we turn to the popular Don Juan pieces played in Germany and Austria in the seventeenth and eighteenth centuries, we are rather better off than in the case of the Faust legend, since both old stage pieces and puppet plays dealing with Don Juan have survived. In the 1680s and 1690s, German versions of Molière were being played, and throughout the eighteenth century there are various more sensational Don Juan plays based usually on French, possibly also on Italian sources. They all contain the traditional murder of the Commander, plus some kind of rustic interlude, plus the final invitation to the statue, and Don Juan's descent, unrepentant, into Hell. In these German plays, Don Juan grows steadily more evil and violent, committing wanton and treacherous murders, even killing his own father.[2]

---

[1] Rosimond's *Le nouveau Festin de Pierre* (first performed 1669) and Thomas Shadwell's *The Libertine* (1675) are by comparison crudely sensational plays which present Don Juan as a monster of depravity.

[2] The motif of patricide enters in the puppet plays. It had occurred in Shadwell, of course, but *The Libertine* is aside from the tradition that leads from France to the popular pieces in German. Rosimond *may* have intended it to be understood that Dom Juan killed his father, but Carrille's 'faire mourir' and Dom Juan's reply are ambiguous (see i, 2, pp. 327f).

I have a given a brief account of the line of development which runs from the early Italian plays on the subject of Don Juan, through France, to the popular stage and puppet theatre in Germany and Austria. There is another line which leads via Italian comedies and operas to da Ponte and Mozart. Anyone familiar with the French Don Juan plays and the naïve popular pieces deriving from them will immediately notice a difference between these works and da Ponte's libretto: da Ponte's Don Giovanni is nowhere near as outrageous as the others. He kills once, but honourably, in a duel and only after trying to warn off his adversary. There is nothing here remotely like the treacherous killings in the German puppet plays. Again, he is a hedonist, but without any trace of the moral sadism which is present in Molière's Dom Juan. As far as Germany was concerned, most early performances of Mozart's opera were in translation and many productions imported extra comic scenes (in spoken dialogue) from the puppet plays of Don Juan. By 1800 or so, the majority of Germans, if they knew of Don Juan at all, will have encountered him in puppet plays or in somewhat popularized and vulgarized versions of the Mozart/da Ponte opera.

It will have been seen that up to the end of the eighteenth century the legends of Faust and Don Juan develop in rather similar ways. Each begins as a denunciation of arrogance and godlessness, a solemn warning to the unrepentant sinner. Each undergoes a long process of popularization. Each is 'reclaimed' for literature in the late eighteenth century: Faust through Lessing and the *Stürmer and Dränger*, Don Juan, as will presently be seen, through Mozart's opera and its interpreters. The Faust tradition has no Molière but otherwise the developments run parallel. Furthermore, in the popular tradition the treatments of the Faust and Don Juan themes become increasingly similar, seeming to invite a comparison of the two 'heroes'. The characteristic German *Volksstücke* and puppet plays are mixtures of sensational material, comedy, and moralizing. In one Don Juan puppet play the traditional call to repentance by the statue was clearly not felt to be enough; an angelic exhortation, copied from the puppet plays of Dr. Faust, has been introduced. I give it here, together with a typical speech from Faust's guardian angel, by way of comparison:

Faust	*Don Juan*
Doctor Faust, du sollst dich bekehren,/Denn du hast die höchste Zeit!/Gott wird dir ja wiederum geben/Und dir schenken die Seligkeit.	Don Juan, Dich bekehre, weil es noch heute heißt, daß der Himmel Dir gewähre, einen guten frommen Geist; . . . der Himmel wird sich Deiner erbarmen, Dich aufnehmen in seine Armen.[1]

In some Don Juan versions Don Juan utters a lament very similar to Faust's traditional *Weheklag* in the chapbooks and puppet plays.[2] From here it was only a short step to the economical device of making one lament do for both characters. We find this in the Faust and Don Juan puppet plays given by E. Wiepking in the mid-nineteenth century. (The style of the lament and the Baroque theme of *Weltflucht* suggest, as so often with puppet plays recorded in the last century, a tradition going back to very much older plays.) Here is the lament, identical in the two pieces, except for minor details of spelling and punctuation:

> Verfluchte Lust der bösen Welt,
> Wie bald bist du vergangen,
> Die Anmuthsrose welkt und fällt,
> Die Dornen bleiben hangen.
> Verfluchter Trieb, der mich verführt
> Und meine Wohlfahrt hat zerstört.
> Weh Dem, der mich verführte.
> Die Fröhlichkeit ist nun dahin
> Und Höllenflammen in meinem Sinn,
> Kein Kühlen wird verspüret . . .[3]

What is more important than such interesting but, in the last resort, superficial similarities is that the ruling characteristics of Faust and Don Juan are played down in such a way that the differences between the two become blurred. In the puppet play Don Juan is represented in the first place as a violent, treacherous and blasphemous person rather than as a womanizer. Even where women play a major part, there is little stress on indiscriminate

---

[1] *Der Schutzgeist des Johann Doctor Faust*, pp. 184f: Strasbourg puppet play of Don Juan, Scheible, iii, 758. Most Faust pieces have a warning song similar to the one quoted here.
[2] E.g. in the early eighteenth-century version *Das steinerne Gastmahl* . . . , Act iii: see Bibliography, section ix.
[3] Both in Engel, *Deutsche Puppenkomödien*. Faust = viii, 55; Don Juan = iii, 80.

wenching. In the Augsburg version Don Juan loves Donna Marillis *and wants to marry her*. Even the Strasbourg play, in which two women figure, emphasizes Don Juan the sinner and killer rather than Don Juan the sexual libertine. However, the oddest puppet play of Don Juan is the Ulm version, which takes up and develops Don Juan's traditional violence and wickedness without *any* hint of his traditional lusting after women. In this play there is no mention of any woman except Don Juan's sister! The lurid deeds and the magical ending are what survive— the skeleton without the motivation. But the Ulm play goes still further; it substitutes a conjuration scene for the traditional statue episode. Don Juan sends Hans Wurst, his servant, to order a meal at the nearest inn, a hostelry which happens to be situated in a churchyard. He wishes to invite the spirits of the dead to supper to see if they can accept such an invitation:

Nun werde ich sehen, ob die entleibten Geister vermögend sind, bei mir zu erscheinen; ich werde sie also einladen auf eine Mahlzeit. Holla, ihr Geister, erscheint bei mir!   (p. 765)

The spirit of Don Juan's father appears and issues his counter-invitation. He demands Don Juan's hand on this, and the terrible grasp of the spirit-hand signals, as in most traditional versions of this legend, Don Juan's descent into Hell. The ending, then, is the expected one but the appearance of the spirit in the first place is motivated in a curiously 'faustian' way—in terms of what appears to be pure intellectual curiosity on Don Juan's part.[1] Conversely, some popular Faust versions include a scene set in a churchyard, in which Faust disinters the corpse of his father in order to use the bones for conjuring.[2] The setting and the appalling manifestation of filial impiety bring the parallel Don Juan tradition to mind. Members of the audience could be forgiven for wondering which piece they had strayed into!

What of Faust's motivation? As has been said, there is in the puppet plays very little stress on learning. What causes Faust to enter on the pact is desire for fame, wealth, power—and love.

---

[1] This may derive from a motif in Dorimon: see below, p. 181. Or it may simply have been suggested by the conjuration scenes in the plays of Dr. Faustus.

[2] E.g. *Fausts letzter Tag*, given by Sophie Seipp in the Landstraßer Theater, Vienna: see E. K. Blümml and G. Gugitz, *Alt-Wiener Thespiskarren*, Vienna, 1925, p. 265.

There is a record of a Faust puppet play given by gypsies in Swabian villages in the early nineteenth century, in which Faust is drawn to the Devil and into the pact *solely* by love. And, in several puppet plays, it is his enslavement to the flesh that keeps him damned when he is almost persuaded to repent.[1]

So Faust and Don Juan were both frequently to be encountered in popular stage pieces and puppet plays which presented them, primarily, as fascinatingly wicked and rebellious characters who finally received their due punishment. When we bear in mind the way in which the differences between the two characters were played down and remember, too, the strong *external* (structural and stylistic) features which the German puppet plays have in common, it is easy to see how parallels came to be drawn even before the Romantic idealization of Don Juan. To put the matter at its simplest: a puppet play about Dr. Faust and one about Don Juan (chosen at random) can instantly be seen as very much more similar to one another in all ways than, say, *El Burlador* and the original *Faustbuch*, or Molière's *Dom Juan* and Marlowe's *Faustus*. The differences had seemingly been narrowed, the pieces existed in the same popular theatrical forms, sometimes side by side in the same repertoire. The first explicit link between the two legends was made, as far as I know, by Franz Horn, writing in 1805: 'Faust und Don Juan sind die Gipfel der modernen christlich poetischen Mythologie.'[2] Horn goes on to refer specifically to Goethe's Faust and Mozart's Don Giovanni, but I think it virtually certain that the strong correspondence between Faust and Don Juan in the popular tradition, especially in the puppet theatre, must have helped him to make the connection. In his insistence on Mozart's *Don Giovanni* and his engaging, if slightly callous, remark that Don Giovanni's descent into Hell is not to be regretted, since it is accompanied by such 'eternal harmonies',[3] Horn seems to prepare the way for E. T. A. Hoffman who, as we shall see, bases his interpretation of *Don Giovanni* intuitively on the music, more or less ignoring what the libretto actually says.

[1] For the play given by gypsies, see A. Zoller, *Bilder aus Schwaben*, Stuttgart, 1834, p. 12; for a Faust damned because of lust, see the puppet play edited by Hamm, 1850, p. 61.

[2] Franz Horn, 'Andeutungen für Freunde der Poesie' in *Luna, ein Taschenbuch auf das Jahr 1805*, Leipzig, 1805, p. 322.

[3] Ibid.

The first attempt to put Faust and Don Juan together into one work is Niklas Vogt's drama *Der Färberhof oder die Buchdruckerei in Maynz*, 1809. In fact, Vogt manages to combine the two in one character! In his Preface, he talks of 'Mozarts Dom Juan . . . , welcher so viele Ähnlichkeit mit dem sogenannten Doktor Faust hatte . . .'. (The form 'Dom Juan' suggests one of the early German translations of *Don Giovanni*, most of which, as has been mentioned, incorporated extra comic scenes from the Don Juan puppet plays. So, since Vogt will undoubtedly also have been acquainted with one or other of the puppet plays of Dr. Faust, the comparison is not far-fetched.)

In Vogt, then, Faust and Don Juan are the same person. Faust is Faust for as long as he pursues truth and Don Juan when he turns to sensual pleasures. The fact that Vogt still subscribes to the old belief that Dr. Faust was identical with the printer Fust further complicates the situation; in the list of characters we find the truly vertiginous entry: 'Faust, Erfinder der Buchdruckerei, unter dem Nahmen Dom Juan.' In Faust's opening monologue, Vogt has tried to achieve this synthesis. Faust, feeling that printing ('gemeines Handwerk') is beneath him, longs for knowledge, fame, riches, and love. And here there are clear reminders of Don Juan:

> Warum soll mich ein lang vergessenes Versprechen
> Von Liebe an ein Mädchen ewig fesseln,
> Da mir der schönsten Weiber Huld entgegen lächelt?
>
> (p. 125)

Again, when Faust gloats over the benefits which magic seems to offer him, he dreams both of 'schöne Weiber/In reizenden Gestalten' and of 'der Wissenschaften/Noch unbekannte Regionen' (pp. 150f).

But any attempt to put two such characters inside one skin is almost bound to fail, as Vogt's treatment of the pact shows. Early in the play Faust had been visited by Saints Hildegard, Catherine, Elisabeth, and Cecilia, representing, respectively, theology, philosophy, law, and poetry. These he had found wanting:

> Was soll dies alles mir? Ich suchte
> Bei euch die Wahrheit und die Wissenschaft,
> Und ihr verweiset mich in's Reich der Träume? (p. 148)

So he had turned to magic. At this moment we would expect the conjuration and the pact. But the pact is held over until the first 'Don Juan' episode, the murder of the Commander:

> Nun bleibet mir die Wahl nicht mehr. Ich muß
> Dem Teufel mich ergeben, um mich hier
> Aus dieser Stadt zu retten, wo man mich
> Auf jedem Schritte schon verfolgt. (p. 159)

This is obviously satisfactory neither for the faustian side of his character (having nothing to do with the 'Four Faculties' scene) nor for the Don Juan in him (for no self-respecting Don Juan of drama, opera or puppet play had ever needed magical assistance to escape from a tight corner).

There would be no point in pursuing the extravagant plot of *Der Färberhof* in detail. The piece has its historical interest as one of the earliest attempts to show a parallel between Don Juan and Faust. But Vogt is incapable of working out coherently the transition from speculation (Faust) to hedonism (Don Juan), let alone conveying any sense of a unified character. He simply gives us an indigestible mixture of the two legends. And one major trait which could and should properly bind Faust and Don Juan together—the reckless and arrogant determination to be true to oneself—of this there is no adequate working out in Vogt, though there are hints enough in da Ponte.[1]

In the Romantic era both Faust and Don Juan were represented as something very near tragic heroes; their ruling characteristics, previously regarded as wicked, were now shown as manifestations of man's divine discontent. The Romantic Fausts have been discussed; the Romantic Don Juan was virtually created by E. T. A. Hoffman in his short tale 'Don Juan. Eine fabelhafte Begebenheit . . .' of 1813. Hoffmann's point of departure seems to have been a disparity, or supposed disparity, between the levels of significance of da Ponte's libretto and Mozart's music. If one looks at the libretto without reading any deeper meaning into it, he argues, one can hardly comprehend how Mozart came to write such music. Unlike Hoffman, we might today prefer to argue that

---

[1] Plot summaries of Vogt can be found in Dédéyan, ii, 198ff and in Weinstein pp. 96f. Another early attempt to link Don Juan with Faust may be seen in C. A. Vulpius' novel, *Don Juan der Wüstling*, 1805, in which Don Juan turns out to have made a pact with the Devil.

much of the greatness of *Don Giovanni* lies in the perfect matching of words and music, but it is not too difficult to see how Hoffmann arrived at his view. If one allowed oneself to become too concerned with the surface extravagancies and improbabilities of the plot, there might indeed—especially if one happened to be of an out-and-out romantic temperament—appear to be a great gulf between words and music.[1]

What is this deeper meaning, hinted at in the music? Man, says Hoffmann, has intimations of transcendental values. The conflict between the real and the ideal is the essence of mortal life. Don Giovanni comes to believe (or is made to believe by the powers of evil) that the ideal is to be found in love, that somewhere there must be a woman who could help him to achieve here on earth the highest happiness (which, in reality, man knows only as a vague longing and which can be realized only in another world). So Don Giovanni goes from one woman to the next but is always disappointed because none lives up to the ideal. Finally he falls into cynicism and avenges himself—through his arts of seduction—on the sex which, he thinks, has failed him.

Anna is Giovanni's opposite, 'ein göttliches Weib', pure and incorruptible. Hoffmann supposes that she had been destined by Heaven to be Giovanni's mate. But he finds her too late and so can only seduce her(!). Turbulent passions have been aroused in her and she now thinks only of revenge. Although she had once thought that she loved Ottavio, she is now indifferent to him.

The first thing that must be stressed in any consideration of this reading of *Don Giovanni* is that it is an imaginative interpretation suggested by the music. It cannot be insisted on too strongly that Hoffman's Don Giovanni is not da Ponte's. (Neither is his Donna Anna, for that matter.) Da Ponte's Don Giovanni is not an embodiment of tragic *Zerrissenheit* but an unscrupulous hedonist whose charm, however, probably appeals to most of us against our will. He justifies his libertinage not by an appeal to any transcendental ideal of womanhood, but by an unproblematic sensuality which rests on the affirmation of 'natural' appetites ('sai ch'elle [le donne] per me son necessarie più del pan che mangio'). His toast: 'Vivan le femmine! Viva il buon vino!

---

[1] Hoffmann describes a performance in Italian, but he will almost certainly have seen one or other of the German versions too, with extra comic scenes imported from the puppet plays.

sostegno e gloria d'umanità'[1] carries implications radically
different from the dualistic view of life on which Hoffmann's
characterization rests.

Dédéyan roundly says that Don Juan was transformed into
Faust by Hoffmann (ii, 203). I would not go so far myself, but
it is certainly true that, in Hoffman's hands, Don Juan becomes a
tragic, quasi-faustian figure. Like Faust, he tries to be more than
man, to achieve on earth more than is vouchsafed to any mortal.
Like all the Romantic Fausts, he is thus condemned to an unceas-
ing, hopeless quest. It is worth noting that the perspective from
which he is viewed is decisive. The old treatments of the theme
presented his arrogance as wicked and saw his attempts to free
himself from accepted morality as criminal. (In the old plays,
Don Juan's servant often expressed the scandalized reaction
of the 'ordinary man' to these licentious and irreligious goings-on.)
But for the German Romantics, holding the view that the ordinary
man is a stunted Philistine, the heroic rebel is entitled to his
own criteria of right and wrong. If these involve an unremitting
and self-defeating quest, he becomes tragic but not necessarily
wicked. There is an obvious parallel to the changing attitudes
towards Faust here.

The growing feeling that Don Juan was a sort of 'second
Faust' led many writers to devote a work to each. The most
famous case is that of Lenau (*Faust*, 1836; *Don Juan*, 1844). Others
are Holtei (1829 and 1834), Braun von Braunthal (1835 and 1842),
Albert Möser (both 1866), and Franz Held (1895 and 1889).
It is hardly a coincidence that all these writers, with the exception
of Holtei, owe something to Hoffmann in the characterization
of Don Juan. From the second decade of the nineteenth century
onwards, Faust and Don Juan became linked, discussed in relation
to one another, compared, contrasted—and always with increasing seriousness, even portentousness. Don Juan and Faust are
usually brought together as contrasting figures. Here is Karl
Rosenkranz, writing in 1836: 'Der Genussucht [*sic*] des Don Juan
. . . steht im Faust . . . die Einsamkeit des Wissensdranges . . .
entgegen'.[2]

---

[1] Pp. 174 and 271
[2] Karl Rosenkranz, *Zur Geschichte der deutschen Literatur*, Königsberg, 1836, p. 148.
For further examples and a discussion of the limitations of this type of formula
see below, pp. 195f.

Of the attempts to confront Faust and Don Juan within a single work, the best known is C. D. Grabbe's tragedy *Don Juan und Faust* of 1829.[1] Here the two men are made rivals for Donna Anna. The plot is rather forced, but Grabbe's chief concern is to show the contrast between the two main characters. When Don Juan appeals to nature: 'das Natürliche,/Mein guter Alter, ist auch wohl das Rechte' (iii, 1), he is placing himself in a long line of Don Juans who have justified their conduct by arguments of this kind. Faust, on the other hand, demands supernatural help to achieve more than human insights. The contrast is epitomized in the famous exchange:

DON JUAN: . . . — *Wozu übermenschlich,*
            Wenn du ein Mensch bleibst?
FAUST: *Wozu Mensch,*
    Wenn du nach Übermenschlichem nicht strebst? (iii, 3)

This antithesis is expressed and developed metaphorically through the analogy with food and drink. It will be remembered that da Ponte's Don Giovanni, when urged by Leporello to give up women, had replied—in surprise rather than indignation, no doubt—that they were more necessary to him than the bread he eats. By contrast, Goethe's Mephisto had ironically commented on Faust's need for more spiritual fare: 'Nicht irdisch ist des Toren Trank noch Speise' (line 301). In Grabbe's play, Faust is set off against a character whose physical appetites are as strong and insatiable as Faust's intellectual ones:

DON JUAN: Die einzge Speise, deren man nicht satt
            Kann werden, ist der Kuß . . . (i, 1)

When called on to consider God, Don Juan replies:

                Die Erde ist so allerliebst, daß mir
                Vor lauter Lust und Wonne Zeit fehlt, um
                An den zu denken, der sie schuf. Ists Gott—
                Nun um so größrer Ruhm für ihn—den Koch
                Lobt man mit dem Genusse seiner Speis
                Am besten. (iii, 1)

Grabbe, that is, uses the metaphor of food and drink in order

---

[1] His sources seem to have been mainly Goethe, Byron, and the Spohr opera (for Faust); Mozart/da Ponte, Byron again, and Hoffmann (for Don Juan).

to show one important difference between Faust and Don Juan. Don Juan rejoices because sensual pleasures feed his appetites without ever cloying, while Faust complains that study feeds his lust for certainty without every satisfying it: 'Tödlicher Durst und nie gestillt!' (i, 2).

And yet a cryptic remark of the Devil's at the end of the play suggests that Faust and Don Juan have something essential in common: 'Ich weiß, ihr strebet nach/*Demselben* Ziel und karrt doch auf *zwei* Wagen!' (iv, 4). To account for this, one has to go back to the very first scene, to Don Juan's praise of ceaseless striving for an unattainable, even indefinable goal. The striving itself, the eternal hunger, is the goal:

> . . . Weg mit dem Ziel—
> *Nenn* es mir nicht, ob ich auch darnach *ringe*—
> . . . Wohl dem, der ewig strebt, ja Heil,
> Heil ihm, der ewig hungern könnte!

This picture of a Don Juan who, in his way, pursues something just as elusive as Faust does, gives the inner justification for placing them together in the play. But this aspect of Don Juan is only hinted at and the unity suggested by the use of words like 'hungern', 'Koch', 'Speise' and 'satt' at various points is only apparent. 'Heil ihm, der ewig hungern könnte' suggests a Romantic quester à la Hoffmann but 'den Koch/Lobt man mit dem Genusse seiner Speis/Am besten' seems like the remark of an unproblematic hedonist. In fact the Devil's words quoted above are likely to come as a surprise on a first reading or viewing of the play. It is the *opposition* of Faust and Don Juan which seems to be the main thing. And here Grabbe's execution is rather inept. For, as soon as Faust has seen Anna's picture, he forgets his lust for knowledge and allows the Don Juan in him to come to the fore so that we now witness a contest between two Don Juans, one using his traditional means of conquest, the other aided by the Devil. What should have been a genuine clash of opposites becomes mere pantomime sensation. However, the contrast between the two men is maintained in one respect, even after Faust has ceased to concern himself with the pursuit of truth and has become the lover. The faustian arrogance and the *limitless* ambition are still apparent. Here is Faust finding fault with his magic castle:

> . . . *Mächtger*
> *Bin ich als alle Lebenden*—das Schloß
> Genügt mir nicht, genügt nicht meiner Neigung
> Für Donna Anna. (iii, 2)

In moments of frustration he shows the madness of Titanism: 'Was ich wünsche, muß ich haben, *oder/Ich schlags zu Trümmern!* (iv, 3). And, most significant of all, he anatomizes passion where he should be experiencing, communicating, and arousing it. It is with some justification that Anna remarks: 'Man sollte lächeln. Flammst du Liebe, und/Philosophierst?' (iii, 2).

Grabbe's Don Juan is not Hoffmann's then, or only intermittently Hoffman's. For Grabbe, the main importance of Hoffmann's musings on the character of Don Juan will have been to persuade him to regard the libertine with as much seriousness as the learned doctor and to suggest a link between the two men as questers after some sort of absolute—even if this link was, as we have seen, rather clumsily and illogically established. There is some sort of parallel with Lessing's championship of the Faust theme here: Lessing certainly encouraged younger men to treat the legend seriously, but their interpretations of its meaning were different from his.

Eugène Robin's dramatic poem *Livia* (1836) has already been mentioned as one of the continuations of Goethe's *Faust*. In the first section of the work, Faust and Don Juan confront each other and discuss their natures. They have this much in common: they are both rebels against society and the laws of Heaven. But the rebellion takes different forms: with Faust, a rebellion of the intellect, with Don Juan, a revolt of the senses. Where Faust torments himself with the unknowable and finds the whole universe too narrow for his soul, Don Juan preaches a gospel of acceptance, maintaining that he is praising God in pursuing God's most beautiful creation, woman (p. 28). Robin's conception of Don Juan is certainly influenced by Romantic views:

> J'adore comme un mage une divinité,
> Une fille du ciel et de l'humanité,
> Un astre, dont je vois incessament la flamme,
> Une Psyché, pour moi visible en toute femme. (p. 32)

But this is altogether a sunnier Don Juan than that of the Romantics: his life is not a vain and embittered quest for an ideal but a

happy progress, happy because a fragment or a reflection of the
ideal can be found in every woman. And so he lives for the present,
untroubled by Faust's existential questions:

> Où vais-je? Comment doit se terminer ceci?
> Je l'ignore.—Après tout, qu'importe? (p. 35)

It is this which makes it possible for Robin's Don Juan—despite
his link with Don Juan the idealist created by the Romantics—
to be set off against Faust. Contrast his 'qu'importe?' with Faust's
'Ce qui me fait souffrir, c'est que, savant, j'ignore' (p. 21).

Gautier, in 'La Comédie de la Mort' (1838), takes as his starting
point the contrast between Don Juan and Faust, in order to point
out the underlying similarity. First we find Faust looking back
on his way of life with bitterness:

> Malheureux que je suis d'avoir sans défiance
> Mordu les pommes d'or de l'arbre de science!
> La science est la mort. (p. 31)

Like Goethe's Faust he thinks that one kiss is better than the total
of all possible wisdom.

> Un seul baiser, ô douce et blanche Marguerite,
> Pris sur ta bouche en fleur, si fraîche et si petite,
> Vaut mieux que tout cela. (p. 31: cf. Goethe, lines 3079f)

Meanwhile, Don Juan curses *his* past life, his quest for an ideal
of womanhood which has always eluded him:

> Femme comme jamais sculpteur n'en a pétrie,
> Type réunissant Cléopâtre et Marie. (p. 39)

He ends by cursing love for it clouds true knowledge:

> N'écoutez pas l'Amour, car c'est un mauvais maître;
> Aimer, c'est ignorer, et vivre, c'est connaître.
> Apprenez, apprenez . . . (p. 40)

So Gautier creates the curious situation in which each wishes
he had been more like the other. His Faust and Don Juan are
Faust and Don Juan as interpreted by the Romantics in both
France and Germany: the despairing seeker after absolute truth
and the despairing seeker after ideal womanhood. They share
the fate of so many of the most typical characters of early nineteenth-century Romantic literature: they are obsessed by the

feeling that the external world is false to the ideals within them. Of all the attempts to bring Faust and Don Juan together in one work,[1] Gautier's is the most strongly imbued with Hoffmann's spirit. There are also, of course, many more works concerned only with Don Juan, in which Hoffman's influence can be felt, and it is to these that we must now turn.

(ii) Hoffmann's influence: 'faustian' Don Juans

'Ce que c'est que d'avoir passé par l'Allemagne.'
(E. Rostand)

The first significant presentation of the 'new' Don Juan in German literature[2] comes with Lenau's 'Don Juan' of 1844, a fragment consisting of isolated episodes dealing with various of Don Juan's loves. The interpretation of Don Juan's character is taken directly from Hoffmann:

Mein Don Juan darf kein Weibern ewig nachjagender heißblütiger Mensch sein. Es ist die Sehnsucht in ihm, ein Weib zu finden, welches ihm das incarnirte Weibthum ist. . . . Weil er dieses, taumelnd von der Einen zur Anderen, nicht findet, so ergreift ihn endlich der Ekel, und der ist der Teufel, der ihn holt.[3]

That reference to the Devil hints at a link with Faust and, in fact, Lenau treats Don Juan's quest in terms which, out of context, could apply just as easily to Faust:

Es fühlt der Geist, der alles will umfassen,
Im einzlen sich verkerkert und verlassen. . . . (p. 403)

---

[1] Half a century later Jean Aicard interprets the two characters similarly, showing a Faust who finally revolts against the intellect and a Don Juan whose pursuit of sensual pleasures has destroyed him as surely as the intellectual life destroyed Faust (Don Juan 89). The last of Max Jacob's three 'Poèmes dans un goût qui n'est pas le mien' (first published in 1922) also figures a Faust and a Don Juan, each of whom is obsessed by the futility of his way of life but cannot escape from it. The most recent attempt to put Faust and Don Juan into one work is by Albert Lepage, 1950. In his Faust et Don Juan, we have a Faust who so regrets his devotion to learning that he turns himself into a second Don Juan.

[2] E. Duller's poem 'Juan' (c. 1835) may have been influenced by Hoffmann; Duller certainly presents Don Juan as a Romantic quester having undeniable links with Faust. Braun von Braunthal also wrote a Don Juan play in 1842, the hero of which was driven on by just the sort of idealism that Hoffmann has ascribed to Mozart's Don Giovanni. But this idealism is unhappily combined with the type of pitiless hedonism, backed up by an appeal to 'nature', that had characterized the Don Juans of older dramas.

[3] Conversation recorded by L. A. Frankl, Zur Biographie Nikolaus Lenau's, 2nd edition, Vienna, 1885, p. 87.

—or, even more striking: 'Zusammenwerfen möcht ich Raum und Zeit' (ibid.). By this, Don Juan means that he would like to be everywhere at all times, in order to possess all women. But his words remind us of Faust's efforts to 'conquer' space and time, as portrayed in various works from the chapbooks on. The root of Don Juan's restlessness lies in the *ennui* to which he is more vulnerable than most men. If Mann's Faustus has a 'rasch gesättigte Intelligenz', Lenau's Don Juan has 'rasch gesättigte Sinne'. In the scene between Don Juan and his brother Don Diego there is an exchange which again shows that, for Lenau, the Don Juan theme is a variation on the Faust theme:

DON DIEGO: . . . willst du dein Erdenlos bestehen,
    Mußt du geschloßnen Auges und verzichtend
    An manchem Paradies vorübergehen. (p. 404)

Don Juan's reaction to this shows the gulf that separates him from the 'common man'. He has his own destiny to fulfil, a destiny inescapably imposed upon him by his nature. So he must follow his own laws: 'Ein anderes Gesetz mein ich zu spüren . . .' (ibid.).

As with Lenau's Faust, so with his Don Juan: the pursuit of the unattainable leads to a mood of emptiness in which suicide is the only possible remaining course of action. (Faust, it will be recalled, stabs himself; Don Juan throws away his sword in a duel and dies voluntarily.) So Lenau takes from Hoffmann the hint of a questing Don Juan for whom all women are pale copies of an ideal and develops it in a way that makes the affinity between this type of Don Juan and the Faust figure quite clear.

In A. Tolstoi's *Don Juan* (1860), we have the most ambitious attempt to work motifs from the Faust legend into a Don Juan drama inspired by Hoffmann. The play has a Prologue in Heaven, modelled on Goethe. As in Goethe, it is the Devil who spurs men on to activity:

    Ich bin der Arzt der Menschheit, der sie hier
    Galvanisirt, daß sich die Spannkraft hebe,
    Und wenn es in der Welt nicht einen Teufel gäbe,
    So gäb' es keinen Heiligen in ihr!
        (p. 17: cf. Goethe, lines 340ff)

The good spirits mention Don Juan as singled out by God for his purposes:

Ihn greifst du [Satan] nicht, such' eine Beute weiter!
Er ist der künft'ge Gottesstreiter,
Und der Erkohrene des Herrn!

(p. 14: cf. Goethe, lines 299–309)

But Satan proposes to destroy Don Juan through pride, through his very exigence in seeking his ideal. Each woman will seem like this ideal until she is once possessed and then he will see her for what she is (p. 15). So Don Juan is made the subject of a wager in Heaven; if he ceases to be discontented with each experience as it comes his way, if he recognizes the ideal in any woman, Satan will have won. As in Goethe, the bet is bound up with the ruling characteristic of the hero, the insatiability of his desires.

The play proper shows Don Juan, the disillusioned libertine, captivated by Donna Anna but afraid that she too will disappoint him. Only after her death does he realize that he had truly loved her. Despairing, he is about to be fetched away to Hell by the statue, when good spirits intervene:

Zurück! du blinde Macht!
Hinweg! laß ab von dem, der glaubt und liebt!   (p. 126)

An epilogue shows us the death of the lay brother Juan after years of repentance.

This ending has its logic. It has constantly been stressed that Don Juan's search for an ideal of womanhood is his way of seeking God. Repeated frustration has made him into a rebel against God. This is why it is worth Satan's while to stake so much of his prestige on the career of someone who is, on the face of it, a mere womanizer—and this is why Don Juan turns to the Church as the most appropriate way in which to express his remorse and his re-won faith. For Anna 'proves' the ultimate attainability of the divine and the goodness of the universe.

Tolstoi's *Don Juan* is inspired, then, by Hoffmann's view of Don Juan; it takes up and treats very freely the main events of the Mozart/da Ponte opera; and it relates the fortunes of the hero to cosmic issues in the manner of Goethe's *Faust*. It seems to me one of the few works to present an idealized, 'faustian' Don Juan, which is not extravagant or merely trivial. The Heavenly wager from *Faust* is restated in terms appropriate for a Don Juan (of the post-Hoffmann era), so that the 'faustian' prologue and the Don Juan play fit together and complement each other.

There would be no point in describing minor work after minor work in which Hoffmann's influence, direct or indirect, can be seen in operation. His view of Don Juan as a seeker after feminine perfection is reflected in works by Ackermann (1845), Möser (1866), Friedmann (1881), Julius Hart (1881), Bernhardi (1903), Gottschall (1906), Anthes (1909), Rittner (1909), Bethge (1910), Heymann (1921), Kratzmann (1939), and Hagelstange (1954). Sometimes the point made is the narrower one that Don Juan turned to libertinage out of shattered faith in woman: Brausewetter (1915), Jelusich (1931). In Hörnigk (1850), Brausewetter, Bonsels (1919), and van Vloten (1922) we find four more attempts to link the Hoffmannesque Don Juan to the figure of Faust. The connection in Bonsel's *Don Juan* is particularly clear, with its Prologue in Heaven and its wager between God and Satan, with Don Juan as its object.[1]

(iii) *Hoffmann's Don Juan in France*

After considering the doleful idealist that Hoffmann made of Don Juan, Bévotte goes on:

... dans la plupart des oeuvres que la fable du *Burlador* a inspirées en France au xixe siècle, retrouve-t-on des souvenirs plus ou moins directs de l'interprétation d'Hoffmann. (i, 252)

Hoffmann was much admired in France and the Don Juan tale was one of the most highly prized of his works, following a translation in the *Revue de Paris* in September, 1829.[2]

A measure of the change in attitude brought about by Hoffmann's interpretation can be taken if we compare Nerval's view of Don Juan, dating from 1828, with the famous romanticized Don Juan of Musset's 'oriental tale' *Namouna* (1832). Here is

---

[1] Rilke wrote two poems about Don Juan ('Don Juans Kindheit' and 'Don Juans Auswahl', both in *Neue Gedichte*, ii, 1908). In the second of these, an angel appears to Don Juan and announces his destiny: to lead women through love to loneliness. There is no direct link with the Romantic Don Juan, but the degree of seriousness with which Don Juan is treated would be unthinkable, had there not been a long tradition of presenting Don Juan in an idealized way. Such hints of this as Rilke possessed were probably picked up from the French poets rather than from German sources.

[2] See M. Breuillac, 'Hoffmann en France', in *Revue d'Histoire Littéraire de la France*, xiii, 427ff and xiv, 74ff, 1906–7, and E. Teichmann, *La Fortune d'Hoffmann en France*, Paris 1961, pp. 133ff.

Nerval in the preface to the first edition of his translation of Goethe's *Faust*:

... si Faust et Manfred ont offert ... le type de la perfection humaine, don Juan n'est plus que celui de la démoralisation ... Combien Faust surpasse ... les amours vulgaires de don Juan ...[1]

And here is Musset in *Namouna*:

> N'en était-il pas une, ou plus noble, ou plus belle,
> Parmis tant de beautés, qui, de loin ou de près,
> De son vague idéal eût du moins quelques traits? ...
> Toutes lui ressemblaient,—ce n'était jamais elle,
> Toutes lui ressemblaient, don Juan, et tu marchais!
>
> (ii, 47)

This Don Juan was quick to catch the French imagination. We have already encountered him, dreaming of a woman who would combine Cleopatra and the Virgin Mary, in Gautier's 'Comédie de la Mort'. Gautier was later to elaborate on this view of Don Juan in a passage which recalls how Lenau had rejected the old conception of the vulgar libertine in favour of the new interpretation:

Don Juan ... représente ... l'aspiration à l'idéal. Ce n'est pas une débauche vulgaire qui le pousse; il cherche le rêve de son coeur avec l'opiniâtreté d'un titan qui ne redoute ni les éclairs ni la foudre.

This is at bottom a religious quest, for he believes that the existence of the ideal within him proves the objective existence, somewhere, of an ideal woman and this, in turn, means that there is a God, the creator of this ideal: 'il ... n'a pas douté de la véracité de Dieu'. Hoffman's view that Don Juan's tragedy comes from his having met Anna too late is echoed by Gautier in terms of pre-Adamite perfection and innocence:

Don Juan, c'est Adam chassé du paradis et qui se souvient d'Ève, avant sa faute,—d'Ève, le type de la beauté et de la grâce.[2]

Examples of Hoffmann's (or, as we should by now perhaps

---

[1] Quoted here from the 1868 edition, p. 7.

[2] *Histoire de l'art dramatique*, Paris, 1858-9, iv, 36f. For the distinction as made by Lenau, see above, p. 176. A somewhat similar point is made by Gobineau in his notes on the Don Juan type, although his dramatic poem *Les Adieux de Don Juan* figures the older, hedonistic Don Juan. For the notes, see L. Schemann, *Quellen und Untersuchungen zum Leben Gobineaus*, i, Strasbourg, 1914, p. 149.

say: Musset's and Gautier's) Don Juan are not hard to find in
the French literature of the mid and late nineteenth century.
E. Jourdain's 'fantastic drama' *Don Juan* (1857) has a hero who
commits suicide because his ideals turn out to be unrealizable.
Villiers de l'Isle-Adam's poem 'Hermosa' (1859) represents Don
Juan as seeking in love what others seek in religion or art or
through the pursuit and wielding of power. Armand Hayem is the
author both of a Don Juan play (*Don Juan d'Armana*) and of a
treatise *Le Don Juanisme*, both published in 1886, although written
somewhat earlier. In the play, Don Juan's remarks on marriage
suggest the Romantic quester once again:

... je me marierais s'il existait une femme à ma taille.—Cette femme ne
l'ai-je pas cherchée toute ma vie, sans la rencontrer?[1]

(iv) *Faustian traits in Don Juans not influenced by Hoffmann*

If we go back to the older treatments of the legend, before
Don Juan was made into a Romantic hero by Hoffmann, we find
the first 'faustian' Don Juan in Dorimon's *Festin de Pierre* (1658).
Here Dom Jouan accepts the statue's invitation not out of pride
and reckless courage, as in previous versions, but out of *curiosity*:

> J'ay veu ce qu'on peut voir Briguelle, sur la terre,
> Les Esprits fors, les Grands, les Sçavans, et la Guerre,
> Il ne me reste plus dans mes pensers divers,
> Qu'à voir si je pouvois les Cieux, et les Enfers,
> Celuy que je vais voir n'est plus dans ces matieres
> Qui souvent font obstacle aux plus belles lumieres,
> C'est un esprit tout pur. . . .
> Allons donc sans tarder. . . .
> L'homme est lasche qui vit dans la stupidité;
> On doit porter par tout sa curiosité. (p. 125)

That last couplet could have been spoken by any Faust. And when
Dom Jouan is confronted by the statue and questioned concerning his attitude to God, he replies:

---

[1] Pp. 120f. Jean Aicard (*Don Juan 89*) portrays an idealist Don Juan in order to
attack an era which was, the writer felt, materialistic, corrupt, philistine, and preten-
tious. The implication is that a fastidious idealist like Don Juan must be repelled by
this age and will concentrate his yearning and effort on the quest for an ideal love.
For a proud and disdainful Don Juan, aware of his superiority to the ordinary man,
see Baudelaire's dramatic sketch 'La fin de Don Juan', *c.* 1853, also the poem 'Don
Juan aux enfers' in the *Fleurs du mal*. A similar characterization can be found in the
sonnet 'À Don Juan', attributed to Verlaine, *c.* 1866.

> Il m'a donné l'esprit, l'ame, la connoissance,
> La force, la raison, le coeur, l'intelligence,
> Et tout cela pour vaincre, et braver les destins
> Et non pour affliger l'ouvrage de ses mains.   (p. 129)

The argument is very similar to that which—implicitly or explicitly—is often urged by Faust.

FAUST: Why should God give me a brain if I am not to exercise it freely?

DON JUAN: Why should God [or, in some versions, nature] give me qualities and not wish me to use them?

These two facets of Don Juan's character—which could have turned him into a 'second Faust' of a type a good deal more interesting than Hoffmann's frustrated idealist—were never really developed. We have seen a brief hint of a Don Juan who involves himself with the supernatural out of curiosity in the Ulm puppet play (see above, p. 166), but one looks in vain for a serious and extended portrayal of Don Juan as an agnostically inclined and individualistic rebel in whom hedonistic urges are combined with a 'faustian' intellectuality: a Don Juan, moreover, sufficiently self-aware to analyse and justify his attitudes. Shadwell's Don John, in *The Libertine* (1675), certainly appeals to 'nature', asserting the claims of his natural urges against the combined pressures of religion, society, and morality —but Shadwell does no more than hint at this and is, for the rest, content to show Don John as a monster abhorrent to every decent man.[1] What of Molière? There might have been a hint for later authors there, but Molière's Dom Juan was too subtle and too shockingly and uncompromisingly rationalistic to have much influence on later presentations of the character. From seventeenth-century France up to the late eighteenth century the popular versions showed Don Juan as unnaturally wicked and took up the magical elements gratefully as a box-office attraction, without making much attempt to examine Don Juan's attitude towards the supernatural. There are various trivial Don Juan works which introduce motifs from the Faust tradition, but these are

---

[1] For the appeal to nature, see *The Libertine*, p. 28. There are other Don Juans who justify themselves by such arguments, for instance, Rosimond's (iii, 4). Later, Coleridge was to remark on this characteristic of Don Juan (*Biographia Literaria*, Chapter xxiii).

usually dragged in uncritically, adding nothing to the characterization. Merely to involve Don Juan with a Gretchen[1] in no way
deepens or enhances our understanding of him. For Leporello's
'in Almagna due cento e trent'una' must surely include a Gretchen
or two and Don Juan's strategies with unsophisticated maidens
had been demonstrated from the early plays onwards. It can even
confuse the issue, for Faust's motives in turning to Gretchen are
vastly different from, and more complex than, Don Juan's
decision to pursue a Zerlina or Rosalba. Some Don Juan works
mention a pact with the Devil and magical assistance rendered
to Don Juan in his adventures,[2] but surely this weakens the
point. What Don Juan worth his salt ever needed more than his
own charm and his own resources?

There is, however, one version which introduces a deliberate
and obvious echo of Goethe's *Faust* in a way that genuinely
adds force to the argument of the play. In Creizenach's *Don Juan*
(1836–7), Don Juan reforms and goes to America (widely regarded
by Germans at that time as a land of limitless freedom and opportunity) in order to start a new life as a pioneer, serving the
community and conquering nature. The description of this new
life is very reminiscent of Faust's dream of a community of free
men living on land wrested from the elements:

> Ist nicht der Strom aus seinem Bett gestiegen
> Dem er in neuer Bahn gebot zu brausen,
> Daß nun an seinem Ufer Städte liegen,
> An seinem Sturz beglückte Männer hausen?
> (p. 58: cf. *Faust*, 10227ff and 11559ff)

So Creizenach's Don Juan, like Goethe's Faust, ends by overcoming his hedonistic urges and developing towards something
better, more altruistic. In this hint that there is something not
merely reprehensible but immature about Donjuanism, Creizenach points forward to two of the most interesting twentieth-
century reworkings of the theme. Before these are discussed,
however, a word must be said about the fortunes of Don Juan
from the mid-nineteenth century onwards.

It has been seen that the Romantics, both in Germany and in
France, idealized Don Juan. This was bound to provoke a

[1] Examples: Mallefille (1848–53) and Königsmark (1869–71).
[2] Vulpius (1805) and Schaden (1820).

reaction. It must be remembered that, in the works that represent or discuss him, his *actions* are still those of a libertine, however much his *motives* may be romanticized. In most of the works influenced by Hoffmann and the French Romantics who followed him Don Juan continues to perform what by any conventional standards of morality are blackguardly deeds, but he is motivated in such a way that the reader is expected to admire, or at least to exculpate him. Often, the libertine is not even punished but is saved through the selfless love of a woman. So, in several works from the mid-nineteenth century on, we find the author taking revenge on this romanticized Don Juan, showing him robbed of his prey, punished in some way for his libertinage, or simply cheated by the passage of time, passed by, and humiliated because he has grown old. For instance, in Gustave le Vavasseur's 'Don Juan Barbon' (1848), an ageing Don Juan has his daughter stolen from him by a young libertine who, to turn the knife in the wound, had learned the arts of seduction from Don Juan himself.

When we come to the discussions of Don Juan by psycho-analysts, we find him suffering yet greater indignities. According to Freudian interpretations his libertinage is the result of an Oedipus complex. For Gregario Marañon Don Juan's indis-criminate pursuit of women is not proof of virility but of emo-tional immaturity, even of a lack of virility. Otto Rank explains the persistence of the Don Juan theme in literature in terms of the survival of ancient myths.[1] For the womanizer to have his virility thrown into question and the out-and-out individualist to be represented as a mere archetype or symbol—these are surely affronts which make being worsted by a younger copy of oneself almost a compliment.

The two most interesting of the twentieth-century works which continue the debunking of the romanticized Don Juan both represent Donjuanism as an adolescent stage in man's development and show Don Juan outgrowing this and, in each case, becoming more like a Faust than a Don Juan. In *Man and Superman* (1903), Don Juan comes to realize that his worship of

---

[1] For a reference to the Freudian interpretations, see Otto Rank, *Don Juan. Une étude sur le Double*, traduit ... par S. Lautmann, Paris, 1932, p. 174. For Marañon, see his *Don Juan et le Donjuanisme*, Paris, 1958, especially pp. 20–30. For the mythical interpretation, see Rank, *Seelenglaube und Psychologie*, Leipzig and Vienna, 1930.

woman was based on a romantic illusion. He was the pursued, not the pursuer, a mere victim of biological necessity:

Life seized me and threw me into the lady's arms as a sailor throws a scrap of fish into the mouth of a seabird.   (p. 668)

As is well known, the play proper works out this variation on the old theme in modern terms, while the analysis of the issues is contained in a dream sequence set in Hell. In this long discussion-piece Shaw shows how Don Juan must inevitably grow tired of pleasure and, longing for something lastingly satisfying and dynamic, turn into a sort of second Faust. The setting in Hell underlines this by merging the two legends. The characters from *Don Giovanni* are introduced by the music associated with them from that opera, but the Devil's music is Mozart's 'grotesquely adulterated' with Gounod's. There are a few passing references to Goethe's *Faust* in addition to this oblique musical allusion. With these pointers in mind, let us see how Shaw implies the transition from Don Juan to Faust.

Life, says Don Juan, is progress, a constant and restless urge towards higher things, a ceaseless process of experimenting and discarding. The ultimate object of the Life Force is to supersede clumsy forms of life and to develop the highest good, which is intellect. Life's 'darling object' is brains—'an organ by which it can attain not only self-consciousness but self-understanding' (p. 663). The Devil (very different from Goethe's Mephisto) holds men back by imprisoning them in a sterile and self-defeating love of pleasure. Hell symbolizes this lazy attitude to life, in which true realities are forgotten. Heaven is the realm of reality and striving. (Here Shaw is nearer to Goethe than in his charac-terization of the Devil.) So Don Juan forsakes Hell for Heaven in order to contemplate and to further the development of the Life Force. His ideal is now the 'philosophic man: he who seeks in contemplation to discover the inner will of the world, in invention to discover the means of fulfilling that will, and in action to do that will by the so-discovered means' (p. 664). His highest joy will now be to assist Life in its struggle towards greater self-awareness and self-knowledge:

I tell you that as long as I can conceive something better than myself I cannot be easy unless I am striving to bring it into existence. . . .
(679f)

That sentiment is worthy of the Faust who wagered his soul on the durability of his divine discontent, who scorned hedonism and security, who came to interpret life in terms of ceaseless striving and evolution and of whom the angels sang:

> Wer immer strebend sich bemüht,
> Den können wir erlösen.   (11936f)

Max Frisch's comedy *Don Juan oder die Liebe zur Geometrie* (1952) is not much more than a witty trifle compared with Shaw's eloquent masterpiece, but the drift of it is somewhat similar. Frisch's Don Juan, too, is an unwilling libertine who longs to escape into a clearer realm where truth is demonstrable and issues are unclouded by emotion. He too resents being driven on by a blind biological urge, but goes even further in his dissatisfaction than does Shaw's Don Juan. He talks of his 'Unwille gegen die Schöpfung, die uns gespalten hat in Mann und Weib. . . . Welche Ungeheuerlichkeit, daß der Mensch allein nicht das Ganze ist!' (p. 81). Longing for woman is a form of drunkenness; it must be overcome if man is to pursue his higher goal (p. 35). Don Juan's goal is pure logic, an intellectual absolute: '[Pater Diego] nennt es Gott, ich nenne es Geometrie' (ibid.). This Don Juan is basically an intellectual for whom woman is no more than an episode; as a type he is nearer to Faust than to Casanova (p. 313). Frisch even goes on to suggest that Don Juan, if alive today, would probably be concerning himself with atomic physics, to find out the truth—'um zu erfahren, was stimmt' (p. 319).

That Don Juan has been represented by both these authors, Shaw and Frisch, as impatient of his way of life and restlessly seeking something higher—this indicates a feeling that the Don Juan legend told of an enormously gifted, restless, and energetic man who had somehow failed to find the right outlet for his energies. In depicting the form his renewed quest might take, each author lights on that other untiring seeker in modern European literature, Faust.[1]

The foregoing account has been mainly concerned with showing how Don Juan came to resemble Faust. We must now turn

---

[1] The characterization of Don Juan in S. Wiese's tragedy *Don Juan* (1840) shows links with Faust as portrayed both by Goethe and the German Romantics. Both E. Rostand (*La dernière Nuit de Don Juan*, 1914) and H. de Montherlant (*Don Juan*, 1956) debunk the idealized Don Juan and the critics and commentators who help to keep him alive.

our attention to the ways in which Faust has approached Don Juan.

(v) *Faust comes to resemble Don Juan*

There has been a strong erotic element in the Faust legend from the beginning. Inevitably so, since the Devil's most persistent and successful mode of temptation has always been through the flesh. Even before the appearance of the Spies Faustbook, Faust was credited with a love life on the heroic scale:

[er] fürete gar vberauß ein bübisch leben/also/ das er etliche mal schier vmbkommen were von wegen seiner grossen Hurerey. . . .[1]

The Spies chapbook returns to the theme of Faust's 'swinish and epicurean life', and gives a catalogue of his mistresses, a chance anticipation of the more famous catalogues compiled by successive servants of Don Juan:

Als Doctor Faustus sahe, daß die Jahr seiner Versprechung von Tag zu Tag zum Ende lieffen, hub er an ein Säuwisch vndd Epicurisch leben zu führen, vnd berufft jm siben Teuffelische Succubas, die er alle beschlieffe, vnd eine anders denn die ander gestalt war, auch so trefflich schön, daß nicht davon zusagen. Dann er fuhr inn viel Königreich mit seinem Geist, darmit er alle Weibsbilder sehen möchte, deren er 7. zuwegen brachte, zwo Niederländerin, eine Ungerin, eine Engelländerin, zwo Schwäbin, vnd ein Fränckin . . . (p. 119)

Then, of course, comes the most famous of Dr. Faustus' passions, his love for Helen. Her arrival is not yet represented as having been staged by the Devil in order to make Faust forget thoughts of repentance; this idea will be introduced by Marlowe. But the insistence on Faust's lechery in the last years of his life is unquestionably intended to show the extent to which he is bound to the Devil.

This attitude lives on in the later German Faustbooks. In Pfitzer, it is explicitly stated that Faust had entered on the pact because of concupiscence (i, 13, note 2). The pact had forbidden marriage, but Faust had reflected that he could no doubt make do with 'cooks and concubines' (i, 9). Later there is a reference to 'daily whoring' (ii, 21). Faust presently wants to marry 'a pretty but humble girl' but, as in 'Spies', he is frightened off the idea of

[1] Ragor, translation of Manlius, 1563. Tille, no. 14.

marriage by the Devil, who promptly procures him Helen for his mistress.[1]

The essential features of this episode were taken up—shorn of the annotations—by the 'Christlich Meynender' into his chapbook. The association of Faust's eroticism with genuine love for a humble girl in this widely read version was one of the factors which would later help to shape Goethe's Gretchen episode.

Meanwhile, other forms of popular Faust literature stressed the theme of Faust's love life to a point where it often became the main concern of the work. In an early eighteenth-century English Faust pantomime it is the apparition of Helen which finally decides Faust to sign the contract, and a pantomime given in Vienna in 1740 substitutes a wager for the usual pact: Faust's soul will fall to the Devil if he proves unable to resist sexual temptation. (The link with the Don Juan tradition is underlined by similarities between the adventures which follow and the traditional rustic episodes in numerous Don Juan plays.)[2] There are puppet plays, too, in which Faust's eroticism provides the central motivation, and one burlesque *Faust* in which Leporello's catalogue of his master's conquests has been openly copied:

Kaspar . . . (schreibt) Die schöne keusche Lukretia, meines Herrn 335ste Geliebte. . . .

(There can be no doubt that this comes from the Don Juan tradition and not from the hint contained in 'Spies', quoted above. The extravagant total and the fact that it is the servant who is keeping the records make it clear enough.)[3]

If we are to imagine the impact made by Goethe's Part 1 in 1808, we must try to shut out knowledge of Part 2 from our minds and recall the extent to which various previous Faust versions,

---

[1] II, 21–2. Pfitzer stresses the lusts of the flesh more than Widmann. It is Pfitzer, for instance, who adds the note that Faust entered on the pact because of concupiscence.

[2] See *The Necromancer* (1724) and the scenario of the Viennese pantomime given in Brukner and Hadamowsky, pp. 41–7.

[3] For the puppet plays, see above, p. 167, also that given by Wiepking in Oldenburg (in Engel, *Deutsche Puppenkomödien*, viii). For the catalogue, see J. J. Engel, *Der travestirte Doktor Faust*, 1806, p. 27. The approach of Faust to Don Juan seems to have occurred for the first time in a serious, 'literary' *Faust* in 1804; in Schink's *Johann Faust*, there are a number of clear similarities to the traditional episodes in Don Juan plays and operas where a woman mistakes Don Juan for her bridegroom-to-be and Don Juan exploits the situation.

from chapbook, pantomime, and puppet play, to Engel and Schink, will have predisposed readers to see the theme of sexual desire as central to the work. Goethe's *Faust* seemed to offer another example of this. Was not the lust for knowledge brushed aside in favour of direct experience of life? And was not Faust's rejuvenation quite specifically linked to the notion that the essence of his desires would be personified in a woman (2437-40)? Mephisto's reference to Helen (2604) would remind early nineteenth-century readers of the role of Helen in the popular tradition, so that what followed would appear to them as a restatement of the traditional theme (the flesh as cause of Faust's ruin)— with the poignant but inessential difference that this fall was brought about unwittingly by an innocent girl who herself became a victim. In fact, this very substitution of innocent victim for devilish succubus underlined the Donjuanesque element in Faust. Even long after the appearance of Part 2 and the resultant awareness that the Gretchen tragedy was only one episode in a long and complex process, the emotional impact of the love tragedy was still sufficiently overwhelming to lead Ferdinand von Feldegg to describe Goethe's Faust as 'a secret Don Juan' (*Der neue Faust*, 1902, p. 150). Open imitations of the Gretchen tragedy, as in Ortlepp's Faust scenes (1833) or Czilski's *Faust* (1843) are not uncommon and the notion that a serious Faust play could lay the main stress on the theme of love must have received a great impetus as a result of Goethe's Part 1.

Later, in France and England at least, this impression will have been strengthened by the sentimentalized version of Part 1 presented by Gounod and Carré in their Faust opera. W. S. Gilbert wrote a perfectly serious Faust play (*Gretchen*, 1879) in which Faust becomes a monk(!) out of bitterness at being betrayed by a woman, then leaves the monastery when shown a vision of Gretchen by Mephisto ('Faustus unfrocked! Faustus unsanctified/Faustus re-butterflied in bravery!'—p. 43). The contrast between false and true love is the theme of the play.

Descriptions of Faust as a 'secret Don Juan' and so on are in one respect misleading. Merely to show Faust as motivated more by the desire for love than by the desire for knowledge is not to turn him into a Don Juan. It is, in my opinion, only justified to talk of a Donjuanesque Faust in cases where he is shown as pursuing woman after woman or where the author

has borrowed material from the Don Juan tradition. (The one
will often involve the other, as when Engel introduces the servant's catalogue of Faust's mistresses.) Such borrowings and
cross-references as one finds usually take the form of more or
less open plagiarism of the Mozart/da Ponte opera.

Among the premature attempts to provide a Part 2 to Goethe's
Part 1, that by Schöne (1823) is conspicuous in its concentration
on Faust's eroticism. True, Schöne's Faust delivers a monologue
or two in which he complains about his doubts and ignorance
and he apostrophizes nature in the style of Goethe's Faust. But
the middle part of the play is taken up with his amours and
Schöne's plot has greater similarities with that of *Don Giovanni*
than with anything in Goethe. In the episode 'Weinberg am Rhein'
Faust is attracted by a blonde girl, dances with her, and woos her
in tones which bring to mind Don Giovanni's wooing of Zerlina.
But there is a bridegroom glowering in the background, playing
the part of Masetto, in fact:

> Mein Bräutigam böse Miene macht,
> Weil ich den Herrn hab' angelacht. (p. 39)

Faust's reply that such a girl deserves better than a crude and un-
appreciative peasant is almost a paraphrase of da Ponte:

Schöne	da Ponte
Der hat ja nicht Gefühl und Sinn	Vi par che un onest' uomo ...
Zu schätzen Deiner Schönheit Werth.	possa soffrir che quel visetto d'oro, quel viso inzuccherato
Wirfst Du Dich, süße Perle, hin	da un bifolcaccio vil sia
Dem Ersten, der Dich nur be- gehrt?	strapazzato? ... Voi non siete fatta per esser paesana. ...
Du kannst die ersten Throne zieren	Là ci darem la mano, là mi dirai di sì;
Mit Deiner herrlichen Gestalt;	vedi, non è lontano,
Komm, laß Dich schnell von mir entführen! (p. 39)	partiam, ben mio, da qui! (pp. 66–9)

Moreover, Goethe's wager has been given a narrower meaning by Schöne. It has, one could almost say, been modified for a
Faust who has been recast as a Don Juan. Discontent with each
experience must mean inconstancy in love:

> Faustina, Engel, Meisterbild des Schöpfers!
> Du gabst Dich liebend mir! An Deiner Brust

Ward mir Genuß—und mit ihm bittre Leiden.
Denn, ach! Du willst den Ruhelosen fesseln,
An deine Hand den wüsten Fremdling schmieden!
Unglückliche! das fordre nicht von mir!
Bei mir hat Liebe keine Dauer,
Ich habe ihrer höchsten Huld geflucht. (p. 171)

This seems a snivelling type of self-justification compared with Don Giovanni's flamboyant claim that his feelings are so boundless that he wishes all women well, that to be true to one would be unfair to the others:

> Chi a una sola è fedele,
> Verso l'altre è crudele . . . (p. 174)

In F. Marlow's *Faust* (1839) Donjuanism forms one well-defined stage in Faust's career. The first part of the work ('Natur') deals with Faust's efforts to penetrate the mysteries of the natural world and he enters on the pact with this intention uppermost. But, as so often in treatments of this theme, he passes from the desire to understand life to the sensual enjoyment of life and it is this stage which is shown in the second part of the work ('Leben'). Here we find Faust abruptly recast in the role of Don Juan. There is an Elvira-like figure, there is an episode with a humble girl, there is the killing of a rival in love. What the author seems to be suggesting by this switch from one legend to the other is that Faust's quest—for knowledge, power, the secrets of nature—and Don Juan's quest for love are two manifestations of the same spirit. Where the faustian qualities are under discussion it is appropriate to maintain thematic links with the Faust tradition; where the erotic urge predominates, motifs are borrowed from *Don Giovanni*. There could be no more practical way of confirming Grabbe's contention that Faust and Don Juan are, fundamentally, pursuing the same end.[1]

The two major works in which Faust is cast as something resembling a Don Juan are those by Lenau and W. Nürnberger. Nürnberger's gloomy masterpiece is discussed elsewhere; let

---

[1] The Spohr/Bernard Faust-opera, dating from 1813, lays the main stress on Faust's pursuit of love, and ends tragically with Faust cursing the sensuality which caused his fall. So it is not inappropriate that the libretto contains echoes of and similarities to *Don Giovanni*, recalling da Ponte's treatment of Anna, Giovanni, and Ottavio, and of the Zerlina episode. In Holtei's and Lenburg's Faust plays of 1829 and 1860, Faust is turned into a womanizer and episodes from Don Giovanni are plagiarized.

us look at the Donjuanesque traits in Lenau's Faust. From the
outset Mephisto seeks to draw Faust away from speculation to
pleasure. Here is his version of Goethe's 'grau, teurer Freund,
ist alle Theorie':

> So eine Dirne lustentbrannt
> Schmeckt besser als ein Foliant.   (p. 29)

Mephisto begins the work of destroying Faust by awakening his
sensual desires. And so to the village wedding scene, where Faust
steals the peasant girl from her 'cuckold-bridegroom'. The
episode is yet another variation on Don Giovanni's pursuit of
Zerlina. Once this first step has been taken by Faust, seduction
becomes a game and a matter of pride:

> Die Sünd ist Spaß, doch kanns mein Stolz nicht tragen,
> Von einem Weib zu werden abgeschlagen.   (p. 55)

The amorality which had generally been implicit in Faust's view
of himself is here translated into a specifically sexual amorality and
the traditional 'faustian' pride and arrogance into specifically
sexual pride and arrogance.

The court episodes of the puppet plays are the obvious model
for the court scenes which follow, but here too there is a link
with *Don Giovanni*, since Maria comes to take on the role of Donna
Anna as interpreted by Hoffmann. Here is Faust addressing Maria:

> Doch, blick ich wieder Euch ins Angesicht,
> So hat die Hölle, der ich zugeschworen,
> Mit einmal ihre Macht an mir verloren . . .
> Ich bin gerettet, hab ich dich errungen!   (pp. 68f)

But, as in the Don Juan tradition, the wooer is interrupted and
murders the intruder.

So there is much in Lenau's *Faust* to remind us of the Don Juan
legend, particularly of the Mozart/da Ponte opera. But it remains
clear throughout that this is a Faust who has turned Don Juan.
He is not a gay and thoughtless hedonist or even an idealist whose
ideal is of the flesh. Lenau's Faust is still 'sick with thought'
(p. 116) for all his restless libertinage. The gulf separating him
from da Ponte's Don Giovanni and Grabbe's Don Juan (both of
whom cheerfully accept the sexual appetite as no more complicated or problematic than the appetite for food or drink) is

clearest in his conversation with Görg in the scene 'Görg.
Schenke am Meeresstrand'. It is Görg who enjoys without
reflecting and without bothering about metaphysics. He will live
while he can and die when he must:

> Ich glaub an diesen süßen Kuß;
> Ich glaube, daß ich sterben muß. (p. 112)

That could have been said by da Ponte's Don Giovanni, but
certainly not by Lenau's Faust:

> Ich habe auf der See die langen Tage
> Mir überdacht des Lebens manche Frage ... (p. 116)

Görg—and Don Giovanni—would ask: what on earth for?

(vi) *Conclusion*

It will have become plain that many of the works that make a
second Don Juan of Faust trivialize him in the process. Faust,
surely, should be a complex character, a personification of western
man's rebellious individualism and his quest for self-realization
in all its forms. To play down the question of knowledge, to
ignore or minimize the lust for power and related traits, and to
concentrate on eroticism—this is to devalue Faust. The original
Faustbook had shown Faust's enslavement to the flesh as one step
in his downfall. And, of course, the authors of important Faust
works who have introduced an erotic strain into their characterization of Faust—Marlowe, Goethe, Lenau, Nürnberger, Mann—
have always integrated this element into his character as a whole.
But with many lesser authors we can almost hear the sigh of relief
as they abandon the difficult question of unsatisfied and unsatis-
fiable curiosity in favour of the intellectually less demanding
theme of Faust's concupiscence.[1] (Artistically less demanding
too; we have seen how many of them took over ready-made
episodes and situations from the Don Juan tradition.) And Faust
is devalued yet further if too much stress is laid on the magical
assistance he receives in his pursuit of women. For in that case
he is, as it were, neither a good Faust nor a good Don Juan.[2]

---

[1] This is particularly clear in Lenburg's *Faust*.
[2] For a Faust-turned-Don-Juan who relies on a magic potion, see the Spohr/
Bernard opera or Czilski's Faust play of 1843. For a Faust who rides off to safety on a
magic cloak when confronted by a jealous bridegroom, see Schöne, 1823.

Faust becomes a rebel because of an impulse which few people since the eighteenth century would regard as wicked. Don Juan, however, is nearly always represented as a wealthy and gifted man who devotes practically all his energies to deceiving and seducing women, holding out expectations which he must know will not be realized, resorting to trickery and impersonation, or at best exploiting his personal charm in a calculating way. Early versions explain this way of life in terms of hedonism and a philosophical appeal to 'nature', but still condemn Don Juan. How then does he become a hero?

Both Faust and Don Juan have benefited from an increasing subjectivity and individualism, and hence an increasing relativity in matters of morals, in modern times. Each made his first appearance as a character in fiction in an age where deviations from the moral norm were promptly condemned. Each was in due course taken up again in an era in which authoritative moral codes were distrusted by a growing minority of the educated and articulate. The fact that these figures are so recognizably true to their own natures will also have helped to make them seem admirable, or more admirable. Both are prepared to go the whole hog, to take what they want, whatever the cost. (It is only in early *Fausts* and in the naïve products of the popular tradition that Faust's sinful folly in underestimating the Devil's price is stressed, and only in *El Burlador* that prominence is given to Don Juan's intention to repent in the end. The very fact that this trait seems to most of us today to be *unworthy* of a Don Juan shows how we have come to regard him as the type of man who goes after what he wants and is prepared to pay for it.) Both Faust and Don Juan are rebels, at first against God and then, in more sceptical ages, against society. Each is obsessed with the feeling that to realize his personal potential is a right and a paramount duty. Because of this both have been admired as rebellious individualists. From the Romantic era onwards, they were regarded specifically as frustrated idealists, men tormented by their inability to be (or experience, or know) something denied to other men. In the case of Don Juan, the main factor is, of course, that Hoffmann represented Don Giovanni as a man tragically led astray, to be true, but engaged in a noble quest. This made it easy for the Romantics to take up Don Juan as another example of someone filled with longing for the unattainable. Moreover, his enormities are, according to this reading, committed in a spirit of vengeance and frustration. This presumably must have had the effect of making them seem less callously hedonistic.

When an explicit contrast has been made between Faust and Don Juan, the result has been nearly always been oversimplification. I have quoted Karl Rosenkranz's rather schematic formulation (see above, p. 171). For Kierkegaard, Don Juan stood for rebellious sensuality, Faust for the rebellious intellect.[1] Similarly, Edmond Haraucourt sees Faust and Don Juan as representing two forms of the individual's revolt against Christianity, which demands a twofold submission:

La tête et la bête se relèvent en révolte, à la fin, et surgissent.
La tête crie: 'Je veux penser!' Et cette révolte s'appelle Faust.
La bête crie: 'Je veux vivre!' Et cette révolte s'appelle don Juan.[2]

Examples of this rather simplistic contrast could be multiplied.[3] The most uncompromising formulation is probably that by Ernst Lert in his book on Mozart: Mozart's Don Giovanni is the 'Faust of the senses', Goethe's Faust is the 'Don Juan of the intellect'.[4] We have seen the same tendency in works of literature. It seems to me that critics and poets alike are presenting a very partial picture of Faust and Don Juan. The two figures can, of course, be used as handy personifications of intellectual and sensual revolt respectively, but they no longer have very much to do with actual characters in identifiable literary works. They have become types, just as 'faustisch' became a mere label for Spengler and those who followed him. For Don Juan is *not* simply a personification of the sensuality which the Church frowns on. The most interesting and searching works devoted to him do dwell on this aspect, to be sure, but on much more besides: the rebel against society, the trickster who charms us against our will, the agnostic or rationalistic challenger of ready-made rules, sometimes the open defier of God, the out-and-out individualist determined to 'be himself' and to work out his own code of

[1] S. Kierkegaard, *Either/Or*, London, 1944, i, 73.
[2] E. Haraucourt, *Don Juan de Mañara*, 1898, Preface, p. xvi.
[3] See for instance K. Engel, *Die Don Juan-Sage auf der Bühne*, Dresden and Leipzig, 1887, p. 9, and C. Rabany, *Carlo Goldoni*, Paris, 1896, p. 264.
[4] E. Lert, *Mozart auf dem Theater*, Berlin, 1921, p. 339.

conduct in an almost Nietzschean sense.[1] Similarly, Faust is *not* simply a personification of limitless curiosity or (as some, going to the opposite extreme, have maintained) a 'secret Don Juan'; he, too, is a good deal more complex, as preceding chapters may have shown.

So most works which present a Don Juan who resembles Faust or a Faust who resembles Don Juan are superficial or confusing. Only a small minority of authors—among them Creizenach, Lenau, Nürnberger, Shaw—manage to add a dimension to their portrait of the one character by implying a link with the other. For the rest, the association between the two figures, insisted on by writer after writer from the early nineteenth century onwards, probably did more harm than good. It must have been one of the factors that encouraged the authors of certain Faust works to adopt the easy solution of turning Faust into a womanizer, and it led to a great number of *Don Juans* in which the heroes were represented vaguely as 'faustian' strivers after an ideal. It seemed to offer an 'instant' characterization of Don Juan. A major reason for the comparative scarcity of independent and searching presentations of Don Juan as a character since the Romantic era is unquestionably that so many writers put him forward as a 'second Faust' and that many more were content to write works which merely debunked or attacked this view.

[1] For examples of 'Nietzschean' Don Juans, see W. van Vloten, *Don Juan Empor!* (1922), S. von Hartenstein, *Don Juan* . . . , (1934), and F. A. Beyerlein, 'Don Juans Überwindung' (1938).

9

Faust and Science in the
nineteenth and twentieth centuries

'There is *nothing* that cannot be explained by science.'
(Sir Ralph Bloomfield Bonington in
The Doctor's Dilemma)

IN their different ways the major late eighteenth-century *Fausts* all respond to new ways of thinking about human personality; they reflect the Enlightenment's faith in human reason (Lessing) or the reaction against this faith on the part of an impetuous young generation (*Sturm und Drang*). Two works at least (the *Urfaust* and Klinger's novel) attempt to come to terms with the implications of Rousseau's teachings about 'natural man' and civilization. Goethe's completed *Faust*—while not exactly 'about' life in contemporary Germany in any obvious and direct sense—certainly takes stock of practically everything that could concern a thinking person of versatile interests in that age, while the Romantic *Fausts* are obsessed by the implications of the Kantian and post-Kantian philosophy, especially inasmuch as it had something to say about the possibility of man's achieving certainty regarding the 'reality' outside him. It is arguable, too, that Platen's 'Fausts Gebet' reflects the poet's reaction to recent advances in astronomy.

William Herschel's observations had shown that the universe was many thousands of times vaster than had previously been imagined. One possible effect of this on man's view of himself and of terrestrial life is put forward in Krüger's essay 'Über das Verhältniß der Erde zum Weltall . . .' in Ballenstedt's *Archiv für die neuesten Entdeckungen*, 1819.[1] Since our earth is such an infinitesimal part of the known cosmos, argues Krüger, old habits of thought which saw man as the measure of things and

[1] Quedlinburg and Leipzig, i, 73ff.

regarded his affairs as the central purpose of the universe must be abandoned. The cosmos must have a purpose which greatly transcends anything dreamt of by man and related to his comparatively insignificant experiences. This feeling that man is dwarfed by the immensity of the cosmos figures in Platen's poem:

> Wenn ich die Sterne, Herr, dort oben, die unendlichen,
> Nachstammle dir, nachzähle dir, nachmillione dir,
> Wie möcht' ich schwingen mich, von Welt zu Welt hin,
>   ewig fort. . . .
> Wir werfen Maulwurfsblicke zwergicht in die Wissenschaft,
> Des Allernächsten Fremdlinge, wie des Entferntesten.

(This shows how scientific discoveries can lead a poet to draw quite different implications from those that the scientist himself draws, for Herschel certainly felt not at all like a mole peering dimly at immeasurable splendour and immensity: 'a knowledge of the construction of the heavens has always been the ultimate object of my observations. . . .')[1]

But the main point I am trying to make is that serious *Faustdichter*, from Lessing to Platen and Lenau, attempt to relate their theme to recent developments in thought and knowledge, to restate it against the background of what the authors think is significant in and for their age. Man's place in the cosmos was seen differently once Herschel's vastly improved telescopes had been trained on distant nebulae; the problem of how much man could know and how reliably he knew it was treated differently after Kant and Fichte. So, too, the quest to discover the source of life is depicted by Goethe in terms of the contemporary quarrel between the 'Neptunists' and the 'Vulcanists'.

Increasingly through the nineteenth century, however, Faust works appear to be written as contributions to a literary tradition rather than in response to contemporary realities; their authors define the faustian urge by looking back at other *Fausts* (especially Goethe's) rather than by looking outwards at the problems

---

[1] *Scientific Papers*, ii, 459. Platen never, to my knowledge refers to Herschel, but his view of the cosmos, with its millions of stars, must be indebted directly or indirectly to Herschel's pioneering work. For a discussion of Herschel's 'expanding universe' in its relationship to Jean Paul's 'Traum über das All', see J. W. Smeed, *Jean Paul's Dreams*, O.U.P., 1966, 30f. Platen had visited Jean Paul in January 1820 and had talked of, among other things, 'einige philosophische Gegenstände' (*Tagebüche*, 30/1/1820). Did these include the philosophical implications of recent advances in astronomy?

which confront the age. An extreme example of a serious, full-length *Faust* which seems almost solely to have been written as a variation on a literary theme is Franz Keim's *Mephistopheles in Rom*, 1890. It is of course impossible to determine which is the chicken, which the egg; did *Faustdichter* see their work as in the first place a contribution to a *literary* tradition because they did not conceive of Faust's thirst for knowledge as a human problem which renews or modifies itself in each generation as the frontiers of knowledge and man's philosophical and religious criteria change, or did they fail to see that Faust's was a contemporary problem at any given moment because they were too preoccupied with the literary tradition? In any case, many—even most—nineteenth-century *Fausts* seem disappointing and trivial and one reason is that they have little or nothing to do with the scientific, philosophical, and religious crises of their age. Now it is clear that art is to some extent engendered of art, and that any view of an art-form which sees the works solely as responses to things and experiences and which does not take artistic traditions into account is inadequate and naïve. But, especially in the case of literature, one hopes to find that each serious taking-up of a tradition is also a response to something in the writer's age and milieu. Furthermore, I am not suggesting that a *Faust* must be 'contemporary' to be valuable —treatments of this legend are, by their nature, more likely to take up perennial problems than are most other works of literature. But even perennial problems—or precisely perennial problems— need to be reviewed and restated as man's knowledge increases and his environment changes.

In Western Europe, the nineteenth century was a period of dramatic advance in scientific knowledge. This in turn changed our environment and our views concerning what man can know and do. Yet the legend which seems most obviously suited to depict man's lust to know, to experience, and to gain power over his environment seems hardly concerned with these themes during the period 1840–1900. Even the changes that the Industrial Revolution was bringing about, in ways impossible to overlook, in man's physical surroundings, are seldom referred to. In Lenburg's *Faust* (1860), Frank, the husband of a woman whom Faust is pursuing, is some kind of unspecified inventor-cum-industrialist. But Faust himself is indifferent to technological novelties:

Ich sah in letzter Zeit zu viel des Neuen;
Mich würde nun das Neueste nicht freuen.   (p. 35)

He is much more interested in Frank's wife than in his inventions. In J. Ernstlieb's *Faust, 2. Theil* (1884), there is a passing reference to the effects of the Industrial Revolution on wildlife:

Der Spanner und der Falter buntes Heer
Wird jährlich dünner und selbst ärmlicher.
Ich fürcht', das macht der viele Kohlendampf.   (p. 30)

But, for the most part, one could read through the plays, novels, and poems written about Dr. Faust in the nineteenth century without gaining much inkling of the changes that applied science was bringing about. What are the reasons for this?

Two probable minor reasons are connected with Goethe's *Faust* and the discussion of it that went on throughout the nineteenth century. One effect of Goethe's work was to help to turn Faust into a sort of second Don Juan in the eyes of many Germans; intellectual questing seemed less important in Faust's motivation than womanizing. Secondly, critical discussion of Goethe's *Faust*, especially of Part 2, had greatly shifted the emphasis from questions of knowledge to questions of activity. Admirers and opponents of the work tirelessly discussed this latter theme (does Faust achieve anything? do his achievements merit salvation? what worthier ideals of activity could be devised for a Faust?). Largely as a result of Goethe's work, Faust came to figure in the imagination of cultivated Germans as a human type whose ruling characteristic is restless activity rather than restless curiosity. And even here, the clear hint contained in Acts 4 and 5 of Goethe's Part 2 that a man's highest ambition should involve an attempt to change and control his environment for the benefit of his fellows was seldom appreciated in the nineteenth century; Faust was more often mocked than praised for his reclamation of land. Not until Lunacharski in this century was Goethe's hint to be taken up again.

A further reason is unquestionably that so many major figures writing in German in the mid- and late nineteenth century were men of the bourgeoisie, primarily concerned with the problem of how man was to live within society, how he was to reconcile his needs as an individual with the demands made on him by society, and how he could satisfy both the practical and the aesthetic sides of his nature in a society that increasingly stressed practical considerations. In the works of writers like Keller, Storm and Stifter, 'ordinary men' figure much more frequently than larger than life rebels, and a modified, 'critical' conformity to social norms is nearer the ideal than any rebellious kicking over the traces.

The shortage of 'scientific' *Fausts* will undoubtedly also be partly due to the fact that the division of poetry and science into two cultures was well under way by 1850 and very marked in the last decades of the century. Despite attempts, especially by the Darwinians, at popularization, science gradually becomes too specialized to be understood in its implications by the intelligent layman in such a way that it can help him to form a unified view of the world. It has often been said that the last European who really managed to survey and unite the sciences and the arts was Goethe. But even Goethe was criticized by the scientists of his day for lacking truly systematic knowledge, particularly in mathematics. And the greatest mathematician of the period, Gauß, is said to have regarded Goethe's work as deficient from a point of view of rigorous thought-content, and appears to have admired only the lyric poetry (cf. Winnecke, p. 31). Yet, when all this has been said, it still remains surprising that the related themes of intellectual curiosity and the capacity to produce change which new knowledge brings with it play so little part in nineteenth-century *Fausts*. To seek further reasons we must look more closely at nineteenth-century attitudes towards knowledge.

The German Materialists had insisted that man and the natural world could be fully described and understood in terms of cause and effect. The secret of life is chemistry, says Moleschott (*Kreis-lauf*, 16. Brief) and, in a famous passage, sums up his view of human personality as follows:

So ist der Mensch die Summe von Eltern und Amme, von Ort und Zeit, von Luft und Wetter, von Schall und Licht, von Kost und Kleidung. (19. Br.)

Accept this view and it follows that man must believe the evidence of his senses and take things as they are. Ludwig Feuerbach: 'Die . . . wahre Aufgabe des Menschen ist, die Dinge zu nehmen und zu behandeln, wie sie sind . . .' (*Wesen der Religion*, p. 43). The

Materialists make constant appeals to empirical methods, whereas the essence of the faustian restlessness is that the senses never take us far enough. For Feuerbach, nature as revealed to man by his sense perceptions is not open to doubt (p. 169), where for successive Fausts, especially in the Romantic era, this had been precisely the area of greatest doubt. If Carl Vogt, Moleschott, and the others are right, man cannot escape from or transcend the human condition; there *is* nothing else. The Materialists' attacks on the Romantic pursuit of unattainable ideals[1] would, for German readers in the mid-nineteenth century, have very obvious application to the Faust type.

More important perhaps than these Materialist views (which, after all, were held only by a small minority) was the growing belief that the march of science would both answer more and more of man's questions and lead to steady progress in improving the quality of human life. Here the ground was prepared to some extent by the Positivists. Auguste Comte, particularly, encouraged the belief that, with the adoption of rigorous scientific methods in all fields, progress would be assured, dreaming of a utopian world-state with a Positivist philosophy as its secular religion.[2] This idea is taken up in an uncritical and popularized form by many of Comte's disciples.[3] The approach to truth, for the Positivists, was a long but basically simple process of collecting data and forming generalizations based on them.[4] The German disciples of Positivism stress that intellectual certainty and material progress will come about by the systematic application of inductive methods:

Auf dieser strengen, *induktiven* Methode beruht die Klarheit und die Sicherheit des einmal Erreichten und in ihr besitzt der menschliche Geist das unfehlbare Mittel zu jenem sichern Fortschritt, welcher allmählich . . . das bis jetzt noch 'rätselhaft' Gewesene in durchsichtige und streng gesetzlich wirkende Elemente aufzulösen vermag. Der heftigste Streit der Gelehrten endet mittels dieser Methode allmählich in einer gemeinsamen Übereinstimmung.(!)

(Kirchmann, *Zeitfragen*, p. 101)

---

[1] See, for example, Feuerbach, op. cit., 28th Lecture.

[2] See Comte, *Cours de Philosophie Positive*, Lessons 48, 51, and 56; also the *Discours*, especially the last chapter.

[3] See L. André-Nuytz, *Le Positivisme pour tous*, Paris, 1868 and E. Littré, *Des Progrès du Socialisme*, Paris, 1852.

[4] Cf. H. Taine, *Hist. de la Litt. anglaise*, 2nd edn., Paris, 1872, v, 397.

Not only did the Positivists declare that all ascertainable facts would eventually become established and all puzzles resolved, they also rejected any pursuit of 'ultimate secrets', everything that Faust has traditionally striven to discover, in fact:

. . . dans l'état positif [=scientific], l'esprit humain reconnaissant l'impossibilité d'obtenir des notions absolues, renonce à chercher l'origine et la destination de l'univers, et à connaître les causes intimes des phénomènes, pour s'attacher uniquement à découvrir, par l'usage bien combiné du raisonnement et de l'observation, leurs lois effectives, c'est-à-dire leurs relations invariables de succession et de similitude.

(Comte, *Cours*, i, 4–5)

'Nothing has been more characteristic of the past two centuries than belief in "progress" as inevitable', says Tuveson (p. 1). In the eighteenth century, the concept of progress commonly depended on the conviction that the universe manifested or reflected a benevolent purpose, and that all men were capable of moral and rational development. Soon the idea of progress through humane rationality became linked with the notion of science as the means by which man can come to command his environment. The first important and detailed expression of this is, as far as I know, in L. S. Mercier's remarkable utopian novel *L'an 2440*, first published in 1770. Mercier's Utopia is influenced both by Rousseau's ideal of the simple life, by the Rationalism and Deism of the *philosophes*, and by a deep conviction that the natural sciences will have a dominant part to play in human progress. Can we plumb nature's secrets? asks Mercier, and answers that this now seems possible, 'pourvu que la chaîne des observations ne soit pas interrompue, et que chaque physicien se montre plus jaloux de la perfection de la science que de sa propre gloire'. Mercier is not thinking of 'pure', abstract knowledge, but of that knowledge which conduces towards men's happiness: 'Le génie peut être puissant, mais il n'est grand que lorsqu'il sert l'humanité.'[1] Already the 'antifaustian' implications of such views are apparent, particularly when one considers the general distaste for all 'futile' (i.e. non-practical) speculation that runs through Mercier's work. By the 1830s, this type of optimism was strengthened by the great impetus in both pure and applied science;

[1] *L'an deux mille quatre cent quarante*, London, 1772, 278 and 283. The book appeared in German as *Das Jahr zweytausendvierhundert und vierzig*, also London, 1772.

people were made dramatically aware of man's ability to make
new discoveries and to change the world through them. The
Great Exhibition of 1851 was seen both as a monument to what
had already been achieved by nineteenth-century science and
technology and as an assurance of continuing discovery and
progress.

As early as 1833 Heine had written:

Die bisherige spiritualistische Religion war heilsam und nothwendig,
solange der größte Theil der Menschen im Elend lebten und sich mit
der himmlischen Seeligkeit vertrösten mußten. Seit aber, durch die
Fortschritte der Industrie und Oekonomie, es möglich geworden, die
Menschen aus ihrem materiellen Elende herauszuziehen und auf Erden
zu beseligen, seitdem—Sie verstehen mich.   (to Laube, 10/7/1833)

An example of a mood of naïve elation directly inspired by a
specific technological achievement can be seen in the following
extract from an anonymous poem celebrating the trial run on
the railway between Heidelberg and Mannheim in 1840:

> Triumph!
> Die Bahn brennt im Dampfe, die Bahnblitze sausen,
> Die Luft selbst erzittert in angstvollem Grausen.
> (quoted by Redslob, p. 218)

Among those who hymned the new age of Rhine steamers and
railway engines were Anastasius Grün and Gottfried Keller.[1]

Optimistic views such as those mentioned above often depend,
implicitly or explicitly, on the belief that man's intellectual powers
evolve. Here the influence of Darwinism was decisive. In Germany,
Darwin's followers thought of the *Origin of Species* and, later, the
Descent of Man as having ushered in a new age in learning. The
tone in which the theory of evolution was discussed by many of
its supporters suggests a pseudo-religion rather than a biological
hypothesis. This can be seen clearly in many of the contributions
to the Darwinistic periodical *Kosmos* (1877ff). Or take the poem by

[1] See Grün, 'Poesie des Dampfes' and Keller, 'Erwiderung auf Justinus Kerners
Lied: "Unter dem Himmel"'. Lenau was against railways; see 'An den Frühling
1838'. The most famous expressions of faith in scientific progress in England are
probably those by Tennyson in 'Mechanophilus' and the 'Ode sung at the Opening
of the International Exhibition'. See too the anonymous book *The Progress and
Prospects of Society*, London, 1841. Among the pessimists were Peacock (*Gryll
Grange*, Chapter xix), William Morris (Prologue to *The Earthly Paradise*) and Matthew Arnold (*Culture and Anarchy*).

Artur Fitger, written for inclusion in an album presented to Darwin by a number of his German admirers in 1877:

> Da kamest Du—und im Getrennten
> Die Einheit fand Dein Forscherblick;
> Den tief entzweiten Elementen
> Gabst Du die Harmonie zurück.
> Du sahst im ewigen Verwandeln
> Der Dinge weitverknüpftes Netz.
> Und in dem rätselvollen Handeln
> Des Weltalls sahst Du das Gesetz.
>   (Quoted in Krause, p. 228)

Haeckel, too, is capable of ecstatic flights:

> Die leuchtenden Strahlen dieser Sonne [= der Entwicklungslehre] haben die schweren Wolken der Unwissenheit und des Aberglaubens zerstreut . . . (*Unsere gegenwärtige Kenntniß*, p. 31)

Darwinism, it was thought, would lead man towards truth. Moreover, since the idea of evolution was applied in the historical, cultural, intellectual, and ethical spheres, it came to be widely held, especially in Germany, that Darwinism, properly understood, guaranteed progress. It may be noted that the final chapter of the *Origin of Species* offers some support for such notions. For Darwin ends with the vision of a revolution in the study of natural history. Scientific investigation will become more and more precise and more illuminating as men come to regard each phenomenon as the result of a complex development governed by factors which we are gradually beginning to understand. Moreover, 'as natural selection works solely by and for the good of each being, all corporeal and mental endowments will tend to progress towards perfection'.[1] These arguments of Darwin's are paraphrased by Ludwig Büchner in his article 'Eine neue Schöpfungsgeschichte' of 1860 (*Natur und Wissenschaft*, i, 248f) and are repeated, often in extravagant terms, by many of the German Darwinists.

It would be tedious and perhaps depressing to multiply examples of this absolute faith in progress. Progress is no longer felt to be something which man might achieve, given

---

[1] Page 489 in the first edition. Darwin also believed that virtuous tendencies might be inheritable (*Descent of Man*, ii, 394). But for a more sceptical view, see Chapters 50 and 51 of the same work.

goodwill, insight and determination; it becomes a law, guaranteed by the evolutionary principle. Phrases like 'das in der Natur waltende große Gesetz des Fortschritts' or 'das Gesetz des Fortschritts oder der Vervollkommnung' become common.[1] In its most rapturous form, the neo-Darwinist belief in progress looked forward to an earthly paradise in which knowledge would have conquered disease and physical hardship, in which the egotistical impulses in men would have yielded to just and humanitarian principles.[2]

Since evolution was held to be at work not only in the physical and instinctual development of animals but in the moral and intellectual development of the human race, many believed that ultimately all man's questions would be answered. On this point the German Darwinists were *plus royalistes que le roi*. Here is Moritz Wagner, after Haeckel the main agent in spreading Darwinism in Germany:

Das Geheimniß des Lebens wird sicher eines Tages ergründet werden. . . . Daß wir heute das Wie noch nicht wissen, ist kein Grund dafür, daß wir es nicht einstmals erkennen und erfahren werden.[3]

What implications do these twin beliefs—in the inevitability of progress and in man's ability ultimately to resolve all his uncertainties—have for Faust? In A. Fitger's poem 'Faust's Schatten an Charles Darwin', Faust addresses Darwin from the grave:

> Von Allen, die ich sah,
> Erhabner Greis, o, fühl' ich Dir mich nah!
> Was ich geahnt, Dir ward es klar;
> Was ich geträumt, Dir ward es wahr;
> Du hast gleich mir des Erdgeists Licht gesehn;
> Ich brach zusammen, aber Du bliebst stehn,
> Und fest im Sturm der wechselnden Erscheinung
> Sahst das Gesetz Du, sahst Du die Vereinung.[4]

---

[1] Cf. Haeckel, *Schöpfungsgeschichte*, passim; Strauß, *Alter und neuer Glaube*, pp. 239f; Wagner, p. 194.

[2] Cf. the anonymous pamphlet *Die Grundlagen der wahren Naturreligion nach Darwin und Haeckel*, Berlin, 1881; also Büchner, *Der Fortschritt . . .*, pp. 35–8. Shaw too believed that evolution would gradually produce a race of men greatly superior in will power and intelligence to his contemporaries: see the chapter 'Wagner as Revolutionist' in *The Perfect Wagnerite*.

[3] Quoted in K. von Scherzer, *Moritz Wagner. Ein deutsches Forscherleben*, Munich, 1888, p. 23.

[4] *Kosmos*, vol. iv (1878–9), p. 337.

Fitger sees Faust as having been superseded by Darwin. Ernst Krause goes further and seems to regard the faustian restlessness as an ailment of man's mental immaturity: 'Das beste und schnellste Heilmittel für die Faustkrisis gibt . . . die Vertiefung in das Studium der Entwicklungslehre an die Hand'.[1] Darwin has given the hint; scientific methods can do the rest: 'Die Mittel und Wege, welche wir zur Lösung der großen Welträthsel einzuschlagen haben, sind keine anderen als diejenigen der reinen wissenschaftlichen Erkenntniß überhaupt, also erstens *Erfahrung* und zweitens *Schlußfolgerung*' (Haeckel, *Welträthsel*, p. 19). Such views certainly help to explain why few scientifically informed people wrote *Fausts* and why comparatively few of the *Fausts* that were written have much to do with the pursuit and application of scientific knowledge. Had he been born into the post-Darwin era, Faust would have recognized that his desire for total and immediate knowledge was childish impatience, and would have set himself to the study of the 'evolutionary theory: that is what Fitger, Krause and Haeckel imply.

In view of what has been said, it is not surprising that such allusions to Materialism or to the belief in progress or, later, to Darwinism as one does find in nineteenth-century *Fausts* are mostly negative—they are made by authors who reject such views and philosophies. First, an example from pre-Darwinian Germany. The notion that science may, one day, solve all man's questions is stated, only to be rejected, in F. Reinhard's *Faust* of 1848. This work certainly takes stock both of advances in the sciences and of the attitudes such advances encourage, but Reinhard is severe on the scientific optimists. Here, as in Goethe's *Faust*, Wagner is the spokesman for an unproblematic belief in progress. Encouraged by recent advances in astronomy, he dreams of a day when men will know all:

> Hat nicht erst spät der Forschergeist erkannt,
> Daß fern im Raume lichte Nebelmassen,
> Geregelt von der Allmacht Hand,
> Zu Welten sich zusammenfassen. . . .
> Darf aber dieser Geist, der in die Werkstatt schaut,
> In der die Allmacht Weltsysteme baut,
> Darf er die Hoffnung freudig nicht begrüßen,
> Es könne einst sich ihm das Ganze noch erschließen?   (p. 35)

[1] 'Über Faust-Stimmung . . .' in *Kosmos*, vol. vi (1879–80), p. 10.

And, as in Goethe, Faust is sceptical:

> Unendlich ist das All und endlich nur das Wissen.   (p. 34)

In fact, Reinhard's Faust returns in the end to a position of faith and comes to repudiate 'sinful' curiosity (p. 88); the implications of this mid-nineteenth century *Faust* are not so different from those of the original Faustbook!

Neo-Darwinistic belief in progress figures in J. Gaulke's *Der gefesselte Faust* (1910), again only to be rejected. Gaulke's Faust learns at the university an optimistic philosophy of ethical evolutionism very similar to that which had been preached by Darwin, Ludwig Büchner, Haeckel, and others. (The dates fit: Faust's professor in this work is of the right generation to have been a disciple of Haeckel, who taught in Jena from the 1860s.) Faust soon finds that reality offers no support for these views. Moral goodness and intelligence do not triumph. There is no evolution towards the Good, the True, and the Beautiful (p. 50). As Klinger's *Faust* had, a century before, set out to destroy eighteenth-century moral optimism, Gaulke's sets out to destroy nineteenth-century scientific optimism—in both cases by reference to man's actual conduct.

In Ferdinand Ritter von Feldegg's *Der neue Faust* (1902) Faust is a scientist who opposes the modern tendency to regard soul as a function or by-product of matter:

> Daß das Leben nicht das Spiel unbewußter Kräfte ist, nicht ein Nervenzellenvorgang allein,—sondern das Werk einer organisierenden, bewußten Seele . . . daß diese Seele von Anfang an ist—nicht der Leib—und sie ihm, nicht er ihr zuletzt gebietet—im Leben wie im Tode . . . Gelänge es uns, dies zu erweisen! . . .   (p. 105)

In a dream sequence (ii, 2) various representatives of modern scientific and philosophical thought are caricatured and pilloried: agnostics, Materialists, physiologists who believe in nothing that cannot be laid bare by the knife and grasped in the forceps, Darwinists. Haeckel, labelled 'Monist', puts in a personal appearance. The modern views figure in the work, but again only to be rejected, scornfully in this case.[1]

The only *Faust* known to me which *accepts* the Darwinistic

---

[1] For a rejection of mid-twentieth-century beliefs in progress through applied science, see A. Schmid, *Faust der Denker*, 1952.

theory and shares the optimism which it helped to generate is
H. Hango's *Faust und Prometheus*, 1895.[1] Faust is the doubting
part of man, and the poem is a dialogue between the doubter and
the hoper (Prometheus). This is a Faust work without God or
Devil: the supernatural dimensions are absent—even the coming
into being of the universe is imagined as having happened
without a creator. The development of life on earth is seen in
Darwinistic terms. There follows an account of the development
of civilization, an account in which the evil and violence in man
are recognized but are set off against his desire for truth and his
nobility. The debate between Faust and Prometheus centres on
which side of man's nature will triumph. Prometheus offers a
glimpse into a utopian future. There will be no more war,
wisdom will overcome folly, national boundaries will be broken
down, disease will be conquered, man will live longer and see a
sort of immortality in his bequest to the next generation. This
vision is very similar to the utopian dreams of the German
Positivists and Darwinists.

Hango's Darwinistic *Faust* certainly seems to bear out the
views of Fitger and Krause; it seems to spell the end of Faust
as we have known him from earlier works. For *Faust und Prometheus* postulates a universe which is complete in itself and is its
own justification. God, inasmuch as he figures at all, is the God
of Feuerbach and his followers, an embodiment of man's ideals
rather than an objective reality. The clear suggestion of the work
is that the faustian urge is to be reconciled to itself and harnessed
to the progress of mankind. What has become of the Faust who
cursed God for imprisoning him in doubt and raved at nature
for withholding her secrets? It is interesting to note that the
view that science will, in the long run, answer all men's questions
had been referred to a few years before in C. A. Linde's *Faust*
of 1887 but only as an excuse for not allowing the theme of
intellectual curiosity to figure in the work! In his dedicatory poem
'An Goethe', Linde explains that his Faust is not to be tempted
by the promise of knowledge since, in this age, science is revelation enough (p. iv). The action of Linde's *Faust* is political and

---

[1] Wilhelm Jordan regarded his Faust version, *Demiurgos*, as a 'poetic anticipation' of Darwinism. (In later works of his, the direct influence of Darwin can be
seen.) In *Demiurgos*, Jordan's approach to the problems of knowing and interpreting
the world is different from Hango's: see below, pp. 213f.

is not concerned with problems of knowledge and doubt at any point.

Even more radical implications for the Faust theme can be seen if we examine a little more closely what most nineteenth-century scientists meant when they talked of finding the answers to man's fundamental questions. Their questions are certainly not those asked by Klinger's Faust, or by Goethe's, or by the Romantic Fausts. Many of the most distinguished nineteenth-century scientists seem to have pursued their work, perfectly convinced that the whole truth will never be known. The great chemist Justus von Liebig is a case in point; he felt that life was inexhaustible and its full meaning undiscoverable. New findings open new possibilities for further study; each answer poses further questions.

Wir ersteigen einen Berg, auf der Spitze angelangt, sieht der umfassendere Blick immer neue Berge sich erheben, die anfänglich dem Auge nicht sichtbar waren.[1]

But this did not lead Liebig to a mood of faustian frustration, rather to a serene determination to find out as much as he could and to encourage others to do likewise. Many scientists were, then as now, simply concerned with getting on with their own piece of research—urgently, no doubt, but very matter of factly as far as questions of 'ultimate truth' were involved. This 'unfaustian' concern with immediate, practical problems is very clear in the letters of Liebig's fellow-chemist and collaborator Friedrich Wöhler, for instance.[2]

From the mid-nineteenth century onwards one finds a growing rift between philosophy and science. Among 'practical', scientifically minded men there is definite hostility towards abstract speculation and vague questions regarding ultimate purpose. H. Debus records Wilhelm Bunsen's dislike of theoretical speculation. 'Das sind ja nur Vorstellungen', he would remark when confronted with a theory which was, in his opinion, insufficiently grounded on empirical data. Debus (pp. 144f) sees this distrust of philosophical pondering as part of a reaction against the

[1] Liebig, *Chemische Briefe*, i, 40. For a similar image, see H. Frerichs in *Kosmos*, vii, 168.
[2] Cf. *Fr. Wöhler. Ein Jugendbildnis in Briefen*, ed. G. W. A. Kahlbaum, Leipzig, 1900.

Hegelian philosophy which had dominated German universities in Bunsen's youth. The same dislike of philosophical systems (and hence of sweeping general ideas) is apparent in Ludwig Büchner: 'Das System ist die *Kindheit* der Philosophie; die *Mannheit* derselben ist die Forschung.' And Moritz Wagner has scant respect for the philosophers, believing them to be incapable of grasping truths which are immediately obvious to the scientist. [1] One may note that this has very little to do with the modern notion of 'two cultures'; it was not a question of the scientists' ignorance or of their inability to understand what the other man was doing; rather a serious *methodological* disagreement which had come about because German systematic philosophy had moved so far away from empiricism. The tendency of some philosophers to regard the scientist's approach as trivial cannot have helped. The scientist, declares Schopenhauer, is concerned only with fragments and details, the philosopher with essentials; the sum total of the empirical discoveries made by scientists only *defines* the problem facing the metaphysician. [2] The opposition between philosopher and scientist is clear if we set off Schopenhauer's opinion of the latter against Liebig's view 'daß der Fortschritt des Menschengeschlechtes *lediglich* durch den Fortschritt der Naturerkenntnis bedingt wurde, nicht durch Moral, Religion oder Philosophie!' (*Briefwechsel*, p. 221).

It is interesting to find Liebig picking up, in one of his lectures, an image common in the *Faustdichtungen*:

Die Natur ist für die Mehrzahl von Ihnen . . . das mit unbekannten Chiffern beschriebene Buch, das Sie verstehen, in dem Sie lesen lernen wollen; die Worte, die Zeichen, in denen sie zu uns redet, sind aber Chiffern besonderer Art, es sind eigenthümliche Phänomene, die Sie kennen lernen müssen . . . (*Reden*, p. 158)

—and he goes on to talk of an 'alphabet' of nature, with which the students will gradually familiarize themselves in the course of their studies. Where Platen's Faust had impetuously and hopelessly desired to grasp nature and the universe in one intuitive

[1] Büchner, *Aus Natur und Wissenschaft*, i, 243; Moritz Wagner, op. cit., p. 210; Werner Siemens too distrusted all ideas that had no practical application—see Matschoß, p. 240.

[2] *SW*., ed. Frauenstädt, 2nd edn., Leipzig, 1891, vi, 151. See too the parable of the two Chinamen visiting a theatre in Europe, vi, 685; also Nietzsche, *Jenseits von Gut und Böse*, §14.

flash, and where Lenau's Faust had cast aside nature's book as being incomprehensible gibberish, Liebig believes that he and his students must try gradually to learn to decipher nature's language. Schopenhauer would doubtless have preferred Faust to Liebig, but Liebig would have regarded Faust as an unscientific adolescent.[1] (Goethe's Faust does, it is true, begin with an impetuous thirst for total certainty concerning the inmost secrets of the universe, then develops towards a more patient viewpoint and an acceptance of the fact that the finite 'reflection' of the divine is all that we can or should hope to perceive and understand. Plainly this is paralleled by a similar change in the attitude of Goethe himself; equally plainly, Goethe's nature studies were a decisive influence in bringing the change about, even if he does not allow scientific study to appear as a major and explicit factor in Faust's development. But I cannot think of *any* post-Goethean Faust who undergoes a similar development from 'superhuman' aspirations to comparative intellectual humility because of scientific studies.)

Ludwig Büchner is another who talks of the factors limiting possible human knowledge in terms very similar to those used by the authors of Romantic *Fausts*; certain puzzles will always remain puzzles, he argues,

... da alles menschliche Wissen mehr oder weniger Stückwerk ist und wohl auch immer bleiben wird, oder da der menschliche Geist infolge seiner durch die Schranken von Zeit und Raum eingeengten Natur wohl niemals im Stande sein wird, bis zu den letzten Gründen der Dinge vorzudringen ... (*Natur und Wissenschaft*, ii, 171f)

But, as in the case of Liebig, the conclusions drawn are different; Büchner accepts the limits cheerfully and sets about the task of explaining and discovering what can be explained and discovered.

---

[1] Lest the foregoing should seem to imply that nineteenth-century *Faustdichter* turned their backs on science in favour of philosophy, that mid- and late-nineteenth-century *Fausts* frequently reflect the authors' responses to contemporary developments in philosophy, it should be said that the only philosopher whose influence is at all prominent in Faust works during the period under discussion is Nietzsche and he only as the creator of the superman who overrides received views on morality. Examples of *Fausts* in which Nietzsche's moral philosophy figures in one way or another: Hutschenreiter (1895), Spielhagen (1898), Gaulke (1910). But Nietzsche's influence is greater in works devoted to Don Juan, a figure who can much more obviously and dramatically be seen living out his scorn for conventional morality.

Haeckel, too, quite serenely conceded that we shall never penetrate to the ultimate secrets:

Die Schöpfung . . . , als die *Entstehung der Materie*, geht uns hier gar nichts an. Dieser Vorgang, wenn er überhaupt jemals stattgefunden hat, ist gänzlich der menschlichen Erkenntniß entzogen . . . Wir gelangen *nirgends* zu einer Erkenntniß der *letzten Gründe* . . . Es liegt das in der Beschränktheit oder Relativität unseres Erkenntnißvermögens.[1]

This type of view figures in Wilhelm Jordan's 'mystery' *Demiurgos* (1852), where Professor Alexander, as a representative example of the sceptical modern scientist, brushes aside all questions of purpose:

> Warum die Dinge, und wozu sie sind,
> Und was am Ende sie bezwecken,
> So fragt, bedünkt mich, nur ein Kind . . . (ii, 161)

Although Jordan himself had been weaned away from the study of theology by D. F. Strauß, he still dreamt of a possible reconciliation between a non-dogmatic Christianity and science, so that Alexander's views, in the passage quoted and elsewhere, are more radical than Jordan's own. Jordan himself seemed to think that science can explain the universe and, in so doing, will render Faust out of date. For Graf Heinrich, the Faust of this poem, complains:

> Wonach sein [=Faust's] Riesengeist gerungen,
> Was ihn durchschauert stolz und tragisch
> Als neue Welt, in seinem Kopf entsprungen,
> Was er nur märchenhaft und magisch
> Um seiner Seele Preis erzwungen:
> Das hat nun die Pygmäenschaar
> Erlangt mit kleinlichem Hanthieren;
> Denn die Natur ward aller Wunder baar
> Und läßt sich klar erkennen, zahm regieren. (i, 118)

The mystery and violence of nature have been reduced to patterns of atoms and 'Einmaleins', and we yawn instead of marvelling. Throwing off the fetters that restricted Faust, we are free but

[1] *Nat. Schöpfungsgeschichte*, pp. 7 and 26. Similar: Carl von Voit, *Über die Entwicklung der Erkenntniß*, Munich, 1876, p. 23, and the anonymous author of *Die Grundlagen der wahren Naturreligion*, p. 52.

P

listless, not knowing what to do with our power and freedom . . .
(119f). So, while the scientists imply that their methods have put
Faust out of business, a poet laments that science has taken the
mystery out of life and robbed Faust of his traditional motive
for allying himself to the Devil.[1]

An extreme instance of a scientist who was out of sympathy
with the Faust cult is the physiologist, Emil Du Bois-Reymond.
His attack on Goethe's *Faust* is a criticism by a scientist of Faust
seen as a quester after learning. Du Bois-Reymond finds it totally
fantastic that Faust, having proof of the existence of a spirit-
world, should not persist in trying to plumb the secrets of nature,
and is clearly pained over Faust's scorn for his scientific instruments, a scorn which he sees as part of a general German deni-
gration of empiricism.[2] Du Bois-Reymond was another of those
who argued that man will never know everything. Even if we
arrived at a law or formula which would explain all the phenomena of the known universe, the possession of this would still
not enable us to solve the ultimate riddles of matter, energy, and
consciousness.[3] This, then, is a scientist's approach to the question of whether we can 'erkennen, was die Welt/Im Innersten
zusammenhält'. It is not difficult to see why, in the nineteenth
century, the scientist and the *Faustdichter* were so seldom one and
the same person. Whether, as a scientist, you agreed or disagreed
with Du Bois-Reymond, the way in which you interpreted the
problem would hardly invite poetic or dramatic treatment,
certainly not treatment in terms of the Faust legend. From its
beginnings to the Romantic era this legend had undoubtedly
owed much of its fascination to the conviction that man's
capacity to ask questions, to perceive what he does *not* know, is
greater than his knowledge, actual or potential. So he is always
aware of the gulf between his desire for knowledge and his actual
knowledge—and he thinks that this gulf is unbridgeable by
normal and 'lawful' human means. In a variety of ways, practising

[1] There has been some discussion of the philosophical ideas in *Demiurgos*. The
most recent and most penetrating study is by Franz Koch (see Bibliography). Koch
shows in what sense Jordan is to be understood when he says that his poem
'poetically anticipates' Darwinism, and goes into the question of Jordan's treatment
of evil and his debt to gnostic ideas.

[2] *Goethe und kein Ende*, pp. 12f, 16–18. For Faust on his scientific instruments, see
Goethe, *Faust 1*, lines 668–75. For Du Bois-Reymond's attack on Faust's salvation,
see above, Chapter 7.

[3] This argument is developed in *Über die Grenzen*. . . .

scientists and scientifically informed laymen in the nineteenth century undermined this conviction.

What of more modern *Fausts*? If the development of science and technology was dramatic in the nineteenth century, it has been sensational in the twentieth. Yet anyone expecting to find the Faust theme used to express significant reactions to recent developments in the sciences will be disappointed. There are costume pieces with little reference to modern problems, such as Kurt Becsi's historical extravaganza set in the sixteenth century, *Faust in Moskau* (1963); there are re-tellings of the chapbook—free and imaginative in Klaus Mampell (1962), mere paraphrase with a little halfhearted updating in Georg Reißer (1954); there are re-workings of Goethe, for example that by M. Ehbauer (1960). Of versions that do deal with our age, some are trivial like John Hersey's *Too far to walk* (1966), others facetious like I. A. Richards' *Tomorrow morning, Faustus!* (1962). Or we find the external trappings of modern life in a work which otherwise has nothing particularly contemporary about it. For example, in R. H. Ward's *Faust in Hell* (1944), there are references to aeroplanes and the radio, but in its restatement of the Faust problem the piece is very like those nineteenth-century *Fausts* which teach that it is wicked to seek illicit knowledge and better to submit to God.

The only serious modern Faust work by a scientist would appear to be Antony Borrow's drama *John Faust* (1958).[1] But even here, if one is hoping for an examination of the problematic nature of modern scientific investigation, one will be disappointed. This is a Faust who is cold, uncompromising, apparently inhuman, because he sees through the pretences by which other men live ('I have penetrated behind every mask'—p. 11). Lonely and bitter, he rejects life and longs for death but is finally reconciled to his lot and learns humility. Apart from a comment on Faust by his father ('It is men like him who will one day find and speak some Word of Power that will wreck the sun'—p. 5) there is little to single out this Faust as a scientist: he could be any type of lonely and hypersensitive scholar.

Why are there so few 'scientific' *Fausts* in modern times? Firstly, of course, the legend has dated in the sense that many of

[1] Mr. Borrow studied Botany and later engaged in microbiological research.

the things that Faust was commonly represented as achieving
with magical aid have long since been matched by applied science.
This became apparent quite early in the era of the Industrial
Revolution. Here is Hans Andersen, writing about railways in
1842:

Oh, what a noble and great achievement of the mind is this production!
We feel ourselves as powerful as the sorcerers of old! . . . Mephistopheles could not fly quicker with Faust on his cloak! We are, with
natural means, equally as potent in the present age, as those in the
middle ages thought that only the devil himself could be!

And, nine years later, Schopenhauer speaks of:

jene Vervollkommnung der Technologie . . . , welche in unsern
Tagen . . . namentlich durch Dampfmaschinen und Elektricität Dinge
leistet, welche frühere Zeiten der Hülfe des Teufels zugeschrieben
haben würden.[1]

What has already, little more than a century later, been achieved
by way of space travel makes Faust's traditional journeyings
through the cosmos seem ridiculous.

What of questions concerning scientific knowledge and the
power over man and nature that such knowledge brings? What
we are concerned with here, to be sure, is not so much the professional views of a few highly-specialized scientists, but the intelligent layman's general notions concerning science and its potentialities. Hardly a month goes by in which we do not read, in some
section of the serious press, of a major breakthrough, achieved
or expected in the foreseeable future, in either pure or applied
science. We are invited to envisage the day when questions regarding the genesis of the universe and the origins of life on our planet
may be solved, when man's conquest of his environment may be
extended to include climate control, sub-marine farming, and
planetary colonization, when genetic tinkering and the control
of memory and temperament may be feasible. (The list could be
extended.) Clearly, to anyone familiar with such forecasts, Dr.
Faust's magical accomplishments must seem very small beer
and his pact almost comically irrelevant in view of the apparent
prospects of achieving knowledge and power through 'legitimate'
means. Take for example the question of the origin of organic

[1] Hans Andersen, *A Poet's Bazaar*, trans. Beckwith, London, 1846, i, 69;
Schopenhauer, *SW*, vi, 263.

life. It begins to look conceivable that this problem will be cracked. At the very least it seems to belong to the category of problems that can be solved piecemeal by a combination of experiment, empirical observation, deduction, and intuition—that is, it is a problem apparently not different in kind from those which scientists have already solved, and *not* a totally different type of question which 'normal' methods of human investigation are powerless to answer. But it was to answer this last sort of question that Faust entered on the pact. It is difficult to imagine a modern Faust concluding a pact with the Devil to discover, shall we say, how DNA and protein came together to form a living cell. Having got thus far, he would expect (or hope) to go further by the same methods. So most modern *Fausts* of any importance are not about this type of hero at all—how could they be? They pick on other possible aspects of the 'faustian' character (Faust as artist in Th. Mann, Faust as a figure caught up in the class struggle in Hanns Eisler).

One modern *Faust* does, it is true, deal with the theme of Faust's curiosity but in a way that constitutes the most radical and uncompromising break with traditional approaches that one could imagine: I am referring to Paul Valéry's *Mon Faust*. In a sketch for the continuation of the section 'Le Solitaire', we find the following:

La vie prit enfin à mes yeux un aspect bien étrange, comme un objet trouvé, un assez petit objet tenu dans la main. On le voit nettement, on le tourne, on le retourne au soleil de la connaissance nette; à quoi ressemble ceci? A rien. A quoi sert ceci? qui l'a fait?

A-t-on le courage de répondre que ce petit objet ne rime, ne ressemble, ne sert à rien. . . . (p. 1411)

We are reminded of that nineteenth-century discussion of whether science merely describes, or whether it can hope to answer questions concerning the 'meaning' of the universe. But even those nineteenth-century scientists who held the former view appeared to believe that there *was* a meaning.[1]

But apart from the question of whether the universe has any purpose beyond that which is defined by its own continued existence, it seems to me that the main problems posed by modern science and technology are not such as can be most appropriately

[1] Strauß is an exception: cf. *alter und neuer Glaube*, p. 222.

treated within the framework of the Faust legend. Most of these problems concern the practical implications of applying scientific knowledge and the resultant moral dilemma faced by the scientist. In modern literature the most telling examination of such questions is not in any Faust work but in Brecht's *Leben des Galilei*. The conflict between science and authority, the relationship of pure to applied science, the duty of the scientist to ensure that his discoveries are not abused—all this is examined in Brecht's play. The ethical dilemma of the scientist and his relationship with authority occurs as a theme in Science Fiction, too, for example in C. M. Kornbluth's short story 'Gomez'.[1] By contrast with Brecht's play or even with Kornbluth's little tale, the Faust works in which the atom bomb and similar hazardous discoveries figure seem superficial. W. Herbst's *Luther und Faust* (1950) would appear to demonstrate that the Faust legend is less adequate to convey misgivings about the abuse of scientific discoveries than is the story of Galileo. The action of Herbst's play takes place in the sixteenth century and Faust (the Humanist, the man of the Renaissance) is set off against Luther. At one point Mephisto mocks Faust's faith in the progress which can be achieved through science:

Ja die Menschen werden nun eines Tages alle Kräfte der Natur kennen und beherrschen! Aber sie werden diese Kenntnis und ihre ganze Naturbeherrschung eines Tages verfluchen! (p. 35)

But the play, with its crude opposition of faith (Luther) and curiosity (Faust), barely touches on the real dilemma. For 'faith' in itself will not solve our problems, nor will progress be achieved except in the first instance through curiosity, nor indeed can 'good' applied science exist without the risk of 'bad' applied science. It is not merely that Brecht is a better dramatist and deeper thinker than Herbst; he has chosen a happier vehicle for the working out of his theme.

The atom bomb figures, too, in Wilhelm Webel's *Spiel vom Dr. Faust* (1951) but the treatment is melodramatic and sententious. Mephostophiles [*sic*] urges Faust to assert his power over

---

[1] First published in 1955. Repr. in *Best Science Fiction Stories of C. M. Kornbluth*, London, 1968, pp. 170–200. Gomez is a young genius in mathematical physics who suddenly perceives the uses to which his theoretical discoveries are likely to be put. He walks out of the top security outfit in which he has been living and working as a sort of pampered prisoner, later pretending to have forgotten the critical equations.

the peoples of the world by hurling the atom bomb down on
their cities. Faust is encouraged to think of himself as an *Übermensch* and the rest of humanity as an antheap (p. 157). But the
problematic nature of scientific curiosity is hardly touched upon
and Faust's readiness to use the bomb in a show of naked force
is no more than a display of arrogance and wickedness. We miss
the point made by Brecht: that the scientist is, morally speaking,
an 'average man' who, because he is intellectually above the
average, has been placed in a situation where impossible demands
are made on him. A work in which the 'Galileo-theme', as we
may now call it, is treated somewhat more searchingly than by
either Herbst or Webels is Edward Byng's *Wiederkehr des Dr.
Faust* (1958). Here Faust discovers how to destroy and revive
memory by means of a preparation he calls 'Lethin' and demonstrates this to his colleagues, using Wagner as guinea pig. But
he soon finds that the powers that be, at home and abroad, want
to exploit his invention for ignoble ends and so destroys both
supplies and formulae, taking his secret to the grave. One passage
in the book calls Brecht's *Leben des Galilei* to mind:

'Aber Faust!' Pracriti erhitzt sich. 'Wohin käme die Wissenschaft,
wenn jeder Forscher seine Entdeckungen der Menschheit vorenthielte,
nur weil sie auch bösen Zwecken dienen könnten! Ich stehe auf dem
Standpunkt, daß der Wissenschaftler die Pflicht hat, die Resultate
seiner Forschungen der Öffentlichkeit zur Verfügung zu stellen.'

'Ich bin anderer Meinung. Solange Wissenschaft und Humanität
Hand in Hand gehen, ergibt sich der Weg des Gelehrten von selbst.
Jedesmal aber, wenn Wissenschaft und Menschenliebe feindliche Lager
beziehen, hat die Wissenschaft bedingungslos zu kapitulieren. Die
Wissenschaft sollte die Dienerin des Menschen sein, ist aber zum
Tyrannen geworden . . .' (pp. 44f)

And so we have the curious spectacle of a Faust *destroying* knowledge. But, in fact, the magic and the pact and all the rest are
the merest trappings;[1] there is no earthly need to evoke the
Faust legend in order to construct a fable about a scientist and
a memory drug.

In general it is the Science Fiction writers who seem to have
assimilated imaginatively into their works the advances of modern
science in a way that the *Faustdichter* have not done. Among the

---

[1] Byng's facetious treatment of the supernatural elements illustrates this: see the
end of Chapter 4, p. 98 above.

themes to be encountered in Science Fiction which are obvious modern treatments of motifs which had often figured previously in Faust versions are: the voyage through the cosmos, consideration of the possibility of intellectual achievement beyond our apparent human potential, the suggestion that some classes of facts and ideas cannot be expressed in human language. The superior, non-human thought processes of planetary visitors or intruders and the non-linguistic communication possible through super-computers—such things are modern counterparts to the old notion of the spirit-language incomprehensible to human beings.

Shaw's *Back to Methuselah* (1921) may be seen as an early example of Science Fiction which brushes aside the traditional faustian urge as not merely irrelevant but childish. The play implies that man's attempts to reach maturity, to use and apply reason, are doomed to failure because he is so short-lived. Real knowledge and the responsibility to use it sensibly cannot be hoped for within a life span of three score and ten. Faust, to Shaw's Ancients, would have seemed like a precocious child playing dangerously and irresponsibly with his knowledge and powers. One of the most interesting modern Science Fiction stories to show a clear thematic link with the Faust theme is C. D. Simak's 'Limiting Factor', a short story originally published in 1949.[1] A spacecraft from earth lands on a deserted planet completely enclosed in a shell of intricate machinery. The earthmen conclude that it is a vast computer, that the race who had inhabited the planet had built it in an attempt to solve all their hitherto unexplained problems, had found it inadequate, and had taken off to colonize a still larger planet which would support a yet more complex computer. So we have reached the stage where the modern Faust feeds his questions into a computer and where the limiting factor is not the bounds of man's understanding or of his sense perceptions, as the Romantics had believed, but the size of computer which it is physically possible to build.

R. Zelazny's 'For a breath I tarry'[2] is a variation on Goethe's *Faust*. As Zelazny's story opens, man has vanished from the earth but the giant computers he created continue to function, keeping

[1] Repr. in *Spectrum. A Science Fiction Anthology*, ed. Amis and Conquest, London, 1963, pp. 68–83.
[2] In *Best Stories from New Worlds*, Panther Science Fiction, ed. Moorcock, ii (1968), pp. 124ff.

the house in order although the tenants have departed. The two chief computers, Solcom and Divcom, roughly correspond to God and Satan. They struggle for power and make a wager concerning the computer Frost, much as the Lord and Mephisto wager on Faust in Goethe. Solcom's question 'Do you know my servant Frost . . . ?' (p. 128) is a direct evocation of Goethe (line 299). Frost 'serves' Solcom by co-ordinating and relaying data concerning the Northern hemisphere. But he (it?) has a hobby: the study of man from what evidence has survived. Presently he is visited by a servant of Divcom, Mordel (Mephisto), who promises to provide him with evidence regarding man, to assist him in his studies, if he will place his services at the disposal of Divcom. Frost has by now gone further in his ambitions: he wants not only to understand man but to become man. And so to the wager on earth: Frost believes that, given sufficient data, he can turn himself into a man. If he succeeds, Mordel will have no claim upon him. If he concedes failure, he will serve Divcom. (He cannot cheat, of course; he can be monitored.) So here too is a clear variation on Goethe. The issue on which the bet hinges is the nature of Faust/Frost; the arbiter is to be Faust/Frost himself. Where Faust had bet on his nature, Frost bets on the possibility of surpassing his. Where, in most versions of *Faust*, man wants to be more than man, here a machine (less than man) wants to become a man. Frost's attempt involves digesting or processing all surviving relics of human culture. There are endeavours to capture an aesthetic mood, to create a work of art. The process is too subtle and depends too much on its details to be summarized. Suffice it to say that Frost finally creates a human body for himself and succeeds in his ambition. Mordel and Divcom have lost. Since Frost is now a man, he is lord over machines so that the loss of the wager involves, in this case, more than simply not winning a servant: the Devil and his agents are themselves transformed into servants. (This brief summary does not do justice to an interesting and witty work. The attempt to examine the 'psychology' of a computer is fascinating.)

Of course, such 'faustian' Science Fiction makes up only a tiny fraction of the total. This is unquestionably mainly due to the fact that doubt as to whether we can attain to knowledge has been succeeded by doubt as to whether we can control the application of that knowledge. Many Science Fiction writers attempt to show the ultimate consequences of man's practical use of modern scientific discoveries and his reactions to the unheard-of, often disastrous situations which arise. Civilization is often shown to have been a veneer; in chaotic circumstances men revert to savagery. Other common features of Science Fiction are attempts to examine men's reactions to the arrival of creatures from another planet, futuristic political parables showing technology as the handmaiden of dictatorship, adventure stories in space, and so on. But there remains enough—and the best of Science Fiction is intrinsically good enough to be taken seriously in such a discussion—to make credible the assertion that the field previously occupied by the *Faustdichter* has now been taken over by the Science Fiction writers, even where there is no obvious link with the Faust legend. And it may be added that scientists do write Science Fiction stories today, where they did not and do not write *Fausts*.[1]

Probably for most people today (except for those holding to some more or less orthodox religious view), the implications of Valéry's *Faust* would seem acceptable: the universe has no 'meaning' except inasmuch as it defines this 'meaning' simply by being. To ask questions which postulate any purpose hidden behind observable phenomena is absurd. (This feeling is unquestionably one of the reasons for the fascination which Kafka's works possess for so many.) The questions which thoughtful people are likely to pose today have little to do with the traditional 'faustian' questions (most of which postulate a transcendental reality and a purposeful universe); rather, they tend to be immensely complicated empirical questions also involving prognostications about future trends. Obvious examples concern the growth of populations, food production, pollution, the rival claims of pressing material needs and more or less intangible long-term interests, the 'balance of terror' and the philosophy of deterrence, supra-national considerations versus national interests, and so on. To answer such questions we may turn to committees and computers but not to spirits which are assumed to know more than any mortal can ever know. Also, as I have

[1] Examples: Fred Hoyle, Isaac Asimov. And see the anthology of Science Fiction stories by scientists: *The Expert Dreamers*, ed. Pohl, Gollancz, 1963, and Pan Books, 1966.

suggested, the central problem has shifted from the likelihood or unlikelihood of being able to find answers to our questions to the problem of how to apply and develop discoveries for the benefit of mankind.

Hence it seems improbable (though not impossible) that we shall see the Faust legend taken up afresh to make any significant statement about man's situation and his problems in the remaining decades of the twentieth century. The type of Science Fiction story which shows human reactions to a sudden environmental threat which science is unable to counter (John Christopher's *The Death of Grass*) or which imagines ways in which technology might come near to destroying humanity (John Wyndham's *The Day of the Triffids*)[1] seems to me much more germane to our state today and in the foreseeable future than any restatement of the Faust fable could be. It is perfectly possible, of course, to take up the Faust figure as personification of man's scientific curiosity which has evolved weapons capable of destroying man—but, as we have seen, this theme can be dealt with in a number of ways, some better suited to it than is the Faust legend. And since, in addition, many metaphysical problems have become physical ones and since few people now find it possible to make a distinction between lawful and unlawful curiosity, Faust has rather had the stuffing knocked out of him. Furthermore, any state of the world which preserves and increases human knowledge is likely to lessen his chances of survival, especially since modern science seems to have driven the pursuit of 'absolute truth' quite out of fashion. Perhaps even the growing awareness that it is scientific research itself which appears to define the limits of knowledge may help to make a state of limited knowledge more acceptable. Faust rebelled against apparently arbitrary limits imposed by God or nature; he is much less likely to rebel against limits gradually revealed by his fellow scientists in the course of their quest for truth. We may see some allegorical reworking of the Faust theme. Faust-as-artist is a possibility; but it is not easy to see how anyone could add very much to what Mann has already said and implied in *Dr. Faustus*.

[1] 1956 and 1951 respectively. Both in Penguins.

Appendix I
Faust and related figures

The special link between Faust and Don Juan has been discussed. Faust and the Wandering Jew—representing two forms of man's rebellion against God—are brought together by more than one writer, although the link seems very tenuous to me. Some sort of relationship can certainly be discovered between the Faust legend and the various stories concerning earlier magicians who made pacts with the Devil, but in most of these cases intellectual curiosity plays no part.

As for more ancient legends, there is clearly an affinity between Faust and Icarus (referred to by both Marlowe and Goethe in the course of their *Fausts*)[1] and between Faust and Prometheus. The youthful Goethe is equally ready to cast himself as Prometheus or as Faust, admiring both as would-be godlike rebels and, a century later, Albert Möser puts words into the mouth of Prometheus that could just as well be spoken by Faust:

> Ihr könnt mir nicht rauben
> Den Götterdrang,
> Nie hemmt ihr den Flug
> Der adligen Seele, ...
> Ich liebte das Licht,
> Ich suchte Vollendung.[2]

For a brief period in the Romantic era, Cain was given the status of a rebellious hero. Since this was the period in which the rebellious side of Faust's nature was being singled out as something admirable, one can see a similarity here too, especially in Byron's *Cain*, where the hero's revolt against his 'enslavement' by

[1] Marlowe in the opening Chorus; Goethe, more obliquely, in the prose scene ('Trüber Tag. Feld') and later, applied to Euphorion, in line 9901.

[2] 'Prometheus' in *Nacht und Sterne*, Halle 1872, p. 114.

God and against the limitations of the human condition is not unlike the faustian rebellion. Cain's resentment of his brother's tame acceptance of God's authority recalls that contempt for the common herd which figures in many *Fausts* from the *Sturm und Drang* onwards.

There are a number of works of English literature from the 1780s on which are more or less recognizably and directly linked with the Faust legend. A somewhat remote cousin of Faust's is the Caliph Vathek in William Beckford's Gothic novel-cum-Arabian Nights fantasy of that name (1787). At the beginning we are told that Vathek had 'studied so much . . . as to acquire a great deal of knowledge; though not a sufficiency to satisfy himself: for he wished to know every thing . . .'. And, after his horrible death, the moral is pointed: 'Such is . . . the chastisement of blind ambition, that would transgress those bounds which the Creator hath prescribed to human knowledge. . . .'[1] But in the body of the book this theme is hardly touched on; the stress is on luxury, wickedness, blasphemy and profanation of religious mysteries. The theme of the pursuit of knowledge has a beginning and an end, but no middle. A similar case is that of Charles Maturin's rambling Gothic novel *Melmoth the Wanderer* (1820), which concerns a man who sells his soul in return for youth. Melmoth's dying confession contains the words: 'Mine was the great angelic sin—pride and intellectual glorying! It was the first mortal sin—a boundless aspiration after forbidden knowledge!' (Chapter xxxii). And again, this particular characteristic has not played any part in the novel.

A much more famous and accomplished work, and one which has a closer link with the Faust theme, is Mary Shelley's *Franken-stein* (written 1816, published 1818). We know from the authoress's preface to the 1831 edition that her imagination was set off by a discussion between Shelley and Byron concerning the hidden principle of life and the possibility that this might be discovered and life synthesized in the laboratory. Although the work contains no overt reference to *Faust*, there are clear similarities.

[1] *Vathek* was first published in 1786 as *An Arabian Tale, from an unpublished manuscript.* . . . This first edition is Henley's unauthorized publication of his trans-lation of Beckford's original manuscript (in French). For the truly farcical story of the various early editions of *Vathek*, see G. Chapman, *Beckford*, London, 1937. My quotations are taken from the first edition, pp. 5 and 210. *Vathek* is now available as a paperback (*Four Square Books*, 1966).

Frankenstein describes his early pursuit of knowledge in terms which recall both the original Faust's wish 'alle Gründ am Himmel und Erden [zu] erforschen' and the desire on the part of Goethe's Faust to penetrate the inner secrets of the universe: 'It was the secrets of heaven and earth that I desired to learn . . .' (Chapter ii). The account of the youthful Frankenstein immersed in the works of Cornelius Agrippa, Paracelsus and Albertus Magnus and even trying to conjure spirits and devils, with its evocation of a no man's land of forbidden and occult knowledge, may even be a deliberate reminder of the Faust legend. Later, at the university, Professor Waldmann's words about the power of science to unlock secrets and unleash hidden forces provoke in Frankenstein the desire to 'unfold to the world the deepest mysteries of creation' (Chapter iii)—a demonstration of intellectual arrogance very like Faust's (especially as seen in Marlowe). Frankenstein soon begins to concentrate his enquiries on the mysteries surrounding the origins of life, thinking of himself as a demigod, a Promethean creator of a new race of men who will owe their existence and their gratitude to him: 'A new species would bless me as its creator and source . . .' (Chapter iv). Again we are near to Marlowe's Faustus, with his dreams of becoming godlike through magic and of gaining power over life and death.

The most discussed works among those which can in some way be regarded as companion pieces to *Faust* are, of course, Byron's dramatic poem *Manfred* (1817) and his fragmentary drama *The Deformed Transformed* (1822). In his day, in fact, Byron was accused of plagiarizing both Marlowe and Goethe, although we now realize that the first of these charges was untrue and most of us would feel that the second was unfair.

Byron's knowledge of Goethe's *Faust* at the time of writing *Manfred* was derived from hearing Monk Lewis translate some scenes verbally in 1816.[1] This reading must have included Goethe's first study scene, since Manfred's Act 1 monologue, set in a 'Gothic gallery', gives the nearest thing to a genuine link with Goethe. But the point made is a different one. Manfred is certainly dissatisfied with knowledge, as was Faust, and is tormented by the dichotomy of knowledge and life, as Faust had been: 'The Tree of Knowledge is not that of Life'.[2] Also Manfred

---

[1] Cf. letters to S. Rogers of 4/4/1817 and to Murray of 12/10/1817.
[2] *Works. Poetry*, vol. iv, edited by E. C. Coleridge, London, 1922, p. 85.

conjures up spirits representing various natural forces. But what he wants is not greater richness and intensity of experience but forgetfulness, self-oblivion, escape from his sense of guilt. Some of his words, in fact, recall Hamlet rather than Faust: '. . . yet we live,/Loathing our life, and dreading still to die'.[1] While his guilt is a major reason for his despair, there are other causes within his character. He is a classic case of Romantic *Zerrissenheit*, a man whose inner life is at odds with the world:

ABBOT: And why not live and act with other men?
MANFRED: Because my nature was averse from life . . .[2]

Manfred is more an anticipation of Lenau's Faust than a copy of Goethe's. Goethe's own comment in a letter to Knebel of 13 October 1817 is a just one; *Manfred* was certainly helped into being by *Faust*, but Byron's work is something very much his own, deriving its peculiar attributes from the poet's inner nature:

Dieser seltsame geistreiche Dichter hat meinen Faust in sich aufgenommen und für seine Hypochondrie die seltsamste Nahrung daraus gesogen. Er hat alle Motive auf seine Weise benutzt, so daß keins mehr dasselbige ist, und gerade deshalb kann ich seinen Geist nicht genug bewundern. . . .

In the case of *The Deformed Transformed* Byron himself (in his 'Advertisement') tells us that the work was founded partly on Goethe's *Faust*, partly on a novel called *The Three Brothers*. This novel, written by one Joshua Pickersgill and dating from 1803, tells of a youth, Arnand, of great gifts and beauty, who is injured and permanently deformed. In his bitterness, he first considers suicide, then enters on a pact with the Devil, pledging his soul in return for renewed physical beauty.

Byron borrows this plot, calling his hero Arnold. Like Pickersgill's Arnand, Arnold contemplates suicide but is held back by the appearance of a stranger in black. There is a pact and the Stranger causes the figures of various famous men noted for their handsomeness to parade before Arnold (there was a similar episode in Pickersgill). Arnold elects to assume the form of Achilles and the transformation takes place, the Stranger assuming the discarded form of Arnold himself and the name Caesar.

[1] Ibid., p. 108.   [2] Ibid., p. 125.

The scene changes to the Siege and Sack of Rome (1527), where Arnold acquits himself with great valour, but shortly afterwards the fragment breaks off.

The main, indeed the only, debt to Goethe is in the figure of the Stranger, the Devil. Goethe, talking to Eckermann on 8 November 1826, says:

Sein Teufel ist aus meinem Mephistopheles hervorgegangen, aber es ist keine Nachahmung, es ist alles durchaus originell und neu, und alles knapp, tüchtig und geistreich.

But Goethe is too kind, as he often is to Byron. The Stranger is only a pale shadow compared with Mephisto. He is mocking and sardonic, a cynical denier, but he lacks Mephisto's savage power of speech. Here is Byron's Devil on the human race:

> And these are men, forsooth! ...
> This is the consequence of giving matter
> The power of thought. It is a stubborn substance,
> And thinks chaotically, as it acts,
> Ever relapsing into its first elements.
> Well! I must play with these poor puppets: 'tis
> The Spirit's pastime in his idler hours.[1]

The passage seems bloodless beside Mephisto's diatribe in the Prologue in Heaven (lines 280–92).

So Manfred shows some resemblance to Faust as a character although the plot of the work has nothing in common with that of *Faust*, while *The Deformed Transformed* has a Devil and a pact, but no Faust.[2]

---

[1] *Poetry*, vol. v, p. 509.

[2] There are two main types of characters in fiction which provide a contrast to the Faust type: characters who are able to accept a limited sphere of activity and limited knowledge, and characters who are quite simply too listless to bother about the problems which trouble a Faust. In German literature the most familiar example of the first is the hero of Jean Paul's *Leben des vergnügten Schulmeisterlein Wutz* (1791). Wutz is content with his lot, can find happiness in the most restricted and humble circumstances and is not even aware that he or his life is limited. To use Jean Paul's terms, the external world and Wutz' inner world of desires and ambitions fit together like the two halves of a mussel shell. When one thinks, say, of Müller's Faust ('ein Löwe von Unersättlichkeit brüllt aus mir') or of Goethe's ('Es möchte kein Hund so länger leben'), one realizes that Wutz is the precise antithesis of such figures. Many novellas of the early nineteenth century contain endearing, if often slightly eccentric and comical, figures modelled more or less directly on Wutz.

The classical depiction of the second type occurs in Goncharov's novel, *Oblomov* 1859). Unlike Faust ('Im Anfang war die *Tat!*'), Oblomov abhors activity and spends

Appendix II
The plan of Madách's *Tragödie des Menschen*

The prophetic visions in which Adam is given hints of future events on earth take up scenes 4–14 of the work. Madách's plan seems to be as follows:

Scene 4. Egypt. Evils of absolutism (oppression and suffering).

Scene 5. Greece. Dangers of democracy (the fickle mob).

Scene 6. Rome. Hedonism.

Scene 7. Constantinople. Religious fanaticism, persecution, obsession with the hereafter.

Scenes 8 and 10. Prague (Kepler). Denial of intellectual freedom impedes progress.

Scene 9. Paris (French Revolution). The Terror: abuse of unbridled freedom.

Scene 11. London (Industrial Revolution). Injustices brought about by conditions of 'free competition'.

Scene 12. A future World State. Arid technological utilitarianism. Totalitarian planning achieves material wellbeing only at cost of individualism and all the frills of life.

---

most of his time at home in a dressing gown. He regards those who have an active business or social life with mixed pity and horror. He puts off even thinking about problems, let alone doing anything about them. Activity, for him, spells boredom: 'Life was divided, in his opinion, into two halves: one consisted of work and boredom—these words were for him synonymous—the other of rest and peaceful good humour' (Chapter v). Contrast Faust's 'Werd' ich beruhigt je mich auf ein Faulbett legen,/So sei es gleich um mich getan!' (lines 1692f). Goncharov's account of Oblomov as a student leads one to wonder whether or not a *deliberate* opposite to the Faust type was intended:

> He was content with what was written in his notebook, and showed no troublesome curiosity even when he failed to understand all that he heard and learned. . . . Philosophers had not succeeded in rousing in him a longing for speculative truth. (Chapter vi)

Perhaps it is no coincidence that the opposing figure to Oblomov within the novel is Stolz, a German.

Scene 14. The distant future. The sun's power is failing and a second Ice Age is ushered in. The few surviving humans eke out a miserable existence. Return to superstition and brutality.

The final scene (15) shows Adam coming to his decision, resolving that—despite everything—existence is better than non-existence, that to struggle and hope is better than to give way to despair.

Appendix III
Translations of passages quoted in the text

(I have translated all passages quoted in foreign languages with the exception of those where the meaning is evident from the context and a few passages where the point made is a stylistic one. References are to page and commencing line number.)

1^5 Everyone should write a *Faust*. . . . The characters of Faust and his fearful companion have a right to all possible reincarnations.

3^{20} He thought the Devil was not as black as he is painted, nor was Hell as hot as men say it is.

3^{27} 'Leave me in peace,' says Dr. Faust to the spirit. And the spirit replies: 'Then stop your questioning and leave me in peace.'

4^4 I *will* know, or I no longer want to go on living: you must tell me.

5^1 . . . for his arrogant curiosity, licence and irresponsibility so stung him and egged him on . . . For as soon as we saw your heart: what thoughts were in your mind and how you could use no-one but the Devil to further such intentions and projects . . . had I had godly thoughts and clung to God through prayer and not let the Devil get such a hold over me, then such harm had not come upon me.

7^{10} God did not give man the noblest of impulses in order to make him eternally unhappy.

8^{27} . . . why should the Devil put an end to atrocities when He, whom men call their Father and Preserver, looks upon them with equanimity?

9^{37} We seek the infinite and everywhere find only finite things.

10¹³ If one day you hope to dwell in Paradise, you must first surrender yourself to the Devil.

14³ The guilty and accursed magician—the ambitious aesthete—the tumultuous and passionate 'original genius'—the superhuman or the complete man according to Goethe—the blasé Romantic—the Utopian striver for a better world—Faust is all those things in turn, according to the temperament of the poet and the ideology in favour at various times.

15²⁶ Oh, poor damned Faust, why am I not a beast which dies without soul, so that nothing more could happen to me . . .

16²¹ And now it comes about that Faust, dissatisfied with ordinary learning, consults magic books and conjures the Devil to his service . . .

16²⁵ Faust's learned discourse in his study as to whether to choose theology or magic.

17²⁰ In external and worldly things, there one may allow reason to decide. For there you can very well calculate and consider that the cow is bigger than the calf, that three ells are longer than one . . . and that it is better for the roof to stand on top of the house than underneath it . . . , for God has given us reason so that we may milk cows and bridle horses and know that a hundred guilders are more than ten . . . But when it comes to the question of how a man shall attain to heavenly bliss, and in all matters of faith, there reason must step down and keep her peace.

17³² For that reason, dear friends, let the natural sciences be. If you do not know what power is in every stone, star, piece of wood, animal or any other creature—knowledge that the natural sciences strive for—then be content with what your experience and common knowledge teach you. It is enough for you to know that fire is hot, water cold and wet; that summer's work is different from winter's; and to know how to attend to fields and cattle, house and children; this is enough scientific knowledge for you. For the rest, consider only how you shall come to knowledge of Christ; he will show you yourself, who you are and what you are capable of. (Luther's 'natürliche Kunst' is not, of course, exactly what we would understand by 'scientific knowledge', but it certainly includes research into, and speculation about, the secrets of nature.)

18⁴ . . . wanted to find out all the deepest, most hidden things on earth and in the heavens . . . fathom the workings of the elements . . .

18²¹ 'Weak mortal! Cease questioning what you ought to adore.'—'But,' said Zadig . . .

18³⁶ Skill, strength of intellect, honour, fame, knowledge, achievement, power, riches: all that is needed to play the God of this world . . .

19⁵ Why has my soul the insatiable hunger, the unquenchable thirst for ability and achievement, knowledge and action, eminence and honour——?

20¹ I feel the Divinity aflame in my veins.

20¹⁸ Why do you keep company with us when you cannot last the course? You want to fly and your head becomes giddy.

21³² Forever teased and tugged about by doubts; a stranger without goal or fatherland . . .

22¹ If Christ is God and if I follow in his steps, even though it be on heavenly paths, I am no more than the shoe which is filled and trodden by his foot . . . If Nature is God, I am only a channel through which she passes in the interests of the whole race. . . . I will firmly assert my stubborn self, sufficient to myself and undaunted; no longer in bondage or subject to anyone, I will pursue my path into myself.

22¹⁶ I have also read hardly any books, for all that is a wretched business; I open only one book, that of my own great genius. If I seek something, it is there for the finding.

22³³ FAUST: Was I created to suffer exquisite torments by a God of hatred who is pleased by suffering?

GOOD SPIRIT: Happiness bloomed all about your path through life.

FAUST: For me, knowledge is the only happiness.

GOOD SPIRIT: Hope flourishes for the patient. Learn to forgo.

FAUST: Hope withered in my sickened breast.

GOOD SPIRIT: May the wreath of virtue adorn your brow.

FAUST: That wreath, too, was torn from me by doubt.

26³³ And the hero's burning desire for truth was cooled in the slime of sensuality.

27¹⁸ . . . every man is more or less a Faust. For nobody is so completely Christian that he would not occasionally wish something to be other than it is; nobody is so patient that he would always and immediately be able to identify his will with the general Will.

28²⁵ I feel happy and elevated in having made this fragment into a whole in a truly German spirit. [Faust has been brought into the sphere of] the greatest and most typical achievements of the German spirit. (Free translation of Müller's rather woolly German.)

29⁴ . . . that striving for the Lofty and the True which is more characteristic of the Germans than of other peoples.

29¹⁷ When the German stops being Faust, the greatest danger is that he will become a Philistine.

30²⁹ In Faust, Goethe depicted the essence of us [Germans], the eternal part which, after each remoulding of our soul, lives on in the new form.

30³⁴ . . . a Nordic heroic saga, a Prussian march, a composition of Bach's, one of Eckhard's sermons, a Faust monologue: all are merely different utterances of one and the same soul, creations of the same will . . .

32²⁵ And so I breathe the deepest emotions of my breast ardently into poetic strains full of foreboding. But alas, the word wretchedly fragments feelings of infinity.

33³ One could also imagine Faust as a writer who wagers his soul's bliss on a work of art and who founders with it.

35¹⁴ . . . that all creatures, even the Devil himself against his will, must try to bring rebellious sinners to repentance.

35²⁵ Believe me, if the whole world were covered with red-hot nails, I would walk around barefoot until the Day of Judgement, if I could then come to heavenly bliss.

36⁸ You have not seen the man who sighs under a heavy yoke, carries life's burden with patience and comforts himself with hopes of the future. In your pride you passed by the hut of the poor and humble man who earns his bread in the sweat of his brow, faithfully shares it with his wife and children and, in the last hour of his life, rejoices that his hard toil is ended.

36¹⁸ MEPH.: You are putting yourself into the hands of evil spirits; the finite being is playing a dangerous game with the infinite. Is that not madness?

FAUST: I do think you're preaching.

MEPH.: Yes: reform. But your ear is deaf to warnings, whether they come from good or evil spirits.

36³⁵ Where you were enjoined to believe, you became presumptuous, proud Faust! At the cost of your peace [of mind] you wished to solve a secret which is hidden from the mortal here below. It is hope and faith which sustain the good man's heart in the maze of this world and lead him on to his fair goal. Your bold spirit rejected patience and faith; you wanted truth but your reward was delusion!

37¹⁸ Devil in his passion, mortal in his weakness, often an angel in his goodness, divine in the flowering of creativity: he is an insoluble riddle! He is eternal and subject to decay, he is day and he is night!

38¹³ Just as many persons and many offices of differing degrees go to make up a kingdom, so there are offices of differing degrees among the devils. For some are lesser devils who tempt men to whoring, ambition and such sins, but some are higher spirits who tempt men to doubt, despair and heresy, such devils as possess the rebellious mobs and the Pope. Certain devils are bidden to concern themselves with this sin, others with other sins. These wicked spirits include idolatrous devils, tyranny-devils, sorcery-devils, curse-devils, drink-devils, marriage-devils, whore-devils and many others who incite and delude men to commit such sins.

40²² . . . everything which we perceive in the form of matter, which we picture to ourselves as heavy, solid and dark but which, stemming—if only indirectly, through affiliation—from the Divine Being, is just as absolutely powerful and eternal as the Father.

43⁹ This purification will . . . continue until all classes of beings, even the mid-point and source or cause of all damnation and ruin, Lucifer, will be laid bare and will long for eternal deliverance, and so he too, as the last enemy, will be lifted up and changed back into his previous glorious figure of light, and so the whole of creation will again appear in its original form.

43³¹ The Devil is the hero of this play; the author did not conceive him as a hideous phantom . . . Goethe wished to show in this character . . . the most bitter wit that disdain could inspire, but together with this an audacious gaiety which can amuse us. In Mephisto's speeches there is a devilish irony which is directed at the whole of creation and which judges the universe like a bad book of which the Devil has made himself the critic.

45³⁶ . . . everything which comes into being deserves to perish.

46³ . . . in a lofty, bold and powerful form . . . Fiery commanding eyes shone out from beneath black eyebrows, between which bitterness, hatred, rancour, pain and scorn had etched deep lines . . . He had the aspect of the fallen angels, whose faces, once illuminated by the Divinity, are now covered by a sombre veil.

46³⁴ Do those people need the Devil whose actions shame him?

47⁵ Thus I in banishment will cool my suffering and feel myself an anti-creator in my destructive work.

48⁸ Mephisto bends down confidentially to him and puts his arm round his neck. Then he whispers very quietly into his ear, so quickly, quickly, that his mouth hardly moves.

48²⁵ I will rest today in the company of this corpse and find relief from my agitated, wild and devilish life, from the horror of my loves and hates.

48³² He hobbles and reels about in the sand, quietly delighted with his wicked plans.

49¹¹ Call me the son of a whore, call me a wicked ape; whatever I am, *I have never created anything*!

49²¹ He climbs up the middle one of the three ruined columns. As he clings apelike to the stone, like a Christ, two other dark shapes hurry quickly to the basalt columns on either side of him.

50³ You wouldn't believe how they are drawn to me, that surging and dancing crowd in there. What shall we bet: not only doctors sign away their souls to devils. What shall we bet: in half an hour all of them in there will be in league with me.

50¹² With these cubes that they call dice the whole crowd will run into my jaws. They are sucking themselves firm and deep into my leg as if I were putting it into a pond for leeches.

50²⁴ Satan has long since passed into fable but men are no better off. They have got rid of the Evil One; the evil ones remain.

51⁸ We have no form of our own; according to your pleasure, we take on any form in which you desire to see us. We shall always appear as in your thoughts.

51³⁶ FAUST: Why must an unquenchable yearning for knowledge burn in my soul?

MEPH.: Be bold enough to admit that your creator is your enemy because he cruelly placed you in this world of night.

52³⁸ For him the battle between good and evil was played out in the soul of his hero and nowhere else. . . . 'The Devil in us: very much so.'

53¹⁷ A man torn in two halves . . . the human animal in Faust's breast, opposed to the spirit and its boundless exuberance.

54⁵ 'Mephisto, answer me: are you the Good and the Evil Beings in one person?'
He smiled dismissingly, but out of his smile spoke something which filled me with horror: God and the Devil one and the same! . . . ghastly thought!

54¹⁷ WANDERER: Truly only Satan could be so lewdly contemptible.

DENIER (ironically): I am only a part of your self! . . . I am only the embodiment of your own thoughts!

55¹² FAUST: I will have no more of this cowardliness. I am the sole source of the evil which I do.

STRANGER: Well then, I die.

DON JUAN: The death of a myth!

59²⁹ . . . a ruinous whore . . . wilful . . . colour-blind.

59³³ Doctor Faustus put on eagles' wings and wanted to discover the most secret things in Heaven and earth, for his arrogant curiosity, licence and irresponsibility so stung him and egged him on that there came a time when he resolved to apply and try out various magical terms, figures, characters and conjurations, so that he might summon the Devil to him.

61¹³ Alas, I have studied philosophy, medicine, law—and unfortunately also theology—thoroughly and with great pains. And here I stand, poor fool, and am no wiser than before.

61²⁴ Instead of living nature into which man was placed by God, his creator, I am simply surrounded, in smoke and mustiness, by the bones of beasts and human skeletons.

62^{14} In the tides of life, in the storm of action I surge to and fro, I am ceaselessly active. Birth and grave, an eternal sea, an ever-changing life. Thus I work at the humming loom of time and fashion the living garment of the Deity.

63^{6} My good friend, grey is all theory and green life's golden tree.

64^{1} FAUST: Fair lady, may I presume to offer you my arm and conduct you home?

        MARGARETHE: I am neither a lady nor fair, and can make my own way home.

64^{7} MARGARETHE: I would give something to know who that gentleman was today. He certainly looked very gallant and is of noble family. I could see that in his face. And otherwise he wouldn't have been so bold.

        FAUST: Welcome, sweet twilight that wafts about this hallowed place. Take hold of my heart, sweet pain of love, that must nourish itself, languishing, on the dew of hope. What richness in this poverty! What bliss within this narrow cell!

67^{23} Our flowers in their artificial splendour blossom through the whole year.

69^{31} He alone deserves the ladies' favours who knows how to protect them vigorously.
He alone deserves freedom, and indeed life itself, who must daily win them anew.

70^{29} I have not yet fought my way to freedom. If I could banish magic from my path and quite unlearn the incantations, then I would stand before you, Nature, as a man alone; then it would be worth while to be a human being.

71^{13} Nature and art appear to flee each other and, before one would expect it, they come together again.

72^{6} See translation of p. 61^{24}.

72^{11} Surely, if this corpse could laugh, it would suddenly burst into laughter at the fact that we are cutting it about and peering into it like this, asking the dead about life.

72^{18} And the scientist's hand crushes many an insect because it would reveal nothing to him of the secrets of its being [literally: creation].

72²² When you trees are decked out in your foliage, your rustling is a confused, complacent prattle; in winter I listen eagerly but can hear only senseless rattling from your branches.

72²⁹ Nature, the friend, has become estranged from him, has turned away from him and holds herself aloof; he is coldly rejected by every blossom, for every blossom says: thou shalt not kill.

73²² In the unpenetrated night of a primeval forest sat Faust on a moss-covered, rotting stump.

73³¹ A moonless night: in the black pinewood, Faust went to and fro, alone and mute. The night was silent as nights are silent: an oppressive whispering, a fantastic play of black shapes, this bending of the treetops and of the pine needles on their stalks.

74¹ And in addition, with a ghostly pallor, the sick, ailing face of the moon shines down.

74⁸ In hateful tangled growths a vast swamp lies rotting here, where many a man went astray. All about was gruesome and frightful, so that mortals felt their courage slip away . . . In the glaring light of the will o' the wisps, many white, dry human bones stare up. Torn-out plumage is driven about by the night wind, and on the marshes the skins of sheep and cattle lie rotting. How the oak bough bends, as if under a weight of stones, almost breaking to the ground; such a wild company of vultures and eagles perch on it in black, sinister hordes.

74²⁵ How wildly seductive was the night, and the world lay, alluring, in the moonlight. . . . Cursed be the dreamy, mild moonlight!

74²⁹ Good old mother Nature, I often used her as my whore.

75¹⁷ The wilds teach me solemn words and the night solves riddles for me.

75²⁴ Oh flashing lightning and cool of the rocks, oh storm and the forest night: take me to you and, as I feel myself to be entirely yours, answer me lovingly. Let my beating heart be engulfed in your abundance, until I cannot separate my own song from the wafting of your breath.

76⁷ When Nature presses me to her bosom, voluptuously splendid in her eternal youth, all snatching and striving after rank and honour seems childish to me.

76¹³ Mighty Nature, on whose bosom the convulsions of my sick breast are eased, where, bathed in the light of Heaven and lulled by the whispering of beloved trees, I forget my cares and my torments, the misery and the curse of the human condition.

77¹⁸ . . . which has come to mistrust all those base things which are called wit, thought, language, learning and the marvels of nature.

77²⁸ Reality is absolutely incommunicable. It is that which resembles nothing, which is represented and explained by nothing and which means nothing.

78¹⁰ . . . whose wings, on top a sonorous triad of colour, resemble a leaf on their underside with insane exactitude. . . . When this cunning creature alighted in the foliage and closed its wings, it disappeared into its environment so completely through assimilation that even the most voracious enemy could not detect it there.

79¹² From early days we had an eye on you, on your quick arrogant brain, your admirable *ingenium* and *memoriam*. They had you study theology, as your conceit devised, but soon you no longer wanted to be a theologian, put the Holy Scriptures aside and thereafter gave yourself up entirely to the *figuris*, *characteribus* and *incantationibus* of music, which pleased us not a little.

79²⁴ It is pure chance how I look, or rather: it comes about in this way or that just according to the circumstances, without my bothering about it. Adaptation, mimicry—you know about that of course—mummery and teasing on the part of Mother Nature, who always has her tongue in her cheek.

79³⁷ One shouldn't let the Philistine have the last word concerning what is sick and what is healthy. Life has many times clutched joyfully at things which have come about by way of death and sickness and has let itself be led on and upwards by such things. . . . What do 'diseased' and 'healthy' matter? Without the diseased, life would never have survived. Who cares about 'genuine' and 'false'?

80²³ Kafka is like a man who translates cracks in slate as if they were hieroglyphs, in order to demonstrate through the absurdity of his translation that the cracks are really only cracks and refute those who make out that the rocks of this world have some meaning.

81⁴ You always evade serious questions! I perceive that the arts of Hell consist in raising dust and that to provoke desire is all that they can do.

83¹⁷ He answers Faust's trickiest questions. . . . 'But,' he says at last, 'I am tired of forcing my understanding back into its old limits. As to the things you ask me: I no longer care to speak of them as a human being and cannot speak to you as a spirit.'

84¹³ FAUST: Have you truths which man does not have?
THE VOICE: Yes, we have.
FAUST: I am yours.

84¹⁸ FAUST: Can you teach me about the incomprehensible Being who rules over us?
HELIM: God alone knows Himself.

84²⁵ FAUST: Let me perceive what no eye has seen, hear what no human ear has ever heard, that which has no sound or name for the son of dust.
MEPH.: Well, wise Faust, you expect great things of the Devil! He is to produce a sound from that which has no sound; your ear wishes to hear what cannot be heard?
FAUST: Leave me if you cannot do this!
MEPH.: All right then. And what else?

85⁷ And now he forces me in despotic commanding tones to keep the promise which I *cannot* keep. I am to teach him what I do not know myself: the mysterious lore concerning those most hidden forces of nature which have never yet been comprehended. What can I do but deceive him with illusion?

85²⁸ The Devil is by no means the worst that there is; I would rather have dealings with him than with many a human being. He honours his agreements much more promptly than many a swindler on earth. To be true, when payment is due he comes on the dot, just as twelve strikes, fetches his soul and goes off home to Hell like a good Devil. He's just a businessman as is right and proper.

86⁸ But not the sort of money that vanishes away again in men's hands. No, money that was minted by man.

86²⁷ But I will deceive him; he isn't counting the nights. . . .
And, when half the time of the pact has run, haven't I
enough power through my arts to escape from his claws? . . .
If you just count the nights as well, you will see that our
pact has run its course.

87²¹ When the farmer hires a labourer, whether in rain, snow
or oppressive heat, the working day is twelve hours and
he has twelve hours' rest to get his strength back. But you
have hounded me night and day, so that the twenty-four
years have shrunk to twelve.

87³⁵ The great men of this world must bow down before me,
looking anxiously to see if I am in a good mood.

88⁷ And that which man is capable of knowing, you shall
know.

88¹⁴ He who is enveloped in dust can know nothing: to him
who was born blind no light can appear. You can only think
through the medium of language, only see nature with
your senses, only think about it according to the laws of
reason.

89¹² FAUST: If I pledge you my heavenly bliss, will [the
true nature of] things be unveiled to me?

LEVIATHAN (after a short consideration): As far as earthly
senses may reach, as far as modes of [human]
thought are attuned to being and non-being,
so far may the light of truth illuminate you!

92¹⁶ All conjurations, making of pacts, summoning the Devil,
—all this is the sorry invention of people who in ignorant
centuries took upon themselves the charge of our souls.
Believe me, if one could force the Devil to bring money,
many a king would have borrowed from Hell in order to
establish a Universal Monarchy.

92³⁵ The mayor bore a stag's head on his shoulders, all the
others, men and women, were adorned with masks from the
capricious realm of grotesque and bizarre fantasy, and each
spoke, cackled, crowed, bleated, neighed or growled in
the tones of the mask which had been assigned to him.

96¹⁴ That would have been possible two hundred years ago.
But now—the Devil has fallen; man's will and behaviour are
free.

98²³ 'Hades here. Whom do you wish to speak to, please? The

Society for the Protection of Young Girls? Sorry, you have the wrong number.'

Then suddenly: 'Hades here. I beg your pardon? Urgent matter of state? Who is speaking? Who please? What was the name? Mephistopheles? With "M", as in "Medusa"? Yes, I understand. With Prince Lucifer in person? Concerning what, please? I'm sorry but I can only put you through to the Prince's private office.'

99² The mistaken belief that our magician was that same Faust who invented printing is widespread among the people.

100²⁵ —that the said Johann Fust, having brought a large number [of his printed Bibles] to Paris to dispose of them, the greater part of them being on vellum and adorned with great letters and vignettes in gold, he sold them at first as manuscripts and did not let them go for less than sixty crowns each; but as he later came to sell them for twenty or thirty, and those who had bought the earlier ones noticed that they were too numerous and too similar one to the other to be handwritten, they brought an action against him for overcharging and pressed him so hard that, having taken refuge in Mainz and not finding himself safe enough there, he went on to Strasbourg . . .

102¹⁹ When Johann Faust, with his two assistants Johann Gutenberg and Peter Scheffer his son-in-law, had invented printing and printed the first Latin Bible, he travelled around with a large number of copies and sold them in the market places, in Paris and elsewhere. He will no doubt have had the books under his cloak. Since the art of printing was new, the buyers could not understand how it was possible that in all copies there was exactly the same number of lines on any given page and that no single stroke was different; so they thought that he was a magician. And because he made an incredible amount of money from his books and made off in his cloak as soon as he had made a good profit and was seen now in this town, now in that, in the market place, that may have caused the legend to spring up. In addition, there is the fact that Faust's assistant, Peter Scheffer, had also gone abroad and was selling books likewise. Now, since Scheffer wore a similar cloak, people will easily have come to believe that he was Johann Faust and will have concluded from this that Faust was in two places at once. And when Johann Faust, as is likely, put on later printed books of his 'Dr. Johann Faust', that is, printed by Johann Faust, the false notion that this reputed magician was a doctor can easily have come about in those dark ages. (Dr. is the normal German abbreviation for 'doctor' and also the first two letters of the German verb meaning 'to print': *drucken*.)

104²¹ For a long time Faust had struggled with the bubble metaphysics, the will-o'-the-wisp morals and the shadow theology without being able to work out a sound, tenable basis for his thought. Furious, he threw himself into the mysterious realm of magic and hoped now to win from nature by force what she conceals so wilfully from us. His first gain was the extraordinary invention of printing.

105¹⁵ Did Paganism, exposed to all the aberrations of human reason, pass on to posterity anything comparable to the shameful monuments which printing has erected during the reign of Christianity? The impious writings of Leucippes and Diagoras perished with them. The art which could perpetuate the extravagances of the human mind had not yet been invented. But now, thanks to the characters of printing and the use to which we put them, the dangerous reveries of Hobbes and Spinoza and their like will remain for ever.

106⁷ And I, with my invention of printing, am numbered among the heretics, and the monks cry aloud from their holes in the monasteries that I am doing them out of their wine, their wages as scribes. And I will do them out of more than that, as soon as men really learn to read.

106²⁰ Johann Faust, a rash mortal, who has invented the art of reproducing books in their thousands without any difficulty: books, the dangerous toys of mankind which have spread many errors.

108¹⁶ I believe that printing is a practical and certain means of spreading insights and knowledge and fighting against obscurantism.

108²⁵ 'And would it not cause you pleasure, my friend, to resume that art which formed the bond between us, to take it up again in continued, purposeful activity?' . . . 'No, I have made my peace with the world.'

113¹ And the legend or story of Faust's life and deeds is so well known in Germany that the players present it on all the stages as one of their principal pieces.

113⁷ The legend of Dr. Faust has amused the mob for long enough and people hardly view such tomfoolery with pleasure any more.

113¹⁹ I found a much more fashionable company than I had expected and they were not sparing with their gracious applause.

114³⁶ The deeply significant theme of the [Faust] puppet play resonated and hummed within me in many tones and keys. I too had ranged through all knowledge and had quickly enough been forced to recognize the futility of it.

117¹⁷ . . . very conscientiously to the tradition as I found it ready to hand in the first place in the chapbooks and puppet plays.

117³² Look at the accursed harvest of the seed you sowed. You brought that girl together with her lover: he is a vagabond. She fled after him with your money because her noble father, objecting not to his poverty but to his vices, refused his consent. On hearing the news of his only child's flight, he hanged himself. The unfortunate girl, abandoned by her husband, ended her life with a dagger. To that beggar you gave money in abundance. He squandered your riches in frenzied delirium and, when he had nothing left but had become accustomed to idleness, he became a highwayman and ended his life on the gallows. You restored his son to that old man. He lived too long to suit this prodigal. In order to come into his inheritance the sooner, he got rid of the old man through poison. But he himself died at the hands of the executioner.

118²³ Oh, Faust! what terrible havoc you have wrought. You left your Gretchen and took up with another girl. She was called Helene and you had much joy of her.

119⁷ See translation of p. 46³.

120³² Take this note or that. You can understand it in this way— or in that way; you can regard it as sharpened from below or as flattened from above.

122⁴ The more interesting phenomena of life probably always have this double aspect of past and future. They demonstrate the ambiguity of life itself.

R

123^{10} . . . that of all the arts it is precisely music which has never thrown off the pious inclination to celebrate its elements.

123^{18} . . . the building-stone of the universe . . . blocks of primeval stone.

124^{31} . . . the second part of the drama, in which Goethe has developed the figure of the faustian leader in such a way that really one is often struck by the similarity when one compares the literary work of that day with the reality of our time.

125^{4} . . . Jewish-Mephistophelian devilry . . . the Mephistophelian (Jewish) spirit.

125^{15} Germany was at that time reeling on the heights of her wild triumphs, about to gain the world by virtue of the one pact which she intended to keep and which she had signed with her blood.

126^{31} And so you want to sell me time?

126^{36} Time? Just time? No, my good friend, that is no Devil's ware. What sort of time, that is what matters! Great time, fantastic time . . . For we purvey the uttermost in this line: soaring flights and illuminations, feelings of liberation and release. . . .

127^{6} A whole hourglass full of inspired Devil's time.

127^{15} Love is forbidden to you, insofar as it warms. Your life is to be cold; therefore you may not love anyone.

129^{23} Parody could be amusing if it were not so dreary in its aristocratic nihilism. Would you expect much happiness and greatness from such tricks?

131^{15} The opera will be swarming with folksongs, lines of Hans Sachs and similar popular material. I am not a retired grammar school teacher who proposes—better late than never—to present his marvelling contemporaries with a drama, but a composer who is constructing a text and makes use of models.

132^{8} HANSWURST: Only yesterday I again heard someone say 'mincemeat' as he went past. And why? Because you are a murderer.

FAUST: I am ill.

HANSWURST: People like you are always ill. What about your friend, the Emperor?

133³ Goethe's *Faust* is continuable ad infinitum . . . There is always a risk in taking a theme which has already been used, or trying—by joining on to earlier works—to open up new points of view for the reader concerning a theme which has [already] been treated by a master's hand.

134¹ Now Faust, to work! Leisure does not befit you.

134²⁶ If you had kept your word to Gretchen, how happy would you be now, a loving couple!

134³² The highest goal beckons also in the humblest sphere.

135²² LUCIFER: I want my share.

    THE LORD (mockingly): You shall have it. Look down to
                earth. See the two trees in the Garden of Eden.
                I curse them—and I give them to you.

135³³ You have snatched me out of my innocent ignorance. Well then, play no tricks, but let me know everything! (Free translation.)

138²⁹ Ah, if only your years would renew themselves so that you were safe from the grave! Yes, then!—But you have been silent; you do not want to complete *Faust*. So I, trembling, have dared to do so.

139¹⁴ Swollen up by the desire for knowledge and the pride of knowledge, I wanted to be a God, wanted to be complete in myself.

139¹⁸ Doggerel! Approximate equivalent:
            Thou virtuous child, oh stay, oh stay!
            She hears me not; she must away.

139³¹ Where again I have given myself up to my old impulse to study, where again, as before, I examine the Divine Revelation of the Scriptures.

140⁵ When Scripture, reason and feeling unite, then true knowledge will be kindled!

140³³ My wager is lost, for the old man [God] was right.

141²⁹ He is now sunk in a deep and powerful slumber; his pale cheeks testify sadly that it has been a long time since he slept so sweetly!

    GRETCHEN'S SPIRIT: Oh friendly Power, which grants to
                these eternal children the lovely, in-
                nocent pastime of hovering around an
                accursed head and relieving a pain
                which they do not comprehend!

142⁹   It is difficult for the stones, witnesses of such a past, to be silent about what they saw.

143²³   Come to my heart, messenger of quiet peace!

143²⁵   If in the dreary course of life you ever confessed that your wild urge was satisfied, then you would be mine.

143³¹   You have striven! You are saved!

144¹⁸   Well now, I will lead him up to Heaven. And this time it will be valid.

144³¹   Where is the moral idea? Do sleep and forgetting suffice to raise the human soul up out of the deadly night of sin?

144³⁸   Director of a Company for the Reclamation of Land . . . more a whimsically pious comedy than a serious representation of the mystery of Divine mercy.

145¹⁰   From the insistent way in which it speaks of weaving, the spirit ought to be called the Spirit of Weaving.

145¹³   After a thousand adventures and wanderings, Faust finds somewhere or other a bit of seashore and a bog at the foot of a mountain, and these appeal to him. To dam up the shore against the encroaching sea, to have the bog drained, this is his highest wish. If only it had been a St. Gotthard Tunnel or a Suez Canal at least—but a bog in a country that did not suffer from overpopulation: that is a modest ambition!

145³²   The true Second Part of *Faust*, in the light of our century: Faust, no egoist, but sacrificing himself and thereby atoning, Faust creating and struggling for humanity and through this banishing the spirit of envy and falsehood, the Devil: this Second Part of *Faust* is still to be written.

146¹⁰   The awe-inspiring pact with the Devil ends like a frivolous farce.

146²²   However prosaic it may sound, it is no less true that Faust instead of going to the court, distributing uncovered paper money and going in search of the Mothers in the fourth dimension, would have done better to have married Gretchen, legitimized his child and invented the electrical machine and the air-pump.

147²³   Faust must pull himself together in warmhearted and lively human activity; not, as the ageing Goethe wished, appearing before us in some utilitarian occupation. No! he is to be converted from his apathy to pure, energetic love of humanity.

149²⁰   That is a completely successful project. You make it clear to the world what an opportunity Goethe missed when he got lost in a poetic haze in his Second Part.

151³² I am the Divinity which is evolving in man. . . . Evolving in me too! How I sought you, God; and what urged me to seek—that was You in me!

152²³ . . . how today a more popular and up to date version of the Second Part is possible and what effect it would have on the [German] people.

153¹⁸ At bottom the fellow hasn't done anything—and for that he's come to Heaven?

155²⁹ Death: No one calls me! My duty is to come unbidden!

156³¹ In the waterfall, with its noise, spray and thunder, I find no trace of greatness! But you are incurable, being immediately uplifted because your God dashes water in your face!

156³⁷ The soul which, after its many struggles, we bring home to the light.

157⁷ I imagine—as might have been—that Goethe was a Bavarian and had the same idea and was alive today. How would he have written *Faust*?

157²⁶ I think I am learning to pray again. One just has to talk with the dead.

165¹ FAUST: Dr. Faust, you are to repent, for it is high time. God will give you bliss again.

DON JUAN: Don Juan, repent. For it is even now still true that Heaven may grant you a good, pious spirit. Heaven will take pity on you and will gather you into its arms.

165¹⁹ Accursed pleasures of the wicked world, how quickly you passed away. The rose of beauty withers and dies; the thorns remain. Accursed impulse which seduced me and destroyed my bliss. Woe to him who seduced me. My happiness is now gone and the flames of Hell fill my mind; nothing will cool them.

166¹⁶ Now I shall see whether the disembodied spirits can appear before me; I will invite them to a feast. Hey there, you spirits, appear before me!

167²³ Faust and Don Juan are the high peaks of modern Christian poetic mythology.

168⁴ Mozart's Dom [*sic*] Juan, who was so similar to the so-called Dr. Faust.

168[17]   Faust, inventor of printing, under the name of Dom Juan.

168[23]   Why should a long-forgotten promise of love bind me for ever to one girl when the favours of the most beautiful women smile upon me welcomingly?

168[27]   ... beautiful women in bewitching forms... regions as yet unknown to science.

168[36]   What has all this to do with me? I sought truth and knowledge among you and you send me off into the realm of dreams?

169[4]   Now I have no more choice. I must make myself over to the Devil to escape from this town where I am pursued at every step.

170[36]   Know that women are more necessary to me than the bread I eat. . . . A toast to the ladies and to good wine, the support and glory of mankind.

171[34]   In Faust, the loneliness of the urge for knowledge is set off against the desire for pleasure in Don Juan.

172[12]   DON JUAN: Why superhuman when you must remain a human being?
         FAUST: What is the point of being human if you do not strive for the superhuman?

172[22]   The fool's meat and drink are of no earthly kind.

172[26]   The only food that one can never have enough of is kisses . . . The earth is so dear to me that, for sheer pleasure and delight, I have no time to think of him who created it. If it is God—well, all the more glory to him; one praises the cook best of all by enjoying his dishes.

173[8]   I know that you are striving towards the *same* destination though rattling along in *different* carts!

173[13]   Away with the goal—do not name it to me, even if I do strive for it. . . . Happy he who strives for ever; yes, hail to the man who could hunger for ever!

174[1]   I am mightier than all living men; the castle does not satisfy me, does not do justice to my love for Donna Anna.

174[6]   I must have what I want or I will shatter it to fragments!

174[9]   It is enough to make one smile. Do you glow with love and yet philosophize?

174[34]   Like a Magus I adore a divine creature, a daughter of the heavens and of humanity, a star, whose flame I see unceasingly, a Psyche, visible to me in all women.

175⁴ Where am I going? How will this end? I do not know.
And, after all, what does it matter?

175⁹ What makes me suffer is that, knowing, I am ignorant.

175¹⁴ Unhappy that I am, having unsuspectingly eaten of the
golden apples of the tree of knowledge. Knowledge is death.

175²⁴ A woman such as no sculptor has ever fashioned, a type
combining Cleopatra and the Virgin Mary.

175²⁷ Do not listen to love, for it is a bad teacher. To love is
to be ignorant and to live is to know. Learn, learn . . .

176¹⁵ My Don Juan is not to be a hot-blooded man, eternally
chasing after women. There is present in him the longing
to find a woman who would be for him the feminine principle
incarnate. But because, reeling from one to the other, he
does not find this woman, he is finally seized by disgust, and
that is the Devil which comes to fetch him.

176²³ The spirit that wishes to embrace everything feels itself
imprisoned within the particular, and forsaken.

177¹ I would like to overthrow space and time.

177¹² If you want to come safely through your earthly span, you
must renounce many a paradise, passing it by with eyes
closed.

177³³ I am mankind's physician, who galvanizes them here on
earth, charging them with new force. And if there were no
Devil in the world, there would be no saint there either.

178¹ You will not lay your hands on him; seek your prey
elsewhere. He is the future warrior in God's cause and the
Lord's chosen one!

178¹⁸ Back, you blind power! Away! Let go of him who
believes and loves!

179¹⁹ In most of the works which the story of the *Burlador*
inspired in France in the nineteenth century one finds more
or less direct reminders of Hoffmann's interpretation.

180³ If Faust and Manfred afford examples of the type of human
perfection, Don Juan is nothing but an example of demorali-
zation. How much Faust is superior to the vulgar amours
of Don Juan. . . .

180⁷ Was there not one, either more noble or more beautiful,
among so many beauties who, from far or near, had at least
some features of his vague ideal? All resembled her, but it was
never she. All resembled her, Don Juan, and you passed on.

180[19] Don Juan represents the aspiration towards the ideal. He is not moved by any desire for vulgar debauchery; he seeks the dream of his heart with the obstinacy of a Titan who fears neither thunder nor lightning.

180[29] Don Juan is Adam banished from Paradise, remembering Eve before her transgression: Eve, the ideal of beauty and of grace.

181[12] I would marry if there were a woman worthy of me. Have I not sought this woman all my life without encountering her?

181[20] All that one can see on earth, I have seen, Briguelle: the freethinkers, the great, the sages, war . . . As far as my thoughts range, only one thing is still lacking: to see, if I can, Heaven and Hell. He whom I am going to see is no longer in that material shell which often prevents the most glorious light from reaching us. He is all spirit. . . . Let us go then without delay . . . That man is a coward who lives in stupidity; one's curiosity should reach out everywhere.

182[1] He gave me wit, soul, knowledge, strength, reason, heart, intelligence: and all that to overcome and challenge destiny and not to mortify the work of his hands.

183[23] Did not the river leave its bed to rush along in a new course at his command, so that now towns lie along its banks and happy men live where it cascades down?

186[5] Whoever strives unsparingly, him we can redeem.

186[14] . . . anger with creation which has split us into man and woman. What a monstrous state of affairs that the human being alone is not a whole!

186[19] Pater Diego calls it God, I call it geometry.

187[9] He led an altogether wicked life, of such a sort that many times he almost died because of his ceaseless whoring.

187[15] When Dr. Faustus saw that the time of his pact was daily nearing its end, he began to lead a swinish and epicurean life and summoned seven devilish succubi with whom he slept. And each one was different from the others, and all so marvellously beautiful that one cannot describe them. For he went with his familiar into many kingdoms so that he might see all women, and chose seven of them: two Dutch women, one Hungarian, an Englishwoman, two from Swabia and one Frankish woman.

188²¹ KASPAR (writing): The beautiful and chaste Lucretia, my master's 335th mistress.

190¹⁸ My bridegroom is looking black because I smiled upon the gentleman.

190²² SCHÖNE: He hasn't the feeling and sense to value your beauty. Do you, sweet pearl, throw yourself away on the first man who desires you? Your glorious form could adorn the highest thrones. Come, let me quickly lead you away!

DA PONTE: Does it seem to you that a man of honour could endure it if such a precious little face, such sugar-sweet features were snatched away by a low peasant? You were not made to be the wife of a peasant . . . There you will give me your hand; there you will say 'yes'; see, it is not far. Let us leave here, my dearest.

190³⁸ Faustina, angel, the Creator's masterpiece! You gave yourself to me lovingly! On your breast I knew happiness— and with it bitter suffering. For oh, you wish to bind the restless one and chain the wild stranger to your hand! Unhappy girl! Do not ask that of me! With me love cannot last; I have cursed its highest grace.

192⁵ Such a girl, aglow with desire, tastes better than a folio.

192²³ And yet—if I look into your face again—Hell, to whom I have sworn allegiance, has suddenly lost its power over me. I am saved if I have won you!

193⁹ During these long days at sea I have pondered many of life's questions.

195¹² The head and the beast finally rise in revolt and tower up. The head cries: 'I wish to think!' And this revolt is called Faust.
The beast cries: 'I wish to live!' And this revolt is called Don Juan.

198⁶ Oh Lord, when I stand before your infinity of stars, naming them haltingly and counting them over in their millions, how I would like to soar away for ever, from world to world. Dwarfishly, we peer at knowledge like moles, strangers to the nearest things as to the most distant.

200¹ I have seen too much that is new recently; not even the greatest novelty would give me joy.

200[6] The bright hosts of butterflies and moths become less numerous each year, even shabbier. I am afraid that all the [factory] smoke is the cause of this.

201[32] And thus man is the sum of heredity and rearing, of time and place, of air and weather, of sound and light, of food and clothing.

202[28] It is on this strict inductive method that the clarity and sureness of our present achievements rests, and it is in this method that human intelligence possesses the infallible means of achieving that certain progress which will gradually be able to resolve everything which hitherto remained a mystery into elements transparently clear and governed by immutable laws. By means of this method, the most violent controversies among scholars will gradually end in common agreement.

203[5] In the positivist state, the human spirit, realizing the impossibility of obtaining absolute knowledge, gives up its search for the origin and purpose of the universe and its quest for the hidden causes of phenomena in order to apply itself solely to the task of discovering, by means of the proper combination of reasoning and observation, the operative laws behind phenomena, that is to say, their unvarying relations of cause and effect and similitude.

203[27] ... provided that the chain of observations is not broken and that each natural philosopher shows himself to be more eager for the perfection of science than for his own fame.

203[32] Genius may be powerful, but it is only great when it serves humanity.

204[8] The spiritualistic religion dominant until now was salutary and necessary as long as the greater number of men lived in misery and had to comfort themselves with [the thought of] Heavenly bliss. But since it has become possible through the progress of industry and economy to extricate people from their material wretchedness and make them happy on earth, since that day—you understand what I mean.

204[18] Very approximate translation: Triumph! the train blazes and steams, flashes and roars; the very air trembles in dread horror.

205[3] Then you came, and your inquiring glance found the unity in what had appeared to be separate; you restored harmony to the deeply divided elements. In the constant process of transformation you saw the elaborate pattern of things and in the mysterious activity of the universe you perceived the law.

205[13] The brilliant rays of this sun [the theory of Evolution] have dispersed the heavy clouds of ignorance and superstition.

206[2] . . . the great law of progress operating in nature . . . the law of progress or perfectibility.

206[17] The secret of life will certainly be solved one day. That we do not yet today know the How is no reason to suppose that we shall not one day recognize and experience it.

206[25] Of all the people I have ever seen, venerable old man, how near do I feel to you! [Echo of Faust's words to the Earth Spirit in Goethe.] Things that I had intimations of were clear to you; things that I dreamed of were proved true by you. Like me, you saw the light of the Earth Spirit; I broke down but you stood firm and, unshakeable in the storm of changing appearances, you saw the law, the unity.

207[3] The best and surest medicine for the Faust crisis is to plunge oneself into the study of the theory of Evolution.

207[6] The methods and paths which we have to follow in order to solve the great enigmas of the world are no different from those of pure scientific knowledge in general: that is to say, firstly *experience* and secondly *deduction*.

207[32] Was it not only late in the day that man's inquiring spirit recognized that far off in space light cloudy masses, guided by the omnipotent Hand, come together to form worlds? This spirit, then, that has seen into the workshop in which God builds world systems—may it not also joyfully entertain the hope that one day the whole might not reveal itself?

208[24] That life is not the play of unconscious forces, not merely a process taking place within nerve cells, but the work of an organizing, conscious soul; that this soul—and not the body—is there from the beginning and that, in the last resort, it is the soul that commands the body and not the other way round, in life as in death. . . . If only we could succeed in proving this!

210[15] We climb a mountain. Having arrived at the peak, we see with our wider-ranging glance ever new mountains rising up, mountains which were not visible before.

211[4] System is the *childhood* of philosophy; its *manhood* is research.

211[20] ... that the progress of humanity was *solely* determined by the progress of scientific knowledge, not through morals, religion or philosophy!

211[26] Nature is for most of you a book written in unknown characters, a book which you want to learn to understand and read. The words and characters in which she speaks to us are, however, characters of a particular sort; they are peculiar phenomena with which you have to become acquainted.

212[23] ... because all human knowledge is more or less fragmentary and will probably also remain so or because human intelligence, as a result of the restrictions placed upon it by the limitations of time and space, will never be capable of penetrating to the ultimate causes of things.

213[3] The Creation, as the coming into being of matter, does not concern us here. This process, if it ever took place at all, is quite beyond the reach of human knowledge. We shall never come to any knowledge of ultimate causes. This is due to the limitations or relativity of our cognitive faculties.

213[13] Why things are and what their ultimate purpose is: only children ask that sort of question, it seems to me.

213[24] The things which [Faust's] giant intellect strove for, the things which filled his proud and tragic mind with a sense of awe, which he could only gain in a legendary and magical way at the cost of his soul: all this the crowd of pygmies have now achieved with their petty carryings-on. For Nature has been robbed of everything miraculous and allows herself to be clearly understood and tamely governed.

216[12] ... that perfection of technology which today, above all through steam-engines and electricity, achieves things which past ages would have ascribed to the help of the Devil.

217[24] Life finally took on for me a very strange appearance, like an *objet trouvé*, a little object held in the hand. One sees it clearly, one turns it this way and that in the light of this clear vision; what is it like? nothing. What use is it? Who made it?

Would one have the courage to reply that this little object
has no rhyme or reason, is not like anything, has no use . . . ?

218²² Yes, men will one day know and command all the forces
of nature! But they will one day curse this knowledge and
their whole command of nature!

219²⁰ 'But Faust!' Pracriti gets excited. 'What would become
of knowledge if every scientist withheld his discoveries from
humanity solely because they could also serve evil purposes!
My view is that the scientist has the duty to place the results
of his research at the disposal of the public.'

'I am of a different opinion. As long as science and humanity
go hand in hand, the path which the man of science must
tread follows automatically. But whenever science and love
of mankind occupy hostile camps, science must capitulate
unconditionally. Science should be the servant of mankind
but has become a tyrant. . . .'

224¹⁸ You cannot rob me of the impulse to be godlike, nor will
you ever check the flight of my noble soul . . . I loved the
light; I sought perfection.

227¹⁷ This strange and ingenious poet has assimilated my *Faust*
and has drawn the strangest nourishment for his hypochondria out of it. He has used all the motifs in his own way so
that none is the same any more, and for this reason I cannot
sufficiently admire his ingenuity.

228⁷ His devil was born out of my Mephistopheles, but is no
imitation. Everything is entirely original and new, everything
is terse, vigorous and witty.

BIBLIOGRAPHY

(i) *Bibliographies (Faust)*

KARL ENGEL, *Bibliotheca Faustiana*, Hildesheim, 1963 (= reproduction of original edition of 1885).

HANS HENNING, *Faust-Bibliographie* (in progress):
Part i (to 1799), Berlin & Weimar, 1966.
Part ii (Goethe), Berlin & Weimar, 1968–70.

(ii) *Chapbooks about Faust*

1587: *Historia von D. Johann Fausten* . . . Quotations from Henning's edition, Halle, 1963 (= Literarisches Erbe, i). I am also indebted to Petsch's edition, Halle, 1911.

1591 & 1592: reprints of 1587 chapbook with additional chapters.

1592: 'P.F.', *The Historie of the damnable life, and deserved death of Doctor John Faustus* . . . I have quoted from B. Ashmore's edition of Marlowe's *Faustus*, London, 1948.

1599: G. R. WIDMANN, *Warhafftige Historien von den* . . . *Sünden und Lastern* . . . , *So D. Johannes Faustus* . . . *hat getrieben* . . . , 3 parts, Hamburg, 1599. Also in Scheible, vol. II, 275ff.

1674: J. N. PFITZER, *Das ärgerliche Leben und schreckliche Ende deß vielberüchtigten Ertz-Schwartzkünstlers D. Johannis Fausti* . . . *Ietzo, aufs neue übersehen* . . . *durch J. N. Pfitzerum.* First published 1674. Edition used: *Stuttgarter Lit. Verein*, Tübingen, 1880.

1725 *Des durch die gantze Welt beruffener Ertz-Schwartz-Künstlerers und Zauberers Doctor Johann Faust's mit dem Teufel aufgerichtetes Bündniß* . . . *Anitzo wiederum aufs neue übersehen* . . . *von einem Christlich Meynenden.* Edition used: Scheible, ii, 76ff.

1844: O. F. H. SCHÖNHUTH, *Des Schwarzkünstlers Dr. Johannes Faust ärgerliches Leben und schreckliches Ende*, Reutlingen, 1844.

1857: ANON, *Dr. Faust's, des berühmten Schwarzkünstlers und Teufelbanners Kreuz- und Querfahrten* . . . , Vienna, 1857. (Retelling of chapbook material with cross-fertilization from literary *Fausts*.)

(iii) *Popular Faust pieces (stage plays, pantomimes and ballets)*

1669: *Commedia vom D. Fausto* given in Danzig, autumn 1669. Contemporary account by Georg Schröder given in *DLE, Barockdrama* iii, 203.

1688: *Das Leben und Todt des großen/ Ertz-Zauberers,/ D. Johannes Faustus/ mit Vortrefflicher Pickelhärings Lustigkeit* . . . given in Bremen, 18/5/1688. Theatre bill in *DLE, Barockdrama* iii, 203. A slightly different bill, apparently of a rather earlier performance in Bremen in J. H. Duntze, *Geschichte der freien Stadt Bremen*, Bremen, 1851, iv, 582f.

1697: WM. MOUNTFORD, *The Life and Death of Dr. Faust, made into a Farce.*
I have used Otto Francke's edition, Heilbronn, 1886.

1724(?): ANON, *A Dramatick Entertainment, call'd the Necromancer/ or,
Harlequin Doctor Faustus* . . . The author, according to Stumme,
is John Rich. I have used the 9th edn., London, 1731.

1724: JOHN THURMOND, *Harlequin Doctor Faustus* . . . , London, 1724
(= ballet-scenario).

1731 or 1736: anon, *Der nach teutscher Comoedien- Engelländischer
Pantomimien- und Italiänischer Music-Art eingerichtete D. Faust.* Given
at the Kärntner-Tor theatre in Vienna and dated Saturday,
9 June. Copy in British Museum. Also given in Brukner &
Hadamowsky, pp. 41ff., where it is tentatively dated 1730. But
the fact that Saturday is given as 9 June suggests either 1731 or
1736.

1738: ANON, *Das ruchlose Leben und erschreckliche Ende des Welt-bekannten
Ertz-Zauberers D. Johann Fausts,* played in Hamburg. Bill in Engel,
Bib. faustiana, item 474.

1742: ANON, *Ex doctrina interibus, Oder die unglückseelige Gelehrsamkeit
dargestellt in dem Leben und verzweiffelten Tode D. Joannis Fausti.*
Theatre bill of 24/5/1742, given in Engel, *Dt. Puppenspiele,*
viii, 7. (A somewhat similar bill, also for 1742, on p. 6 of the
same work.)

c. 1762: ANON, *Der Münchener Faust,* ed. Payer von Thurn in *Chronik
des Wiener Goethe-Vereins,* xxvi (1912).

1767: *In doctrina interitus Oder: Das lastervolle Leben, und erschröckliche
Ende des Weltberühmten und jedermänniglich bekannten Erzzauberers
Doctoris Joannis Fausti.* Given by J. F. von Kurz in Frankfort, 1767.
The bill in Engel, *Dt. Puppenspiele,* viii, 9f. Also in Brukner &
Hadamowsky, 51–3.

(?) 3rd quarter of eighteenth century: anon, *Das Zingerlische Faust-Spiel,*
ed. Payer von Thurn in *Chronik des Wiener Goethe-Vereins,* xxv,
1911. (Faust play performed by Tyrolean peasants.)

Early nineteenth century: anon, *Das Prettauer Faustus-Spiel,* ed. W.
Hein in *Das Wissen für Alle,* i, Vienna, 1901, pp. 681–3, 697–9,
718–20, 737–9, 757–9, 776–9. (Austrian peasant play.)

(iv) *Faust puppet plays* (in order of publication)

Puppet play given by gypsies in various Swabian villages in early
nineteenth century. Account in A. Zoller, *Bilder aus Schwaben,* Stuttgart,
1834, pp. 12–14.

F. H. VON DER HAGEN, 'Das alte und neue Spiel vom Dr. Faust' in
Germania, Berlin, 1841, 211–24. (Extracts from version presented
by Schütz and Dreher in various North German towns.)

'Doctor Faust oder der große Negromantist', Berlin. Given in Scheible, v, 747 ff.

'Doktor Johann Faust. Schauspiel in zwei Theilen', Ulm. In Scheible, v, 783ff.

'Faust. Eine Geschichte der Vorzeit', Cologne. Scheible, v, 805ff.

'Johann Faust', Augsburg. Scheible, v, 818ff.

'Der weltberühmte Doktor Faust', Strasbourg. Scheible, v, 853ff.

Das Puppenspiel vom Doctor Faust . . . , Leipzig, 1850. The editor, according to Engel, is Wilhelm Hamm.

Das Puppenspiel vom Doctor Faust, ed. Karl Simrock, Leipzig, 1850.

'Das Puppenspiel Doctor Faust', ed. Oskar Schade, in *Weimarisches Jahrbuch f. dt. Sprache, Lit. u. Kunst*, Hannover, 1856, v, 241–328.

'Doctor Faust'. Given in Oldenburg. In Engel, *Dt. Puppenkomödien*, Oldenburg, 1874–9, viii, 3ff.

Das Schwiegerlingsche Puppenspiel vom 'Doktor Faust', ed. A. Bielschowsky, Brieg, 1882.

'Der Schutzgeist des Johann Doctor Faust' (lower Austrian), in *Dt. Puppenspiele*, ed. Kralik and Winter, Vienna, 1885, 157–93.

'Doctor Johann Faust. Volksschauspiel vom Plagwitzer Sommertheater', ed. Tille, Oldenburg & Leipzig, 1890 (= *Dt. Puppenkomödien*, x: *Ergänzung der Engel'schen Sammlung*).

'Das fränkische Puppenspiel von Doktor Faust', ed. R. Petsch in *Zeitschrift des Vereins f. Volkskunde*, xv, Berlin, 1905, 245–60.

Das alte deutsche Faustspiel . . . bearbeitet durch Paul Braun, Munich, 1924.

Ein Kärntner Spiel vom Dr. Faust, ed. G. Graber, Graz, 1943 (= *Kärntner Forschungen*, 1).

F. Brutschin, *Faust. Volks-Schauspiel in 4 Akten*, Lucerne, 1948.

(v) *Faust ballads*

(a) *England*

Numerous black-letter exemplars, usually of 20 stanzas. Versions are easily accessible in:

The Shirburn Ballads, 1585–1616, ed. A. Clark, Oxford, 1907, pp. 72–5 and:

The Roxburghe Ballads . . . , ed. Ebsworth, Hertford, 1887, vol. vi, part 2, pp. 703/5.

(b) *Germany*

A. TILLE, *Die dt. Volkslieder vom Doktor Faust*, Halle, 1890; photographic reprint, Tübingen, 1969.

Tille gives some examples, pp. 192ff. Large numbers of German Faust ballads have been published at various times. Since they differ from one another only in details, I give a selection here:

H. COMMENDA, 'Eine weitere Fassung der Faustballade', in *Jahrbuch f. Volksliedforschung*, vii (1941), 196f.

L. ERK and F. A. BÖHME, *Dt. Liederhort*, i (Leipzig, 1925), 655f.

A. JEITTELER, 'Das Volkslied von Faust', in *Germania*, xxvi, 1881, 352–6.

J. MEIER, 'Die älteste Volksballade von Dr. Faust', in *Jb. f. Volksliedforschung*, vi, 1939, 1–29.

R. PETSCH, 'Ein Lied vom Dr. Faust', in *Jb. der Sammlung Kippenberg*, ix, 1931.

A. SCHLOSSER, *Dt. Volkslieder aus Steiermark*, Innsbruck, 1881, pp. 348–50.

(vi) *Literary treatments of the Faust theme* (chronological order)

1592(?): CHRISTOPHER MARLOWE, *Doctor Faustus*. I have quoted from the B-text of 1616, according to the edition of W. W. Greg, Oxford, 1950.

1755–67(?): G. E. LESSING, *Faust*. (Lost. Survives only in fragments and brief descriptions. See *Sämtl. Schriften*, ed. Lachmann and Muncker, Berlin and Leipzig, 1886ff, iii, 380ff; xvii, 51, 148, 239. Also in Tille, nos. 277, 328 and 332 and in Geißler, i, 295ff.)

1756: J. F. LÖWEN, 'Die Walpurgis Nacht. Ein komisches Gedicht . . .', in *Poetische Werke*, Hamburg and Leipzig, 1760, 275–334.

1773: J. M. R. LENZ, 'Fragment aus einer Farce, die Höllenrichter genannt'. Many editions.

1773/75: J. W. VON GOETHE, *Urfaust*. Quoted from L. A. Willoughby, *Goethe's Urfaust and Faust, ein Fragment* in Blackwell's German Series, Oxford, 1943.

1775: P. WEIDMANN, *Johann Faust. Ein Allegorisches Drama*. Many editions, including one in paperback: Österreich-Reihe, vol. 242, 1964.

1776: FRIEDRICH (MALER) MÜLLER, 'Situation aus Fausts Leben'.

1778: FRIEDRICH (MALER) MÜLLER, 'Fausts Leben, dramatisiert'. Many editions of this and the preceding work. I quote from Geißler (i, 312ff).

1778: J. F. SCHINK, 'Doktor Faust: ein komisches Duodrama', in *Theater-Journal für Deutschland*, 6. Stück, Gotha, 1778. Given by Tille, no. 309. Slightly revised as 'Der neue Doktor Faust', 1782. Adapted for the puppet theatre (see Scheible, v, 884ff) and as a *Singspiel* (in Brukner and Hadamowsky, 64ff).

1782–3: ANON, *Faust, der zweyte* . . . , 2 vols., Stettin, 1782–3. A long *Trivialroman*, using Faust's name in the title for catchpenny purposes.

1790: J. W. VON GOETHE, *Faust, ein Fragment*. For edition used, see under *Urfaust*, 1773–5.

1791: F. M. KLINGER, *Fausts Leben, Taten und Höllenfahrt.* Many editions; I have referred to chapters when quoting.

1792: A. W. SCHREIBER, *Szenen aus Fausts Leben*, Offenbach, 1792.

1793: ANON, *Faustus. A Fragment of a Parody* . . . , London, 1793. In fact, not so much a parody as a paraphrase of Klinger, covering the ground up to Faust's signing of the pact.

1794: J. N. KOMARECK, *Faust von Mainz* . . . , Leipzig, 1794.

1795: J. F. SCHINK, 'Prolog zu einem dramatischen Gedichte: Doktor Faust', in *Berlinisches Archiv der Zeit und ihres Geschmacks*, i, 2 (1795). Given by Tille, no. 348. Most of this will be taken up into the *Faust* of 1804.

1796: J. F. SCHINK, 'Doktor Faust's Bund mit der Hölle', in *Berl. Archiv d. Zeit* . . . , ii (1796), 70ff. This is the 'prosaic' pact which prompted Schiller to write his famous *Zenie*. It will be taken up in revised form into the *Faust* of 1804.

1797: F. J. H. VON SODEN, *Doktor Faust. Volks-Schauspiel in 5 Akten.* Edition used: Wendriner, iii, 151ff.

1798 ANON, *Faust der große Mann, oder seine Wanderungen durch die Welt* . . . , 2 parts, Vienna and Prague, 1798.

1800: J. F. SCHINK, 'Doctor Faust. Romanze aus einer noch ungedruckten Oper', in W. G. Becker's *Almanach und Taschenbuch zum geselligen Vergnügen*, Leipzig, 1800. In Tille no. 433. A summary in verse of Faust's career.

1801: L. TIECK, 'Anti-Faust oder Geschichte eines dummen Teufels . . .', in *Nachgelassene Schriften*, ed. Köpke, Leipzig, 1855, i, 127ff. Pokes fun at the Faust vogue of the day, but expresses reverence for Goethe's *Fragment*.

1801: K. F. BENKOWITZ, *Die Jubelfeier der Hölle oder Faust der jüngere*, Berlin, 1801.

1803: A. VON CHAMISSO, 'Faust. Ein Versuch'. A fragment. In all editions of Chamisso's works.

1804: J. F. SCHINK, *Johann Faust, Dramatische Phantasie, nach einer Sage des sechzehnten Jahrhunderts*, 2 parts, Berlin, 1804.

1805: C. A. VULPIUS, 'Doctor Faust in Insprug [*sic*]' in *Bibl. des romantisch-Wunderbaren*, Leipzig, 1805, i, 37ff. Retelling of an incident from the Faustbook.

1806: ANON (= J. J. Engel?), *Der travestirte Doktor Faust*, Berlin, 1806.

1808: J. W. VON GOETHE, *Faust. Der Tragödie erster Teil.* Since most editions give line-numbers, I have given line-references when quoting.

1809: C. C. L. SCHÖNE, *Faust, eine romantische Tragödie*, Berlin, 1809.

1812–3: F. GRILLPARZER, 'Waldgegend' in *SW* (*hist.-krit. Gesamtausg.*), ed. Sauer, Abt. 2, vol. iv, Vienna, 1924, pp. 239–43. A fragment of 49 lines, part of Grillparzer's plan to continue Goethe's Part 1.

1813: J. SCHNERR, 'Das Gastmahl des Doktors Faust', in *Erheiterungen*, Aarau, 1813, ii, 313ff. An invented anecdote told in the style of a folk ballad.

1813: L. SPOHR and J. C. BERNARD, *Faust. Romantische Oper.* Composed 1813, first performed 1816. Edition used: *Faust. Große romantische Oper* . . . von J. C. Bernard. Musik von Louis Spohr (=*Breitkopf and Härtels Textbibliothek* no. 90, Leipzig, n.d.—about 1880).

1815: E. A. F. KLINGEMANN, *Faust. Ein Trauerspiel* . . . , Leipzig and Altenburg, 1815.

1816: E. VON GROOTE, *Faust's Versöhnung mit dem Leben*, Cologne, 1816.

1816: W. SEYBOLD, *Der umgekehrte Faust oder Frosch's Jugendjahre*, Reutlingen, 1816. Apparently one of two projected volumes. Incoherent and confused attack on various trends in German cultural and intellectual life.

1817: A. VON ARNIM: *Die Kronenwächter.* Book 2 contains an episode intended to present Faust as the sixteenth century saw him.

1820: A. VON PLATEN, 'Fausts Gebet'. Poem.

1821: N. VOGT, 'Faust'—the 12th poem in the collection *Rheinische Bilder*, Frankfort on the Main, 1821. Faust identified with Fust, the printer.

1823: C. C. L. SCHÖNE, *Fortsetzung des Faust von Göthe* . . . , Berlin, 1823.

1823: J. VON VOß, *Faust, Trauerspiel mit Gesang und Tanz*, ed. Ellinger, Berlin, 1890.

1824: H. HEINE, early plan for a *Faust*: see E. Wedekind, *Studentenleben in der Biedermeierzeit* . . . , ed. Houben, Göttingen, 1927, 120f.

1825: G. SOANE, *Faustus. A Romantic Drama*, London, 1825.

1829: C. VON HOLTEI, *Dr. Johannes Faust. Melodrama* . . . Edn. used: C. von H., *Theater*, Breslau, 1845. 178ff.

1830: 'PATER BREY' (pseud), *Die gezähmten Zecher in Auerbachs Keller* . . . , Frankfort on the Main, 1830. Contemporary satire.

1830(?): FR. TH. VISCHER, 'Faustische Stimmen', in *Ausgew. Werke*, ed. Keyßner, Stuttgart and Berlin, 1918, i, 12–14. 4 poems. The dating is tentative.

1831: H. HARRING, *Faust im Gewande der Zeit*, Leipzig, 1831. (Satire on the age.)

1831: F. C. VON MÜFFLING, 'Zum Faust, der Tragödie von Goethe' (bound MS. of 95 pp. in British Museum. Catalogued under printed books).

1831: G. PFIZER, 'Faustische Szenen' in Cotta's *Morgenblatt für gebildete Stände*, xxv (1831), pp. 633f, 639f, 641f, 649f, 657f, 662–4, 665f.

1831: K. ROSENKRANZ, *Geistlich Nachspiel zur Tragödie Faust*, Leipzig, 1831.

1832: J. W. VON GOETHE, *Faust.* Regarding quotations, see comment on Part 1, 1808.

1833: L. BECHSTEIN, *Faustus, ein Gedicht*, Leipzig, 1833. Retelling of chapbook material.

1833: J. D. HOFFMAN, *Faust. Eine Tragödie von Goethe. Fortgesetzt von J. D. H.*, Leipzig, 1833.

1833: E. ORTLEPP, 'Aus einem Faust', in *Der Komet. Ein Unterhaltungs-blatt . . .*, 4. Jg., 1833, nos. 113–16, 129–30, 133–6. Scenes from an uncompleted Faust play.

1834: 'W. JEMAND' (= W. Langewiesche), 'Faust', in *Lies Mich! Ein Taschenbuch für gesellige Unterhaltung*, Iserlohn, 1834, ii, 317ff. Retelling of Faust's story in verse.

1835: BRAUN VON BRAUNTHAL, *Faust. Eine Tragödie*, Leipzig, 1835.

1835: H. SCHIFF, 'Johann Faust in Paris 1463' in *Novellen und Nicht-Novellen*, Berlin and Königsberg, 1835, 28–68. Concerns Fust, the printer.

1836: J. I. BAGGESEN, *Der vollendete Faust* (= vol. iii of his *Poetische Werke in dt. Sprache*, Leipzig, 1836).

1836: N. LENAU, *Faust. Ein Gedicht*. Edn. used: *Sämtl. Werke*, ed. E. Castle, Leipzig, 1910ff, ii, 1–123.

1837: ANON, 'Faust in Hamburg', in *Hamburg wie es ist und—trinkt*, n.F., i. Abt., pp. 1–86, Hamburg, 1837.

1838: ANON, 'Der dritte Theil des Faust', in *Phönix*, ed. E. Duller, Frankfort on the Main, 1838, 462–4. A fragment of one scene only. The intention was to pursue Faust's fortunes in Heaven and those of various other characters from Goethe, including Wagner, on earth.

before 1839(?): GÉRARD DE NERVAL, 'Faust'—dramatic fragment, published posthumously. Edition used: Goethe, *Faust et le second Faust*. Traduction de G. de N., ed. M. Allemand, Paris, 1962, 294–313. For the tentative dating, see G. de N , *Oeuvres complémentaires*, ed. Richer, ii(1961), p. 479.

1839: L. AURBACHER, 'Geschichte des Doctor Faustus', in *Ein Volks-büchlein*, Munich, 1839, part ii, 1–50.

1839: P. J. BAILEY, *Festus, a Poem*. First published 1839. I have used the edition of 1852.

1839: A. LUTZE, *Faust in Auerbach's Keller zu Leipzig. Lustige dramatische Szene*, Berlin, 1839.

1839: 'F. MARLOW' (= L. H. Wolfram), *Faust. Ein dramatisches Gedicht*, Leipzig, 1839.

c. 1840: F. W. GUBITZ, 'Faust und Mephisto in Mitte des neunzehnten Jahrhunderts', in *Gedichte*, Berlin, 1860, i, 269–82.

c. 1840: A. LUTZE, 'Doctor Faust. Entwurf einer Schluß-Scene', in *Gedichte*, 3rd edn., i, Cöthen, 1863, 228–33.

1841: ANON, *Leben, Tod und Höllenfahrt des weltberühmten Doctor Daus. Einaktige Parodie des Göthe'schen Faust*, Leipzig, 1841.

1841: IDA GRÄFIN VON HAHN-HAHN, *Die Gräfin Faustine,* first published 1841. I have used the English translation of 'A.E.I.', 2 vols., London, 1845.

1841: J. E. NÜRNBERGER, 'Faust junior. Dramatische Skizze', in *Ernste Dichtungen,* Kempten, 1841, 117ff.

1842: H. P. GRATTAN, *Faust; or the Demon of the Drachenfels* . . . Edn. used: *Dick's Standard Plays,* no. 573, London, 1884. A melo-dramatic tear-jerker, with less debt to Goethe than is the case with most nineteenth-century English Faust plays.

1842: WOLDEMAR NÜRNBERGER, *Josephus Faust. Ein Gedicht.* First published under the pseudonym 'M. Solitar' in 1842, with the title *Faust. Ein Gedicht.* I have used the second edition, Landsberg, 1847.

1843: S. J. ST. CZILSKI, *Faust. Ein dramatisches Gedicht,* Halle, 1843.

1846: H. BLAZE DE BURY, 'Marguerite', in *Intermèdes et Poëmes,* Paris, 1859, 289–301.

1848: FR. REINHARD, *Faust,* Düsseldorf, 1848 (unfinished).

c. 1849: LEMAN REDE, 'The Devil and Dr. Faustus', in *Cumberland's British Theatre,* London, n.d., vol. xlv, no. 367.

1849: ANON, *Mephistopheles als Volksmann* . . . , Carlsruhe, 1849. Parody of Goethe's 'Hexenküche' scene for purposes of political satire.

1849: H. VON BEGUIGNOLLES, *Hilario. Dramatische Studie zu Goethe's Faust,* Leipzig, 1849.

1849: M. CARRÉ, 'Faust et Marguerite. Drame fantastique . . .', in *Bibliothèque Dramatique* . . . , xxx, Paris, 1849. Freely adapted from Goethe. Differs from the libretto of 1859. (There Faust is saved; here he is damned.)

1851: 'TERTULLIAN FABER' (Xaver Schmid), *Der neue Faust,* Rastatt, 1851. To avoid confusion, it should be mentioned that Schmid's *Studien zu einem neuen Faust,* Salzburg, 1856, is the same work under a new title.

1851: H. HEINE, *Der Doktor Faust. Ein Tanzpoem* . . . , Hamburg, 1851. Written 1847.

1853: D. K. [ALISCH], *Faust, der zu spät bekehrte Demokrat* . . . , Berlin, 1853. (Political satire.)

c. 1854: J. HALFORD, *Faust and Marguerite* . . . *A Grand Operatic Extrava-ganza,* London, n.d. (=c. 1854). A parody of Goethe's part 1, ending with the reform of Faust.

1854: W. JORDAN, *Demiurgos. Ein Mysterium,* 3 parts, Leipzig, 1854.

1856: I. TURGENEV, 'Faust. Novelle in neun Briefen', in *Erzählungen von Iwan Turgénjew,* trans. Bodenstedt, i, Munich, 1864, 1–93.

1858: VILLIERS DE L'ISLE ADAM, 'Chanson' (=no. 7 of the 'Fantaisies Nocturnes'). Edition used: *Œuvres complètes,* x, Paris, 1929, 29f.

1859: CHARLES GOUNOD, P. J. BARBIER and M. CARRÉ, Faust opera, freely based on Goethe. Editions of libretto: Paris, 1859 and 1860. French/English parallel text published by the Grand Opera Syndicate, Covent Garden, London, n.d. (= 1900).

1859: JULIUS GROSSE, 'Ein Bild' (poem addressed to Faust). In Grosse's *Aus bewegten Tagen*, Stuttgart, 1869, 196f and in the *Gedichte*, Berlin, 1882, 80f. Also given by Geibel in his *Münchener Dichterbuch*, Stuttgart, 1862, 172–4.

c. 1860: CARL STEIN, *Doctor Faust oder Struwelpeter's Urbild. Weinachts–Zauberkomödie* . . . , Berlin, n.d. (=c. 1860).

1860: A. LENBURG, *Faust. Ein Gedicht*, Berlin, 1860.

1861: IMRY MADÁCH, *Az ember tragediája*. I quote from the German edition: *Die Tragödie des Menschen. Aus dem Ungarischen übersetzt von L. Dóczi*, Stuttgart, 1891. English translations by W. M. Loew, 1909; C. P. Sanger, 1933; C. H. Meltzer and P. Vajda, 1933.

1862: FR. TH. VISCHER, *Faust, der Tragödie dritter Theil*. First published pseudonymously in 1862. I have used the revised edition, Tübingen, 1886.

1862/3: G. PFARRIUS, 'Schein und Sein. Erzählung aus dem 16. Jahrhundert', in *Westermanns Monatshefte*, Oct. 1862 (pp. 1–16), Nov. 1862 (121–45), Dec. 1862 (235–55) and Jan. 1863 (347–62).

1864: C. E. MÖLLING, *Faust's Tod. Eine Tragödie in funf Aufzügen*, Philadelphia, 1864. Also in English translation, *Faust's Death*, Philadelphia, 1865.

1864: S. MOSER, *Göthe's zweiter Faust oder Der geöffnete Walpurgissack* . . . , Weissenburg, 1864. Shortened version of Goethe's Part 2 with a facetious and, in parts, scurrilous commentary added.

1865: ANON, *Faust, eine tragi-komische Fastnachts-Posse (frei nach Herrn v. Goethe)* von einem Melancholicus, Berlin, 1865.

1865: E. GEIBEL, 'Fausts Jugendgesang' and 'Historische Studien', first published in *Neue Gedichte*, 1865. Edition used: *Ges. Werke in 8 Bdn*. Stuttgart, 1888, iii, 10f and 33–7.

1866: R. DEHNICKE, 'Der neue Faust (Fragment)', in *Gedichte (aus seinem Nachlasse)*, Berlin, 1866, 85–136. Not a true Faust work: contemporary political satire with Faust's name in the title for catchpenny reasons.

1866: A. MÖSER, 'Doctor Faust in Salzburg'—versification of traditional episode. Edition used: *Schauen und Schaffen, neue Gedichte*, Stuttgart, 1881, 240–3.

1869: ADOLF MÜLLER, *Faust. Tragödie in fünf Acten. Als zweiter Theil zu Goethe's Faust*, Leipzig, 1869.

1869: F. STOLTE, *Faust. Dramatisches Gedicht in 4 Theilen*, Hamburg, 1869.

c. 1875: 'GOETHE DER SCHWÄCHERE', *Faust. Der Tragödie dritter und unwiderruflich letzter Theil,* Berlin, n.d. (=*c.* 1875). Burlesque of Goethe, relying heavily for comic effect on echoes of Goethe's verse in incongruous contexts. A weak example of its kind.

1877: LOUISE M. ALCOTT, *A Modern Mephistopheles.* Novel, first published in 1877. Edition used: Boston, 1889.

1878: A. FITGER, 'Faust's Schatten an Charles Darwin', a poem, in *Kosmos,* 2. Jg., vol. iv, Leipzig, Oct. 1878–March 1879, 335–8.

1879: W. S. GILBERT, *Gretchen. A play, in four acts.* London, 1879. Also in W. S. G., *Original Plays,* 2nd series, London, 1881, 151ff.

c. 1880: O. LINDERER, *Schuster Faust und seine Grete* . . . , Berlin, n.d. (=*c.* 1880). Burlesque of Goethe: Faust as Berlin cobbler.

1880: R. BAUMBACH, 'Der Adept', in *Lieder eines fahrenden Gesellen.* First published 1880. I have used the 3rd edn., Leipzig, 1881, 172–4.

1880: H. E. JAHN, *Faust. Eine Satire,* Rostock, 1880. Contemporary satire.

1883: ANON, *Faust. Der Tragödie dritter Theil,* Vienna, 1883. A parody, not a serious continuation. Its only claim to interest is as one of many works of the 1870s and 1880s which made fun of Wagner and of Wagnerism.

1883: J. STURM, 'Faust und Mephistopheles', in *Neue Christoterpe, Ein Jahrbuch,* ed. Kögel, Baur and Frommel, Bremen, 1883, p. 311.

c. 1884: J. ERNSTLIEB, *Faust. Zweiter Theil. Dramatische Dichtung,* Mannheim, n.d. (=*c.* 1884).

1886: W. G. WILLS, *Faust, in a Prologue and Five Acts* . . . , London, n.d. (=1886). A free and abridged version of Goethe's Part I.

1887: C. A. LINDE, *Faust. Eine Tragödie. iii. Theil zu Goethe's Faust,* Darmstadt, 1887.

c. 1888: 'J. VRCHLICKÝ' (=Emil Frida), 'Faustulus'. The poem was translated by E. Albert and appeared in his anthology *Neuere Poesie aus Böhmen* . . . , Vienna, 1893, 300–3.

1888: ADOLF MÜLLER, *Doctor Faust's Ende. Tragödie in fünf Aufzügen,* Blankenburg, 1888.

1888: 'S. REINHOLD' (=Georg Zapf), 'Faust's Jugend', in *Faust's Jugend. Ahasvers' Tod. Zwei Gedichte,* Tachau, 1888. The poem presents a sombre Faust brooding on the transience of life and unable to believe in God.

1890: E. ALBRECHT, 'Faust und Ahasver', in *Die Gesellschaft,* Leipzig, 1890, iii, 1317–19. A single scene in rhymed verse joining on to the end of Goethe's Part I, and dealing with Faust's grief over Gretchen's death.

1890: FRANZ KEIM, 'Mephistopheles in Rom', in *Ges. Werke,* Munich and Leipzig, 1912, iii, 1–113. A serious continuation of Goethe, *not* a parody as stated—or conjectured—by E. M. Butler.

1891: ANON, *Der Militairische Faust. Eine Höllenparodie vom Famulus Wagner*, Berlin, 1891.

1891: HANS SCHILF, *Faust. Tragödie in fünf Acten*, Leipzig and St. Petersburg, 1891.

1893: A. GEIGER, 'Ein moderner Faust', in *Im Wandern und Stehenbleiben*, Carlsruhe, 1893, pp. 99–199.

1895: H. HANGO, *Faust und Prometheus*, Leipzig, 1895.

1895: 'FRANZ HELD' (=Franz Herzfeld), 'Faust's Monolog', in *Trotz Alledem!*, 2nd edn., Berlin, 1895, 70–2.

1895/96: E. HUTSCHENREITER, *Moderne Faust-Scenen*, 2 parts, Dresden, Leipzig and Vienna, 1895–96.

1898: F. SPIELHAGEN, 'Faustulus', first published 1898. Edition used: *Sämtl. Romane*, Leipzig, 1903–10, xxvi, 1–247.

1900: ALFRED HAHN, *Faust fin de siècle*, Berlin, n.d. (= 1900). Burlesque. Tries to show how Faust and Mephisto would fare if pitchforked into the modern world.

1902: WALTER VON DER ELBE, *Khâli, oder 'der Ausgleich'*, Leipzig, 1902. Faust's quest for truth and his attempt to resolve the paradoxes of life. The answer seems to lie in a rather indigestible combination of Western humanitarianism and Oriental mysticism.

1902: FERDINAND RITTER VON FELDEGG, *Der neue Faust*, Linz, Vienna and Leipzig, 1902.

c. 1906: ANON, *Faust. Der Tragödie Abschluß*, Leipzig, n.d. (=*c.* 1906).

1908: STEPHEN PHILLIPS & J. COMYNS CLARK, *Faust. Freely adapted from Goethe's dramatic poem*, London, 1908. An emasculated and bowdlerized version of Part 1. Ends with Faust's salvation.

1910: J. GAULKE, *Der gefesselte Faust*, Berlin, 1910.

1914: F. BUSONI, *Doktor Faust*. Libretto written 1914 and published 1920. Music composed between 1916 and 1924, but unfinished at Busoni's death. Completed by F. Jarnach. The opera was first performed in 1925. I have used the first edition of the libretto, Potsdam, 1920. See too under Busoni in General Bibliography.

1916: ANON, *Faust. A Play in 4 Acts*, London, 1916. Indebted mainly to Marlowe, rather less to Goethe.

1916: E. L. ENGELHARDT, *Faust, ein deutscher Mythos*, Artern, 1916.

1916: G. S. VIERECK, 'Dr. Faust's Descent from Heaven', in *Songs of Armageddon*, New York, 1916, 35–8. Faust as the 'pilgrim of passion'—a donjuanesque Faust, in fact.

1918: A. V. LUNACHARSKI, *Faust and the City*. Written in 1908, recast in 1916, published in 1918. Edition used: A. V. L., *Three Plays*, transl. L. A. Magnus and K. Walter, London and New York, n.d. (= 1923), 1–134.

1919: F. AVENARIUS, *Faust. Ein Spiel*, Munich, 1919.

1919: RUDOLF PAYER VON THURN, *Doktor Faust. Ein Gelehrtenschicksal*, Vienna and Leipzig, 1919.

1920: 'c. p. TORBRECH' (=Carl Borchert), *Eine Faust-Phantasie*, Nuremberg, 1920.

1921: HANNAH STAHN, *Faustus redivivus*, Dresden and Leipzig, 1921.

1923: R. A. ÉDON, *Mephisto. Eine Faust-Paraphrase*, Vienna, 1923.

1924: PAUL DEGEN, *Doktor Faust. Ein Spiel in 4 Akten*, Greifswald, 1924.

1925: E. WIEPRECHT, *Jung-Faust. Eine ernsthafte Faust-Parodie, der deutschen Jugend gewidmet* . . . , Großenheim, n.d. (according to Dabezies, 1925). The work dates from 1923. A version in which Faust is made to stand for the spirit of German youth.

1926: M. DE GHELDERODE, *La Mort du Docteur Faust*. Written and first published 1926. Edition used: *Théâtre*, v, Paris, 1957, 207–85. A rather facetious version from the fringes of Surrealism. It employs the device of allowing Faust and Mephisto to be aware that they are figures within a literary tradition.

1927: HERMANN HESSE, 'Ein Abend bei Dr. Faust', in *Fabulierbuch*, Zürich, 1947, 191–7. Faust theme as vehicle for contemporary satire. The wittiest example of this type known to me.

1927: ERNST KRATZMANN, *Faust. Ein Buch vom deutschen Geist*. Finished by 1927, first published 1932. I have used the 2nd edn., Vienna and Leipzig, 1938.

1929: KARL ZAPFE, *Faust. Der Tragödie 3. Teil*, Leipzig, 1929.

1932: ANON, *Jung Faust an die Menschheit* . . . , Vienna, 1932. According to Dabezies, the author is M. Blümelhuber.

1933: A. GSTÖTTNER, *Der Wanderer. Dramatische Dichtung*, Salzburg, 1933.

1934: A. GROßMANN, *Faust (Erfüllung)*, Berlin, 1934.

1939: DOROTHY L. SAYERS, *The Devil to Pay*. First published 1939. Edn. used: D. L. S., *4 Sacred Plays*, London, 1948, 105–212.

1940: R. PANNWITZ, 'Mechristophiles Himmelfahrt', in *Vierteljahrdrücke*, 1940, no. 3, 24–33.

1940: PAUL VALÉRY, '"Mon Faust" (Ébauches)'. Written 1940, appeared 1941 as 'Études pour "Mon Faust"'. First published with the definitive title in 1945. Edn. used: P. V. *Œuvres*, ii, 276–403 and 1410–15 (=*Bibl. de la Pléiade*, vol. 148, 1962).

1944: R. H. WARD, *Faust in Hell*, Ilkley, 1944.

1947: TH. MANN, *Doktor Faustus. Das Leben des deutschen Tonsetzers Adrian Leverkühn, erzählt von einem Freunde*. First published 1947. Edn. used: S. Fischer, Berlin, 1960.

1950: W. HERBST, *Luther und Faust. Ein dramatisches Spiel*, Berlin, 1950.

1951: W. WEBELS, *Ein Spiel vom Doktor Faust*, Essen, 1951.

1952: HANNS EISLER, *Johann Faustus. Oper*, Berlin, 1952. The libretto; the music was never composed.

1952: AUGUST SCHMID, *Faust der Denker*, Affoltern, 1952.

1954: G. REIßER, *Man suchte stets geheime Künste. Die Geschichte eines Doktor Johann Faust*, Hamburg, 1954. Modernized and shortened version of 'Spies'.

1958: ANTONY BORROW, *John Faust, a drama in three acts*, Ashford, 1958.

1958: E. J. BYNG, *Die Wiederkehr des Dr. Faust. Novelle*, Munich, 1958.

1960: M. EHBAUER, *Der Faust in der Krachledern . . .*, Munich, 1960.

1962: K. MAMPELL, *Die Geschichte des berüchtigten Zauberers Doktor Faust . . .*, Frankfort on the Main, 1962.

1962: I. A. RICHARDS, *Tomorrow morning, Faustus!*, London, 1962.

1963: K. BECSI, *Faust in Moskau*, Vienna, 1962.

1966: JOHN HERSEY, *Too Far to Walk*, London, 1966.

(vii) *Bibliography to Chapter 9: Faust and Science*

KINGSLEY AMIS *New Maps of Hell*, London 1960. (Survey of Science Fiction.)

GÜNTHER ANDERS, *Die Antiquiertheit des Menschen*, Munich, 1961.

MATTHEW ARNOLD, *Culture and Anarchy . . .*, London, 1869.

JOHN BAILLIE, *The Belief in Progress*, O.U.P., 1950.

R. BLUNCK, *Justus von Liebig*, Berlin, 1938.

W. BOLIN, *Ludwig Feuerbach*, Stuttgart, 1891.

J. W. BRAUN, *Goethe im Urtheile seiner Zeitgenossen*, iii, Berlin, 1885. Contains a number of comments on the scientific writings. See especially pp. 262 and 279.

LUDWIG BÜCHNER, *Aus Natur und Wissenschaft*, 2 vols., Leipzig, 1862 and 1884. (Collection of essays, reviews, etc.)

LUDWIG BÜCHNER, *Der Fortschritt in Natur und Geschichte . . .*, Stuttgart, 1884.

LUDWIG BÜCHNER, *Die Darwin'sche Theorie . . . 6 Vorlesungen*, 5th edn., Leipzig, 1890. (First published 1868.)

J. B. BURY, *The Idea of Progress*, London, 1920.

E. M. BUTLER, *The Saint Simonian Religion in Germany*, C.U.P., 1926.

A. M. CLERKE, *The Herschels and Modern Astronomy*, London, 1895.

AUGUSTE COMTE, *Cours de Philosophie Positive*, 6 vols., Paris, 1830–42.

AUGUSTE COMTE, *La Philosophie Positive . . .* résumé par Jules Rig, 2 vols., Paris, 1881. (= Comte's 6 vols. in much abridged form.)

AUGUSTE COMTE, *Die positive Philosophie von A.C. im Auszuge von Jules Rig*. Übersetzt von J. H. von Kirchmann, 2 vols, Heidelberg, 1883. (Translation of Rig's edition plus brief account of Comte's life and works.)

AUGUSTE COMTE, *Discours sur l'Ensemble du Positivisme*, Paris, 1848.

AUGUSTE COMTE, *Der Positivismus in seinem Wesen und seiner Bedeutung*, übersetzt von E. Roschlau, Leipzig, 1894. (Translation of the *Discours*.)

CHARLES DARWIN, *The Origin of Species* . . . , London, 1859.
CHARLES DARWIN, *The Descent of Man* . . . , 2 vols., London, 1871.
H. DEBUS, *Erinnerungen an Robert Wilhelm Bunsen* . . . , Cassel, 1901.
EMIL DU BOIS-REYMOND, *Über die Grenzen des Naturerkennens*, Leipzig, 1872.
EMIL DU BOIS-REYMOND, *Goethe und kein Ende*, Berlin, 1882.
IFOR EVANS, *Literature and Science*, London, 1954.
L. FEUERBACH, *Das Wesen der Religion* (= 30 lectures given in Heidelberg, 1848/49). Edition used: Kröner, Stuttgart, 1938.
M. GEBHARDT, *Goethe als Physiker*, Berlin, 1932.
E. HAECKEL, *Natürliche Schöpfungsgeschichte*, Berlin, 1868.
E. HAECKEL, *Ziele und Wege der heutigen Entwicklungsgeschichte*, Jena, 1875.
E. HAECKEL, *Gesammelte populäre Vorträge*, 2 vols., Bonn, 1878/79.
E. HAECKEL, *Über unsere gegenwärtige Kenntniß vom Ursprung des Menschen*, Bonn, 1898.
E. HAECKEL, *Die Welträthsel*, Bonn, 1899.
W. HERSCHEL, *The Scientific Papers* . . . , 2 vols., London, 1912.
JOYCE O. HERTZLER, *The History of Utopian Thought*, London, 1923.
J. H. VON KIRCHMANN (German Positivist), *Zeitfragen und Abenteuer*, Leipzig, 1881. See too under Comte.
Kosmos. Zeitschrift für einheitliche Weltanschauung auf Grund der Entwicklungslehre, Leipzig, 1877ff.
E. KRAUSE, *Charles Darwin und sein Verhältnis zu Deutschland*, Leipzig, 1885.
J. VON LIEBIG, *Chemische Briefe*, 2 vols., 4th edn., Leipzig and Heidelberg, 1859.
J. VON LIEBIG, *Reden und Abhandlungen*, Leipzig and Heidelberg, 1874.
J. VON LIEBIG, *Briefwechsel mit L. F. Schönbein*, Leipzig, 1900.
E. LITTRÉ, *Conservation, Révolution et Positivisme*, Paris, 1852.
F. MATHÉ, *Karl Friedrich Gauß*, Leipzig, 1906.
C. MATSCHOß, *Große Ingenieure*, Munich and Berlin, 1937.
W. MAY, *Ernst Haeckel*, Leipzig, 1909.
J. MOLESCHOTT, *Der Kreislauf des Lebens*, Mainz, 1855.
J. MOLESCHOTT, *Kleine Schriften*, Giessen, n.d. (=c. 1862).
G. MÜLLER-SCHWEFE, 'Fortschrittsglaube und Dichtung im victorianischen England', in *Anglia*, 77, 1959, pp. 145–72.
W. PREYER, *Darwin. Sein Leben und Wirken*, Berlin, 1896.
E. REDSLOB, *Die Welt vor 100 Jahren*, Leipzig, 1940.
J. RIG, *see under* Comte.
E. ROSCHLAU, *see under* Comte.
SIR CHARLES SHERRINGTON, *Goethe on nature & on science*, 2nd edn., C.U.P., 1949.
J. B. SIDGWICK, *William Herschel. Explorer of the Heavens*, London, 1953.
HUGO SOMMER, *Die positive Philosophie Auguste Comte's*, Berlin, 1885.

D. F. STRAUß, *Der alte und der neue Glaube*, Leipzig, 1872.

D. F. STRAUß, *Briefwechsel zwischen Strauß und Vischer*, 2 vols., Stuttgart, 1952/53. (= *Veröffentlichungen der deutschen Schillergesellschaft*, 18 and 19.)

J. SULLY, *Pessimism*, London, 1887.

E. L. TUVESON, *Millennium and Utopia*, University of California Press, 1949.

R. VIRCHOW, *Göthe als Naturforscher*, Berlin, 1861.

C. VOGT, *Bilder aus dem Thierleben*, Frankfort-on-Main, 1852.

C. VOGT, *Köhlerglaube und Wissenschaft*, Giessen, 1855.

MORITZ WAGNER, *Die Entstehung der Arten* . . . , Basle, 1889. (= Post-humous collection of Wagner's essays and papers.)

A. R. WALLACE, *Contributions to the Theory of Natural Selection*, London, 1870. Translated into German as *Beiträge zur Theorie der natürlichen Zuchtwahl*, Erlangen, 1870.

F. A. T. WINNECKE, *Gauß. Ein Umriß seines Lebens und Wirkens*, Brunswick, 1877.

T. ZIEGLER, *Die geistigen und sozialen Strömungen des 19ten Jhts.*, Berlin, 1899.

(viii) *Bibliography* (*Don Juan*)

A. E. SINGER, *A Bibliography of the Don Juan Theme. Versions and Criticism.* (= *West Virginia University Bulletin*, Series 54, Nos. 10–11, April, 1954.)

(ix) *Popular stage plays, pantomimes, etc., about Don Juan*

1700: *Histrio Gallicus, comico-satyricus, sine exemplo: Oder Die Welt-berühmten Lust-Comödien Des . . . Herrn von Moliere . . . in das Teutsche übersetzt* . . . , Nuremberg, 1700. vol. i, 12–110 = 'Des Don Pedro Gastmahl'—a reasonably faithful version of Molière.

Early or mid eighteenth century: *Das steinerne Gastmahl, oder die redende Statua, samt Arie welche Hanns-Wurst singet; Nebst denen Versen Des Eremiten, Und denen Verzweiflungs-Versen Des Don Juans* . . . , no place, no date. 24 pp.: parts of the action only in the form of a summary. Not from Molière. Derives from other French Don Juan plays and/or Italian sources.

1752: 'Das steinerne Todten-Gastmahl oder Die im Grabe noch lebende Rache, oder Die aufs höchste gestiegene endlich übelange-kommene Kühn- und Frechheit' = theatre bill from Dresden, dated 11 January 1752. Given by Engel, *Die Don Juan-Sage auf der Bühne*, 187f.

1757: 'Le Festin de Pierre, Des D. Pedro Todten Gastmahl . . .' = theatre bill of 16 February 1757 in *Theaterzettel der Schuchischen*

Gesellschaft aus Regensburg (1756–7)—collection in Göttingen University Library.

3rd quarter of eighteenth century: *Der Laufner Don Juan. Ein Beitrag zur Geschichte des Volksschauspiels*, ed. R. M. Werner, Hamburg and Leipzig, 1891. (= *Theatergeschichtliche Forschungen*, iii.)

1782: *Don Juan or the Libertine Destroyed*, London, 1782. Pantomime. Another version, different in some details, London, 1784.

1783: MARINELLI, 'Dom Juan, oder Der steinerne Gast. Lustspiel in vier Aufzügen nach Molieren, und dem spanischen des Tirso de Molina el Combidado de piedra für dies Theater bearbeitet mit Kaspars Lustigkeit', in *DLE*, Reihe Barock: Barocktradition im öst.—bayerischen Volkstheater, ii, 1936, 53–96. Ed. Rommel.

c. 1818: W. T. MONCRIEFF, *Giovanni in London; or, the Libertine Reclaimed.* Edition used: *Dick's Standard Plays*, London, n.d. (= *c.* 1875), No. 104, pp. 815–30. Farce in the form of a ballad opera.

(x) *Don Juan puppet plays* (in order of publication)

'Don Juan oder der steinerne Gast' (Strasbourg), in Scheible, iii, 725ff.

'Don Juan. Ein Trauerspiel in 4 Aufzügen' (Ulm), in Scheible, iii, 760ff.

'Don Juan und Don Pietro' (Augsburg), in Scheible, iii, 699ff.

'Don Juan oder: Der steinerne Gast', in Engel, *Dt. Puppenkomödien*, Oldenburg, 1874–79, iii, 23ff.

'Don Juan, der vielfache Mörder oder Das Gastmahl um Mitternacht auf dem Kirchhofe', in Engel, *Dt. Puppenkomödien*, iii, 69ff. (Extracts only.)

'Don Juan der Wilde oder Das nächtliche Gericht oder Der steinerne Gast oder Junker Hans vom Stein' (lower Austrian), in *Dt. Puppenspiele*, ed. Kralik and Winter, Vienna, 1885, 81ff.

(xi) *Literary treatments of the Don Juan theme* (chronological order)

c. 1630: TIRSO DE MOLINA(?), *El Burlador de Sevilla y Convidado de Piedra.* Editions used: 'Cambridge Plain Texts', C.U.P., 1954 and German translation by C. A. Dohrn: 'Der Verführer von Sevilla' = *Spanische Dramen*, Berlin, 1841, i, 1–156.

1640s: J. A. CICOGNINI, *Il Convitato di Pietra.* Edn. used: Bévotte, *Le Festin de Pierre avant Molière*, 369–424.

1658: DORIMON, *Le Festin de Pierre ou le fils criminel.* In Bévotte, op. cit., 17–134.

1659: J. DE VILLIERS, *Le Festin de Pierre ou le fils criminel.* In Bévotte, op. cit., 151–275.

1665: MOLIÈRE, *Dom Juan ou le Festin de Pierre*, first performed 1665, published 1682. I have used W. D. Howarth's edn. in *Blackwell's French Texts*, 1958.

1669: ROSIMOND, *Le nouveau Festin de Pierre ou l' Athée foudroyé*. Edn. used: V. Fournal, *Les Contemporains de Molière*, Paris, 1875, iii, 313–77.

1675: THOMAS SHADWELL, *The Libertine*. Edn. used: *Complete Works*, ed. Montague Summers, London, 1927, iii, 19–93.

1677: TH. CORNEILLE, *Le Festin de Pierre*. Edn. used: *Œuvres de Pierre et Thomas Corneille*, Paris, 1850, 378–421.

1736: CARLO GOLDONI, *Don Giovanni Tenorio o sia Il Dissoluto*. Edn. used: *Opere* (I Classici Mondadori), Milan, 1935ff, ix, 209ff.

1787: W. A. MOZART and L. DA PONTE, *Il Dissoluto punito o sia il Don Giovanni*. I have used the vocal score arranged by Ernest Roth and published by Boosey and Hawkes.

1797: FR. SCHILLER, 'Don Juan' (fragment of a ballad). A reading of Don Juan's character suggested by da Ponte's libretto and stressing Don Juan's arrogance. The fragment was completed by Adalbert Rudolf about 1885; this completed version can be found in Engel, *Don Juan auf der Bühne*, 175–83.

1805: C. A. VULPIUS, *Don Juan der Wüstling. Nach dem Spanischen des Tirso de Molina*, Penig, 1805. The subtitle is misleading; *not* based on *El Burlador*.

1813: E. T. A. HOFFMAN, 'Don Juan. Eine fabelhafte Begebenheit . . .' An essay in interpretation of *Don Giovanni*, wrapped up as a fantastic tale. Dates from 1813. Edn. used: *Werke*, ed. Ellinger, Berlin and Leipzig, n.d., i, 72–83.

1819–24: BYRON, *Don Juan*. Edn. used: *Works: Poetry*, vi, ed. E. H. Coleridge, London, 1924.

1820: A. VON SCHADEN, *Der deutsche Don Juan*, Berlin, 1820.

1828: J. B. BUCKSTONE, *Don Juan. A Romantic Drama in Three Acts*. First published 1828. Edn. used: *Dicks' Standard Plays*, No. 828, London, 1887.

1830: BLAZE DE BURY, 'Le Souper chez le Commandeur', in *Poésies Complètes*, Paris, 1842, 1–72.

1830: A. PUSHKIN, 'Der steinerne Gast', in *Alexander Puschkin's Dichtungen*, trans. R. Lippert, Leipzig, 1840, ii, 203–42.

1832: A. DE MUSSET, 'Namouna. Conte oriental'. Edn. used: *Poésies complètes*, ed. Allem, Paris, 1957, 239–70.

1834: C. VON HOLTEI, *Don Juan. Dramatische Phantasie*. First appeared as 'von einem deutschen Theaterdichter', Paris (!=Leipzig), 1834. I have used this edition. There is also a more modern edition, Berlin, 1923.

1834: P. MÉRIMÉE, 'Les Ames du Purgatoire', in *Colomba, La Vénus d'Illes. Les Ames du Purgatoire*, Paris, n.d., 295–399.

c. 1835: E. DULLER, 'Juan', in *Gedichte*, Berlin, 1845, 151–5.

1836: ALEXANDER DUMAS (Dumas père), *Don Juan de Marana* [*sic*]. Edn. used: *Théâtre complète*, Paris, 1899, v, 1–100.

1836–7: TH. CREIZENACH, 'Don Juan', in *Dichtungen*, Mannheim, 1839, 1–60.

1840: S. WIESE, *Don Juan. Trauerspiel in fünf Acten*, Leipzig, 1840.

1842: BRAUN VON BRAUNTHAL, *Don Juan. Drama in fünf Abtheilungen*, Leipzig, 1842.

1844: A. DE. GOBINEAU, *Les Adieux de Don Juan. Poëme dramatique*, Paris, 1844.

1844: N. LENAU, 'Don Juan: dramatische Szenen'. Edn. used: *SW*, ed. Castle, Leipzig, 1910ff, ii, 402ff.

1844: JOSÉ ZORRILLA Y MORAL, *Don Juan Tenorio*. German translations by G. H. Wilde (1850) and J. Fastenrath (Dresden and Leipzig, 1898). I have used the latter.

1845: E. W. ACKERMANN, 'Don Juan und Maria. Commedia infernale', in *Aus dem poetischen Nachlasse von E. W. A.* . . . , ed. Raupach, Leipzig, 1848, 129–50.

1847: F. MALLEFILLE, *Les mémoires de Don Juan*. I have used the German translation in 11 vols., Leipzig, 1848–53.

1848: G. LE VAVASSEUR, 'Don Juan Barbon', in *Poésies Complètes*, Paris, 1888/96, i, 115–50.

1850: R. HÖRNIGK, *Don Juan. Tragödie*, Potsdam, 1850.

c. 1853: BAUDELAIRE, 'La Fin de Don Juan'. Sketch for a projected Don Juan play, first published posthumously. Edn. used: *Œuvres complètes*, Paris, 1939: *Œuvres posthumes*, i, 79–81.

1853: V. PRECHT, 'Don Juan'. Poem in *Düsseldorfer Künstler-Album*, Düsseldorf, 1853, pp. 20f.

1854: N. HÜRTE, *Wahrhaftige Historie vom ärgerlichen Leben des spanischen Ritters Don Juan und wie ihn zuletzt der ††† geholt* . . . , Reutlingen, 1854.

1856: P. F. TRAUTMANN *Don Juan in Wiesbaden. Schwank in einem Akt*, Berlin, 1856.

1856: VILLIERS DE L'ISLE-ADAM, 'Hermosa. Poème', in *Œuvres complètes*, x, Paris, 1929, 37–108.

c. 1857: FR. SPIESSER, *Don Juan, oder: Der steinerne Gast. Seine Thaten und sein furchtbares Lebensende* . . . , Cassel, n.d. (=c. 1857).

1857: BAUDELAIRE, 'Don Juan aux enfers', in *Les Fleurs du mal*.

1857: E. JOURDAIN, *Don Juan. Drame fantastique* . . . , Paris, 1857.

1858: A. WIDMANN, 'Don Juan de Maranna [*sic*]. Ein romantisches Schauspiel', in *Dram. Werke*, Leipzig, 1858, ii, 1–176.

1860: A. TOLSTOI, *Don Juan*. Edn. used: *Don Juan, dramatisches Gedicht*. Transl. C. von Pawloff, Dresden, n.d. (=c. 1863).

1866: PAUL VERLAINE (?), Sonnet 'À Don Juan'. Usually attributed to Verlaine; originally published under the signature 'Fulvio'. In P. V., *Œuvres Posthumes*, Paris, 1903, 143.

1866: A. MÖSER, 'Don Juan'. First published in *Neue Sonette*, Leipzig, 1866, p. 47, then in *Gedichte*, 2nd edn., Leipzig, 1869, p. 226.

1869–71: W. VON KÖNIGSMARK, *Ein neuer Don Juan . . . Ein Sittengemälde aus der Neuzeit*, 5 vols. in 2, Berlin, 1869–71.

c. 1870: 'FERNANDO DEL CASTILLO', *Don Jouan. Romantisches Lustspiel . . . aus dem Spanischen übersetzt*, Madrid, 1820. Author's name, place of publication and date are all fictitious. Not a play in any practical, stageable sense: pornography in dramatic, rather than narrative form, figuring the main characters from Mozart/da Ponte.

1874: J. BARBEY D'AUREVILLY, 'Le plus bel Amour de Don Juan', in *Les Diaboliques*. Edn. used: Paris, 1934, 95–133.

1880: S. LIPINER, *Der neue Don Juan. Tragödie in fünf Akten*, Stuttgart, 1914.

1881: A. FRIEDMANN, *Don Juan's letztes Abenteuer. Drama in zwei Akten*, Leipzig, 1881.

1881: JULIUS HART, *Don Juan Tenorio. Eine Tragödie in 4 Aufzügen*, Rostock, 1881.

1883: PAUL HEYSE, *Don Juan's Ende. Trauerspiel in 5 Akten* (=*Dram. Dichtungen*, xiii, Berlin, 1883).

1884: PAUL VERLAINE, 'Don Juan Pipé', published in *Jadis et naguère*, 1884. Edn. used: *Œuvres complètes*, Paris, 1923, i, 413–18. (Don Juan as rebel and blasphemer.)

1886: A. HAYEM, *Don Juan d'Armana. Drame en 4 actes*, Paris, 1886. See too General Bibliography.

1887: G. B. SHAW, 'Don Giovanni explains' (short story). Edn. used: *Short Stories, Scraps and Shavings*, London, 1934, 97–118.

1889: J. AICARD, *Don Juan 89*, Paris, 1889.

1889: FRANZ HELD, *Der abenteuerliche Pfaffe Don Juan*, Leipzig, 1889.

1891: R. MANSFIELD, *Don Juan, a play in 4 acts*, New York, 1891.

1894: FRANZ HELD, *Don Juans Ratskellerkneipen*. The 2nd edn. of 1895 has been used.

1895: H. ROUJON, *Miremonde*, Paris, 1895.

1896: W. WEIGAND, 'Don Juans Ende. Ein Lustspiel in einem Akt', in W. W., *Moderne Dramen*, Munich, 1900, ii, 1–38.

1897: RUDOLF VON GOTTSCHALL, *Der steinerne Gast. Roman*, Berlin, Eisenach, Leipzig, 1897.

1898: O. J. BIERBAUM, 'Don Juan Tenorio', in *Kaktus und andere Künstlergeschichten*, Berlin and Leipzig, 1898, 123–76.

1898: E. HARAUCOURT, *Don Juan de Mañara. Drame en cinq actes*, Paris, 1898.

1900: M. BARRIÈRE, *Le nouveau Don Juan*, 3 vols., Paris, 1900. An aesthetic Don Juan with some resemblance to the hero of *À Rebours*.

1900: F. VON HORNSTEIN, *Don Juans Höllenqualen. Phantastisches Drama . . .*, Stuttgart, 1900.

1900: O. A. H. SCHMITZ, 'Don Juan und die Kurtisane', in *Don Juan und die Kurtisane, fünf Einakter*, Munich, 1914, 5–47.

T

1902: RUDOLF STRAUß, *Die Waffe des Don Juan*, Vienna, 1902.

1903: O. C. BERNHARDI, *Don Juan*, Berlin, 1903.

1903: G. B. SHAW, *Man and Superman*. Edn. used: *The Bodley Head Bernard Shaw*, ii, 489ff.

1906: RUDOLF VON GOTTSCHALL, 'Don Juans hohes Lied', in *Späte Lieder*, Breslau, 1906, 71f.

1908: R. M. RILKE, 'Don Juans Auswahl' and 'Don Juans Kindheit', in *Neue Gedichte*, ii.

1908: O. A. H. SCHMITZ, *Don Juanito. Komödie in 4 Aufzügen*, Berlin, 1908. Reworked as *Ein deutscher Don Juan*. 1909.

1909: O. ANTHES, *Don Juans letztes Abenteuer. Drama*, Berlin, 1909. Also as opera libretto: Paul Graener, *Don Juans letztes Abenteuer. Oper in 3 Akten*. Dichtung von Otto Anthes. Textbuch, Vienna and Leipzig, 1914. This is the edition I have used.

1909: TH. RITTNER, *Unterwegs. Ein Don Juan-Drama in drei Akten*, Berlin, 1909.

1909: CARL STERNHEIM, *Don Juan. Eine Tragödie*. Edn. used: Munich, 1921.

1910: H. BETHGE, *Don Juan. Tragikomödie*, Leipzig, n.d. (=1910).

1912: A. LEMBACH, *Don Juan. Ein Drama in drei Akten*, Berlin, 1912.

1913 (written): ARNOLD BENNETT, *Don Juan de Marana. A Play in Four Acts*, London, 1923.

1914 (written): E. ROSTAND, *La dernière nuit de Don Juan*, Paris, 1921.

1915: A. BRAUSEWETTER, *Don Juans Erlösung. Roman*, Brunswick, 1915.

1919: W. BONSELS, *Don Juan. Eine epische Dichtung*, Berlin, 1919.

c. 1921: C. LEYST, *Don Juans Mission. Drama in 3 Akten*, Berlin, n.d. (=c. 1921).

1921: R. HEYMANN, *Don Juan und die Heilige. Roman*, Leipzig, 1921.

1922: LUDWIG ENGEL, *Der Don Juan vom Jungfernstieg. Ein Hamburger Roman*, Leipzig, 1922.

1922: W. VAN VLOTEN, *Don Juan empor! Roman*, Basle and Leipzig, 1922.

1925: J. E. FLECKER, *Don Juan. A Play in Three Acts*, London, 1925. Loosely based on Molière. A rather halfhearted attempt to transplant the events to England and update them.

1928: ERICA GRUPE-LÖRCHER, *Der wiedererstandene Don Juan. Roman*, Reutlingen, 1928 (=vol. 333 in *Enßlins Roman- und Novellenschatz*).

1930: J. DELTEIL, *Don Juan*, Paris, 1930.

1930: S. VON DER TRENCK, *Don Juan—Ahasver*, Gotha, 1930.

1931: M. JELUSICH, *Don Juan. Die sieben Totsünden. Roman*, Vienna and Leipzig, 1931.

1931: ERIC LINKLATER, *Juan in America*, first published 1931. Edn. used: London, 1962.

1932: A. SCHIROKAUER, *Don Juan auf der Flucht. Roman*, Berlin, 1932.

1933: A. HEIMERDINGER, *Don Juan. Balladenzyklus*, Berlin, Leipzig, Munich, 1933 (=*Gegenwart und Zukunft*, vol. ii).

1934: S. VON HARTENSTEIN, *Don Juan. Ein Leben Liebe, Laster, Heiligkeit*, Vienna, 1934.

1937: BENN W. LEVY, *The Poet's Heart. A Life of Don Juan*, London, 1937.

1937: ERIC LINKLATER, *Juan in China*, first published 1937. Edn. used: London, 1961.

1937: HUMBERT WOLFE, *Don J. Ewan*, London, 1937.

1938: F. A. BEYERLEIN, 'Don Juans Überwindung', in *Don Juans Überwindung, Ende gut—alles gut. Zwei Novellen*, 2nd edn., Bielefeld and Leipzig, 1938, 5–113.

1939: E. KRATZMANN, 'Don Juan in Venedig', in *Regina Sebaldi*, Vienna, 1939, 51–76.

1948: 'CHRISTIAN SCHNELLER' (=C. A. Mayer), *Der Sturz. Eine Don-Juan-Tragödie*, Munich, 1948.

1950: FRANK THIESS, *Don Juans letzte Tage. Novelle*, Vienna and Linz, 1950.

1952: MAX FRISCH, *Don Juan oder Die Liebe zur Geometrie. Komödie in fünf Akten*. Edn. used: *Stücke*, Frankfort on the Main, 1962, ii, 7–85.

1952: M. ZÉVACO, *Don Juan*, Paris, 1952.

1954: RONALD DUNCAN, *Don Juan*, London, 1954.

1954: R. HAGELSTANGE, *Die Beichte des Don Juan*, Olten, 1954.

1957: O. BRÜES, *Don Juan und der Abt*, Rothenburg o.d. Tauber, 1957.

1958 (written 1956): HENRY DE MONTHERLANT, *Don Juan. Pièce en trois actes*, Paris, 1958. Quotations from this edn. Revised and reissued under the new title *La Mort qui fait le trottoir*, Gallimard, 1972.

1958: GWYN THOMAS, *The Love Man*, London, 1958.

1963: ANTHONY BORROW, *Don Juan, a comedy*, Lympne Hythe, 1963.

(xii) Don Juan and Faust together in the same work

1809: N. VOGT, 'Der Färberhof oder die Buchdruckerei in Mainz', in *Die Ruinen am Rhein*, Frankfort on the Main, 1809, 109ff.

1829: CHR. D. GRABBE, *Don Juan und Faust*. Many editions; I have given scene references only.

1836: ADOLPHE DUMAS, 'La Fin de la comédie ou la mort de Faust et de Don Juan'. Unpublished. Account in Bévotte, ii, 93–5.

1836: EUGÈNE ROBIN, *Livia. Poème dramatique*, Paris, 1836.

1838: T. GAUTIER, 'La Comédie de la Mort'. Edn. used: *Poésies complètes*, Paris, 1924, ii, 3–49.

1846: G. HESEKIEL, *Faust und Don Juan . . .*, 3 parts, Altenburg, 1846. A *Zeitroman*. No link with Faust and Don Juan as known from their respective legends.

1864: E. DUTOUQUET, *Une Aventure de Don Juan*, Paris, 1864. Faust and Juan are discussed in the first section, 'Faust'.

1883: EMIL VON SCHONAICH-CAROLATH, 'Don Juans Tod' in *Gesammelte Werke*, Leipzig, 1907, i, 101–26. Makes Faust and Don Juan twins!

1922: MAX JACOB, 'Poèmes dans un goût qui n'est pas le mien'. The last of the three deals with Don Juan and Faust. First published in *Cornet à dés*, 1922. I have used the 13th edition, Paris, 1945, pp. 34f.

1960: ALBERT LEPAGE, *Faust et Don Juan. Pièce en trois actes*, Brussels, 1960. First written as a radio play, 1950.

(xiii) *Collections of source material*

(a) *Faust*

F. BRUKNER and F. HADAMOWSKY, *Die Wiener Faust-Dichtungen von Stranitzky bis zu Goethes Tod*, Vienna, 1932.

H. W. GEIßLER, *Gestaltungen des Faust . . .* , 3 vols., Munich, 1927.

F. HADAMOWSKY, see F. BRUKNER.

A. TILLE, *Die Faustsplitter in der Literatur des 16. bis 18. Jahrhunderts . . .* , Berlin, 1900.

K. G. WENDRINER, *Faust-Dichtung vor, neben und nach Goethe*, 4 vols., Berlin, 1913.

(b) *Don Juan*

G. DE BÉVOTTE, *Le Festin de Pierre avant Molière*, Paris, 1907.

O. MANDEL, *The Theatre of Don Juan*, Univerity of Nebraska Press, Lincoln, 1963.

(c) *Faust and Don Juan*

J. SCHEIBLE, *Das Kloster. Weltlich und geistlich. Meist aus der älteren deutschen Volks-, Wunder-, Curiositäten-, und vorzugsweise komischen Literatur*, 12 vols., Stuttgart and Leipzig, 1845–9. Vols. ii, iii, v and xi contain material on Faust and/or Don Juan.

(xiv) *General Bibliography*

JOHN AUSTEN, *The Story of Don Juan*, London, 1939.

G. BERGSTEN, *Thomas Manns Doktor Faustus*, Lund, 1963 (= *Studia litterarum Upsaliensis*, 3).

G. G. DE BÉVOTTE, *La Légende de Don Juan*, 2 vols., Paris, 1911.

GENEVIÈVE BIANQUIS, *Faust à travers quatre siècles*, Paris, 1935.

Blätter der Knittlinger Faust-Gedenkstätte und des Faust-Museums, Knittlingen, 1956ff.

M. VON BOEHN, *Goethe, Faust. Mit einer Einleitung: Faust und die Kunst*, Berlin, 1932.

J. BOLTE, 'Über den Ursprung der Don Juan-Sage', in *Zeitschrift für vergleichende Litteraturgeschichte*, n.F., xiii (1899), 374–98.

ELISABETH F. BOYD, *Byron's Don Juan. A critical Study*, London, 1945.

M. BREUILLAC, 'Hoffmann en France', in *Revue d'Histoire Littéraire de la France* xiii (1906), 427–57 and xiv (1907), 74–105.

F. BUSONI, *Über die Möglichkeit der Oper und über die Partitur des 'Doktor Faust'*, Leipzig, 1926.

E. M. BUTLER, *The Fortunes of Faust*, Cambridge, 1952.

F. BYLOFF, *Das Verbrechen der Zauberei*, Graz, 1902.

H. C. CHATFIELD-TAYLOR, *Goldoni*, London, 1914.

F. CHRYSANDER, 'Die Oper Don Giovanni von Gazzaniga und von Mozart', in *Vierteljahrsschrift für Musikwissenschaft*, iv (1888), 351–435.

W. CREIZENACH, *Versuch einer Geschichte des Volksschauspiels vom Doktor Faust*, Halle, 1878.

W. CREIZENACH, *Die Bühnengeschichte des Goethe'schen Faust*, Frankfort on the Main, 1881.

A. DABEZIES, *Visages de Faust au 20e siècle* . . . , Paris, 1967.

C. DÉDÉYAN, *Le Thème de Faust dans la Littérature Européenne*, 4 vols., Paris, 1954–61.

S. DENSLOW, 'Don Juan and Faust. Their parallel development and association in Germany 1790–1850', unpublished dissertation, Virginia, 1941. (A much shortened version published in the *Hispanic Review*, x, 1942, 215–22 as 'Don Juan and Faust'.)

E. J. DENT, *Mozart's Operas*, 2nd edn., O.U.P., 1947.

J. DOOLITTLE, 'The Humanity of Molière's *Dom Juan*', in *PMLA*, lxviii (1953), 509–34.

ALFRED EINSTEIN, *Mozart, His Character, His Work*, trans. Mendel and Broder, O.U.P., 1945.

(HANNS EISLER), *Sinn und Form. Sonderheft Hanns Eisler*, Berlin, 1964.

K. ENGEL, *Die Don Juan-Sage auf der Bühne*, Dresden and Leipzig, 1887.

A. ENSLIN, *Die ersten Theater-Aufführungen des Goethe'schen Faust*, Berlin, 1880.

G. FERCHAULT, *Faust. Une légende et ses musiciens*, Paris, 1948.

L. A. FRANKL, *Zur Biographie Nikolaus Lenau's*, 2nd edn., Vienna, 1885.

R. VON FREISAUFF, *Mozarts Don Juan 1787–1887. Ein Beitrag zur Geschichte dieser Oper*, Salzburg, 1887.

H. GOUHIER, 'L'inhumain Don Juan', in *La Table Ronde*, Paris, Nov. 1957, 67–73. On Molière's *Dom Juan*.

H. G. GRÄF, *Goethe über seine Dichtungen*, Frankfort on the Main, 1906. See *Drama*, vol. ii for Goethe on *Faust*.

A. GRAF, *The Story of the Devil*, trans. E. N. Stone, London, 1931. Originally published in Italian, 1889.

G. GUERRINE, *F. Busoni*, Florence, 1944.

A. HAYEM *Le Don Juanisme*, Paris, 1886.

H. HECKEL, *Das Don Juan-Problem in der neueren Dichtung*, Stuttgart, 1915.

F. HELBIG, 'Die Don-Juan Sage, ihre Entstehung und Fortentwicklung', in *Westermann's Jahrbuch*, xli, Brunswick, 1876–7, 637–50.

E. HELLER, 'Faust's Damnation: the morality of knowledge', in *The Artist's Journey into the Interior*, London, 1966, 3–44.

H. HENNING, 'Faust als historische Gestalt', in *Jahrbuch der Goethe-Gesellschaft*, xxi, Weimar, 1959, 107–39. (See too under K. Theens.)

E. HIRSCH, 'Die drei großen Sagen vom Don Juan, vom ewigen Juden und von Dr. Faust', in *Altes und Neues*, v, Wiesbaden, 1873, 324ff.

F. HORN, 'Andeutungen für Freunde der Poesie', in *Luna, ein Taschenbuch auf das Jahr 1805*, Leipzig, 1805, 297ff. (Discusses Faust and Don Juan.)

F. HORN, *Poesie und Beredsamkeit der Deutschen*, first published 1823. Includes discussion of Faust and Don Juan, with particular reference to the puppet plays. Reprinted in Scheible, v (1847), 670–92.

F. HORN, *Psyche. Aus Franz Horn's Nachlaß*, ed. G. Schwab and L. Förster, Leipzig, 1841. See i, 198f for discussion of Don Juan.

S. KIERKEGAARD, *Enten-Eller*, 1843. Edn. used: *Either/Or*, trans. D. F. and L. M. Swenson, London, 1944.

C. KIESEWETTER, *Faust in der Geschichte und Tradition*, Leipzig, 1893. Reprinted Hildesheim, 1963.

FRANZ KOCH, 'Wilhelm Jordans "Demiurgos"', in *Abhandlungen d. Preuß. Akad. d. Wissenschaften, Phil.-hist. Klasse*, Jg. 1942, pp. 3–48.

J. F. KOEHLER, *Historisch-kritische Untersuchung über das Leben und die Thaten des . . . Doctor Johann Fausts . . .* , Leipzig, 1791. (Early attempt to reconstruct the life of the historical Faust.)

E. LERT, *Mozart auf dem Theater*, 3–4th edn., Berlin, 1921.

J. LESSER, *Thomas Mann in der Epoche seiner Vollendung*, Munich, 1952.

A. LIRONDELLO, *Le Poète Alexis Tolstoï*, Paris, 1912.

DOROTHY E. MACKAY, *The Double Invitation in the Legend of Don Juan*, Stanford Univ. Press, 1943.

C. A. MANNING, 'Russian versions of Don Juan', in *PMLA*, xxxviii (1923), 479–93.

THOMAS MEDWIN, *Journal of the Conversations of Lord Byron . . .* , London, 1824.

J. MEIßNER, *Die englischen Comödianten zur Zeit Shakespeares in Österreich*, Vienna, 1884.

A. MEYNIEUX, 'Pouchkine et Don Juan', in *La Table Ronde*, November 1957, 90–107.

G. MICHAUT, *Les Luttes de Molière*, Paris, 1925. (Chapter iv deals with Dom Juan.)

W. G. MOORE, *Molière, a new criticism*, Oxford, 1949.

W. G. MOORE, '"Dom Juan" reconsidered', in *MLR*, lii (1957), 510–17.

E. MÜLLER-GANGLOFF, 'Faust und Don Juan', in *Vorläufer des Antichrist*, Berlin, 1948, 26ff.

C. NIESSEN, *Faust als Schmutz und Schund*, Emsdetten (Westphalia), 1964. (Deals with the censorship and bowdlerization of Goethe's *Faust* throughout the nineteenth century.)

O. NIETEN, *Chr. D. Grabbe, sein Leben und seine Werke*, Dortmund, 1908.

G. N. NISSEN, *Biographie W. A. Mozart's . . .*, Leipzig, 1828.

G. OREGLIA, *The Commedia dell'Arte*, trans. L. F. Edwards, London, 1968. Gives Don Juan scenario, pp. 43–55.

MAX OSBORN, *Die Teufelliteratur des xvi. Jahrhunderts*, Berlin, 1893.

JOHN PALMER, *Molière. His Life and Works*, London, 1930.

ROY PASCAL, 'Lunatscharski: "Faust und die Stadt." Zur Deutung des "Faust"', in *Gestaltung Umgestaltung. Festschrift zum 75. Geburtstag von H. A. Korff*, Leipzig, 1957, 129–38.

C. E. PASSAGE, *The Russian Hoffmannists*, The Hague, 1963.

R. PETSCH, *Lessings Faustdichtung*, Heidelberg, 1911 (= *Germ. Bibl.*, ii, 4).

L. PETZOLD, 'Don Juan in der volkstümlichen Überlieferung', in *iv. Int. Congress for folk-narrative research in Athens. Lectures and Reports*, Athens, 1965, 354–63.

G. J. PFEIFFER, *Klinger's Faust*, Würzburg, 1890.

K. PRIEGER, *Urtheile bedeutender Dichter, Philosophen und Musiker über Mozart*, 2nd edn., Wiesbaden, 1886.

C. RABANY, *Carlo Goldoni*, Paris, 1896.

DANIEL ROGERS, 'Fearful Symmetry: the ending of *El Burlador de Sevilla*', in *Bulletin of Hispanic Studies*, xli, 1964, 141–59.

OTTO ROMMEL, *Die Alt-Wiener Volkskomödie*, Vienna, 1952.

G. ROSKOFF, *Geschichte des Teufels*, 2 vols., Leipzig, 1869.

K. SCHIFFNER, *Wilhelm Jordan*, Frankfort on the Main, 1889.

R. SCHIRMER-IMHOFF, 'Faust in England', in *Anglia*, lxx (1951), 150–85.

GÜNTHER SCHMID, *Chamisso als Naturforscher*, Leipzig, 1942.

ERICH SCHMIDT, 'Faust und das 16. Jahrhundert', in *Charakteristiken*, 2nd edn., Berlin, 1902, pp. 1–36.

TH. SCHRÖDER, *Die dramatischen Bearbeitungen der Don Juan-Sage in Spanien, Italien und Frankreich bis auf Molière einschließlich*, Halle, 1912 (= *Beihefte zur Zeitschrift für romanische Philologie*, xxxvi).

M. SCHWENGBERG, *Das Spies'sche Faustbuch und seine Quelle*, Berlin and Leipzig, 1885.

HANS SCHWERTE, *Faust und das Faustische*, Stuttgart, 1959.

OSWALD SPENGLER, *Der Untergang des Abendlandes*. First published 1918–22. I have used vol. I, 33–47th edn., and vol. II, 16–30th edn., Beck, Munich, 1922–3.

G. STUMME, *Faust als Pantomime und Ballett*, Leipzig, 1942.

N. SUCKLING, *Paul Valéry and the Civilised Mind*, O.U.P., 1954. (Chapter 7 deals with Valéry and Goethe.)

ELIZABETH TEICHMANN, *La Fortune d'Hoffmann en France*, Paris, 1961.

KARL THEENS, *Doktor Johann Faust*, Meisenheim am Glan, 1948. (Brief history of the growth of the legend and accounts of the various Faust works through the ages.)

KARL THEENS, *Faust im zwanzigsten Jahrhundert. Festschrift für Karl Theens zum sechzigsten Geburtstag*, Knittlingen, 1964. (Contains Hennings' survey of the more important Faust works of this century, pp. 7–32.)

E. VOLHARD, *F. M. Klingers philosophische Romane*, Halle, 1930.

O. WALZEL, *Heines Tanzpoem Der Doktor Faust*. First published 1917, repr. Hildesheim, 1962.

R. WARKENTIN, *Nachklänge der Sturm- und Drangperiode in Faustdichtungen des 18. und 19. Jahrhunderts*, Munich, 1896.

L. WEINSTEIN, *The Metamorphoses of Don Juan* (= *Stanford Studies in Language and Literature*, xviii), Stanford, California, 1959.

INDEX

(Some items, although not dealt with in the text, are described briefly in the Bibliography; these are included in the Index—see Preface, p. vi.)